GREAT SHOOTERS OF THE WORLD

By
SAM FADALA

STOEGER PUBLISHING COMPANY

DEDICATION

For Joe Vigneri, M.D., and Gene Thompson,
Educator—My Wyoming Friends

Cover Art and Design: Cat Alfano
Production Artist: Anthony Fischetto
Editor/Prod. Mgr.: Charlene Cruson Step

Photo Credits: p. 9 (Neg. #410927) and p. 10 (Neg. #410782), by Shackelford, courtesy Department Library Services, American Museum of Natural History; pp. 63, 64, courtesy St. Martin's Press; pp. 99, 100, 101, 104, courtesy *Outdoor Life* magazine; p. 102, courtesy *Field & Stream;* pp. 134, 137, from *The Ben Lilly Legend* by J. Frank Dobie, © 1950 J. Frank Dobie, by permission of Little, Brown and Company; p. 140, photograph by J.S. Ligon; p. 183, courtesy Marlin Firearms Co.; pp. 214, 220, from *The Hunter Is Death* by T.V. Bulpin ($30), available through Safari Press, P.O. Box 3095, Long Beach, CA 90803; p. 240, courtesy Sturm, Ruger & Co., Inc.; pp. 254, 256, 257, 259, courtesy Col. Charles Askins; p. 273, from *Wilderness Hunting and Wildcraft* by Col. Townsend Whelen, reprinted by Wolfe Publishing Co.; p. 282, photograph by Geo. Tate, courtesy Weatherby, Inc.

Published by Stoeger Publishing Company
55 Ruta Court
South Hackensack, New Jersey 07606

ISBN: 0-88317-160-0
Library of Congress Catalog Card No.: 90-71238
Manufactured in the United States of America

Distributed to the book trade and to the sporting goods trade by Stoeger Industries, 55 Ruta Court, South Hackensack, New Jersey 07606

In Canada, distributed to the book trade and to the sporting goods trade by Stoeger Canada, Ltd., Unit 16, 1801 Wentworth Street, Whitby, Ontario L1N 5S4.

PREFACE

Not all great men and women are famous. Some of the shooters in this book attained worldwide acclaim in the course of their lives; others did not. Most people will recognize the names Annie Oakley, Buffalo Bill and Theodore Roosevelt. Few readers, however, will remember Cotton Oswell, early settler of South Africa and patron of Dr. David Livingstone. Many of us know Jack O'Connor and Elmer Keith only because we are shooters. Their names are not taught in American history classes. And unless you are a student of the Nile, Sir Samuel Baker will not ring a bell. Not all famous names—but all great.

Hunters, such as Selous, Bell and Oswell, spent more days afield in a year or two than most of us can claim for a lifetime. They walked daily where life can be snuffed by claw or hoof. The marksmen—the sharpshooters or trick shooters such as Annie Oakley and Ad Topperwein—spent thousands of hours stropping their natural talents to a razor's edge. The experimenters—Ackley and Weatherby, for example—shaped brass cartridge cases into new forms for study, and burned pounds of powder in testing new creations. Pope was the barrelmaker nonpareil. Dr. Mann—the shooting empiricist without peer. Harvey Donaldson—the wildcatter supreme. John Browning—the inventor of a century.

These are their stories. The river of time has eroded the banks of memory, carrying many interesting, entertaining and worthwhile details of life to the ocean of lost facts. Where biographical data are lacking, I have tried to supply clues regarding the personalities and impact of the great shooters. Where only chards of facts remain, I have tried to cement the pieces together to form a whole. No biography is ever complete. No human story is ever fully told. However, anyone interested in shooting will further his knowledge and appreciation of the grand sport by listening to these echoes of history as they reverberate in the canyon of memory. Not that all of our shooters are of the past. Modern shooters, too, grace these pages—Dr. Lou Palmisano, inventor of the most accurate cartridge in the world, Colonel Charles Askins, modern-day safari expert, Fred Huntington, father of the modern reloading press, and Bill Ruger, gun designer.

My intention in this book is to "tell it like it is," or was, rather than escalate, glamorize or dilute the facts. The ivory hunters, for example, lived in accord with their times. Game was teaming over Africa, most of it perishing to drought, fang, claw and natural catastrophe. The hunters of the era saw no reason to restrict themselves, as we limit our hunting today. Their trackers, skinners and camp helpers were treated to fresh meat at every opportunity. Looking at the numbers of animals taken on an African trek, a modern sportsman may tend to cry out, "Game hog!" However, we must view the record in relation to the era, which was the 19th and early 20th century. Game in America was sometimes depleted at great rates during this time frame also. The United States Congress of 1870, for example, decided that the only way to defeat the Plains Indian was through oblique, not direct, attack; hence, the order was given to the U.S. Army to destroy the bison, which represented food, shelter and clothing to the Red Warrior of the West. Free ammunition was handed out. Salted bison tongues, of no great actual worth, were acquired at a dollar each as the ammo wagons forged westward, supplying the "buffalo runners." Examine the facts as they are. Consider them in the light of their times. Judge only within the framework of history.

During the course of investigating the lives

of these great shooters, and their impact upon the world of shooting, I searched the holdings of many libraries and read numerous old books and magazines. Shooters of historical fame, such as Teddy Roosevelt and Buffalo Bill, had millions of words dedicated to their lives. Other shooters were remembered in only one or two documents. I found, for example, but a single work on William Cotton Oswell, a treatise by Colonel Townsend Whelen. That one source was relied on, coupled with shreds of mention in a few other places. Wherever possible, multiple records were used in synthesizing an account of a great shooter. When information was unavailable, however, the biography had to be built upon a single-layered foundation.

Photographs of many of the shooters, especially those of former eras, were often difficult to come by, faded or not up to fine-grained contemporary quality. No matter, for the vintage look of some of them only add, I think, to their nostalgic appeal. I believe you'll enjoy the photos for their well-rounded look at the people, their accomplishments and the period in which they lived.

ACKNOWLEDGMENTS

Sincere thanks to George Martin, Executive Director of NRA Publications, and to the National Rifle Association for generous permission to reprint illustrations from *American Rifleman* magazine. Thanks also to Dave Wolfe and the Wolfe Publishing Company for their support. Also, to all the firms and institutions—the American Museum of Natural History, *Field and Stream* magazine, Little, Brown and Company, Marlin Firearms, Sturm, Ruger & Company, and The Woodbine Company—that graciously allowed us to reprint photographs/illustrations. Last, but not least, a special hug for my wife, Nancy, who helped me with the research and photography.

ABOUT THE AUTHOR

Sam Fadala is currently Technical Editor for *Rifle Magazine* and *Handloader Magazine*, Feature Editor for *Muzzleloader Magazine* and Special Projects Editor for *Guns Magazine*. Since he began freelancing in 1969, his articles have appeared in *Gun World, Bow and Arrow Hunter, Outdoor Life* and *Sports Afield*. He has written many books, most recently *The Book of the 22: The All-American Caliber*, another Stoeger publication. As a boy, Fadala thrived on the outdoor life and now spends many hours shooting modern rifles, muzzleloaders and longbows. He is an avid hunter who has stalked most of the western U.S., Canada, Alaska and has been on safari in Africa. Casper, Wyoming, is where he and his family presently call home.

CONTENTS

1

ROY CHAPMAN ANDREWS: WORLD EXPLORER

Adventurer. Explorer. That was Roy Chapman Andrews—and a great hunter and rifleman, too, although he was never noted as such in most circles. But what else would you call a man who collected more wild animals with rifle than most dedicated sportsmen could ever come close to equaling in two lifetimes?

Although Roy would become famous as a naturalist, he spent his early life as a tenderfoot hunter and outdoorsman. His hunting interest followed precisely the path trod by all of us who harvest wildlife. Hunting coincided with a strong love of animals and a desire to know as much about them as possible. Two early favorites, the *Handbook of North American Birds* and *Robinson Crusoe* blended perfectly to describe his nature. Roy would become a dedicated student of wildlife and an inveterate vagabond. His sparkling career as a naturalist was nurtured by early hunting.

When Roy was in grade school, his father Ezra, a wholesale druggist, gave the boy a single-barreled shotgun. "The greatest event of my early life was when, on my ninth birthday [January 26, 1893], Father gave me a single-barrel shotgun. Previous to this I had been allowed to shoot Grandfather's muzzle loader once or twice, but it was too much for me to negotiate with its forty-inch long barrel," he said in his autobiography, *Under a Lucky Star*. Roy's mother, Cora May Chapman, was against the idea of her son having

the firearm, but it was his all the same. Roy used it straightaway to bag a duck, which was prepared for supper.

In the marshes of Beloit, Wisconsin, Roy's birthplace, he next went goose hunting. But there was a problem. The young lad made a good stalk, and his aim was true. But the three geese he shot turned out to be decoys belonging to one Fred Fenton, a man entirely disliked by the elder Andrews. Roy got a brand new double-barreled hammergun the week of his decoy shooting. Father could not have been too displeased with him.

Andrews sold the single-barreled arm for three dollars, since he no longer needed it. His double-barreled hammergun was enough. In the Preface of *Meet Your Ancestors*, a 1946 anthropology title, Andrews said, "All my life I have been a sportsman. Beginning with whales, I have shot big game and dangerous game in most countries of the world." Andrews went on to say that he pursued evidence of ancient man with similar hunting instinct. *Taxidermy and Home Decoration* by William T. Hornaday taught the young man how to mount specimens. His work was good enough to command money, even when Roy was still in grammar school. Although he was an animal-lover of the highest order, he never did care for reptiles, having been frightened by a snake as a youngster. His aversion to reptiles was somewhat matched by his attitude toward school. He simply was not a great student in elementary or high school—except for science and literature. In these subjects he excelled.

A grave accident befell Roy in his youth, or rather the accident belonged to Monty White, a young English instructor who was accompanying young Andrews on a duck hunting trip. White dropped a paddle from the boat into the icy water. As he lunged forward to retrieve it, he tipped the vessel over. Roy almost drowned, but, sadly, Monty *was* drowned. A farmer saw Roy trudging toward his house, drenched and freezing. He saved the lad with blankets and shelter. Andrews could never forget the incident.

The young taxidermist went on to graduate from Beloit College in 1906—with honors. His study habits had improved markedly from his earlier days, and Roy's degree read *cum laude*. His intelligence and curiosity had blossomed, as affirmed through his good marks. However, he admitted that he did not labor long and hard in the making of his excellent grades. In fact, he did not feel well-educated after graduating from college. But at least now he knew what he wanted to be: a naturalist.

THE ADVENTURE BEGINS

It was July 6, 1906. Teddy Roosevelt was president. Roy Chapman Andrews had ventured all the way from Beloit, Wisconsin, to New York City. He stood outside of the American Museum of Natural History. For the first time, he saw the structure that had occupied his thoughts for so long. But there was no opening for him. He told the man in charge that mopping the floors would be a sufficient post, if only to be allowed access to the treasures of the museum. He was hired. He worked for 40 dollars a month under Jimmy Clark in the Department of Taxidermy. In keeping with his desire to be a part of the museum, even if he had to scrub floors, he was entrusted with mopping the tiles of the taxidermy department each morning. "They were not ordinary floors to me and I didn't mind scrubbing them," he said. "Those floors were walked on by my scientific gods."

But imminent was his first real assignment. He was to go after whales along the Pacific coast of Alaska for the museum. And whaling he did go. In fact, on the first week of the 1908 expedition, he killed three whales himself, using a harpoon gun. He was now a hunter of museum spec-

imens. In fact, his career would have been a dismal failure had Roy not been a hunter. It was his outdoor lore, his enthusiasm for the hunt, and his marksmanship that brought many treasures to the museum for awaited study and display.

Andrews engaged in trapping to obtain certain species for collection. On uninhabited islands he trapped Sambar, boar, monkey and giant lizards for the museum. But he continued to hunt at every opportunity. He looked for the small as well as the large. On one adventure, he even found a species of ant hitherto unknown, which was named in his honor.

He continued for about six years to do considerable whaling and gathered great and new data on whales from all the oceans. During that time Roy hunted in several countries. In Korea, with a hunter as his guide, Andrews set out to locate and dispatch a tiger that was killing livestock. A village elder implored Roy to track down and kill the animal. Three weeks of tracking and labor brought no tiger. Meanwhile, the beast added more people to its list of victims. At one point, Paik, the guide, wanted to follow the feline into a cave he thought the animal had entered. Roy, being an agreeable sort of chap, decided that was not a bad idea. He'd go along. But the tiger evacuated the cave through a rear entrance. No tiger charged that time, but later a boar struck from the brush at Paik. Roy Andrews fired three rifle shots before the boar was downed. The man-eating tiger was never dispatched, however.

More Korean hunting was in store for Roy, for Roe deer and other species of collectible (and edible) wildlife. And there was always adventure for the naturalist/hunter. Roy ran into Manchurian bandits on one trek, but he got along well with them, explaining who he was and what he was doing. However, people back home believed that Andrews was now a corpse lying in a faraway land that Americans knew little about. As with Mark Twain before him, Roy's demise had been "greatly exaggerated." A memorial service in honor of the "deceased" Roy Chapman Andrews was held in his home town. Few things are more embarrassing than showing up after your funeral. But, of course, Roy eventually did.

Traveling to Russia, Roy hunted for two months with a Russian prince. Finally, Andrews returned to the museum to resume his normal duties. His superiors believed, however, that he

Roy Chapman Andrews led several Central Asiatic Expeditions for the American Museum of Natural History in the early 1900s. Carrying two rifles on most of his adventures, the 250-3000 Savage lever-action and the 6.5mm Mannlicher carbine, he found that smaller calibers minimized the damage to scientific specimens.

was capable of greater things. The director of the museum implored Roy to continue with his education, for obvious reasons of advancement. Roy completed his Ph.D. at Columbia University in 1913.

That same year Andrews gathered up another degree as well—a marriage certificate. In October Roy married Yvette Borup, the sister of one of the party members who had accompanied Admiral Peary to the North Pole. Surely Yvette would understand Roy's appetite for adventure. She was a photographer and her camera skills came in handy on the expeditions her husband would eventually make. During his study of whales, their efforts produced Andrews's first book, *Whale Hunting with Gun and Camera*, which was published in 1916.

Andrews's experience as an explorer and his insatiable thirst for discovery naturally evolved into his leading the Central Asiatic Expeditions

on behalf of the Museum. The first expedition, in 1916, to Tibet, Southwest China and Burma, was one of the largest of its kind. Andrews led 40 men—assorted experts in geology, paleontology, archaeology, topology—plus eight automobiles and 150 camels into the Gobi Desert in search of fossils, living animals, birds, vegetation and whatever they could unearth in order to study the area.

Hunting was of course an integral part of the exploration. Another tiger, the "Great Invisible," had earned his appellation through grim accomplishment. No matter how stalwart the hunter, the odds are in favor of the big cat. Also known as the Blue Tiger, Roy saw him once, but never claimed his hide. The tiger went on to kill a total of about 100 men, women and children—an unsatisfactory end to another adventure. Roy did not travel alone now. Yvette levied no complaint (at least not in those early years of nuptial bliss)

Andrews's third Asiatic Expedition in the 1920s led him again into the Gobi Desert, where camel travel was relied on. The digs uncovered the first-known dinosaur eggs as well as skeletons of the oldest and largest land mammals known at that time.

about Roy's wanderlust. Andrews hunted near the Burmese border for a time, searching as much for camp food (and perhaps for the sheer joy of hunting) as well as specimens. An infection in his hand caused him great concern; then malaria struck.

But Roy Chapman Andrews went on. He used a 6.5mm Mannlicher rifle for some of his hunting. He considered 200-yard shooting within his and his rifle's ability. He was also a "binocular man," and with the glass located many wild animals. The Chinese called his binoculars "Thousand-mile eyes." On the China trip, Roy took 3,100 specimens for science: 2,100 mammals, 800 birds, and 200 reptiles. Yvette took 8,000 feet of film. Rumors of Roy being a secret agent for the government seeped up from the undergrowth, but nothing in my research verified the suggestion. Naturally, world politics were such that having a spy in China at the time would not have been out of keeping with American interest.

Roy Chapman Andrews loved hunters as well as hunting. For example, Carl Akeley, about whom Roy later wrote, was a great friend of his. But Andrews did succumb to what I call the "Old Hunter Syndrome," stating in his later years that "I kill animals for food or science . . . [not sport]." That was a bit of fluff sometimes known to emanate from hunters who have had a wonderful time in the field—properly using the animals they have harvested, enjoying every thrilling moment of it all, and then later making up unwarranted excuses for hunting. In a more candid moment, Andrews said, "Some men tell me that they never get excited when they hunt. Thank God, I do." He was certainly excited when he hunted rams in China.

Almost in a daze, I lifted my rifle, saw the little ivory bead of the front sight center on that gray neck, and touched the trigger. A thousand echoes crashed back upon us. There was a clatter of stones, a confused vision of a ponderous bulk heaving up and back—and all was still. But it was enough for me; there could be no mistake this time. The ram was mine . . . I yelled and pounded the old Mongol on the back until he begged for mercy; then I whirled him about in a war dance on the summit of the ridge. I wanted to leap down the rocks where the sheep had disappeared but the hunter held my arm. (from *Mongolian Plains*)

Yes, Roy Chapman Andrews hunted only for science and food.

Roy became especially animated about one man-eating tiger taken in China. Roy's friend Caldwell had quite an encounter with her, firing several times at close range with buckshot. None of the pellets penetrated deeply to stop the cat on the spot. But the tiger did succumb. "Next day I followed the blood trail with a lot of natives and found her dead nearly a half mile away. Her whole face and neck were full of buckshot but most were flattened against the heavy bones and hadn't penetrated. I think she bled to death."

The Chinese brought the tiger back to the village and a mother who had lost a child to the cat began beating it with a stick while screaming curses at the lifeless animal. The villagers took all but the hide, which Roy kept. They sopped up the blood with rags, and wore them to ward off disease and bad spirits. The meat they sold for medicinal purposes—a little bite would render "tiger-courage" to its consumer. The bones, whiskers and claws were stewed into a jelly and turned into pills, which the Chinese druggists sold to ailing patients.

Afterwards, Roy and his hunter friend discussed the ballistics of the situation. Andrews was a smallbore fan. Recall his 6.5mm rifle. But he did not have faith in Caldwell's 22 Savage Hi Power for tigers. "I believe the .22 Hi Power you've got is just about as bad [as a shotgun]," he told him. "It hasn't enough shocking power for dangerous game." Caldwell had taken several tigers with a 303 Savage, but he found the 22 Hi Power quite deadly on the big cats. He insisted on it.

Caldwell attested, ". . . the Savage Company sent me out this rifle and the first time I ever fired it was at a tiger. You ought to have seen what that tiny bullet did to him! He was a big tiger, too—a man-eater that had killed several people in this very village." (from *The Heart of Asia*) Andrews-proffered a theory about the 22 Hi Power's effect on the tiger, warning Caldwell that he must not expect the same results on the next tiger he tried the little cartridge on.

Andrews believed that the full stomach of the cat had contributed to its demise. "I've seen the same thing happen when I've shot woodchucks with a hardnose .22 Hi Power bullet. They just blow up if I get them through the body when the stomach is packed with food; if it is empty, I lose my 'chuck.''

In *Across Mongolian Plains, A Naturalist's Account of China's 'Great Northwest,'* Andrews spoke of hunting with the 250 Savage. Considering that he was a collector of specimens, the smaller calibers made sense—less destruction for specimens that were to be mounted for the museum. However, it seems that Roy did admire smaller cartridges in general. In hunting antelope, he preferred his 250 Savage. ''The one I killed was 400 yards away, and I held four feet ahead when I pulled the trigger.'' Andrews assured the reader that the shot was legitimate. ''I mentioned that the antelope I killed was four hundred yards away. I know how far it was, for I paced it off. I may say, in passing, that I had never before killed a running animal at that range. Ninety per cent of my shooting had been well within one hundred and fifty yards, but in Mongolia conditions are most extraordinary.''

Andrews went on with his hunting and explorations. He led two more Asiatic Expeditions and, on the third one in the 1920s, his group discovered the first known dinosaur eggs as well as skeletons of the oldest and largest land mammals known at that time. The energetic—no, frenetic—man, very physical, an outdoorsman, a

Andrews admired and often used the lever-action Savage in caliber 250-3000 Savage. Here Bill Fadala demonstrates the Savage Model 1899 (later known as the Model 99).

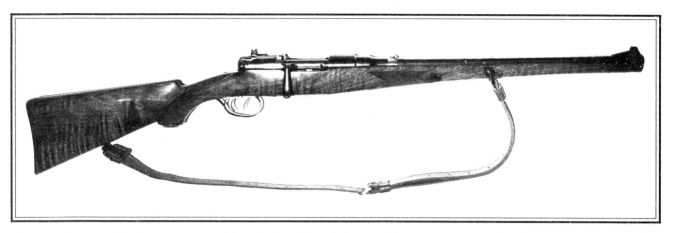

The great naturalist Andrews gave his reliable Mannlicher to his son, George. "For his protection he had the Mannlicher rifle that was my constant companion during more than a quarter of a century." (from *An Explorer Comes Home*)

hunter, found it impossible to settle down to a routine life in any city. In fact, he believed that city living was much more dangerous than the perils he faced in his whole life of exploring the world.

Andrews's wandering proved too much for his marriage, and Yvette finally divorced Roy in 1931. They had had two boys, George Borup and Roy Kevin, and once Yvette stopped traveling with Roy, the man seldom saw either his wife or his children. It seemed too important to Andrews to be known as the naturalist who first discovered dinosaur eggs, or the deliverer of the huge whale that was suspended in the museum for all to study. Time passed. Yvette was killed in a car accident in Spain. Four years after the divorce, Andrews married Wilhelmina Anderson Christmas, with whom he shared the remainder of his life.

In January of 1935, Roy Chapman Andrews became director of the American Museum of Natural History, the institution that had supported his naturalist/hunting interests and to which he had contributed so much. He continued with the directorship until 1941, when he retired from the position at age 57. But his career was far from over. He lectured, wrote monographs and authored many books, those already mentioned, plus *Camps and Trails in China, On the Trail of Ancient Man, The New Conquest of Central Asia, This Business of Exploring, This Amazing Planet, An Explorer Comes Home, Beyond Adventure: The Lives of Three Explorers* (himself,

Admiral Peary and Carl Akeley), and others. One of his last books was *In the Days of the Dinosaurs*, published a year before his death.

Andrews received many medals and honors in his lifetime, among them the Hubbard Medal of the National Geographic Society, and was elected to memberships in a host of scientific organizations. He had received an honorary Doctor of Science degree from Brown University in 1926 and another from Beloit College two years later.

When Roy finally gave up hunting for good, he left his favorite Mannlicher carbine to his son, George—

> For his protection he had the Mannlicher rifle that was my constant companion during more than a quarter of a century. To its bullets had fallen game in almost every country of the world. Two notches on the stock were reminders of how it had saved my life from Chinese brigands. In Arctic snows or tropic jungles it never failed. (from *An Explorer Comes Home*)

The famous naturalist/rifleman died on March 11, 1960, in Carmel, California, from a heart attack. He was 76 years old. Roy Chapman Andrews had led a full life, the kind many of us dream about. We may have adventure in our souls, but Andrews was able to live it out. And it all began with a boy of nine who had a strong hunting instinct—and a gun.

2

COL. CHARLES ASKINS: MODERN MARKSMAN

"Unrepentant sinner." That's how Colonel Charles Askins referred to himself in the title of his autobiography, *Unrepentant Sinner*. And that about sums him up. No regrets. The Colonel lives his life as he wishes to live it. I had the good fortune of meeting Askins on a jet plane bound for South Africa. I didn't know he was on board, but when I looked up, there he was, unmistakable in his appearance, as Keith or O'Connor would be to a shooting fan. I was in for a surprise. I walked up the aisle toward him and stood waiting by his seat to greet the man. He looked up. "Hello, Sam," he said. "I've read your stuff in *Rifle Magazine*. It's good." Then the Colonel introduced me to his son, Bill, who was as generous as his father in making a fellow feel important.

Charlie Askins had an interesting beginning. He led a Huckleberry Finn youth in Texas, where he was born in 1907. He played pranks, such as dropping a circus tent over an elephant, tethering a billy goat to the school bell on the second floor of the building (which earned him expulsion by the headmaster), and shooting a bully in the calf of the leg after the lad stole Charlie's horse and road him in a race.

He loved adventure of every kind, and that appreciation for excitement burns in the man's soul to this day. At one point in his youth, he became the youngest member of a posse. He didn't get to shoot the bank robbers and killers who were rounded up by the group, for he was the kid of the

bunch and his job was to hold the horses. But it was young Askins who had spotted the campfire smoke that gave the bandits away. He was ready for action, and was influenced by the wildness of his Texas home.

It was his father, though, who made the greatest impact on his life. Charles Askins Sr. was the firearms editor of *Outdoor Life* magazine. There was no big living in it at the time, but there was a certain prestige to it as well as a multitude of guns to test and ammo to enjoy. That he followed in his father's footsteps is no surprise. Major Charles Askins was a hero to his son. Today, many years after the passing of the Major, the Colonel says, "My Old Man has now been gone for years but I still miss him." The Colonel thought he was "the greatest admirer of a father" a kid could be. And he was. The two "batched it" a lot. One gathers that Charlie's mother was off teaching school in town, and that neither the junior nor senior Askins saw much of her.

Colonel Askins (the real family name was Erskine, but the Colonel doesn't know why it was changed) didn't view his father in the light of worshipful unreality. He saw the man as he really was—and he liked what he saw. "My Old Man, unfortunately, had utterly no ambition to better his station in life. He had never had anything. He was a poor man, lived a poor man and died in the same deplorable state. He was without drive, without incentive, without aggressive spirit. His life was bound up in his guns, his dogs, and his horses and he was quite content to live so. For all that he was the best father a man ever had and I revere his memory.'' (from *Unrepentant Sinner*).

How many boys bitten by the bug of shooting had a dad who knew as much about firearms as Askins Sr.? Very few. Charlie came early into a battery of longarms that would serve to put him on the same trail his father had taken: toward being one of the foremost authorities on hunting and shooting in the world. His first big game hunting rifles were a Model 95 Winchester in 30-40 Krag, a Model 99 Savage in 250-3000 Savage, another of the same in 300 Savage and a Model 94 Winchester in 25-35 Winchester chambering. Why lever-actions? Lever-actions were the order of the day. But there was another reason—Askins's left-handedness was better served by the lever gun.

Young Charlie loved to hunt, another characteristic picked up from the Major, who hunted almost every day of his life. ''When wars, or other mundane affairs, did not interfere he went hunting every day, seven days a week.'' Although the Major fought in the Spanish-American War, and even though his record of service brought him a commission at the beginning of World War I, he could not be called a professional soldier. That is, he did not spend an entire career in the Army.

Field & Stream magazine hired the Major as a dog handler. Although he was not big on training dogs, he took the job. His first article wasn't about dogs, either; it was on choosing the proper shotgun. In fact, not one of Major Askins's dog stories was about hounds. After his editorship with *Field & Stream*, Askins Sr. enjoyed a tenure of about two dozen years as firearms editor of *Outdoor Life* magazine. He also wrote for *Recreation* magazine and later *Sports Afield* magazine as the gun editor, a position he held for about 12 years. He wrote six books on guns and hunting, including his classic title, *Ballistic of the Shotgun*.

Colonel Askins would follow in his father's footsteps, for he would become even more recognized as an arms authority. His work would be read by millions of enthusiasts for many years. The Colonel is currently an arms editor with *Guns Magazine*. Everyone agrees that he's among the most candid of the arms authors. But we're getting ahead of our story.

AN EXPERT SHOOTER EMERGES

It was time for Charles to venture out a little. He spent a summer in the CMTC, Citizen's Military Training Corps, an organization similar to the ROTC program today. By not completing the tour, he did not receive his commission. He did, however, show a great many people that he could shoot. ''At the end of camp, we fired over the 'A' course which started at 200 yards, then moved back through 300, 500 and 600 yards, with both slow and rapid fire. Regular army sergeants conducted all the preliminary training and organized the actual firing. They gave me a rough time over being a port-sider and I was compelled to switch shoulders.'' Charlie alternated shoulders. He shot from the left shoulder for regular offhand, and from the right for rapid fire, using the Model '03 Springfield rifle with its right-hand bolt. He won the CMTC championship.

Next summer, the CMTC people marked Askins as a hopeful for the National Matches at Camp Perry, Ohio. En route to the shoot, he met two men who would become his friends, one a life-long amigo—George Parker. Parker ended up earning his commission by returning to CMTC camp the next year. That fact would play a role in Askins's life later on when George's commission helped him land a job with the U.S. Border Patrol. Parker and Askins solidified a friendship about which Parker said in the Foreword of the Colonel's autobiography, ''There was never a time when there was a doubt in either of our minds that we would go to hell for each other.'' He wasn't one to heap compliments on everybody, but when it came to the Colonel, he couldn't say enough.

Meanwhile, Charlie was growing impatient. He finished high school and in fact taught grades kindergarten through eight for a short while in a one-room school. He lasted only one year. An eighth grade kid as big as Charlie required a little discipline, and after the correction took place— Askins broke his nose with a stick of stove wood—the young man's teaching career was over.

The U.S. Forest Service came next. Charlie believed that his father helped him get the job through the editor of *Outdoor Life*, who knew the right people in the Denver area, where the magazine was published at the time. The young man became a firefighter in the Flathead National Forest of Montana. Then the Major decided to give

Col. Charles Askins, one of the most experienced modern shooters in the U.S. A member of the Forest Service, the U.S. Border Patrol and the National Guard, all before he served military duty in WWII, Askins promoted competitive shooting. He was so accomplished that he brought home 534 medals and 117 trophies from state and national shooting competitions.

The Colonel (left) has hunted on nearly every continent and has made over 30 African safaris. Here, as a younger man in safari dress, he talks with Ad Topperwein, another shooting great who left behind a legend related in this book.

the lad a crack at college. Charlie attended a small four-year teacher's school. But he quit and, at age 20, headed back to the U.S. Forest Service. Adventure began to hound Askins again. He was in on a little manhunt for a desperado who attacked a game warden, and he had a close call with a grizzly bear. After these episodes, and the termination of the summer fire season, Charlie returned home.

He played game warden for a while, which brought more adventure. Then he returned to the Forest Service in a full-time capacity. His job in-

cluded watchdogging grazing rights on public land. A man would be granted so many acres for so many head of livestock. Charlie had to see that these rights were not violated by the running of excess animals. The Apaches were raiding livestock from time to time, and this brought more action into Askins's life. There was even some gunplay, which didn't disturb the young man at all.

Prohibition went into effect when stalwarts of the government decided Demon Rum had to be controlled. As with any taboo, the new law invited immediate disobedience. Meanwhile, the U.S. Border Patrol, now only six years old, had a new fight on its hands. Since it was illegal to distill alcohol in the U.S., one of the best ways to make a fast dollar was to import the stuff. And Mexico was ready to be a prime exporter. Of course, this meant the Border Patrol had a real job to do, forestalling the smuggling of firewater from Mexico.

Enter George Parker. Parker was already a member of the Patrol. He knew Askins would be perfect for the job, and he advised him to join. The two pals didn't work the same district. Parker ended up on the Arizona-Mexico border, Askins on the Texas-Mexico border. Now there was some real adventure to be had, as Askins relates:

The Hudson came to a stop just as I set foot on the ground. The officer who was in the rear seat also alighted. The driver of the

gov't vehicle threw the door open on the left side and hit the ground. He stepped down just as a gunman sitting behind the driver of the old Hudson swung a Model 94 carbine behind the driver's head and let go at the Patrol officer in front. He was struck in the head by the .38-55 bullet and fell dead. The bullet broke up in his skull and a major [bullet jacket] fragment exited and by a strange coincidence struck the patrolman alighting from the back seat in the head. It did not kill him but knocked him unconscious. Thus in the space of two heartbeats and with only a single round, the contrabandista had knocked out two patrolmen and had only myself to contend with.

I ran around behind the smuggler's car and opened fire. I shot the gunman through the eye, the bullet exiting through his temple.

Askins hunted all sorts of dangerous game, including the Cape buffalo, pictured here by artist Philip R. Goodwin. But Askins tailored his own loads and developed his own medicine for the tough African beast. He put up a 416 on the old .404 casing as reshaped in a Fred Huntington die.

I kept right on firing and shot the driver through the kidneys. He later died. A third smuggler in the back seat cautiously poked a sixshooter up over the back seat and got shot through the hand for his pains.

It paid to be a champion shooter when you were on the Border Patrol. At the close of the shootout, Askins heaped his wounded partner, as well as the dead patrolman, into the patrol car and headed for the station. This was before the days of car radios. Later, the chief of the Patrol told Charlie, "Nice shooting."

But the "nice shooting" was not all good for Askins. Too many gunfights marked his career. For political reasons, it might be a good idea if he were transferred to a station where gunplay would be less likely. "To pacify the District Director I am going to assign you to a horseback station. You are going to Strauss," said the Chief. Charlie was happy. He loved horses. He loved out-of-the-way places. This assignment was just right for him. Although not that far from El Paso, the exact locale of duty was in New Mexico. "A fine desert country where there were no towns, precious few inhabitants, a ranch here and there, and the opportunity to get back on a horse again was simply great!" said Askins.

By this time, Charles had married, a fine union based on mutual respect as well as love. Dorothy was totally supportive of her young husband and his work. After five years of marriage a son, Charles Askins III, was born to the couple. "Major Charles Askins was properly delighted and opined that we'd have to make a shooting man of him."

Charles continued with the Border Patrol for a total of five years of service, but a new era was opening for him. He had joined the National Guard. And his ability as one of the country's greatest handgun target shooters was brought to wide attention. He had shot on the Border Patrol and had won many prizes. In fact, it was Askins who promoted competitive shooting in the Border Patrol. Now in the National Guard, his great ability would be more broadly appreciated. He, to put it in Askins's own words, "Knocked off the National Individual Pistol Championship. Along with this I won three NRA national matches." Charles went on to win championship after championship. In due time, Askins had won 534 medals and 117

trophies in state and national shooting competitions. He had truly proved himself one of the best marksmen of the era.

Now it was time to move on from the Border Patrol. Charlie landed other work—not the sort that pays that well, nor did it provide as steady a check as a man likes, but it was the type of job that fit Charles Askins II to perfection. He became a writer. He did well. In 1940, at age 33, Charlie made 4200 dollars with his pen. That was good money at the time. *Outdoor Life* was paying him 300 dollars an article. Meanwhile, Askins had been state champion pistol shooter of Texas five times, and his shooting with the National Guard also continued in full force. A second son, Bill, was born.

When the U.S. entered World War II, Askins went immediately into the fray. Of course he was put to work where he could do the most good, in all manner of armament, and finally the important task of reclamation. Tanks, for example, could be returned to duty, as well as many different types of firearms. Captain Askins was in charge of that duty, to go into an area and reclaim what could be salvaged. This, too, was a shooting part of the war, and there was plenty of danger.

Then tragedy.

Askins was devoted to his wife and his family. A "tough hombre" who was willing to shoot it out on the border or the battlefield, he melted into a caring and concerned man when it came to his family. "After a full day's reconnaissance I came back into the battalion hqrs as the staff was just preparing to eat," reported Askins.

"Here's a cable for you, Captain," said the adjutant.

Askins read, "Your son, Charles Askins III, struck by auto which resulted in his death." Askins remembers his feelings. "To be killed I had always more or less looked forward to [expected to happen], but to have my son swept away was a catastrophe of such enormous proportions that I was left utterly numb. I staggered away to my tent and went inside, laced the flaps and gave myself over to my grief." Charles Askins III, whom they called Chuckie, was hit by a car as he proceeded to school—he was only six. He lingered for three days before dying.

"Is Poppy coming to see me?" the boy asked as he lay in the hospital.

"Yes," his mother soothed him, "They are

going to put Poppy on a B-17 and fly him back here." Poppy never arrived. The boy told his mother, typical of his bravery, "Mommy, I never even cried when the car hit me." Brother Bill was at this time one year old. The knowledge that he had another son was the only thing that kept the Army man sane, he said.

In the African theater, Askins had pioneered battlefield recovery of important tools of war. He

was, by duty, the Battlefield Recovery Officer for the entire U.S. Army. Then came the Battle of the Bulge and Major Charles Askins, for there had been another promotion, was in the thick of it. Finally, the war ended, but there was more military duty. Colonel Askins made 138 jumps with the 82nd Airborne Division and XVIII Airborne Corps, the Spanish Army and ARVN Forces. He also found himself in Vietnam for 14 months as

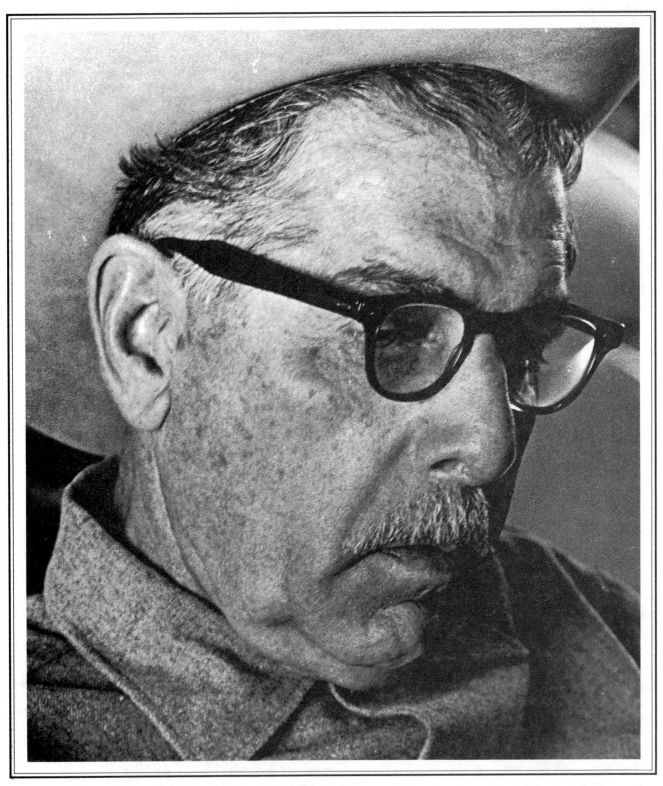

Like his father, Charles Askins enjoys writing about firearms and his shooting adventures. For nine years, he wrote for *American Rifleman* magazine and today, in his 80's, he still pens for *Guns Magazine*.

chief adviser on marksmanship to the Vietnam military.

A PROVOCATIVE WRITER NOURISHES THE PUBLIC

But his career as arms author has lasting importance to us. Askins spent nine years as a writer for *American Rifleman* magazine, during which time he wrote over 100 articles. He also worked for Petersen Publishing Company, writing from the platform of experience. The Colonel has a heyday with editors. He admits that there are great ones, such as George Martin—anyone in the business of arms authorship has to agree with that assessment—but he considers that most editors "taken by and large, are opinionated, prejudiced and arbitrary. They have had precious little hunting experience—ask the next one you meet how many times he has shot on safari—and all are given to tampering with your copy and garbling your meaning. Unfriendly words. But Colonel Askins is not about to take them back. An editor at *American Rifleman* magazine once explained to the Colonel that ". . . most of the letters we get from our 1.5 million readers are critical of your stories. You are, if truth was told, a provocative writer."

When he was 80, Askins claimed that he had grown just a little weary of it all, and that maybe it was time to slow down. At that point he had gone on more than 30 African safaris. "I've finally gotten pretty much a belly full," he said. But it wasn't true. That year, 1987, the Colonel had plans to hunt Wyoming, and to spend a little time with an outdoor writer who lives in that state. But he had to cancel out. It seems he was called to another safari in Africa. Which number? Even the Colonel wasn't sure.

Dangerous game, from bears to Cape buffalo, intrigued Askins. He's hunted all but one continent, taking game of all description, except the sheep, for which he said he never had a desire to climb. George Parker said something about Askins that marks the man: "I have never known any person more gentle with an animal." That denotes the real hunter, for hunters love animals; they are simply realistic enough to know that game population dynamics fluctuate, and that harvesting the wildlife crop makes sense.

Moreover, Askins is an incurable gun crank. King of the wildcatters, P.O. Ackley, (see next chapter) created a multitude of fine home-grown cartridges. Askins hunted with a whole batch of his own design. He admitted one day that a fellow could get by with factory cartridges, but it might be dull. For example, when he wanted a Cape buffalo cartridge, he put one of his own together. "The .458 Mag. certainly will do the job," he said, "but as an inveterate handloader I had to develop my own medicine for the tough African buffalo. My 416 is put up on the old .404 casing as reshaped in a Fred Huntington die." He shot five Alaskan "brown bear," now classified as ordinary grizzly bears, even though anyone who can tell the difference between a cat and a canary can see that the two bears differ significantly. He said of these brutes, "If one of the bites-back kind of critters takes the seat out of my pants one of these fine afternoons it won't be because I shot it with a .270 pipsqueak. I believe in the big calibers for big game." The Colonel classifies the 222 Remington, 223 Remington, 243 Winchester, 6mm Remington and the 270 Winchester as "penny ante stuff." He also believes that the 7mm-08 and 308 Winchester are "for the birds."

Most of us live uneventful lives, which is just the way we want it. There is a Chinese curse that supposedly goes, "May you live in interesting times." War may be interesting. Hard economic times may keep you hopping to earn your bread and butter. Political upheaval, I suppose, can really keep the pot boiling. But as I say, most of us prefer smooth sailing. Colonel Askins, I think, is different. He has welcomed the adventurous events of life with open arms. As these words are published, the Colonel is an octogenarian who still seeks excitement. He is probably off somewhere right now trying to find a Cape buffalo or an elephant, and hoping silently that the animal will decide to charge instead of going the other way. "After all is said and done," wrote Colonel Askins in 1987, "when I look back over eight decades I find little to deplore. I'd turn in my suit with the sense that if I had it to do over again I'd not change an iota of those 80 years."

3

P.O. ACKLEY: KING WILDCATTER

No one knew of course that when Parker Otto Ackley was born on May 25, 1903, he would become the world's most renown wildcatter. He knew, though, as a boy that he loved firearms. At a tender age he was a woods hunter and went about restocking his Stevens Crackshot 22 rimfire rifle. The full-length Mannlicher-style stock was one of the few Ackley ever made. He was inherently a metalworker, not a stockmaker. It was his penchant for changing chunks of steel into meaningful objects that allowed the man later on to wildcat just about every factory cartridge he could lay his hands on, from the smallest to the largest centerfires. He couldn't stand looking at a factory-originated case, it seems, without necking it up or down, blowing it out, or in some manner altering its design. It's a good thing. Ackley's creativeness brought about many useful, exciting and worthwhile cartridges that have contributed to great shooting everywhere.

P.O.—he didn't care to be called Parker, a name he inherited from his mother's side of the family—was raised on a farm in Granville, New York. He'd planned to be a farmer himself, and earned a degree in agriculture from Syracuse University, where he graduated magna cum laude in 1927. He had taken a number of engineering courses along the way, which helped provide a foundation for the work that would one day place him among the best-known barrelmakers in the country. After college, Ackley returned to the rural

life as a scientific farmer. With a wife and family to support, he felt he could make a good living for them from the land. He proved to be a productive farmer, too, yielding fields of the best-looking potatoes anyone in the area had ever seen. But those 'taters just didn't sell. Parker couldn't get a dime a bushel for them.

The Great Depression was on. The stock market crash of 1929 wiped most of the farmers out. Ackley was able to hold on a little longer than his neighbors, but it became clear that farming wasn't going to provide a living at that time in that place. Besides, P.O. had seen an advertisement in the *American Rifleman* magazine. A gunshop owned by Ross C. King was for sale, in Roseburg, Oregon. Parker didn't jump at the chance, but he did think it over. A late spring freeze that killed his crops helped him decide. Ackley would head west. He would buy the King gunshop and move his family to Oregon. A man could do worse. King wanted two thousand dollars for the operation—lock, stock and gun parts. But he didn't need it all at once. P.O. could pay a thousand now and the other thousand when the shop began to bring in a profit. On Memorial Day in 1936, the Ackley family was off to Oregon.

The Depression was bad everywhere, but it was worse in the East. Oregon was a pretty good place to have a gunshop. The populace owned and used firearms. Guns were tools. And guns often broke down or required modification. Many repairs were needed, and Ackley was there to do the job. But he wanted to be more than a repairman.

Barrelmaking filled his mind. You couldn't take up barrelmaking around Roseburg in those days, so P.O. made contact with an old friend, Ben Hawkins. Ben owned a gunshop back East where barrels were made. The chief barrelmaker of the shop, an expert who, at age 12, had been apprenticed in the trade in Germany, became Ackley's tutor. P.O. was totally dedicated to his studies. He was forced to leave his family in Oregon. They were provided for, of course, but Ackley could not learn barrelmaking the way he intended to, and transplant his family at the same time. Away from home, he made barrels seven days a week, day and night, for one full year. Ackley returned to Oregon an accomplished maker of accurate barrels. As Colonel Charles Askins wrote much later, "During three decades, Ackley has made 23 barrels for me. By far, most of these tubes have been for wildcat calibers. I have yet to find any of them that were not splendidly accurate." That endorsement is like having your music applauded by Mozart. Askins, himself the subject of Chapter 2 is one of this country's most experienced shooters and big-game hunters.

Nestled in his Oregon shop, P.O. built a hand-powered deep-hole drill and rifling machine. He had funds to tool up for only one caliber. He chose the 22, not simply for its obvious all-American popularity, but because he could rebore a 22-caliber barrel to a larger one if he had to. Things were going along well, but something happened to skyrocket Ackley's business. U.S. Hubble, of Tensleep, Wyoming, put in an order. The old Army scout wanted a Model 98 Mauser rebarreled to 257 Roberts. Ackley went to work. Blame the machinery if you will, but for whatever reason, the barrel did not delight its maker. At least that's the way P.O. saw it. He found everything wrong with the finished product and very little right. The barrel was placed in a corner, and it may have rested there for quite some time. But U.S. wouldn't have it. Hubble had ordered a 257 Roberts and he would have a 257 Roberts, right now. Ackley finished the job. He watched the mails for a letter of complaint. Instead, U.S. Hubble wrote a letter of praise, not to P.O., but to Fred Ness, then editor of The Dope Bag, a regular and important column in the *American Rifleman* magazine. U.S. loved Ackley's work. "I never got caught up after that,"

P.O. Ackley in his workshop. Although he graduated from Syracuse University with high honors in agriculture, it was the engineering courses that he applied to metal-working that eventually earned him the distinction "Mr. Wildcat."

Ackley reported to Lester Womack, his one-time student and good friend.

World War II got in the way of things. In order to make barrels, you needed barrel blanks. Such materials were not to be had. The war effort claimed them all. Back in his college days, P.O. had been commissioned in the Reserved Officers Training Corps, ROTC. He would be working on guns again, and soon, but not in his own shop. He was sent by the U.S. Army to the Ogden Ordnance Depot in Utah to initiate a repair program. It was so successful that it blossomed into a full-scale arsenal overhaul operation. Ackley was proving his worth. He was also meeting some of the king pins of shooting: Fred Barnes, the well-known bullet-maker, Elmer Keith, the famous rifleman of Chapter 14, and Ward Koozer, a gunmaker of renown.

Koozer had real impact on P.O.'s life. The

P.O. Ackley's world—the professional gunshop. Here gunsmith Dale Storey works at his lathe. Ackley spent many hours using such machinery to "invent" wildcats or make barrels.

two got together and decided to open their own gunshop in partnership after the war. They had their eyes on a place run by George Turner of Cimarron, New Mexico. By 1944, P.O. had accumulated enough points to be granted a discharge from the Army. He and Koozer were off to New Mexico to launch their new venture.

It wasn't that Ackley disliked Cimarron. The area was simply too isolated. A gunshop could thrive only if it got materials, and only if it could send its finished products and repairs to customers without delay. That meant decent rail service. The Ackley enterprise moved to Trinidad, Colorado, where a shop was built in the heart of that little city. Ackley began turning out the Turner mount, now known as the Ackley Snap-In mount.

P.O. Ackley, center, always made the time to assist others. Mr. Wildcat shared his knowledge in his books and in the classroom. For many years, he taught gunsmithing at Trinidad State Junior College in Colorado.

The shop also provided barrels and finished custom rifles. But there was just too much shop traffic. The shop had to be moved again—out of town. It didn't help. People just drove out to get to it.

The war ended and thousands of GIs came home. They needed work. Many of them opted for careers in gunsmithing. Ackley already had a name going for himself, so he was singled out. In two years, P.O. received about 4,000 letters from returning servicemen who wanted to apply the GI Bill to learning the gunsmithing trade. Obviously, the Trinidad shop could not accommodate even a small percentage of that number.

Dean C.O. Banta of Trinidad State Junior College also saw a need for gunsmith training. He hired the best man in town to head a gunsmithing school at the college—P.O. Ackley. The program was started in January 1947 and it is still popular to this day. That's how Lester Womack became a student of the gunsmithing art under Ackley's wing. So did many others. Parker was dedicated. The doors of the shop were open from eight in the morning until ten at night. Students were anxious to build experimental projects as well as complete their course work. P.O. was just the man to steer them—safely—in the right direction.

A very important study of military rifle-action strength ensued. That work has remained a standard for decades. Gunmakers wishing to know the integrity of a given military action can turn to the Ackley-inspired data. They need go no further. "The Strength of Military Actions," written by P.O. Ackley, remains an subject of study to this hour. It appeared in the *Handbook for Shooters and Reloaders*, a 1959 spiral-bound publication.

THE INNOVATIVE CARTRIDGE KING

Ackley was well on the road to being King of the Wildcatters before he began teaching at Trinidad. He had been altering factory cartridge cases for years. These were modified mainly through fire-forming. Fire-formed cases are built by altering the chamber dimension of a rifle and then shooting standard ammunition in the new chamber. The result is a so-called "blown-out" cartridge—a wildcat—for there are no factory rifles chambered for it. The wildcat cartridge offers essentially two advantages over the original. First, it has more case capacity. Therefore, it can hold

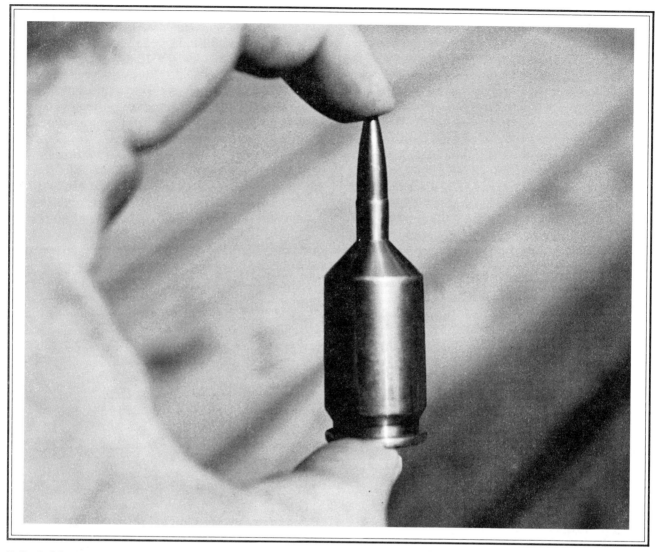

P.O. Ackley couldn't stand looking at a factory case without necking it up or down, blowing it out, or in some way altering its design. This dummy cartridge, chambered for no particular firearm, clearly illustrates what can be done when a professional metal-worker wants to alter a brass cartridge case.

more powder. More powder means greater velocity and energy over the original round. Increased capacity is gained through creating a straight-walled case from a slope-shouldered one. Furthermore, the neck of the cartridge can be reduced in length through fire-forming, which means that part of the brass once used to form the neck of the cartridge is now pushed forward to create a larger capacity body. Short necks posed no problems. In fact, reduced bullet friction from a short neck could offer a little lower breech pressure. Second, the new design had a sharper shoulder angle, which, at least in theory, offered a more efficient burning chamber for powder. (For more on wildcat cartridges, see *The Handloader's Manual of Cartridge Conversions* by John J. Donnelly and *The Book of the Twenty-Two*, Chapter 27, both titles published by Stoeger Publishing Company.)

Ackley's wildcats were far-reaching in design and many examples of good ones abound. The reader interested in studying the Ackley lineup—about 52 rounds of his own design—should check loading manuals, the above book on cartridge conversions and of course the *Hand-*

book for Shooters and Reloaders—the 1959 copy if you can find one—and the more complete 1962 (Volume I) and 1966 (Volume II) editions, which have been available in hardbound and softcover. However, you just can't talk about P.O. Ackley without looking at a few of his innovative cartridges. Three are particularly interesting.

One is the 17 Ackley Bee. Ackley did some fine work on 17s. He interested a number of shooters in the sub-bore high-velocity 17, including the one behind this keyboard. Ackley's little 17 Bee is a somewhat improved 218 Bee cartridge case, with sharper shoulder and straighter wall, necked down to 17 caliber. It launches the 25-grain pill at 3800 feet per second, not quite the zip associated with the superb 17 Remington, but fast enough, and the slight Bee design works well in single-shots, such as the Thompson/Center Contender pistol. Dale Storey as well as other gunmakers have constructed almost miniature rifles based on the Contender action with relatively short rifle barrels and compact stocks, chambered for various cartridges. One of Storey's mini-rifles in 17 Ackley Bee is a real hummer.

Another cartridge is the 7mm/308 Ackley. This little number was made legitimate by Remington in 1980, so it is no longer considered a wildcat. It offers mid-length action chambering

Wildcats have a solid place in the shooter's scheme of things. Dale Storey chambered the 218 Ackley Bee in this mini-single-shot rifle built on the Thompson/Center Contender action.

with a cartridge that essentially duplicates the venerable and excellent 7×57 Mauser (7mm Mauser). Volume I of the *Handbook* says, "The 7mm/.308 is a very fine 'wildcat' made by necking the .308 Winchester case to 7mm, and of course it is very similar to the same case necked to .270." Further remarks suggest that in terms of performance, the round sails on the heels of the 270 Winchester and 280 Remington. Ackley data shows a bullet of 140 grains leaving the muzzle at about 3000 feet per second in this little round. Today, the cartridge is called the 7mm-08 Remington and chronographed ballistics closely match the original data presented by Ackley about 30 years ago. That is truly far-reaching inventiveness in the world of shooting. In conjunction with work on this book, a Sako mid-length action rifle was tested in 7mm-08 Remington caliber and it was extremely accurate. Furthermore, Remington factory ammunition proved to be loaded to meet full advertised ballistics.

The third Ackley cartridge highlighted here is the 7mm Ackley Magnum. Personal prejudice colors this canvas. As noted by RCBS in their Cartridge Board on the 7mm Remington Magnum, my favorite all-around big-game cartridge is Remington's Big 7. Is it ballistically similar to the old Ackley number? You bet. Ackley noted that his 7mm Magnum drove a 160-grain bullet at 3124 feet per second muzzle velocity. Today, the hottest 7mm Remington Magnum factory ammunition chronographed in my tests develops a muzzle velocity of about 3165 feet per second. That is with RWS brand ammunition. My best handloads better that muzzle velocity by a few feet per second, but not in all rifles. Rifles vary, sometimes considerably, in the velocities they produce in accord with bore friction, chamber dimension and other factors. Once again, Ackley was ahead of his time. The 7mm Ackley Magnum is not identical to the 7mm Remington Magnum. I even prefer the case design of the latter (slightly). However, it is certainly a fraternal twin, if not an identical one.

Ackley wasn't the only gunsmith to wildcat cartridges in the earlier days of this century. There were others. But P.O. was not content producing one, two, ten or even 20 wildcats and calling them good. His lineup is perhaps the longest. Furthermore, and this is important, his writing on the subject has promoted a greater under-

standing of the wildcat. Ackley was honest. His wildcats were not his children. If he didn't like one of them after developing it, he said so. Although I cannot agree with his own remarks about the 7mm Ackley Magnum—I think it was a great cartridge—P.O. stated that "the 7×57 Improved should prove to be a much more interesting cartridge because it drives the various weights of bullets nearly as fast as the Magnums with considerably less powder, it is more flexible and barrel life is much better, and after all, the 7mm Improved with the right bullet is sufficiently powerful for almost any type of big game."

THE PROOF IS IN THE SHOOTING

And Ackley knew first-hand about that. Perhaps he was not a dedicated big-game hunter—he didn't roam the continent in search of trophy animals, like some of the other great shooters discussed in this book. But he did his share of hunting. He was greatly interested in the performance of cartridges in the big-game field, and for a period of time he traveled to Texas annually to hunt deer. In the *Handbook* (Volume I), P.O. explains his style of hunting:

Every year I make my annual South Texas deer hunt sort of an experimental hunt. The first deer I shoot with my .257 Roberts Improved, and believe me, it never fails, no matter it seems, where I place the shot. The second deer I usually try out something new on. This past season I decided to try the .17 Javelina. Before some of you start yelling; Texas allows any center fire cartridge to be used on deer. Some counties prohibit rimfires but this is the only calibre restriction in game regulations. I won't go into the details of the hunt because it is not the purpose of this report, and mind you, I am not unequivocally recommending the .17's for big game, but in this particular instance the results were rather startling, at least to me.

Ackley went on to describe the deer harvest using the 17-caliber rifle: "I shot a running deer at a range of 125 to 150 yards, the shot entering the left side high, just ahead of the pelvis." The result? An immediate dispatch.

Ackley was also very good about data-gathering. He had a network of informants, as it were, men who hunted with Ackley wildcat (and other) cartridges, and who reported the results of their experiences to Mr. Wildcat. Thereby, Parker compiled a wealth of field information. He returned some of this information to the shooting public in his books. The 1959 title began with a work by Les Bowman, Wyoming guide and shooter. "How Big a Rifle Do You Need?" provided a forum for Bowman to discuss his opinions about big game cartridges for the "average" sportsman. Since Les owned a ranch and had, in his career, many hunters under his wing in the field, he gathered a great body of practical information on big game cartridge effectiveness. Ackley saw to it that some of that information was made public in his book.

The 1959 version of the *Handbook* contains an article on killing power in which the kinetic energy formula is compared with "impact energy" and pounds-feet theories. Hosea Sarber, the well-known game warden of Petersburg, Alaska, writes on "Rifles for Alaska" in this edition, too. Then P.O. and A.E. Ellinger jointly compose "Bore Capacity in Rifle Shells." The 1959 book includes numerous interesting topics for those interested in ballistics. Bullet performance, sectional density, the chronograph, time of flight factors, headspace and dozens of important shooting topics are broached. Later Ackley works would continue with a presentation of excellent materials prefacing the data portion of the book. In Volume I of the 1962 *Handbook*, Parker tells the interesting story of Allyn H. Tedmon, who was born in 1884 and enjoyed many interesting hunting and shooting experiences. P.O. did not have a one-track mind. The King Wildcatter appreciated shooting on many different levels.

P.O. was a fine teacher. He was realistic. He did not encourage the young men in his classes to wed themselves to a gunsmithing career without understanding that the hours would be long, the pay sometimes meager. He admitted that a working wife helped him leap many a financial abyss. Teaching was fine, but P.O. was a man of enterprise. He began operating P.O. Ackley, Inc. out of Trinidad. And in 1951 he said good-bye to the classroom. Maybe he would have stayed longer; however, stockholders in his company decided to sell to Easton Engineering, which in turn demanded that business be carried out from the Easton home base in Salt Lake City, Utah. Ap-

parently, Ackley had a choice, and he chose enterprise over the classroom. He worked with Easton for a while in Salt Lake, but you can guess what came next—his own shop. P.O. was creative. He had already owned his own business. Although he was essentially his own boss in teaching, building and operating a program, he wanted to get back into a P.O. Ackley shop. He quit Easton.

His new shop thrived. The far-reaching Ackley was a businessman as well as a technical-mechanical metalwork wizard. He hired a few women employees for his Salt Lake operation. They were good. Ackley found that the ladies were interested in the job itself, and in doing that job well. They did not care about personal gunsmith-

Ackley autographing a copy of one of his books. He imparted much knowledge about shooting and cartridges through his writing. He also gathered considerable field information from others, which he included in his titles.

ing and pet gunmaking projects. When one lady was asked about her shooting battery, she admitted to owning no firearms. If not interested in guns, why did she want to work for P.O. Ackley? Because it was a good job. She helped in the process of barrelmaking and she was proficient at what she did. Ackley began to phase out of the barrelmaking business. He expanded his writing with columns in *Guns & Ammo* and *Shooting Times* magazines. His truthful approach couched in modesty made him and his columns popular.

Colonel Askins had much to commend about

King Wildcat and his innovations. In his November 1980 *American Rifleman* article, Askins spoke of the 17 Bee discussed above, but also of the other end of the spectrum, the 475 Ackley Magnum, 375 Magnum brass necked up to accept bullets of almost 48 caliber weighing 600 grains. Using 90 grains of powder, the 475 Ackley Magnum pushes the 600-grain bullet at 2250 feet per second muzzle velocity. Askins also mentioned the interesting 228 Ackley Magnum—interesting because this wildcat demanded much more manufacturing attention than most. A belt was swaged onto the head of a 30-06 Springfield brass. The case was shortened. Then it was formed and necked to accept a bullet of .227-inch diameter. Thus, the 228 Ackley Magnum, which P.O. called the 228 Belted Express, was a 22-caliber cartridge built on a shortened 30-06 case, but made to fire .227-inch bullets instead of .224-inch bullets. These 70-grain bullets could be driven at over 3600 feet per second. There is also a 230 Ackley. Why? Because some states forbid caliber 22 for big game. Therefore, Ackley came up with a 23-caliber cartridge that fired a 75-grain bullet at 3500 feet per second muzzle velocity.

Of Ackley, the man, Askins says, "Indicative of Ackley's modesty are his comments about the 6mm Ackley Mag. He says, 'This is another over-capacity cartridge which in no way compares to the .243 and the 6mm Rem. in their various versions. The case is made by shortening and necking the .300 H&H brass to accept the 6mm bullet. The 6mm Mag. I'd not recommend. It is inefficient, hard to make, and it lacks flexibility.' Ordinarily, pride would prevent a fellow being quite as honest as this!"

P.O. Ackley passed away in Salt Lake City, Utah, on August 23, 1989. At 86, he'd turned his lathe for the last time. Yes, new cartridges will be made and old ones will fade against the backdrop of history. But Ackley's contributions to the shooters of the world—from his involvement in button rifling to the creation of so many wonderful wildcats—will remain indelible.

4

SIR SAMUEL BAKER: BIG GAME HUNTER

Sir Samuel Baker was a 19th-century Englishman who lived for hunting and adventure. While not as well-known as Selous or Bell to modern shooters, Baker led as interesting a life, and perhaps occupies a higher niche in world history as an explorer of note. From 1861 to 1865 during the time of the U.S. Civil War, he investigated the Nile River. He was an opinionated man. His ideas on shooting were adamant, carved in granite with the chisel of experience. Yet these opinions "hold water" even in the reservoir of modern shooting technology—for the most part.

A real English knight, Baker was perhaps in a negative sense a zealot of English hierarchy. He sometimes exhibited an intolerance toward the natives who were hired to tend camp and trod the hunting and exploration trail. It was not uncommon for him—who stood probably six and a half feet tall and weighed a bounteous 250 pounds— to administer corporal punishment to a native who failed to carry out the nobleman's wishes with dispatch. But judge him for his deeds, and in the light of his time. He was a person of courage and strength, never known to recoil from danger or hardship.

Samuel White Baker was born in London in 1821. As with Selous and W.D.M. Bell (see separate chapters), the quest for adventure catapulted him from his homeland. He left when he was in his mid-twenties. Africa. Ceylon. India. He had heard and read of these far-off lands, wild

and untamed. Baker believed that he would find what he was looking for in these places. He was right. Trained as a railroad engineer, Baker's passion was for hunting and exploration. Were he living in our times, he may have been an astronaut. However, his outer space had to be those territories yet untamed by civilization. His appetite for exploration was fed by the hand he wed, according to the documentation. Baker, at age 41, married a Hungarian noblewoman in 1860. With her he explored the Nile. Some biographers disclaim Lady Baker's heritage. Regal or not, her resources apparently furthered Baker's ambition to journey on virgin soil.

While Baker would be known to the general public as an explorer, he was an inveterate hunter and ballistician. He was one of the few hunters of his day to do autopsies on downed game in an attempt to study wound channel and bullet behavior. Frankly, Sam shot an example of just about everything that crossed his path, from sand grouse to elephants, with monkeys and baboons taking up the slack in between. Again, no disparagement intended. Sir Samuel was a great man because he was a leader who could make things happen.

BAKER'S BIG-BORE THEORIES

Of particular interest to modern shooters are Baker's theories and experiences with the firearm of his day. Ballistic power in Sir Samuel's time meant large projectiles. High velocity as we know it was out of the question. The big bore was king. However, Baker had a penchant for massive rifles beyond the norm, even for the time period. He wrote, ''My battery consists of one four-ounce rifle (a single barrel) weighing twenty-two pounds, one long two-ounce rifle (single barrel) weighing 16 pounds, and four double barreled rifles . . . weighing fifteen pounds each.'' Of course, the reference to ounces is the heft of the projectile each rifle fired. The four-ounce ball, for example, weighed about 1750 to almost 1900 grains, depending upon exact missile diameter and style—compare that to a modern 180-grain 30-caliber bullet. In short, Baker was no lover of small tunnels in rifle barrels. However, in spite of a romance with the heavy bullet, Sir Samuel preferred the ''round ball,'' as we would call it, over the conical. While the elongated projectile had the mass, Baker claimed the spherical missile was deadlier in stopping the charge of dangerous game. Coming from a man who fired upon hundreds of elephants and buffaloes, his point of view must be taken seriously. Writing for the *Field* magazine of March 23rd, 1861, Baker said:

I strongly vote against conical balls for dangerous game, they make too neat a wound, and are very apt to glance on striking a bone. The larger the surface struck the greater will be the benumbing effect of the blow. . . . In giving an opinion against conical balls for dangerous game, I do so from practical proofs of their inferiority. I had at one time a two-groove single rifle, weighing 21 pounds, carrying a 3 oz. belted ball, with a charge of 12 drachms powder. This was a kind of ''devil-stopper,'' and never failed in flooring a charging elephant, although, if not struck in the brain, he might recover his legs. I had a conical mould made for this rifle, the ball of which weighed 4 oz., but instead of rendering it more invincible, it entirely destroyed its efficacy, and brought me into such scrapes that I at length gave up the conical ball as useless.

The 12 drachms referred to by Baker translate to 12 *drams*. The term drachm was used interchangeably with dram, and did not refer to the apothecary weight of 60 grains. Nonetheless, Baker's 12 drachm load represents a powder charge of 328 grains of black powder. Baker had great influence on shooters of his time. Lieutenant James Forsyth, later Captain Forsyth, referred often to Baker in *The Sporting Rifle and Its Projectiles* (1863). Baker influenced many others with his big-bore proposition. He was the Elmer Keith of his day, or Elmer Keith was the Baker of our era. Riflemaking had progressed sufficiently by Baker's time to allow the production of double-barreled rifles that could be regulated—both barrels striking close to the same point of impact on the target. Therefore, Baker combined the big bore with the double gun, giving two rapidly delivered, powerful blows on dangerous game.

In the middle years of the 19th century, the English riflemaker was struggling with various aspects of his art, as were his American counterparts during the same span of firearm history. Baker's theories on rifling were being put to the test. Not to say that Sir Samuel had individually invented anything new. However, his concept of deep grooves for the round ball was absolutely correct. He also called for, but did not always end up with, a slow rate of twist for the spherical missile. James Forsyth and Major Shakespear echoed the slow-twist sentiment. Baker had special rifles made up to illustrate his ideas. The rifles proved that a rapid rate of twist combined with shallow grooves could cause a ''stripping'' of the ball on the lands, also called ''tripping over the rifling.'' Instead of being guided by the lands, the ball rode over the top of them. Baker commissioned the building of rifles with deeper grooves, to help remedy the stripping problem. Furthermore, Baker deduced that a slower twist plus deeper grooves would allow a larger powder charge, with commensurate higher velocity. Previously, one way to remedy the stripping problem in faster-twist rifles was to reduce the powder charge, which lowered the velocity of the projectile so that it would not trip over the rifling. This brought a reduction in power and a higher trajectory.

In his own words, Sir Samuel said:

In 1840, I had already devoted much attention to this subject, and I drew a plan for an experimental rifle to burn a charge of powder so large that it appeared preposterous to the professional opinions of the trade.

Sir Samuel Baker, knight of England, elephant hunter of Ceylon and explorer of the Nile country. Baker was a 19th-century proponent of the big bore and the round ball, even for dangerous game.

I was convinced that accuracy could be combined with power, and that no power could be obtained without a corresponding expenditure of powder. Trajectory and force would depend upon velocity; the latter must depend upon the volume of gas generated by explosion.

The experimental rifle, built by Gibbs of Bristol, weighed 21 pounds, with a barrel length of 36

An inveterate hunter and ballistician, Baker was one of the few hunters of his day to do autopsies on downed game in an attempt to study wound channel and bullet behavior. He had a few exciting moments with one of the more dangerous animals of any land, the crocodile.

inches. The rifle was designed to fire a round ball of three-ounce weight. This was a belted ball, which means precisely what it implies, a sphere of lead girdled by a raised rib integral with the missile itself. Sir Samuel also had a mould built for a four-ounce conical bullet for the same test rifle. Oddly enough, the rate of twist was 1:36, which would suit the large conical better than the ball; however, the ball fired well anyway for this reason: There was so much volume in the huge bore that pressures were not high, even with heavy powder charges. Velocity was modest, probably no higher than 1500 feet per second. Therefore, the ball was not going fast enough to strip.

Later tests revealed that a turn in 90 inches was quite adequate for stabilizing large-caliber round balls. Furthermore, Baker designed his rifle as a two-groove, with "exceedingly deep" grooves. The deep groove created a tall land. The high land gripped the ball fiercely with considerable "bite," further ensuring that it would not strip. Baker's big bore did not require that the projectile be hammered home. It could be pressed downbore with a loading rod. The round ball was fitted with a greased linen patch, while the powder charge was introduced to the breech in a unique manner: Envision a long loading rod with a one-ounce cup on the end. The cup is filled with powder. Rather than pouring the powder downbore, the rifle is reversed, muzzle pointing downward. The muzzle is slipped over the end of the loading rod containing the powder on its tip. The ramrod is slid up the barrel until the end with the cup of powder touches home in the breech. Then the rifle is ro-

tated muzzle-up. This puts the entire powder charge in the breech, without granules becoming lodged in the rifling by pouring downbore in the usual fashion.

The Baker-designed rifle went on to serve its master admirably. When the explorer first visited Ceylon in 1845, he found a country where hunters did not use the rifled arm. The smoothbore was preferred. Baker reported that these smoothbores were loaded with double charges of powder and a hardened ball. (Records show that round balls were heat-treated to harden them, although details of the process and degree of hardness attained by the heat treating process were not available.) Sir Samuel remarked that the smoothbores withstood the heavy charges of powder *somehow*. The reason they did not burst has to do with the statement made earlier concerning the large volume of bore and consequent reduced pressures. According to Baker, these were 14-bore and 16-bore firearms for the most part. Baker stated that he was the first hunter to introduce rifled firearms to Ceylon, which is probably true. The hunting was dangerous. Samuel related that "Before breechloaders were invented, we were obliged to fit out a regular battery of four double rifles for such dangerous game as elephants, buffaloes, etc., as the delay of re-loading was most annoying and might lead to fatal accidents."

Good luck did not always carry the black-powder hunter out of the path of destruction. Great ballistic force was needed to deliver a telling blow that would stop a charge. How much power? Immense. The chart below reveals the sort of sheer ballistic force Baker was dealing out with

Rifle Bore	Bore Dia.	Powder Charge	Bullet Weight (grains)	Rifle Weight (pounds)	Recoil (ft.–lbs.)	Muzzle Velocity (f.p.s.)	Velocity 100 yds. (f.p.s.)	Muzzle energy (ft.–lbs.)	Energy 100 yds. (ft.–lbs.)
4	1.052"	14 dr.	1882	24	158.4	1450	1217	8832	6222
4	1.052"	12 dr.	1250	20	102.4	1460	1099	5912	3351
8	.835"	10 dr.	862	16	85.0	1654	1193	5232	2720
10	.775"	273 gr.	670	11	79.8	1600	1117	3829	1866
12	.725"	110 gr.	547	7½	42.5	1384	985	2324	1185
12	.725"	191 gr.	599	13	50.3	1584	1111	3356	1650

The table above is extracted from the work of W.W. Greener. The figures for each caliber are not universal and riflemakers did not adhere to strict bore dimensions. Rifles were often constructed with unique bore sizes for which the gunmaker would build moulds to match the individual rifle bore. Therefore, it is possible to find, for example, two 4-bore rifles that shoot projectiles of different diameter.

Baker shot an example of just about everything that crossed his path, from sand grouse to elephants. He learned quickly that the pachyderm was smart—and dangerous.

his largest blackpowder firearms—note that his largest rifle had more foot-pounds of energy at 100 yards than the present-day 458 Winchester has at the muzzle.

A well-documented case of how tenacious a charging animal can be comes from W.T. Thom, recorded in his book, *Wild Sports of Burmah and Assam*, a London printing, 1900. According to the account, the hunters were in pursuit of the Asian seladang or gaur, of the wild cattle family, similar in size to the African Cape buffalo. The victim of the hunt was a Captain Syers, a police commissioner for the Federated Malay States. Syers and his partner were armed with 577 double rifles, yet they were unable to stop the final charge of the seladang. The animal was hit solidly with multiple missiles, but would not fall. At close range, the bull charged again. Syers scored two hits with his 577 rifle, but the animal did not swerve from his mission. The man was struck full on by the bull. It's not unusual for a buffalo to knock its intended victim down and then gore or trample him. As Syers careened to the earth, the bull attacked him. Meanwhile, Syers' partner fired two more 577 bullets into the seladang, but these did not drop the animal either. The bull's horn caught Syers in the chest and penetrated. The man held on for 11 hours, then died. The bull had absorbed 15 bullets, most of them in the shoulder area, before succumbing. The concensus of opinion—a bigger rifle would have saved Syers' life.

Baker was a wolverine by nature. He would pursue his game through any sort of territory until he got his shot. Incidentally, not all of his shooting with the big bores was from close range. Some shots were very far, even by modern standards. Fortunately, there were eye witnesses to many of these long-range strikes, or the feats may have gone unrecorded for fear of disbelief. In Ceylon, Baker was in pursuit of water buffalo, animals of great tenacity, if not quite on par with the Cape buffalo of Africa. "One of the bulls," said Baker in his book, *The Rifle and the Hound in Ceylon*, "from this herd had separated from the troop, and had taken to the lake; he had waded out for about four hundred yards, and he was standing shoulder deep. This was a fine target, a black spot upon the bright surface of the lake, although there was not more than eighteen inches of his body above the water." Baker proved his marksmanship. He

was confident of two things: He could hit the bull and the blow would be fatal. The modern ethic would be to hold fire, of course, but this was Ceylon, devoid of hunters, replete with wild animals, and it was the 19th century—Sir Samuel would shoot. He explained:

I rode to the very edge of the lake, and then dismounting, I took a rest upon my saddle. My horse, being well accustomed to this work, stood like a statue, but the ball dropped in the water just beyond the mark. The buffalo did not move an inch until the third shot. This hit him, and he swam still further off; but he soon got his footing, and again gave a fair mark as before. I missed him again, having fired a little over him. The fifth shot brought luck, and sunk him.

Baker continued to try long shots the rest of the day until his shoulder "was so sore from the recoil of the heavy rifle . . . that I was obliged to reduce the charge to six drachms, and give up the long shots." The retrieved buffaloes revealed that the huge round balls had penetrated deeply, in spite of the range. Those of us who hunt with muzzleloaders today are often surprised by the inordinate penetration of the lead ball. However, owing to the terrific mass of Baker's projectiles, momentum was high. And it was that high momentum that promoted projectile penetration. High mass meant high retained energy, as the Greener table discloses. The ballistically inferior shape of the round ball was therefore overcome to a degree by the sheer caliber of the big-bore rifle. Furthermore, Baker demanded huge powder charges, and his rifles *were built to take them*, unlike some muzzleloaders of his day, and ours.

CAMPING IN HIGH STYLE

While Sir Samuel, English nobleman, was up to roughing it if he had to, he didn't if he didn't have to. On one hunt, accompanied by the Honorable Stuart Worthy, E. Palliser, Esq., and Lieutenant V. Baker, Samuel's brother, the host was attended by four personal servants. The camp had a cook, four housekeepers, and fifty coolies. There were two tents. One held four beds and a dressing table. The other housed a dining room, complete with linen and fine table service. Provisions were plenty, if not profuse: wine, both sherry and Mad-

When Sir Samuel explored during the last century, travel with porters was common. What was uncommon, however, was Baker's lavish camp and luxurious provisions.

eira, brandy, curaçao, biscuits, sugar, coffee, tea, hams, tongues, sauces, pickles, mustard, sardines, tins of soup, preserved meats and vegetables, currant jelly, macaroni, vermicelli, flour, plenty of soap for bathing and candles for light. This was Sir Baker's truck, but not all of it.

"Although I can rough it if necessary," admitted the knight, "I do not pretend to prefer discomfort from choice. A little method, and a trifling extra cost, will make the jungle trip anything but uncomfortable." Of soap and candles he said, "No one knows the misery should either of these fail—dirt and darkness is the necessary consequence." Of course, Lady Baker was along on many of the hunting trips, which prompted further care in keeping a comfortable camp. Lady Baker did hunt. Her husband recounted in *The Nile Tributaries of Abyssinia:* "Early on the following morning the lions were still roaring, apparently within a hundred yards of the camp. I accordingly took a Reilly No. 10, double rifle, and accompanied my wife, who was anxious to see these glorious animals, and who carried my little Fletcher No. 24 [about 50 caliber]."

Is it true that Baker had no genuine feeling for the native people? No. In his eight years as planter/hunter in Ceylon, he founded a settlement and a sanatorium, both affording aid and comfort to the people of the country. Furthermore, he was party to the anti-slavery movement. That seems incongruous with his attitude toward the non-European; however, he was a man with a sense of fairness beneath his exterior lordshipness.

Sir Samuel White Baker continued to explore the duration of his days. Fortunately, his pen worked as well as his rifle and he left many books behind. Among them were: *The Rifle and the Hound in Ceylon,* 1854, *Eight Years' Wanderings in Ceylon,* 1855, *Ismalia,* 1874, *Wild Beasts and Their Ways,* 1890, and other titles. Several of his books were bestsellers in their day. This Ishmael of the last century visited not only Ceylon, Africa and India, but also Japan, Cyprus, Syria, and even America.

Baker died in England on December 30, 1893. He was among the first shooters to have test rifles built, and to try these firearms in the field. He promoted the building of better bullets as well as rifles. And he will always be remembered by students of gunnery as the thinker and shaker who helped develop the big-bore "elephant rifle" of his era.

5

W.D.M. BELL:
"KARAMOJO" IVORY HUNTER

If your name were Walter Dalrymple Maitland Bell, you would probably prefer "DWM," which is exactly how this famous ivory hunter was known. Bell was especially admired by American sportsmen because he was an experimenter throughout his shooting career. His field of experience was well-planted with many different trees of knowledge. When he spoke or wrote of his shooting ideas, people paid attention, for WDM Bell was an authority in his time, with vast credits to back his claims.

WDM Bell was born in Scotland in 1880. His upper middle-class merchant father probably wanted Walter to plant his feet precisely in Papa's well-defined and staid tracks. But the young man's destiny was written with the ink of adventure.

Bell's friends and teachers considered him intelligent. And they admired him for his physical prowess and courage. Before his twenty-first birthday, the restless young man had been engaged as an apprentice seaman, a professional hunter who culled lions for the railroad in Uganda (the lions made hors d'oeuvres of the workers as they tried to lay track), an ivory hunter, a prospector in Canada during the 1897 Gold Rush and a scout in the Boer War. Bell's gold-seeking qualified him as a North American pioneer, as well as a pioneer to Africa.

Bell also worked for a gunsmith in his early years, when he learned the fine art of regulating the barrels of big-bore double rifles. This experience qualified him as a practical gunsmith, but his work with the big rifles left him with a lifelong monkey riding on his back--flinching. Indirectly, WDM's flinching made him even more famous than he ordinarily would have been.

Because of WDM's sensitiveness to the big bores, he hunted elephants with a deer rifle. His hatred for big-bore firearms led him to the little 276 Rigby, which is no more than a 7×57mm Mauser shooting the 173-grain, full-metal-jacketed bullet at about 2200 to 2300 feet per second muzzle velocity. Bell strode into the ivory field, dropping 700 of a total of 1,011 elephants with the comparatively tiny 7mm rifle. John "Pondoro" Taylor, author of *African Rifles and Cartridges*, stated that Bell was very happy with the little 276 Rigby, calling it his favorite. However, Taylor laid no bouquets upon the diminutive 7mm round, saying it was minimal for African shooting. In fact, Bell himself did not recommend the 7mm for African sportsmen. The great ivory hunter never advised the 7mm for pachyderms. It was a "Do as I say, not as I do," proposition. Bell preferred the light recoil of the 7mm, and in the hands of the great "Karamojo," a name derived from the African district where Bell hunted, the tiny rifle performed miracles. WDM was a wonderful game shot. He was so good that he also employed the even smaller 6.5×54mm cartridge with its 160-grain bullet departing the muzzle at only

2200 feet per second. To Bell, the modest 318 Westley-Richards, another of his favorites, was also a competent big game instrument in Africa.

Bell's superb marksmanship was widely acclaimed and verified by many hunters and writers of the day. He and the little rifle became unified in character. Bell was the ivory hunter who used a slight 7mm rifle. Many forgot that Bell did not advise the 7mm for big game applications. Bell was written about, and he also wrote of his own hunting exploits. In his celebrated book, *Karamojo Safari*, long out of print, but still available from used book dealers, Bell explained the dropping of a departing bull elephant with a brain shot:

Of course, sometimes that kind of shot fails . . . The timing may be a fraction out. Or the bullet may be deflected. And in this connection the otherwise incomparable 7mm. bullet came under suspicion in my mind. There began to arise those times when one felt everything was all right and yet failure was registered. I began using a .318 bullet of 250 grains with long parallel sides—like an enlarged .256 bullet in fact—for those slanting through-the-neck shots. At once the inexplicable misses ceased.

Bell labeled his .318-inch 250-grain bullet a four-diameter projectile, the length of the bullet being approximately four times its caliber. The great hunter felt that the 318 was proficient in the African big game field, especially for the brain shot, because of its good sectional density. In *Karamojo Safari* Bell stated that the big bores did not enjoy the length for diameter advantage of the 318, with 465 and 470 bullets offering 2.5 calibers and the

Every shot counted if Bell was to make a living at ivory hunting. His hunting style was to get razor close before firing with his little 7mm rifle. A premier shooter, he was noted by many as the finest shot in his Karamojo district.

Ivory hunting was a venture between the natives and the Europeans, jointly pursuing jumbo wherever the big pachyderms led them. The elephants were used as camp food as well as for their ivory, and Bell was especially fond of trunk meat stewed with vegetables.

577 only 1.5 calibers in length to diameter ratios. While Karamojo Bell liked 318 bullets, he said:

> I hated the .318 case, with its mean-looking powder space—it is merely a .30 U.S.A. Springfield .30-06 case—its miserable shoulders hardly wider than the bullet. But for some inexplicable reason the effect on the recipient of that bullet is startling and not to be observed in the case of any other bullet that I have used, and that includes everything up to the 800-grain bullets driven by 120 grains of Cordite . . . both triggers of a double .400 wired together.

DWM preferred the custom rifle. Both his 276 and 256 rifles were hand-built by noted gunmak-ers. But the great hunter felt he had to apply his own gunsmithing talents to the 256, whittling away on the rifle until it weighed but five pounds. Bell was a rifle lover. He believed in personalizing a special rifle in order to gain the most from it. He admired quality, and his appreciation of good craftsmanship is clearly seen from his own elated remarks. When he received a custom rifle made by Fraser of Edinburgh he wrote, "A genius in his own line. I shall never forget the unpacking of that .256 in the wilds of the African bush, the ripping open of that tin-lined case that looked so incredibly small. There, wrapped in grease-proof paper, lay the oily little rascal. Out in the hot sun it was but a moment's work to strip off the mercurial grease Fraser used for protecting his steel-work on tropical voyages." Bell's enthusiasm

During Bell's days in turn-of-the-century Africa, he often encountered the natives of the land, proud warriors like these.

spills from the page. We visualize the little rifle in his hands, the hunter tracing his fingertips over its lines. "What a thrill to just handle it," exclaimed Karamojo. The rifle connoisseur of today finds a special line of communication with DWM Bell, a shared appreciation. Bell was soon in the field with his new rifle. He went forth to bag 12 elephants with 12 shots from the little 256. But the hunter was to be denied immediate continued success with his prize—the 256 began to fail because of bad ammunition, with split necks and ballistic problems. Bell lost an elephant over it. The ivory hunter returned to his faithful 276 Rigby.

That Bell was a great shooter is akin to saying that it snows in Alaska. He was a great hunter of almost boundless energy. Bell hunted often with his warrior companion Pyjale. The two literally ran after their quarry until WDM could negotiate for a clear brain shot. The ivory hunter wore out 24 pairs of boots in one season, averaging, he estimated, about 73 miles on foot for every jumbo brought down. In spite of their sandals, the native hunters who joined Bell in the bush had to quit the work within a given framework of time because the soles of their feet would not hold up to the continued walking and running over the harsh terrain. Bell was tough, all right. He often lived for days on sour milk and "biltong," which was a kind of jerky or dried meat.

WDM Bell was a businessman as well as a hunter. He made a living from the land, just as shrimp fishermen today garner a livelihood from the sea. From Bell's careful records, we are able to understand the nature of ivory hunting, a business carried out during a time when the wilds of Africa were truly wild. The areas were teeming with creatures of all kinds, and we must not apply the morals and game laws associated with today's circumstances to a time that was nothing like our own.

Bell's best day would include 1,643 pounds of ivory derived from 21 tusks taken from 11 elephants. One jumbo had only a single tooth. This amounted to 78 pounds average weight for an earnings of 863 British pounds. His best year afforded an income of 7,300 British pounds, with 3,100 spent for overhead, leaving a profit of 4,200 pounds. Of course, as a businessman he also incurred losses. His worst year saw no profit at all. The red part of the ledger overshadowed the black

by a total of 1,837 pounds. By and large, however, Bell's labors in Africa afforded him a comfortable existence back in Scotland. He earned over 100,000 early 20th-century dollars plying his trade as an ivory hunter.

While his 276 Rigby-Mauser accounted for ivory, it also brought in camp meat. He enjoyed pursuing the game that fed his party and himself and was fond of elephant trunk meat cooked with vegetables. He hunted Cape buffalo, too. Again, we can't measure a distant time with a modern yardstick. Bell shot between 600 and 700 Cape buffalo in his career, a considerable tonnage, though in no way comparable to losses due to recent droughts in Africa. In one stint, the hunter-marksman collected 23 buffaloes for 23 shots. All were used for food.

BULLET PLACEMENT IS THE KEY

But, wait, Karamojo used a 22 Savage Hi-Power when he dropped those two dozen buffs. Hunting a 1500-pound hooved devil like a Cape buffalo with a 22-caliber rifle is like stopping a freight train with a hairpin. In keeping with Bell's philosophy of shot placement instead of bullet momentum, the great hunter found the 22 Savage Hi-Power much to his liking and quite effective. Firing an 80-grain bullet in his rifle, Bell directed the missile to the vitals of the animal. With his pipsqueak 22-caliber rifle, Bell bagged 25 lions and 16 leopards, along with the buffs. Bullet placement. That was the key to success. Bullet placement overcame the obvious lack of cartridge power for Bell. He was, of course, a brilliant shot. The projectile usually found its mark—not the head of an elephant, but those few square inches—a four-inch area, it was noted—that represented a boulevard to the brain—not the neck of a Cape buffalo, but the exact juncture where the missile would penetrate and shatter a vertebra.

Bell used iron sights. Although he was not opposed to the telescopic sight, glass aiming devices were simply not that prevalent in his day. He was a passionate hunter—not for ivory alone, and not always to feed his men in camp—but for the love of the hunt itself. At home in Scotland, he harvested the red stag and wrote of his adventures in "The Neck Shot," in the January 1950 issue of *American Rifleman* magazine. Bell used the 22 Hi-Power for these good-sized stags. The

An interesting relationship between Africans and Europeans evolved because of the big game hunt. Although an unfortunate prejudice existed among many "white hunters," the black tracker was highly respected for his skills in the bush.

renowned hunter explained, "The .22 Hi-Power cartridge, for example, has completely ousted the .275 and the .303 from several large forests." He used the 70-grain bullet for stags. The thesis of Bell's article matched its title—make a neck shot with a rifle of modest power, and the harvest will be quick and humane. The reader might guess that WDM was a fan of the 220 Swift. He said of that great cartridge, "The .220 Swift seems to be the cartridge expressly designed by Providence, acting through the agency of Winchester Company experts, for the humane killing of wild animals at distances hitherto considered risky or even impossible, provided that the neck shot is selected as the target." Bell was consistent. His regard for smaller rifles combined with good marksmanship and proper bullet placement resided with him for a lifetime.

Bell continued to employ many different rounds in his hunting career. The field experimenter in him would not be denied. The 303 Lee-Metford was the first cartridge he had used in Africa, with its 215-grain round-nose "solid" bullet. We know he liked the 256, although his success with that cartridge was thwarted by poor ammunition performance. The 318 Westley Richards earned the great hunter's respect and admiration, too. He almost had a covenant with the 22 Hi-Power, even against dangerous game, where he and the cartridge "agreed" to get things done in style, the hunter guiding the bullet and the bullet penetrating to effect a clean harvest. He was a fan of the 220 Swift, too, directing its high-speed little pill where it counted on the game animal target.

When World War I struck, Bell left the Congo, selling his gear and heading directly to England to enlist for duty. He joined the Royal Flying Corps and won a military cross for aerial intelligence over East Africa. He earned the rank of Major, and as a fighter pilot was cited for bravery, as well as unerring marksmanship. The two traits had served him well throughout his hunting career, and now as well in military duty. After the war, he wrote about his hunting adventures in *Wanderings of an Elephant Hunter*, published in 1923, and later *Karamojo Safari*, which appeared in 1949. *Bell of Africa*, a biography about the famous shooter, was posthumously printed in 1961.

In 1954, DWM Bell was dead. We wish to know more of his life, but must content ourselves with what we have. The smaller facts have fallen through the crevices of time, but the larger truths pertaining to his exploits, his idiosyncrasies as great hunter and riflemen, his tenacity, innate abilities and bravery, have remained on the surface of memory. Walter Dalrymple Maitland Bell was one of the greatest of the great shooters of his, or any other, era.

6

JOHN BROWNING: AMERICAN ARMS DESIGNER

The train depot in Ogden, Utah, is of particular interest to anyone who loves the era of steam engines. I remember the huge steam locomotives pulling, sometimes pushing, long strings of railroad cars through the town of my youth. Their power was absorbed by the earth and riveted back into every building on the block and through your feet as you watched them throttle by. The diesel engines that replaced the iron giants lacked both acoustic character and visual elegance. It was the nostalgia of the old-time trains that drew me to the station house, but it was the small gun museum within that held me spellbound and filled me with awe.

The museum was designed to honor John Moses Browning, known broadly as the greatest firearms inventor of all time, an irrefutable title. The Winchester rifles alone merit a book: the single-shot design of 1885, the famous Models 1886, 1890, 1892 and 1895. And the 1887, 1893, 1897 and 1906 Winchesters that sprang from the Browning mind as well. Don't forget the design that still lays fair claim as being the most successful "deer rifle" of them all—the 1894, or Model 94 Winchester "30-30."

John Browning's genius lay behind all of the basic Colt auto pistols. He was responsible, too, for the BAR (Browning Automatic Rifle) and for the 50-caliber machine gun. Every standard issue machine gun in World War II was parented by Browning. All branches of the armed forces employed these big guns. Even the 303 British machine gun, used on the Spitfire and Hurricane RAF (Royal Air Force) fighter planes in the Battle of Britain, were of Browning design. Essentially, no modern shooter with a liberal interest in firearms can escape the influence of John Moses Browning. He was a giant in his field. His success was as deep as his interests, whether they were semi-automatic shotguns, over/under shotguns, pistols or rifles. His gun designs still excel. The Browning over/under remains one of the finest-handling shotguns in the world.

John Browning's fascination with firearms was as natural to him as inhaling. His father, Jonathan, a strong link in a family chain dating back to 1600 America, was himself a maker of guns. Jonathan was born in Sumner County, Tennessee, in October 1805. With no formal schooling to guide him, the man learned his lessons at the foot of experience and the hand of ingenuity. In his early teens, he was given a worn flintlock rifle in lieu of seven days of farm service. The firearm was considered worthless. Jonathan tinkered in the shop of a friendly blacksmith, repaired the gun and sold it back to the former owner for four dollars.

Jonathan continued to work in the blacksmith shop, where he learned all major aspects of metalsmithing. He became a self-tutored gunsmith, and his good mind brought him well beyond the shore of repair to the ocean of invention.

John Moses Browning, premier firearms designer. This portrait hangs in the Browning Museum in Ogden, Utah, the town of Browning's birth.

Moving to Nashville, Jonathan learned more of the gunmaking business from a "real" gunsmith and would eventually handcraft his own barrel. The gunsmith, Samuel Porter, liked the boy and was willing to train him, knowing that Jonathan's search for knowledge would lead him to his own shop one day. And it did. This is not intended as Jonathan Browning's story so much as the background of John Moses's life, for the elder Browning's influence on his son is paramount to understanding the man who would become the world's greatest arms designer. Jonathan Browning became noted for his repeating rifles, including a longarm with a revolving cylinder, and another with a "harmonica" slide. The slide constituted a five-shot magazine consisting of a rectangular bar of iron with essentially multiple chambers. The bar slid through an aperture in the breech, presenting a fresh load each time it was indexed.

Jonathan Browning's legacy to his son was at least three-fold. First, he gave him a geography of wide open spaces. The elder Browning, having become interested in the Church of Jesus Christ of Latter-Day Saints, moved from Tennessee to Illinois and eventually to the valley of Salt Lake, a place where the newly formed Mormon Church could prevail in peace. Brigham Young chose Mr. Browning to act as gunsmith to help provide firearms for the Mormons moving westward. In 1852 Jonathan himself was encouraged to load his own wagons and family of 10 children to make the trip. (Before his death, Jonathan would have three wives and father a total of 22 children, divided equally among girls and boys.) There in Ogden, Utah, John Moses would be born on January 23, 1855. Second, because the elder Browning was a gunsmith, his son would continually be exposed to firearms in his youth. Guns were a part of John's life from the start. And third, Jonathan, it is said, encouraged his son's inventiveness. He provided gunwork early in John's life and allowed his son to take over in the shop when he was frequently away.

At age 10, John Moses made his first firearm. The crude instrument, in essence detonated as a matchlock would be, brought home three birds for supper first time out. The young inventor's mother, Elizabeth Clark, was on his side, seeing the provision of table fare a testament of gun-building success. The father, however, was dubious, for during dinner, he happened to ask about the origin of the birds. John told his father about the gun. The elder Browning asked to see it. According to the book, *John M. Browning, American Gunmaker*, by Browning and Gentry, the father finally said, "You're going on eleven; can't you make a better gun than that?" And so he did.

BROWNING'S FIRST RIFLE

John made his first "real" rifle in 1878. He was 23 years old. The story goes that John was studying a particularly overcomplicated single-shot rifle when he remarked to his father that he could make a better model himself. Ever-encouraging, the father suggested he do just that. "I know you could, John Mose. And I wish you'd get at it. I'd like to live to see you do it." (from Browning and Gentry, page 59) In that year, John built two single-shots. One, with a forward lever, apparently achieved little success. The other eventually bore the name "Winchester." Today, we find the rifle represented in Browning's B-78 single-shot. Browning's first patent, No. 220,271, for

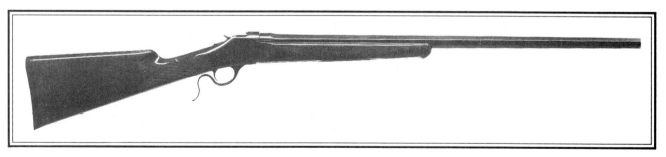

The 1885 Single Shot Rifle was the first patent John Browning sold to the Winchester Repeating Arms Company. It launched a long, lucrative career of firearms inventions, many of which are still being produced today.

The author tries a Model 71 Winchester, a rifle descended directly from the famous Model 1886 Winchester designed by Browning. It is difficult to find a contemporary shooter who has no experience with a rifle originally developed by Browning.

the single-shot cartridge rifle was granted in May 1879.

The year 1879 was a poignant one, filled with highs and lows. John had celebrated his marriage to Rachel Teresa Child on April 10. But on June 21, his father, at age 74, passed away. The elder Browning had lived to see his son build that rifle. When he'd left his shop to John, Jonathan must have known that the road to arms invention had been but lightly tread upon by his son. There were many more steps to come.

The Winchester Repeating Arms Company, owned by Oliver F. Winchester and based in New Haven, Connecticut, was contacted and saw the Browning single-shot. Thomas Bennett, general manager at the time, boarded a train for Ogden to see the factory that produced this "BROWNING BROS. OGDEN UTAH" firearm. The brothers had produced about 600 of the rifles between 1880 and 1883. That year, John Moses sold the manufacturing and sales rights to Winchester for the sum of $8,000. It was a sizable lump of green in those days and a landmark that provided essential working capital. The firearm was introduced to the shooting public as the 1885 Single Shot and was produced by Winchester in an incredible array of calibers until 1920.

Two more designs emerged, a bolt-action repeater, U.S. Patent No. 261,667, which possessed little of specific interest except that it had a tubular magazine, and another repeater, No. 282,839, a lever-action model with tubular magazine, now in the Ogden museum. Meanwhile, the Browning retail store thrived, run by John's three half-brothers as well as his full-brother, Matt, who may have helped with some of the early design work. The Winchester patent money was hard at work, freeing John's inventive mind. Although there is evidence that Browning did design firearms on paper, the usual engineering style, he proved to be more a sculptor in steel than a draftsman. Many of his firearms were created essentially by hand-building a prototype, then preparing drawings of the actual rifle *after the fact*.

By October 1884, Browning was ready to unveil one of the finest lever-action, big game rifles of all time, the design that would become known as the Winchester Model 1886. Much later, the '86 would evolve into the Model 71 Winchester; however, in its original form the rifle may well have been the best piece of machinery

a late 19th-century hunter of big game could ask for. Here was a rifle capable of handling the larger blackpowder cartridges. It was foolproof in function, sufficiently accurate for hunting, and smooth-actioned and steady with good balance. The two '86s of my personal ownership were as reliable as the rising of the sun. The '86 was a most impressive rifle, and Browning did not show it to Winchester until the patent was secured. The inventor may have received around 50,000 dollars for this patent. The gun enjoyed immense popularity and the Winchester company manufactured nearly 160,000 continuously through 1935.

Browning's patents were purchased outright, rather than by payment of royalties. The genesis of the arms invention to follow is not easily sorted out. There were other models that briefly saw the light of day, but that never made it to production, even though Winchester did buy patents on some of them. Winchester did, however, want a shotgun. Reportedly, Browning suggested a pump-action model. Winchester believed that the lever-action model was all but synonymous with the company name, and that's probably why the Model 1887 lever-action Winchester shotgun was born (No. 336,287). Remember, of course, that by purchasing a patent, even for a firearm that Winchester had no intention of producing, the use of the same design by a competitor was precluded entirely. In other words, Winchester's patent purchases for arms never produced was a shrewd business maneuver.

In short order, during 1885, 1886 and 1887, Winchester had the best single-shot cartridge rifle, the best repeating lever-action big-game rifle, and what must have been the best repeating shotgun offered in that specific time niche, all from the Utah inventor. Shortly thereafter, Browning sold Winchester designs for pump-action shotguns and a 22-rimfire rifle. Winchester issued this latter model as the 1890. Not only was this rifle a completely workable repeating 22, but it spurred the invention of the later-to-be-famous Model 62 Winchester "pump," which any carnival shooting-gallery fan will remember with nostalgia. Many of my immediate shooting friends owned a 62. I did too—also the sleeker Model 61, which was eventually offered in 22 Winchester Magnum Rimfire as well as 22 Short, Long and Long Rifle.

The oft-told story in all Browning literature

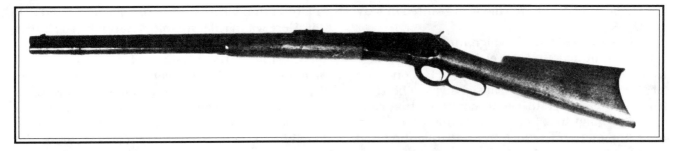

The lever-action Model 1886 Winchester was an extremely popular Browning-designed rifle. Offered in 10 calibers, production totaled nearly 160,000 when it was discontinued in 1935.

concerning the 22-rimfire rifle is an interesting one. Apparently, this time John Moses sent a drawing of the rifle, rather than the usual working model. Winchester's cognoscenti decided after studying the design that the rifle would not function if it were built. So John Browning built one. Of course it worked—splendidly.

In the late 1880s, Browning got the idea of a gas-operated firearm by watching the energy expended at the muzzle of a rifle, that energy manifested in the flattening of minor vegetation in front of the gun. The idea allegedly went from concept to inception in about a day and resulted in a gas-operated model that would fire almost a thousand rounds a minute. John applied for a patent for the first gas-operated firearm in January 1890. That same year, Bennett wanted a rifle similar to the great Model 1886 for the Winchester line, only smaller in size. He also wanted it chambered for more petite cartridges, the 25-20, 32-20, 38-40 and 44-40, which were all popular at the time. Winchester had already tried to minia-

turize the 1886, but the plant engineers had not been successful.

According to the literature, Bennett offered 10,000 dollars for a miniaturized Model 1886 if the design could be delivered within three months, 15,000 dollars for a two-month delivery date. Browning offered a challenge: the design within thirty days for 20,000 dollars—or no charge. The rifle would be free to Winchester. In short, the time limitation would give Browning 18 working days to make the prototype rifle. Winchester offered a contract containing the three figures and three dates (without the no-charge clause that Browning had offered). Browning received the 20,000 dollars for his Model 1892. Winchester, however, was the greater benefactor. Had Browning gone with royalties, his returns on the 1892 would have been staggering. Manufacture of the model totaled over one million when it was finally discontinued in 1941.

The rather remarkable Model 1895 Winchester also became a reality during this time. It

The most famous sporting rifle in the world—the Winchester Model 94 (cutaway view)—was a Browning creation and was Winchester's first lever-action rifle made for smokeless powder cartridges. Acknowledged as the company's most successful rifle, it is still being produced in numbers that reach into the millions.

was a rifle of strong, smooth action, and a favorite of many, even today. The Model 1895, patented a year earlier than its name, was the first lever-action rifle of the era to have a box magazine. The shooter did not have to concern himself with the point of one bullet detonating the primer of the cartridge in front of it, as in the tubular magazine. Everyone knows that eventually a president of the United States—Teddy Roosevelt—would consider the '95 in 405 Winchester chambering a favorite. But the 1895, in spite of its box magazine and action strength, would never come close to achieving the popularity of John Browning's U.S. Patent No. 524,702. The patent was applied for on January 19, 1894, and granted on August 21 of the same year. That rifle—the Model 94 Winchester—is still in production, recently with an improved Angle-Eject configuration.

Winchester did not benefit from all of Browning's ideas. During the 1890s when Browning was experimenting with gas-operated and automatic weapons, the inventor devised an automatic shotgun, which he offered to Bennett, then president of Winchester, in 1902. Browning had a hunch that this type of firearm, a totally new concept, would sell like frankfurters at a picnic. Rather than an outright sale, Browning wanted royalties. Bennett refused and later regretted the decision. The Browning/Winchester association had lasted almost 20 years to the benefit of both parties—as well as the shooting public.

New business relationships were explored—Fabrique Nationale of Belgium, Colt in the U.S., Remington and others—which brought worldwide attention to Browning's genius. Colt became the first U.S. firearms manufacturer of automatic pistols with the Model 1900, based on Browning patents (and C.J. Ehbet's patents) of 1897. At the same time, Fabrique Nationale had an auto pistol, too, which served the European market. The semi-auto rifle of Browning design, first patented

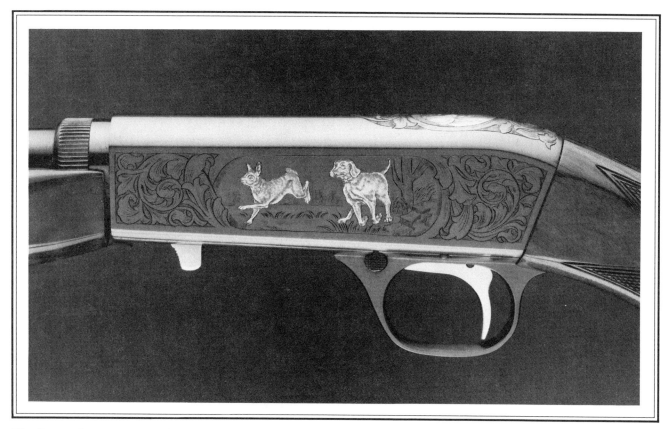

The Browning name remains on many modern firearms. The Browning 22 Automatic Rifle was first manufactured in 1965 by the Belgian firearms firm, Fabrique Nationale. Available in a variety of grades, this Grade VI with engraving was introduced in 1986.

in 1900, became the Remington Model 8 Auto-loading Center Fire Rifle in 1906. This evolved into the Model 81 Woodmaster in 1936 and was offered in calibers 30 Remington and 32 Remington, as well as 25 Remington and 35 Remington. Not a pretty rifle, at least not to my eyes, it worked well for many thousands of hunters. Another semi-auto rifle gained prominence, the blowback-operated model we know today as the Browning 22 Rimfire Automatic. It was offered in 1914 by Fabrique Nationale, and then as the Remington Model 24 in 1924. The Browning 22 Automatic version was introduced by FN in 1965 and is still being produced. In 1911 the U.S. Government adopted the Browning 45 Government Pistol as its official sidearm, while in 1917, the Browning Automatic Rifle became its official longarm. And in 1918, Browning tested his 50-caliber machine gun, which eventually saw extensive use in World War II.

There were so many Browning designs—the military models alone are endless—that our tribute to Browning's inventiveness touches only the surface of his efforts. The inventor passed away of heart failure in the office of his son, Val Browning, at Fabrique Nationale in Liège on November 26, 1926. He had turned down an honorary degree, saying he had not earned it. He'd turned down the rank of colonel. He didn't know how folks in the West would view that title. His principles were not to be compromised. Jonathan Browning's influence upon his son remained strong throughout a lifetime. John Moses Browning's influence upon the world of shooting shall remain strong as long as firearms are built and enjoyed, for although many of his designs are no longer in functional use, they remain important stepping stones to what has come to be.

If you're ever in Ogden, Utah, stop at the train depot. You'll see a lot of firearms lore in a small captivating space.

7

BROR BLIXEN: ROGUE HUNTER OF AFRICA

A bit of a rogue. That's how friends and neighbors described Bror Blixen. And he was. He was stocky, thick, tough and rugged. Blixen was a natural for the hinterlands of Africa—good-natured, robust, with nerves of tempered steel. The native of Africa, where Bror spent most of his life, has a habit of renaming people. The black trackers on one of my trips called a professional hunter "Ngongoni," meaning wildebeest. The gentleman had a handlebar moustache as the wildebeest has "handlebar horns." The nickname was fitting. Another fellow who wore a hearing aid was aptly dubbed "radio man." Blixen became known to native Africans as "Wahoga," the waddler, because he was short and thick, although his portrait denies it.

What no one could dispute was the fact that Bror was born to hunt. He loved shooting from the start. "I cannot say how old I was when I had a gun in my hands for the first time, but that my fingers itched to hold a weapon rather than a book is beyond question," said the hunter, who became a gifted marksman.

Born in 1886, Baron Bror von Blixen-Finecke ("Bror") was a twin son of a Swedish baron and Danish countess. Bror was no stranger to wealth, although money of his own was hard to come by in adulthood. In borrowing he was speedy. In paying back he was sluggish. Early life on the Swedish family estate included hunting. "The woods and fields swarm with game, from deer to hares

and birds," said Bror of his homeland. He was required to attend school, of course, but his education was, in his own words, "a fiasco." Bror admitted that the "daily grind of the classroom cannot fail to be a minor hell for a boy who has grown accustomed to roam about under God's sky without let or hindrance." After an agricultural education, Blixen was given charge of a tenant farm on the estate. But he was not entirely content with the work.

Eventually, his itch for adventure was scratched by two uncles. Aage Westerholz, an uncle of his future wife, wanted Bror to take over his rubber plantation in Malaya. There would be hunting. But Malaya? No, said Blixen's own uncle, Count Frijs, who had been on safari in Africa. Africa was the land of opportunity. Besides, what could Malaya offer compared with the wildness of the Dark Continent? Bror became engaged to Karen (Isak) Dinesen, a girl he had known for a number of years. He called her "Tanne." We know her as the author of *Out of Africa*. Her talented writing prompted Ernest Hemingway to remark in 1954, as he received the Nobel Prize for literature, that Dinesen deserved it more. The romantic souls of Tanne and Bror naturally chose Africa. "We would milk cows and grow coffee instead of cutting slits in the rubber trees," chortled Bror enthusiastically.

Bror left Sweden for Africa with plans for his bride-to-be to arrive after the 700-acre farm they had purchased was sold. The money for the farm came from Karen's family, who considered Blixen a bounder, but they gave the cash anyway. (Bror may have had the title, but the Dinesens had the money.) Blixen left for Africa. Tanne followed. They were married in Kenya. Blixen would become one of the best-known hunters of the land, a leader in organizing the professional safari, and his book, *African Hunter*, would give us a worthy record of the times in East Africa.

Bror fell in love with the Dark Continent, its people and its smorgasbord of game. "The train plows its way forward across the plain between whole regiments of giraffes, gnu, antelopes, graceful gazelles (Grant's and Thomson's), ostriches, and zebras," he wrote. While von Blixen's masterpiece would never rival the literary triumph of his wife's works, it proved a valuable source of Africana, for Bror was well-read, a far better student than he admitted—alert, pensive and a natural historian as well as a hunter. He was a fine writer, too. "Nairobi in 1913 was more like an empty old anchovy tin than anything else," he wrote. From Nairobi, Blixen struck out for his farm.

BEANS VERSUS BEASTS

Farming wasn't easy. Soon von Blixen learned that the gold he was seeking was not in breeding livestock nor in running a ranching operation. "Gold meant coffee," Bror discovered. But coffee beans could not be ground into gold nuggets, either. The baron was an agriculturist by education, but a hunter at heart. He was already

Bror Blixen lived for adventure, and the taking of this three-horned rhino in African in 1932 was only one of the many episodes written in his hunter's book of experiences.

hunting before the first coffee plant sprouted, a well-documented fact illustrated in his diary. Bror explained that "The soil was cleared. The coffee fields were marked out. The cultivator's hopes swelled in my breast." Yes, but "Summer went and autumn came—the autumn of 1914. The war. The price market was chaotic." Bror lamented that "Difficulty upon difficulty arose. The plantation had to be sold—my home was broken up. I stood there in the forest empty-handed. But I still had my sporting rifle." Born to shoot, Bror was a lot happier with a rifle in his hand than a hoe. Game laws were stringent, which was good for a would-be professional hunter.

"Game is protected by so many laws and regulations, and their observation so elaborately and strictly enforced, that the authorities have an absolutely effective control over the increase or diminution of various species," noted von Blixen. In such an atmosphere, guided hunts paid off. Poaching as is known now in Africa was less troublesome. Revenues brought in by hunters paid for a staunch game department. Bror was ready to take his place among the professional hunters of Africa with a 7×50 Zeiss binocular and a small battery of firearms.

After World War I, Blixen began his life's work in earnest. He lived in the golden era of big-game hunting in East Africa. He would ply his trade into the late 1930s, a rather brilliant career at that. His ability as a naturalist was exceeded only by his charming manner as a "white hunter." He was sought after by many rich and famous hunters and aligned himself with the notables of the region, including the Honourable Denys Finch-Hatton, son of the Thirteenth Earl of Winchelsea and Nottingham. Denys would befriend not only Bror, but Bror's wife as well. The long love affair between Denys and Karen was well-publicized. As for Blixen, he didn't seem to give a damn.

Besides, he was occupied with his own flirtations. Bror immediately fell in love not only with African game, but with the carefree native maiden. His amours brought Karen the malady of syphilis. Quite ill from the disease, she was forced to return to Europe for medical attention. But Blixen's free lifestyle continued. He would be known as a pioneer of the safari industry. Apparently, no one put on a better hunt than the amiable von Blixen. Because the game depart-

ment held stewardship over the wildlife of the region and power over hunters both native and European, hunting was stable. Trophies were available. And clients were happy. Bror liked the adventure of African big-game hunting. Presumably he was good about instilling his clients with the same enthusiasm. Blixen enjoyed the hunt for its own sake, and any sort of danger that might accompany an outing.

That's why he liked the Cape buffalo. Once Bror and his trusted gunbearer, Abdulla, were charged by an entire herd of the deadly bovines. The two men made a run for it. But you don't outrun buffalo. So Bror stopped and shot the lead animal. "The animal tottered and fell," he reported. "A gap was formed in the assault column, and next second the avalanche of buffaloes rushed past, the thunder rolled on, the cloud of dust was wafted slowly away on the wind," and the day was saved—an exciting way to make a living. Bror observed, "Of all African animals, the buffalo is the only one which has a hereditary instinct, when wounded and pursued, to leave his tracks, lie in ambush, and attack from the flank." Blixen made a study of the buffalo and studied all of the game he hunted. Although the large numbers of beasts he dropped seems an inordinate amount, it wasn't. As noted elsewhere in this book, times were different during the Golden Age of African hunting. There was a terrific amount of game, and usually a lot of mouths to feed. A safari camp might have 20 working natives in it these days, but most of the transporting is accomplished by truck, not the backs of porters. In the early 1900s, goods were man-carried from one place to the next, and that manpower had to be fed.

Blixen made the usual silly sounds concerning the photo-safari, how admirable it was, and how wonderful to get close and take the picture of a wild animal. He even said that a picture was worth more than a trophy on the wall or floor. But in fact he continued hunting with rifle rather than camera his entire career, although he did lead a few photographers on their celluloid quests. All the same, he held an intense interest in the fauna of the land. He had a trained chimpanzee, which was not unusual. He also had a tame hyena—not your average household pet. But a hand-raised Cape buffalo? Yes. "We were together day and night," said Bror. Moreover, "If Lottie suspected that I was in the slightest danger, she would attack to defend me." Lottie grew into a full-scale buff, about the size of a small car. "Our friendship lasted till Lottie died . . . I mourned for her sincerely. . . ," lamented Blixen.

Bror's brand of Africana rings with the clear tones of truth. His accurate judgment was trusted by all who came in contact with him. Nothing he said or wrote was stained by exaggeration. Of course he had a lot to learn when he arrived from Sweden. And he absorbed much, replacing early superstitions about the country with facts. Of elephants, for example, he discovered:

> When I came to Africa it was not long before my ideas of the elephant, his nature and mentality, were thoroughly revised. Like most other people, I thought him a mild, good-natured animal. And what is he in reality? When you are out shooting one day and suddenly find yourself the hunted instead of the hunter, with death trumpeting furiously hard at your heels, it is no use appealing to the elephant's mildness and good nature.

Blixen fell into the trap we all slip into, giving wild animals human characteristics. He ended up pronouncing the pachyderm "savage and vindictive." Many times Bror was called in to hunt an elephant that was not only raiding the fields of the natives for food, but also destroying them for whatever reason. His experience paints us a stark picture:

> You need not be a coward for your hair to stand on end with fear when you are charged by an elephant. You suddenly become so fearfully small. There is a thing called sportsman's nerves which is responsible for many misses—and there is ample excuse for an unsteady hand. A mistake of a fraction of a second, the smallest error of judgement in distance or hit, may be as good as a death sentence, and heaven help the man who has not a clear brain at the decisive moment. Unless the bullet from your large-caliber gun hits heart or brain you may as well send your remembrances to those at home; so he who goes elephant-hunting had better take a few lessons beforehand in the creature's anatomy.

Bror admitted, "I am not ashamed to say that I was frightened myself. The man who declares that he is not afraid of elephants is either an ignoramus or a liar."

Blixen had many adventures in hunting, and not all of them with wild animals. He awoke one morning to find his clothes missing. Absent also were his rifle and the rifle case that went with it. "A thief had been at work during the night and pinched all my belongings," he declared. Marobe was the culprit. The man didn't want Bror's rifle. He wanted what had been in the gun case, for Blixen had used the enclosure to bank some money. Marobe didn't know that Bror had already removed the bulk of the cash. A certain humor followed the theft. Bror was left with only blanket and pillow to clothe himself. Under these circumstances he encountered a tremendous bull elephant. Of course, he could only watch the activities of the huge jumbo that gamboled before him. "He paid no attention to me, but simply ignored my existence. I sat for hours wearing my blanket and pillow—I think I must have presented a rather curious appearance."

And how did the clever crook steal von Blixen's belongings? "A brown stain on the mosquito net afforded the solution to the problem; the thieving scoundrel had blown opium smoke under the net, which had made my sleep so heavy that he had been able to carry out his evil plans undisturbed. The inhaling of opium explained, too, why my head had felt so heavy and my legs so stiff when I had been awakened." The elephant that Bror missed out on, a huge tusker, was subsequently taken by another hunter, whom Blixen put on the trail of the animal. Its tusks weighed a total of 285 pounds and brought 250 English pounds on the ivory market. As for tusks, Bror was not truly an ivory hunter. He was a professional hunter, a safari leader. But of course he hunted elephants for their cash value when the opportunity presented itself.

A PASSION FOR LIONS

Lions were a passion with Blixen, too. There is a time to shoot and a time to hold fire. The man who claims that he approaches his game, sights on it, then returns the safety to "on" while merely viewing the quarry that is at his mercy may deem himself a great sportsman. In fact he is a fraud who was sold a tag in good faith to be a part of an

Blixen was known as "Wahoga," or waddler, by the African natives because he was short and squat. Posing with a young "pygmy" girl, however, creates the illusion of much greater stature.

important biologically sound harvest. Indeed you may pass up a shot at a young animal. Certainly letting a small specimen go because you are holding out for an old-timer is admirable. But a hunter who goes home without game to lift his pride is no hunter at all. That was not Blixen-Finecke. Bror was realistic. He was true to himself. He shot game for food. He shot game for value (ivory). And he led clients to game as part of his livelihood. That is why the following is important in understanding the nature of a man who had a clear shot at a fine trophy, but declined to send a single bullet, not as a brag, but as an appreciation for an event in nature. ''A red flame spurted up behind the rocks to eastward, and against the fiery background there stood out the silhouette of a splendid male lion.'' Although urged by his gunbearer to shoot, Blixen said, ''One could not shoot a vision like that to pieces.'' The waddler knew when to fold his hand instead of throwing his cards on the table.

Von Blixen describes many experiences involving lions in his diary. In the movie version of *Out of Africa*, Tanne chases the kingly beasts away from the oxen with nothing more than a whip. This episode may seem like Hollywood veneer covering the plain wood of truth, but Blixen reports its accuracy in *African Hunter*. When Bror was a scout on the Tanganyika front during the war, he was at one point forced to move off

hastily. He had to leave the camp behind with Tanne in charge. She would be responsible for transporting the wagon, drawn by 16 oxen, following after her husband. On the third night out, lions attacked the oxen. Two had attached themselves to the backs of the bovines. The teamsters fled camp. Karen had no firearm, for they had been left ''stowed among the baggage.'' She flew forward with nothing but a whip in hand, slashing at the cats. The felines fled from the whirling whip. One ox died moments later from its wounds, while the other was saved. Lions fascinated Blixen. He reported a thundering herd of Cape buffalo that he and a hunting companion had to dodge. Bror said, ''Then we discovered the cause of the panic; on the back of the largest buffalo— a regular giant—rode a lion, with his claws round the buffalo's throat and his teeth in its neck.''

Blixen learned of the African people during his years of perpetual safaris. He studied the Masai closely, noting their habits well. As already admitted, he had a great admiration for the Masai

Bror Blixen was a professional hunter, a safari leader, not an ivory hunter—but he hunted elephants for their cash value when the opportunity presented itself. These elephant tusks weigh an average 115 pounds per tusk and brought big money in the heyday of African hunting.

All in the name of adventure, and Africa was pure adventure for many hunters of the 19th and early 20th centuries, as Tanne and Bror Blixen both described in their books. After their divorce, Tanne remarked that if she had had one last wish, it would have been to go on safari once again with Bror.

women, from whom he contracted venereal disease. He knew also the Wambouti or pygmy people (who do not care for the term "pygmy"). He admired the Wambouti, finding their style of life interesting. He applauded their courageous hunting deeds. He was intrigued by the superstitions of the natives, and he studied the reaction of the people to all events that befell them. Blixen did not live alongside the natives as an observer—he lived among them. His lifestyle made him a part of Africa.

Perhaps too much a part, some thought. "I say, Blixen, you really oughtn't to let your wife live in a tumbledown place like this," admonished his highness, the Prince of Wales, for whom Blixen was serving as guide at the time. "I natu-

rally felt ashamed—though my wife had never complained—and inwardly promised to set things right," said Bror repentantly. Of course, the home remained in the same condition.

Bror moved not only in the circle of natives and the Europeans of Africa, he also had many famous friends and clients from all over the world. The Prince of Wales and Denys Finch-Hatton were among them of course; Frederick Selous (see separate chapter), another renowned African hunter, was another. And Ernest Hemingway, with whom he both hunted and fished, was more than an acquaintance. Bror wrote of a Hemingway fishing adventure: "Hemingway is a gigantic fellow weighing, I am sure, over a hundred and ninety pounds, with shoulders like a wrestler and a chest like Hercules. With the big, strong Hardy rod quivering under the colossal forces at work on both sides, he slowly began to haul in. But the fish did not give way. It was as though the hook had become fastened to the sea-bottom." The boat was being towed out to sea under the power of the hooked fish. Who was captor? Who was captured? "Hemingway toiled at reel and line like a galley-slave at his oar. . . . A shark! A disgusting giant shark, of the hammer-headed species—I am sorry, but I have no idea what its Latin name is. There was great disappointment and annoyance on board; when one goes out lion-hunting one is not pleased to get a hyena." The shark, hooked in a fin only, died of heart failure, Bror decided, for it expired soon after surfacing. Hemingway was half-dead, too, said Blixen, but they doused him with cold water and "poured a strong brandy down his throat."

Literary speculation suggests that Baron von Blixen became the fictional hunter Robert Wilson in Hemingway's successful short story, "The Short Happy Life of Francis Macomber." Perhaps. Other conjecture proffers that an episode from the adventures of John A. Hunter, African safari guide, served as the germ of the story. Writers of fiction weave countless events into one story and many lives into one hero, with the copious glue of imagination to stick these events and human traits together coherently. It doesn't matter whether Bror was the model for Robert Wilson or not. That he could have been Wilson is enough.

Bror Blixen also knew Sir Charles Markham and Lady Beryl Markham, the aviator. Mrs. Markham, the subject of a recent television presentation, was a fine photographer as well as pi-lot—and a close friend of Denys Finch-Hatton. When Denys's airplane crashed near Voi in 1931, killing the man, it was rumored that he was en route to meet Mrs. Markham. Baroness Karen von Blixen would never recover from syphilis, nor perhaps from the loss of Denys Finch-Hatton. She left Africa never to return. Thirty years after her first safari with Blixen, Karen admitted that "If I should wish anything back of my life, it would be to go on safari once again with Bror Blixen."

Baron Bror von Blixen-Finecke returned to Sweden at last. Perhaps it was ill health that moved him first to America, where he managed an estate for a wealthy man, and finally back to his homeland. He suffered from malaria, and though there is no written indication of syphilis working its full evils on the rogue, the disease may have exacted its toll anyway. After living the life of a professional hunter, he and Karen divorced. Blixen married again. That marriage, too, ended in divorce, followed by a third marital disaster.

In 1946 Bror Blixen died in Sweden as the result of a car crash. A fitting end, perhaps—to live an action-filled life, and to die that way. He had lived a full life in his 60 years, a life that touched many people. He was a bit of rogue, all right, and, yes, a bounder. But he was also one of Africa's great professional hunters and a true character who was loved even by those who had little reason to admire him. Judith Thurman, author of *Isak Dinesen: The Life of a Storyteller*, a St. Martin's Press book, summarized Bror Blixen's character in one sentence: [he was]

". . . one of the most durable, congenial, promiscuous, and prodigal creatures who ever lived."

8

BUFFALO BILL: SHOWMAN SHOOTER

"Fake," "fraud," "phony," "fool," cried detractors. Bill Cody was called all of these, and that was in polite company. Harsher words were saved for men-only cracker-barrel discussions. Showman? Sure, Buffalo Bill was that. He knew how to create a carnival atmosphere. He knew how to draw the public. And anyone who studies this famous shooter, for he certainly was that, too, would have to admit that Cody could turn a story about picking up a lady's handkerchief into a full-blown rescue from marauding Indians. However, William Frederick Cody's contribution to shooting is as real as rain in Ketchikan and as solid as the Washington monument. He was a showman. But he was neither a fake nor a fraud. He simply took the truth in both hands, and gave it a strong tug, which stretched things a mite. He was an actor. He played roles. He was also an excellent marksman and a highly accomplished horseman, as well as a western figure of historical importance. His impact on shooting was very real.

Buffalo Bill promoted marksmanship—not the kind of marksmanship most of us are interested in today, of course, but sharpshooting, the sort of rifle-work many of us used to perform for our own pleasure and that of local onlookers before we found out that only benchrest groups were worthy of our undivided attention. Buffalo Bill's reputation as a marksman and hunter was tarnished in many ways. There was still plenty of "wild west" in America during Cody's early days.

His time was transitional, for he was born into the Old Wild West, but he survived into the 20th century. He kept alive what was rapidly dying, except in the pages of history books—the myth as well as fact of the "Old West." He began a career of riding, shooting and hunting very early in his life. Had he not started young, he would have missed the last of the buffalo shooting, which became obsolete before his death.

William Cody did have a Pinocchio nose. Some biographers think he stretched the truth about his date of birth; he was criticized about being too young to have performed the feats he boasted of in his early career as hunter and "Indian fighter." Bill said he was born in 1845. However, the family Bible, which wouldn't contain a falsehood, would it? records that Bill was born on February 26, 1846. The U.S. Census concurs. Cody was careless about dates anyway, and I don't buy the idea that he lied about his birthday to make his youthful tales more believable. Had he done so, why shave off just one year? Why not cut back to 1843 or 1842? Bill just got the year wrong. That's all.

Bill Cody's father, Isaac, son of Philip and Lydia Manton Cody, was born in Toronto Township, Peel County, Upper Canada in 1811. Isaac found himself in Ohio at age 16. He married Martha O'Connor, who died in childbirth in 1835. Isaac then married Rebecca Sumner, who also experienced an early demise. In 1840 Buffalo Bill's

Buffalo Bill pictured with his imperial-style beard. Forever famous for romanticizing the Old West, he fashioned the Wild West show around his own experiences: Pony Express relays, stagecoach attacks, bucking broncos and Indian raids.

father married for a third time. His wife was Mary Ann Bonsell. Mary Ann, perhaps a ''school marm''—the usual tapestry of biography is once again woven with a mysterious shuttle—would be William Frederick Cody's mother. Isaac Cody was the type of man referred to as a leader of the community. Sometime Indian trader, he managed farmland for William F. Brackenridge, after whom Buffalo Bill may have been named. Isaac was very successful as a leader of men on the Brackenridge property; his services were highly sought after. However, he had an urge to ''go west'' in pursuit of California gold. Isaac wanted to be a pioneer.

In 1841 in LeClaire, Scott County, Iowa,

Mary Ann Cody gave birth to Samuel, and five years later, to William. Will, as they called the boy, was already in trouble at age one. He wasn't in hot water, just water, as a boat overturned, spilling the lad into the river. He was saved by a hired hand who dove into the water and retrieved the child. Isaac's plan for western adventure and gold panning materialized as far as resigning from his position at Brackenridge Farms. The would-be pioneer prepared for a covered wagon trip west. But Isaac fell ill and did not make the journey of his dreams. He went into the stagecoach business instead, but sold it in 1852. Tragedy struck a year later when Samuel, Bill's older brother, was killed at age 12 when he fell from a horse.

Isaac's wanderlust was a thirst unslaked, so the elder Cody moved on again, this time to Salt Creek Valley, Kansas, near Fort Leavenworth. There Isaac found himself involved in the slavery issue, in principal if not substance. His moral convictions were rewarded when a member of the other point of view stabbed him. Isaac did not die from the wound, but he did expire in 1857, leaving the Cody family devoid of monetary provision.

The spade of biography digs deeper into early Cody roots and turns up one Philip Cody, who died in 1743. His will was signed Coady, by the way, not Cody. Descended from Irish kings? Some biographers think so. Others say no. The fascist Mussolini claimed that Buffalo Bill was from the Italian ''condottieri'' class, which refers to a group of carefree Italian adventurers. Of course, Mussolini's imagination was superseded only by Jules Verne's.

Bill worked hard as a youth. He was an ''express boy,'' delivering messages by horseback. He got into an argument with another lad and ended up stabbing the fellow, which may have precipitated Bill's leaving town on a teamster's wagon. Bill was in many skirmishes in his early days. He also met some very interesting people who no doubt shaped his ideas about the West. Among these was Kit Carson, who was 50 years old when he made Bill's acquaintance. Cody also met Jim Bridger, who was perhaps the most famous mountain man of early Far West exploration.

Next, the Pony Express. Russell, Waddell and Majors, principals in the venture, had decided to connect the isolated reaches of the west via a mail escort system—the Pony Express. Bill Cody was probably 14 or so when he became a rider for the company. Express stations about 15 miles apart were maintained all the way from St. Joseph, Missouri, to Sacramento, California. Fast horses to cover the nearly 2,000 miles demanded riders equal to the task. Young Cody was one of them. Bill's mom feared that the young man would ''shake himself to pieces'' galloping 45 miles on horseback in one day. But for a 125 dollars a month, when a dollar was a dollar, Will figured the shaking was worth it. This author lives along a stretch that was considered the most dangerous part of the Pony Express journey, from Red Buttes on the Platte River to Sweetwater Station at Three Crossings in what is now the state of Wyoming. Young Cody chose that portion of the run for himself. It's claimed that Bill made one of his delivery trips of 322 miles in 21 hours and 40 minutes. And then outlaws tried to steal the 14-year-old's horses as the lad was cooking sage hens. Bill got away through clever riding. And he was, make no mistake, a horseman. Early motion pictures of Cody astride a horse still exist, and no one can dispute his ability to straddle a steed.

When the Civil War broke out, with official declaration in April 1861, Bill was a Pony Express Rider. Conflict over the slavery issue had already affected the elder Cody; some thought the old wound was what eventually killed Isaac. Bill did not enter the war because he had to return home to his mother, who was sick at the time. As soon as she recuperated from her illness, Cody wanted to enlist. In spite of his Pony Express connection and manly life, Bill, still a minor, needed his mother's permission to sign up. His mother said ''No!'' And the lad obeyed her command.

But Cody got into the fracas without a uniform. He joined Chandler's group of ''jay-hawkers,'' and with that unruly band rode out to wreak havoc in Missouri. They raided. They stole. They burned. They created terror. But this type of illegal war was not to Cody's liking, in spite of the righteous cause. Besides, his mother found out about his activities. Bill's ''war effort'' ceased immediately. Cody left home to become a wagon driver, but soon returned to his failing mother, who died on November 22, 1863. After that, he was able to enlist as a private and served with the Seventh Kansas Volunteer Cavalry.

In 1866, Bill was 20 years old and married. He had tied the knot with Louisa Frederici on March 6th. In his home town of Salt Creek Valley,

Buffalo Bill would not have been named "Buffalo" were it not for his 50-caliber Springfield rifle, "Lucretia Borgia." With this he was able to drop 11 buffalo with 12 shots from a galloping horse. Records indicate that this expert shooter killed 4,280 buffs in 17 months.

they established "The Golden Rule Hotel," presumably prompted by his sensible wife. Eventually he left behind the hotel—and his wife—with whom he experienced a rocky relationship. Many believed the hotel failed because of Bill's generosity. He spent money lavishly and didn't mind "putting friends up" at the hotel as non-paying guests. But Cody's true nature sought adventure. And adventure he would have. By 1868, Bill had been supplying buffalo meat to the workers on the Union Pacific Railroad and became a scout for General Sheridan as well.

THE "BUFF" IN BUFFALO BILL

Bill Cody made $500 a month with the Goddard Brothers supplying meat to the railroaders, and he did a great job. Railroad records show that Bill killed 4,280 shaggies in 17 months. Shooting from a running horse, Buffalo Bill was noted to drop 11 buffs for 12 shots with Lucretia Borgia, his 50-caliber Springfield "needle gun" breechloader. Obviously, his sobriquet of "Buffalo" Bill was well earned.

He enhanced his new title further by accepting a special challenge: a contest between himself and Billy Comstock, Chief Scout for Gen. Wallace. Comstock was said to be quite a buffalo hunter. William Cody thought he was the better man. Twenty miles east of Sheridan, Wyoming, the two engaged in slaying buffs from horseback. Comstock used a Henry rifle, with its great magazine capacity and repeating fire. But Cody's riding ability, as well as fine marksmanship, won the contest for him. All of Buffalo Bill's animals lay in a circle, because the rider's horse cut off the headlong flight of the beasts rather than allowing them to stampede at will. Comstock's kills trailed over a distance of three miles.

That Cody was Chief of Scouts with the U.S. Army Fifth Cavalry between 1868 and 1872 is part of U.S. Army record. Lt. General Sheridan wrote glowingly of Cody's courage and ability. The famous general credited William with lifesaving tactics. That he shot "Tall Bull," a leading Indian chief from 30 yards, the notes say, is quite probably factual. Cody had participated in 16 Indian fights, including the defeat of the Cheyenne in 1869 under Brevet Major Gen. Eugene Carr. This general said of Cody that he performed "extraordinarily good services as trailer and fighter . . . his marksmanship being very conspicuous."

Cody's reputation as a scout expanded while he served as a hunting guide for various parties of note, one being the Grand Duke Alexis of Russia in 1872. Buffalo days and Indian Wars melted away, however. Cody turned his horse, Brigham, named for the Mormon leader, away from the field for a while (not for long, though). But Cody's fame did not wane. People remembered the man who shot bison from horseback. In fact, his legend was so widely known that many dime-novel writers of the day used Buffalo Bill as the protagonist hero in many of their stories. One author, Ned Buntline, sensationalized a story that later became a play. He convinced Buffalo Bill to play in the melodrama, which Cody did in 1872. The famous buffalo hunter stayed with the role for 11 seasons—in between scouting and guiding hunting parties. In one of his last Indian skirmishes in 1876, he killed Yellow Hand, an episode that later became known as the "first scalp for Custer."

SHOOTING AND SHOWMANSHIP COME TOGETHER

The hunters whom Cody had guided helped to spread the word about the man who rode like the wind ". . . the horse set off at top speed, running alongside the rear buffalo. Raising his old gun, 'Lucretia Borgia,' Cody killed the buffalo with one shot." (from Sell & Weybright's *Buffalo Bill and the Wild West*) That was how they remembered this man of the plains. That image would easily lend itself to a "Wild West" show. Cody's previous theater experience and his own innate abilities would serve him well. The prototype for what became Buffalo Bill's Wild West show in 1883 may have been "The Glory Blowout" of 1882, held at North Platte, Nebraska, as a Fourth of July celebration. Cody was in charge of production, and a rodeo-like contest for cowboys, which was his idea, along with a demonstration of a buffalo hunt, proved very popular to the crowd. Cody decided to expand these ideas into a show of his own. And that is how his shooting and showmanship came together.

Doc W.F. Carver claimed that it was he who actually thought up the Wild West show. Carver was a member of Cody's first show, which was a flop. After that, Carver, who lost money of his own in the hapless venture, spent a great deal of time trying to "debunk" Buffalo Bill. Carver opened a rival show. He even sued Cody and wrote attacks on his character and integrity. But Buffalo Bill's revamped show eventually moved forward anyway. The show had but three stars: Johnny Baker—the "Cow-boy Kid," Annie Oakley—"Little Sure Shot" and Buffalo Bill himself—all accomplished marksmen. Without doubt, these sharpshooters were the top drawing cards, in spite of the Indians (Sitting Bull was there) and cowboys and all the regalia.

Buffalo Bill's Wild West was one of the longest running shows of its kind—a total of 30 years, although it suffered its down years, change of management and the rivalry of many other com-

One of the posters that advertised Buffalo Bill's Wild West show. "No tinsel! No Gilding! No humbug!" The exhibition featured Major Frank North, who as commander of the Pawnee Scouts, enrolled Indians in the show, Annie Oakley (Little Sure-Shot), Doc Carver (the first year), and Johnny Baker (the Cow-boy Kid). With shooting demonstrations, "wild" animals and plenty of regalia, the show pleased thousands of people worldwide.

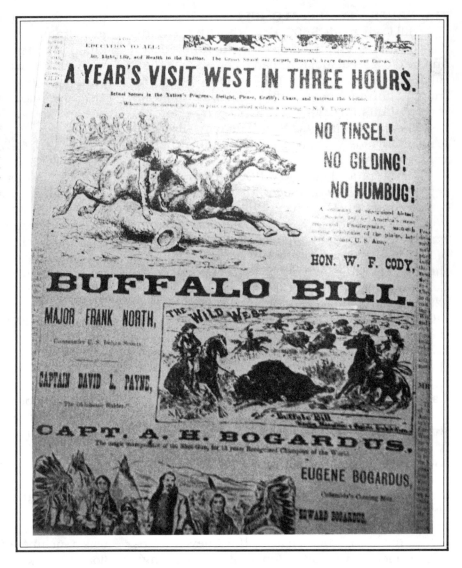

petitive "exhibitions." In 1887 it played in London for Queen Victoria's Jubilee and made other European stops that ensured its international success. Another highlight was in 1893 when it was highly applauded at the World's Columbian Exposition in Chicago.

Despite Bill's reputation as a fighter of Indians, he was also a friend to many of them, Sitting Bull in particular, and he employed them in his show when he could. While it pleased the audience, it in turn gave the Indians some wampum as well as a larger world view.

About Bill's shooting, detractors claimed he was a total fraud. He was known to shoot shot (fine pellets) from his rifles they said. Under a cir-

cus tent, what else could have been used? Certainly not "real" bullets. Even the small shot encapsuled in those cartridges probably rained down on the audience at times. Later on, when Ad Topperwein (see separate chapter) tried using bullets instead of shot, he was reputed to have caused the collapse of a circus tent by undermining its structure with bullet holes. Don Russell, in his book *The Lives and Legends of Buffalo Bill,* sums up the shot cartridge quite well. "A number of detractors, beginning with Dr. Carver, made much of Bill's 'trickery' in using small shot fired from a rifle instead of rifle bullets. It is said that both Dr. Carver and Cody used rifle bullets at their first performance—and got a big bill from a greenhouse owner eight blocks away!'' Russell states further that a ''gun expert'' said Cody used

the .44/40 W.C.F. shot cartridges with a thin paper bullet which dropped off from the shot charge after it left the muzzle, but did protect it from leading the rifling. The charge was about 20 grains of black powder, a half charge or 'midrange load' and 1/4 ounce of No. 7½ chilled shot. At 20 yards, the average range which Cody shot the glass balls, the pattern was about two or three inches across.

Captain A.H. Bogardus, champion pigeon shot of America, was an important star in William F. Cody's Wild West show. Even though his face was recognizable, it was little Annie Oakley who stole the show.

That's good shooting, if the above load and pattern stand as correct. A two-inch or three-inch pattern at 20 yards requires excellent marksmanship in order to hit such a small aerial target. Buffalo Bill was supposed to have broken 76 out of 100 glass balls tossed into the air--with his rifle while riding horseback at a full gallop. With a shotgun, he broke 78 of 100. Naturally, we tend to suspect some of the claimed shooting feats of the past, though in Bill's case, as in Annie Oakley's, shooting was done in front of thousands of witnesses. Buffalo Bill was as good a marksman as he claimed to be. The story about Wild Bill Hickock regularly hitting a dime at 50 yards with a rifle comes to ear somewhat suspiciously. I still have excellent vision. I placed a dime in a bush at 50 yards and could see it, but with iron sights it would have been a very difficult target to hit *consistently.*

Buffalo Bill's shooting was much more down-to-earth in its claims. One witness to Cody's marksmanship, A.B. Snyder of North Platte, flatly stated, '' 'Well, the best they've told about old Bill's shooting was no exaggeration.' '' (p. 320, Russell) Bat Masterson claimed that Cody was also a deadly revolver marksman, and that he ''would ride his horse full tilt into a herd of buffalo and with a pistol in either hand and the bridle reins between his teeth, was almost sure to bring down that day's supply of meat on the first run.''

Cody was not noted for carrying a sidearm regularly. He seems to have gone around unarmed most of the time. He was not a fast-draw artist, which is mostly western mythology anyway. He was not a western-style dueler, either, in spite of his dime-novel reputation. Bat Masterson said nobody challenged Buffalo Bill because his reputation as a marksman was renowned. There were numerous witnesses to Bill's shooting. And to call his use of shot cartridges ''trickery'' sounds a bit ludicrous. Bill attracted detractors, however, for whatever reason. There is the ''wig story,'' for example. Robert Altman's fictional movie, *Buffalo Bill and the Indians,* shows a wig, and rumormongers of Bill's time said so, too. But biographers state that there was no wig, and that Cody's flowing locks were real.

His image was certainly his own. Bill entered a law suit in the Supreme Court of New York in 1911 against the Yankee Film Company for presenting his image on film. Cody won. ''Buffalo Bill

Buffalo Bill is still honored through the Buffalo Bill Historical Center in Cody, Wyoming, the town named in his honor. The famed Winchester Collection of firearms is housed here, as well as a fine display of Plains Indian artifacts.

has a sort of copyright on the goatee of the peculiar form and color that adorn his chin," said the court. In fact, Bill did not wear a goatee at all. His style of beard is known as an imperial, the same style worn by Napoleon III.

What was he like, really? All information suggests that fame "went to his head" far less than it affected many other entertainers and per-

sonalities of his time or ours. Bill was beloved in England, for example, but as the New York *Herald's* London reporter said, "He has a fine sense of humor and laughs at himself when he sees his mantel covered with invitations." He also was embarrassed, the reporter stated, by the "mass of flowers received daily from female admirers."

Annie Oakley gave a glowing account of

Cody's character. She traveled with him for 17 years, and said, "His word was better than most contracts." She also said that he was so generous he was an "easy mark" for "every kind of sneak and goldbrick vendor." Annie reported that Bill treated all people equally, and that a "teepee or a palace were all the same to him." And she suggested that Cody died a relatively poor man in 1917 because of his generous nature. Cody considered himself a public figure, of course, and a famous man, but he seemed to handle his fame with considerable grace.

Colonel William Frederick Cody did a lot for shooting in his time, but in addition, he left behind an image of Scout and Trailmaster that was bright and lustrous. He admired the Wyoming hills and called them "the foothills of Heaven," and in the region he admired so much a town was named for him—Cody, Wyoming. It should have been named for him. Bill established the city in 1895–1896 because he loved the Big Horn Basin and wanted to see the area enjoyed by others. In that town there was the Irma Hotel, named for his daughter, a livery stable, a newspaper and a school. Today, there is something else in Cody, Wyoming, a place of special interest to shooters and students of western lore: the Buffalo Bill Historical Society, which houses the famous Winchester Collection. The museum is known world-wide. (Anyone who visits Yellowstone Park should stop in; Cody is just on the outskirts of the park). William Cody also inspired the Rough Riders and The Boy Scouts of America. And he had a dam named for him, the Buffalo Bill Cody Dam above Cody, Wyoming. Cody's dam supplies water to irrigate the Basin, just as Bill said it could do.

Showman? Sure. Dime-novel hero? Yes. Promoter? You bet. But William Cody was much more than any one of these labels, and for our purposes he certainly deserves to be included in a book about great shooters. He inspired a great many people, spanning two time frames—the Old West and the transitional West. He painted a picture of the Old West for thousands of individuals who lived too late to see it for themselves. And he influenced a great many others who read about his exploits. His many writings have been enjoyed by millions of people. Buffalo Bill helped to capture and freeze forever one of the most interesting slices of American history.

9

JIM CORBETT: HUNTER OF MAN-EATERS

"Fear stimulates the senses of animals, keeps them on their toes, and adds zest to the joy of life; fear can do the same for human beings. Fear had taught me to move noiselessly, to climb trees, to pin-point sound; and now, in order to penetrate into the deepest recesses of the jungle and enjoy the best in nature, it was essential to learn how to use my eyes, and how to use my rifle." These are the perceptions of Jim Corbett—the intrepid hunter of man-eaters, and the best-known tiger hunter of his time. Corbett's work entailed the most fascinating hunting in history, for each killer cat had its own personality and left its own legacy on a village.

Corbett was a great man in his own right, a person any of us would have been proud to know, and even more pleased to call friend. His words reveal the fiber of the man. While detractors are always waiting to toss dirt on the flame of a man's biography—William Cody certainly had his share—not one shovelful was heaped on Corbett, his life or his career.

Jim Corbett's mother, Mary Jane, was a 23-year-old widow with four children when she married Christopher William Corbett, Jim's father, in 1859. Corbett, a widower with one daughter and two sons, proceeded to father three more daughters and six sons, one of whom was Edward James Corbett, born July 25, 1875. Mrs Corbett was a remarkable woman, strong and reliable, with a fine sense of duty. She established an excellent

Victorian home for her family. Music and books provided a centerpiece to a cultured life. She played the piano and won many prizes for her efforts. Mary Jane's sense of self-denial and high moral character were transferred to her son, Jim, who lived a lifetime of the same ideals.

Christopher Corbett, a soldier with the rank of Apothecary in the First Afghan War (1839-1842), served as Assistant Surgeon on the battlefield. After his soldiering ended, he took on a position with the postal service in 1862. Corbett was appointed postmaster in the Himalayan resort of Naini Tal, a station on a lake in the high country of India at 6,400 feet above sea level. Although there was railroad travel from Delhi to Rampur, Naini Tal, at that time, was quite out of the way. Christopher was presented with a plot of land at Kaladhungi. There, to accommodate his large family, he built a generous home—Gurney House. This was located about a thousand feet higher in elevation than Naini Tal within range of the often snow-clad Cheena (or Naini) peak. The comfortable Gurney House, which was staffed with servants, was reported intact as of a couple decades ago. It probably stands to this hour.

Jim's father died when the lad was six years old. Twice widowed now, Mrs. Corbett carried on her duties and kept the family intact. Under the wing of an old and trusted family gardener, Jim, when he was about nine, took to the jungle on forays that sometimes lasted several days. He

Jim Corbett: great hunter of man-eaters. Corbett overcame all fear when he stalked tigers and leopards in India. As an officer in the two world wars, he taught his men survival tactics and became their symbol of courage.

learned to imitate the calls of jungle animals, a talent he later used to delight school children during his lectures on wildlife. He learned to prepare skins for specimens. His interest in shooting was a progression. His first shooting instrument was a catapult, probably a simple sling, rather than a slingshot. Jim launched smooth stones from his catapult, missiles gathered along the banks of streams. From the catapult, young Corbett graduated to a longbow, in fact, a straight or flatbow, and not the true longbow of thick core and narrow limb. Next came a muzzleloader. These were worthy tools, but Jim's first big hunting adventure did not come until the young man carried his 450 blackpowder Martini rifle. This he learned to shoot in the Naini Volunteer Rifles.

Although 12 was the usual age of induction, the Volunteers took him at 10. As Jim put it, "Volunteering was very popular and was taken very seriously in India in those days, and all able-bodied boys and men took pride and pleasure in joining the force." Jim's captain was heavy on discipline. He wanted, and had, the best cadet company. Jim liked the regimen and uniform. "Our uniforms . . . were of dark blue serge of the quality guaranteed to stand hard wear," said Corbett, "and to chafe every tender part of the skin they came in contact with, and, further, to show every speck of dust." There was drill, but there was also shooting. One day Jim was asked to prove his marksmanship for a visiting officer. The encounter was brief, but the officer left an indelible message, for when the lad suffered a poor showing, lack of performance was met with encouragement and calm instruction. In his pristine uniform, the visiting soldier got down "in the oily drugget" of the range beside Jim, adjusted the rear sight to 200 yards, which the boy had forgotten to do, and with a pat on the shoulder bade the young marksman to try again. Jim did well. "When I have been tempted, as many times I have been, to hurry over a shot or over a decision, the memory of that quiet voice telling me to take my time has restrained me and I have never ceased being grateful to the great solider who gave me that advice."

The regular Sergeant-Major of the Volunteers surprised Jim when he offered the boy a service rifle and "all the ammunition you want, provided you keep the rifle clean, and return me the empties." Jim promised. He now had a 450 Martini

for the holidays. "So that winter I went to Kaladhungi armed with a rifle," said Jim.

The good rifle the Sergeant-Major had selected for me was dead accurate, and though a .450 rifle firing a heavy bullet may not have been the best type of weapon for a boy to train on, it served my purpose. The bow and arrow had enabled me to penetrate farther into the jungles than the catapult, and the muzzle-loader had enabled me to penetrate farther than the bow and arrow; and now, armed with a rifle, the jungles were open to me to wander in wherever I chose to go.

His muzzleloader had taught him ammo conservation. Now he would spend no ammunition plinking. The 450 Martini was for game only, especially junglefowl and peafowl. "I can recall only one instance of having spoilt a bird for the table," said Jim.

THE FIRST TIME

Jim and the deep jungle had been like two north pole magnets. Fear repelled the boy from entering the dark places with only bow and arrow or muzzleloader. Now his confidence mounted. He was no longer afraid. Adventure beckoned and Jim had a good rifle with which to answer it. The boy no longer skirted the dense growth that surrounded the clearings. He plunged in. One day Jim was perched on a rock, awaiting the approach of 20 or 30 junglefowl led by a cockbird in full plumage. Jim never fired until he had a backstop. As he waited for the bird to present him with one, he detected a motion. A leopard was coming straight at him, fast. The birds smashed their wingtips against the air, lifting wildly skyward at the approach of the big cat, which had apparently been put to flight by someone or something near the main road. The leopard did not weave from his course, continuing by chance straight for Jim, who was riveted to the boulder in the tight ravine. The cat stopped at the edge of the ravine, slightly above Jim. Jim fired. The big bullet flew amidst a cloud of smoke that obscured the boy's vision. The leopard leaped the ravine over Jim's head, landing on the opposite bank.

"With perfect confidence in the rifle, and in my ability to put a bullet exactly where I wanted to, I had counted on killing the leopard outright and was greatly disconcerted now to find that I had only wounded him," said Corbett. He reloaded his rifle and immediately took the trail of the cat, afraid to wait lest the animal find a cave or thicket in which to hide. Jim followed the spoor until 20 yards before him stood the cat, only its tail and one hind leg showing. Jim maneuvered until he could see the head. "The range was short, and I had taken my time, and I knew now that the leopard was dead, so going up to him I caught him by the tail and pulled him away from the blood in which he was lying. It is not possible for me to describe my feelings as I stood looking down at my first leopard." The young hunter stood trembling, both from fear and excitement. "I could have screamed, shouted, danced and sung, all at one and the same time. But I did none of these things, I only stood and trembled, for my feelings were too intense to be given expression in the jungle, and could only be relieved by being shared with others."

Jim attended an American Methodist school, and after that went to work for the India railway, first as a fuel inspector. When coal replaced wood in the steam engines, Corbett's job as inspector terminated. But Jim continued with the railway, a manager by age 20, and for many years thereafter, with long tenure at the ferry station of Mokameh Ghat. When he arrived at Mokameh Ghat, he had five days to learn his duties, which he did, with the help of senior station master Ram Saran. They remained friends for many years.

As a youth, Corbett lived in Naini Tal, India, in Gurney House, a huge "estate" built by his father to accommodate their large family. About 1899 Jim (standing) posed with (left to right) his brother Tom, his mother, Mary Jane, and his sister, Maggie, of whom he was particularly fond. Corbett never married.

Famine ruled the area. Jim managed to quell many near-uprisings. He was admired by members of all castes and social positions, which helped him overcome adversity. Jim not only shared with his workers on every occasion, he also helped his brothers and sisters with their educational expenses. With his own money he started a school for the sons of his workmen. "The idea originated with Ram Saran, who was a keen educationist, possibly because of the few opportunities he himself had had for education." The institution, which Jim named the Ram Saran School, thrived, but only after certain caste problems were solved by architecture. The school worked so well that the Indian government eventually took it over, raising its status to a Middle School. The government also bestowed honor on Ram Saran by naming him Rai Sahib, a title of distinction. Jim was an organizer. After the school came a recreation club with Tom Kelly, who was Ram Saran's counterpart on the broad-gauge railroad, and a dedicated sportsman. Land was cleared for a playing field; hockey and football ensued.

"My work was never dull," wrote Corbett. Time never hung heavy in his hands. He was responsible for running the steamers that ferried thousands of passengers annually at the Ganges River crossing, not to mention the million tons of goods that flowed through Mokameh Ghat. Jim also involved himself in numerous enterprises and adventures. One adventure included a cobra in his bath. "On this cemented wall my foot slipped, and while trying to regain my balance a stream of water ran off my elbow on to the wick of the lamp and extinguished it, plunging the room into darkness." Few things race the heartbeat more than a cobra in your bathroom with the lights out, the door closed and no window to climb out of. "I was frightened to move for fear of putting my bare foot on it," said Jim. The exits were latched from the bottom. In order to open a door to escape, Jim would have had to pass his bare hand along the floor to disengage the bolts. Ground level is where he did not want to be.

"The fact that the cobra was as much trapped as I was in no way comforted me," said Jim. An associate had been in a somewhat similar predicament not long before, and he didn't make it. "The unfortunate man had tried to fend off the cobra with his hands, and while doing so was bit-

ten twelve times on hands and on legs." The fellow died from his bites. Jim hoped that when he did not show up for dinner, a friend might come looking for him. He waited. Each drop of water that trickled down the man's legs were imagined as the forked tongue of the snake licking his bare skin for a place to bury his fangs, to paraphrase Corbett's words. A servant came who introduced a lamp to the room by ladder from the outside. A heavy bathmat was flung over the snake, while Jim beat a hasty retreat before the Cobra could recover his composure.

But larger predators of man were to loom in Jim Corbett's life. The leopard. The tiger. Killer leopards. Killer tigers. Man-eaters both.

MAN-EATERS MENACE THE COUNTRYSIDE

By the early 1900s, Jim Corbett was known as an expert with rifle, a good hunter and a brave man—attributes necessary to tackle a man-eater. In those days, the human/cat population was more in balance than now. The Indian population totaled around 200 million with a lot of tigers and leopards. Today there are 700 million people and fewer tigers and leopards. Cat encounters were commonplace in the India of Corbett's time. Now and then, for various reasons, a tiger or leopard turned to human flesh.

Between 1907 and 1911, it is said, killer tigers and leopards accounted for the deaths of over 1000 villagers. The Chowgarh man-eater alone killed 64 human beings before it was stopped. Man is a mighty creature when armed with fighting tools. Unarmed, he lacks the tooth and claw to defend himself against a small bobcat, let alone a man-eating leopard or tiger. That is why the unarmed citizens of India once suffered under the domination of the big cats. The villagers were not allowed sufficient armament to defend themselves. "Firearms were strictly rationed," said Corbett, "and for our forty tenants the Government allowed us one single-barreled muzzle-loading gun." When pigs and porcupines came to raid the crops, they were discouraged with the use of this one muzzleloader. By night, farmers watched their fields. They could not allow animals to wreak havoc on a food supply already too limited to nourish the populace.

The cats were unique. They were not a plague or virus you could name, but couldn't see, such as malaria. They were tangible villains with tooth and claw. No matter how sincere a person was in suggesting that the killer cats were simply doing "what was natural" for them under the circumstances, the sight of a corpse mangled by one of the animals could bleach the bambi-ism out of the most dedicated animal-lover. What to do? Catch the man-eater and put an end to his career. That's where Corbett came in.

Corbett had to travel in order to do this. But he did not worry for his loved ones at home, such as his sister Maggie. As Jim put it, "Her safety gave me no anxiety, for I knew she was safe among my friends, the poor of India." The friends Corbett spoke about were in fact the workers on his estate.

Since Jim lived in the Kumaon district, much of his hunting was for the man-eaters there. One particular tigress, the Muktesar man-eater, had had an unfortunate encounter with a porcupine. Losing an eye and sustaining painful wounds from the porcupine's barbs, some 50 quills were still embedded in her hide. She was angry and dangerous. To cross her path would mean attack. The cat did not even eat of her first victim, an Indian lady cutting grass, who unwittingly walked right up to the hidden feline. The animal crushed her skull with one blow. The victim died so suddenly that when found the next day, her sickle, full of grass, was still clutched in her hand. The tigress retreated from her victim by a mile, taking

Corbett with the Bachelor of Powalgarh, a man-eating tiger he killed in the early 1900s. Huge cats such as this were responsible for the deaths of hundreds of people. The Panar Leopard, for example, killed over 400 villagers before Corbett set out after it.

Indian villagers carrying home the Bachelor of Powalgarh circa 1910.

refuge in a depression under a fallen tree.

During the next attack, a man invaded the animal's radius of domain. He came to chip firewood from the very tree that formed a roof over the tormented cat's head. The man fell across the tree, dead. Corbett surmised that the cat was attracted by the blood. She ate a little of her second victim and moved on.

Thus began the career of a mankiller. The next day she killed her third human. A way of life was evolving for the man-eater of Muktesar. Sportsmen of the area pursued her with no success. Corbett knew of the cat, but felt it wrong to interfere until asked to help. He was asked. Carrying a 500 express rifle, he left Naini Tal at noon and walked 10 miles to a bungalow where he spent the night. The chase was on. By this time, the cat had killed upwards of two dozen people.

The hunted animal had developed a special wariness. Jim would try to bait her, but he knew that his shot would come after dark. The tiger would not readily come to a dinner party in its honor by the light of day. Moonlight cocktails, perhaps. Jim got his chance.

Clouds had obscured what light there was that night. "I would have to depend on my ear," said Jim. He missed by a few inches, the bullet crashing into the dead bait instead of the tiger. The hunter sat in the rain, cold and dejected. With the rising of the sun, his men came with a pot of tea. But Jim got a second chance. The end of the man-eater came at two yards. "I leant forward and with great good luck managed to put the remaining bullet in the rifle into the hollow where her neck joined her shoulder. The impact of the heavy .500 bullet deflected her just sufficiently for her to miss my left shoulder.''

"While I was hunting the Champawat man-eater in 1907 I heard of a man-eating leopard that was terrorizing the inhabitants of villages on the eastern border of the Almora district," Corbett reported. Between the Champawat and Panar man-eaters a total of 836 human victims had suffered, far surpassing the 64 count of the Chowgarh man-eater. By the time Corbett had a chance to hunt the Panar Leopard, the cat had killed around 400 persons. Corbett had returned to Naini Tal after dispatching the Champawat man-eater. He was engrossed in the duties of making a living when the Government asked that he tackle the leopard. However, several man-eaters were working simultaneously and Jim had to hunt the Muktesar Man-eater first. After that successful hunt, Corbett agreed to try his hand in stopping the killer leopard of Panar.

Jim was not familiar with the Panar area. He and his small party of men struck out on foot and darkness found them miles from the district. With a full moon igniting the skies, the men took temporary repose in a school courtyard. They roasted a leg of mutton. Corbett was resting that evening, smoking a cigarette, his back arched against the locked door of the school building, when a leopard's head appeared over the wall not far from the roasting spit. The cat dropped into the courtyard, grabbed the meat and made off with it. The cook thought it was a dog and began chasing the animal. On seeing it was a leopard, he made an immediate U-turn and flew headlong for Jim. His speed coming back doubled his speed going. Jim laughed. The cook reminded him that it was his dinner that had been carried off into the night.

When Jim reached the area, he was greeted by a young man, sobbing at his feet. The fellow recounted a harrowing experience with the leopard. He and his wife had been eating in an elevated open room. The cat leaped to the balcony, entered the room and seized the woman by the throat in an attempt to carry her off. She grabbed her husband, who was able to wrench her from the cat's jaws. She survived, although badly injured. "To get help for the woman I would have to go for it myself and that would mean condemning the man to lunacy, for he had already stood as much as any man could stand." The young wife, a girl of about 18 years, was in serious con-

dition. The cat, in order to get a better purchase on her body, sank its claws into her breast. The deep gashes in her breast, as well as on her neck, had already turned septic in the now boarded room of buzzing flies. Corbett gave the young wife little chance for survival, so he spent the night outside the domicile.

The young husband warned Jim that the leopard would return and kill him unless he were safe behind a wall and that he must come inside. But Jim told him to close himself in and wait until morning. No leopard came. The first hunt for the Panar Leopard, which transpired in April of 1910, ended in failure.

A second hunt was mounted in September of the same year. At last, Jim Corbett and the man-killing leopard would meet. The night of truth was dark. Jim had built a blind in a tree. He was elevated above the ground where he could watch two goats that had been tethered as bait. The cat approached and, ignoring the bait, began to tug at Jim's blind, trying to drag him down. "After his initial pull, [he] had now got the butt ends of the shoots between his teeth and was jerking violently, pulling me hard against the trunk of the tree." Corbett was armed with a 12-gauge double-barrel shotgun loaded with multiple projectiles. The only sighting aid Jim had was a strip of white cloth tied around the muzzle of the shotgun.

"Having killed four hundred human beings at night, the leopard was quite unafraid of me," said Jim. He was "in his element and I was out of mine." The animal continued in its attempt to rip the hunter from his perch and almost succeeded. "Several times he had nearly unseated me by pulling on the shoots vigorously and then suddenly letting them go." The cat finally tired of trying for the human prey, so he dashed to one of the goats. Jim was forced to wait for the turmoil to settle. "I could not save the goat," he explained. Jim fired at the cat. The leopard flew backwards and disappeared. Corbett's men called out. The hunter told them to light torches and come to him, which they did. Jim had to be helped down from his perch, because the cat's tugging had tightened the knots so securely that the ropes could not be untied. They had to be cut. Corbett wanted to head for the village, allowing the cat, if wounded and not dead, to stiffen up. But the men were anxious to see an end to the killer. They talked Jim into taking a brief look. After all, they had fire torches and Jim had a gun.

The leopard sprang from the undergrowth. The men, who had promised not to run, reversed their direction and fled like turpentined kittens. Jim didn't hold it against them. "I have seen a line of elephants that were staunch to tiger turn and stampede from a charging leopard," he said. In their haste to retreat, pieces of their torches had broken off, leaving little islands of flickering light on the earthen floor of the field, by which the hunter aimed. The charge of shot struck the leopard in the chest. The fastest hundred yard dash in history stopped. "*Oh, no.* He won't be angry with us, for he knows that this devil has turned our courage to water," Jim heard one man say.

"Had I been one of the torch-bearers, I would have run with the best," Jim allowed. The hunt for the man-eating Panar Leopard was over. "The cold night-wind blowing down from the north had brought on another attack of malaria, and now that all the excitement was over I was finding it difficult to remain on my feet," the intrepid hunter admitted. He wanted a cup of hot tea.

Too old to join the Army in 1914, Jim's part in World War I came in 1917 in the rank of Captain. His duty was to take a labor force of 500 men from the Kumaon district into France. After the war, Major Corbett brought back 499 of his men. Then he saw fighting in the Third Afghan War, after which, at about 45 years of age, he settled for a while at Naini Tal to take care of his mother, his sister Maggie, and stepsister, Mary Doyle. His mother died in 1924; Mary, in 1940.

Jim raised a second labor corps for World

Tigers in India were often shot at night from above in a machan. Good marksmanship and steady nerves were the watchwords. And Jim Corbett had both.

War II. It consisted of 1400 Kumaon men. When Corbett was commissioned Lieutenant-Colonel in February 1944 to teach the 14th Army how to survive in the jungles of Burma, he was not well. Typhus reduced his body weight by about 40 percent. Malaria struck in Burma.

Jim Corbett finished his days in Africa. There he fished, for he was an avid flyfisherman, and he wrote his books. Maggie says that Jim typed with one finger, making four copies of each book. Although Corbett was not maligned, a few doubted that he wrote his own books. All evidence says he did, however: *Man-eaters of Kumaon*, 1944; *The Man-eating Leopard of Rudraprayag*, 1948; *My India*, 1952; *Jungle Lore*, 1953; *The Temple Tiger and More Man-eaters of Kumaon*, 1954; and *Tree Tops*, 1955 (posthumous). Jim dedicated *Man-eaters of Kumaon* to "the gallant soldiers, sailors and airmen of the United Nations who during this war have lost their sight in the service of their country." He donated all royalties from the book to St. Dunstan's Hostel for Indian soldiers blinded in the war. The Book of the Month Club (USA) produced 250,000 copies in its first printing. Jim's work was translated into several different languages and a 1948 Universal-International movie was made, entitled "The Man-Eater of Kumaon."

Jim Corbett died at the age of 80 in 1955, enveloped with honors. He had killed the leopard of Rudraprayag at age 63, ending that animal's attacks on the pilgrims visiting the shrine in that area. He had restored a village in India and given it away. Corbett National Park in the Kumaon countryside was named for him. He had been chosen to escort Princess Elizabeth and the Duke of Edinburgh to Treetops the very day that the princess was named queen. He was awarded the Kaiser-i-Hind Gold Medal. He was a Companion of the Order of the Star of India and an Officer of the Order of the British Empire. He earned the Freedom of Forests distinction. He was allowed to roam at will in all of India's game preserves. In 1976 the government of India commemorated Jim's 1875 birth with a postage stamp. And a race of tigers—what better tribute to the famous hunter—was named in his honor with the scientific name *Panthera tigris corbetti*.

10

SAMUEL COLT: CROWN PIECEMAKER

"God made men. But Sam Colt made them equal." Those, or similar words chipped from the same stone, summarize the impact of Sam Colt on the shooting world. Colt was a businessman. His passion was to build a repeating sidearm, intended neither for offense nor defense, but for whatever application the owner deemed fitting. Sam said his invention was a peacemaker, a name attached to the Colt 1873 sixshooter after Sam's death. As it turned out, the Colt sidearm saw action extensively on both sides of the law—by people standing up for human rights and by people taking them away. Colt was born to invent something. He tinkered with one idea or another from boyhood. And even though he was not really a design genius, he was innovative and possessed a futuristic business mind. Our major interest in the famous Mr. Colt lies with his fabulous sidearm—a gun that remains one of the finest ever built.

It's never easy to fit all the pieces of a life-puzzle together a century later. Sam Colt's story is no exception. His life was complex. But many of the man's dealings were committed to paper in one form or another—letters, patents, litigation, even a problematical marriage license.

Sam Colt's father, Christopher, was born into a world of poverty. But leaving Hadley, Massachusetts, for Hartford, Connecticut, was the beginning of better times for Colt. The story goes that young Christopher rescued one Sarah Caldwell by stopping her runaway horses. The act of bravery brought him into the Caldwell circle at a most propitious time. Town officials, including Major Caldwell, had just studied a list of those who were seeking or already receiving monetary help from the city. Call it 19th-century welfare, if you will. Colt was on the list and was found undeserving, for he had been in Hartford too short a time to be eligible. On the brink of being told to get out of town, the lad was saved by none other than Major Caldwell's favorite and entirely spoiled little girl, Sarah, the apple of her father's eye. In truth, the Major didn't see much in the rescue. Any of a dozen other men could have grabbed the reins of his daughter's steeds.

But Christopher endeared himself to the Caldwell family. Instead of being told to leave town, he was invited as a hero to the Major's residence. The Major had the town clerk destroy Colt's extradition papers. Two years later Christopher and Sarah were married. They had seven children—three girls and four boys. Samuel was born on July 19, 1814. Christopher gained considerable wealth. He was involved in the Triangle Trade: African slaves traded for West Indies sugar, which was then sold to England. He also fared especially well between 1805 and 1808, bettering his father-in-law's income with a simple plan: buy low, sell high. Christopher Colt smelled inflation coming. He didn't care what merchandise he bought, as long as the product could be sold later for a profit. "Prices are never going down," Colt concluded. But they did fall. He would have gone under had his father-in-law not floated a couple of loans. By 1820 Christopher was bankrupt. Sarah, the victim of consumption, died on June 16 the following year.

Except for Sam, Christopher Colt's offspring fared poorly. Father Colt remarried in 1823. His new wife, Olive Sargeant Colt, took over the sad Colt budget, and for the first time pulled the reins in on spending and borrowing. Sarah had pampered her children at the expense of borrowed money. Olive tried her best, but she finally gave up on the Colt kids and family finance. The children were "farmed out," as they say, to other families. Young Sam Colt, age 11, was indentured to a farmer for two years. He didn't suffer like Annie Oakley when she was sent to help on a farm for her keep, but Sam did not love the pastoral life.

Biographers agree that the boy took his special possession, a horse pistol, to the farm. Sam had received the pistol when he was only seven years old and some historians claim Sam shot the pistol, firing gravel and stones in place of lead balls. Supposedly, the single-shot pistol gave Sam a desire to have a repeater. One day he would build a firearm capable of shooting several times before it had to be reloaded, he said.

Sam wasn't interested in the Classics, nor did reading the Bible enthrall him. He was happy that the farmer observed the Sabbath only because it meant a day off. Young Colt devoured the *Compendium of Knowledge,* a book of scientific data. And he liked explosives. He had already blown a toy cannon to bits, after which Christopher took away the soldiering outfit given by Sarah. Now, through reading and personal experience with explosives, Sam was ready to blow something else to pieces—a raft.

Sam learned the power of advertising early in life. "Sam'l Colt will blow a raft sky-high on Ware Pond, July 4, 1829," he announced to all. The flashy announcement drew a crowd. The idea was to detonate an underwater charge via a galvanic spark. Sam wrapped his wire in tarred cloth (or at least something that was waterproof). The explosion didn't exactly lift the raft sky-high. The underwater charge blew near shore, sending a geyser of mud and water into the air and all over the holiday finery of the crowd, who saw the blowup as a mean prank. They would fix Sam'l Colt. They might have tarred and feathered Sam had Elisha Root not stepped in. His intercession was good for Sam. It was also a red letter day for the young mechanic who had come to see Colt's underwater explosion, for Root would one day be the country's highest-paid factory manager in the Colt plant.

Sam Colt had had enough of farming. When a chance to leave presented itself, the boy took it. The new Mrs. Colt had been badly shaken by the suicide of 21-year-old stepdaughter, Sarah. She feared that if she didn't pull the family together, more grief would befall the children. Mr. Colt had begun a textile plant and Sam was called home to join the enterprise. He didn't stay long. He was sent to school, probably at Olive's insistence, for Christopher Colt found his son a willing and excellent worker and was in no hurry to see him go.

Off to Amherst Academy went Sam and with him his inventive ways. He was always trying to blow something up. Finally, an explosion propelled Sam out of school. Although only slight damage was done to school property, Amherst officials decided that Sam Colt was not the kind of pupil the institution was interested in. So back to Hartford he went.

Christopher Colt had another career move in mind for Sam. He would make a seafaring man of him. Sixteen-year-old Sam was put aboard the Boston brig *Corlo* in 1830. The ship carried Christian missionaries who vowed to set right the cockeyed religious principles of the Oriental people. Supplies to sell and trade provided a more practical cargo. Young Colt hated the sea and vowed to stay on dry land for the rest of his life once he got off the *Corlo.* Little did he know that he would become one of the most traveled men of his time.

On board ship, Sam carved a wooden revolver from a discarded tackle block. The story of a child prodigy creating a working wooden model of a revolver grates on the sensibilities of some biographers who can't buy it and who discredit the story as folklore. We don't know if the wooden revolver story is a fabrication, or whether the youngster actually did create a model to illustrate his idea of a repeating firearm. It is clear that one year of sailor life, during which Colt "saw the world," was enough for him. Christopher bade him back to Hartford. Soon after Sam's return,

Portrait of the famous entrepreneur, Samuel Colt, as he appeared in the 1850s. Colt became well-recognized around the world as the man who manufactured repeaters, the man who presented lavishly engraved firearms to prominent people, and the man who changed the world of shooting.

he presented his father with a handgun model. This we do know, because the elder Colt sought gunsmiths to produce a metal prototype of his son's gun.

Two prototypes were manufactured. Neither was worth two cents. The Colt design was said to be at fault, but Sam blamed shoddy workmanship on the fact that one of the prototypes exploded upon firing and the other wouldn't shoot at all. Sam wasn't hurt because he shot the revolver remotely with a pull-string. That's how much he trusted the device. Christopher advised his son to give up on a repeating sidearm. But Sam knew there was a need for one.

In the early days of westward U.S. expansion, neither the Indian warrior nor his bow and arrow were primitive in terms of their ability to wage war. The Indian was a good soldier. And the bow had proved deadly for centuries the world over. Archery tackle had it all over the firearm when it came to repeated shooting. The bow was powerful. One arrow could kill a man with total certainty. The muzzleloader was another story, however. After a soldier fired his weapon, he was in for a reloading session that included introducing a fresh charge of powder downbore followed by a projectile that had to be rammed home on top of the charge. Then he had to prime the pan with powder for igniting. Even after the advent of the percussion cap, the blackpowder reloading pro-

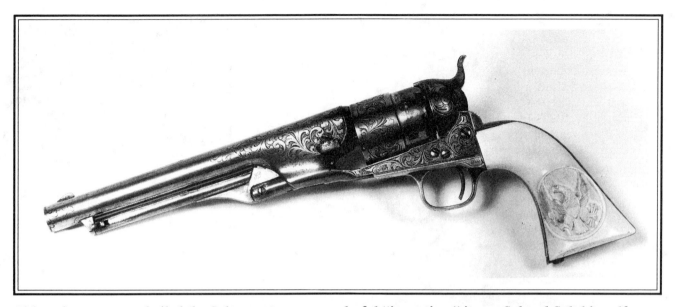

Although many users hailed the Colt repeater as a wonderful "invention," it was Colonel Colt himself who promoted the firearm ingeniously. With great fanfare, he often presented elaborately engraved, ivory-stocked models, such as this one, which was given to General Jack Casement, as a token of his appreciation for favors already granted, or favors anticipated.

cedure was still tedious and time-consuming. While the soldier reloaded, the Indian brave advanced at high speed with all intent of making a pincushion of the rifleman.

Sam Colt, despite his tender age, knew full well that the tables would turn as soon as a repeat-fire weapon was put in the hands of settlers and soldiers. His aim was business more than patriotism, however. When his handgun finally emerged, he sold it to whomever would buy it. Sam pursued the idea of a repeating sidearm even though experts insisted that his model was unworkable. But he would have to finance his own idea.

In a money-making scheme, Colt toured as "Dr. Coult" of New York, London and Calcutta. He had seen these places in his travels. No falsehood there. But of course Sam Colt was no doctor. Nor did he pretend to cure anyone. He had a one-man carnival show. He sold tickets for 25 cents each, for which the buyer had a jolly good time sniffing laughing gas. The cholera scare was on, and at one point Sam was forced to act as a healer. He tried to tell the people who enlisted his aid that he was no medical man. But they had a pretty good idea that laughing gas might be beneficial to ward off the curse of the dreaded cholera disease.

Sam was hailed as a competent doctor when several of his "patients" were cured. The people who thought they benefited from Dr. Coult's remedy were never ill in the first place. They were simply frightened by the least symptom and, once treated, they got well in a hurry. Consider that Colt was still in his teen years when he began traveling as Dr. Coult. He continued as Dr. Coult for four years before returning to the repeating revolver.

THE REPEATER BECOMES A REALITY

Sam tried Europe with a prototype revolver that functioned correctly, and in 1835 he obtained patents in France and England. In February 1836, he received his first U.S. patent, which resulted in a Colt monopoly on revolvers that lasted over 20 years. And on March 5, 1836, Colt burned his brand on the world of firearms manufacturing. He opened the "Patent Arms Manufacturing Company" in Paterson, New Jersey, with a showroom and sales office in New York City. Sam Colt was only 21 years old.

The Paterson Colt, (the No. 1 Pocket or "Baby Paterson") as it came to be called, had a 5½-inch barrel (later a nine-inch barrel) and a folding trigger—no trigger guard. The trigger flopped forward for use when the hammer was cocked. The revolver shot a round ball of about 28 caliber. The Paterson had a five-shot cylinder without swinging loading rod beneath the barrel. You got your five shots, and then a fresh or reloaded cylinder was installed. The Paterson had considerable impact on the firearms industry.

Colt's repeating sidearm was no astounding innovation, though. Every aspect came from previous concepts. However, Colt's revolver embodied the best of existing ideas rolled into one handgun. The pawl and ratchet of the Colt that caused the cylinder to revolve dated back to the 17th century. But in the Paterson's operation, the nipples that held the percussion cap in place were recessed well into the rear portion of the cylinder. The cylinder was positioned on a central rod or arbor, and the barrel, which was forged separately, slid onto the arbor and was held in place by a locking pin that could be swiftly removed. Drawing the hammer rearward cocked the piece, while at the same time activating a pawl that in turn pushed against a ratchet at the rear of the cylinder. This revolved the cylinder. All working aspects of the Colt revolver had to be carefully timed, but that was no problem for the Paterson. Colt's revolver was reliable.

The invention was not immediately greeted with cheers of praise, however. The Paterson Colts sometimes malfunctioned because of the blackpowder that fouled the barrels; small parts, such as the springs and cylinder stop, occasionally broke; and add to that the drawbacks of high price and multiple discharges. Reliable most of the time, but not perfect.

While Sam's revolver was not entirely new, his ideas of assembly-line mass production were innovative. Along with the revolver, Colt produced longarms—initially the No. 1 and No. 2 Ring Lever rifles, the 1839 Carbine and the 1839 Shotgun. These were produced in basically three pieces: the barrel assembly, the cylinder and the stock frame. The Paterson manufacturing facility became the most modern gunmaking plant at the time. In the six years of operation, the Colt plant turned out nearly 5,000 arms: 2,850 handguns (six different models) and 1,912 longarms. As head of the operations, Colt was to act as consultant designer, engineer, demonstrator and salesman. And when it came to the assembling phase, Sam trained some of the men himself, in the workings of the guns and in their use.

Guns sales were slow, but Sam's penchant for advertising certainly got his product into the public eye. Despite the failure of the ring lever arms in the 1837 U.S. Government trial at West Point, Sam set out on a promotional tour, personally showing his revolver where he thought it would do the most good. He had special models made up for special people who were in a position to buy his handgun. It was Yankee ingenuity, not bribery. Although Colt was a success early in life, it was because he got started as a youngster, not because everything fell into place automatically. The man had so many ups and downs that a book could be filled with his successes and failures. In addition, he had a propensity for spending the profits before they actually showed up on the ledgers. Loan after loan kept the enterprise afloat.

So did man's warlike nature. At one of the darkest hours in the Colt story, a time when the entire enterprise could have disappeared in the quicksand of the business world, a war with the Seminole Indians in Florida burst forth. The government, under Lt.-Col. William Harney, bought about 50 rifles, followed by the Republic of Texas, whose Rangers were fighting the Camanches. Texas was the best customer, and they purchased the No. 5 Holster or "Texas" Paterson, along with rifles. But general government bias against the guns plus inadequate sales forced Sam to close the doors of the Paterson plant in 1842.

Ever the entrepreneur, Colt continued to seek government sales, but this time for waterproof ammunition and underwater harbor defense systems. He even worked with Samuel Morse on the telegraph during this period. But Sam was destined to be a gunmaker and war, again, proved to be his best ally.

WALKER AND WAR SPARK THE COLT EMPIRE

The Mexican War had broken out and a Captain Samuel Walker, an experienced veteran who had used the No. 5 Paterson in Texas and Mexico, came to see Colt. Walker was convinced that the world—especially the cavalry—needed an improved Colt revolver. With heads together, the new design became the Colt Walker, a hefty 44-caliber improved Texas Paterson. Manufactured by agreement with Eli Whitney Jr., son of the cotton gin inventor, the gun debuted in 1847. It brought Colt immediate success.

Colt was charged. His next step was to work on an improved design and organize his own gunmaking facility, which he located in Hartford. By 1850 he had one of the most profitable, well-organized, well-known private armories in the U.S. Elisha King Root, who had witnessed Colt's underwater fiasco years before, became factory superintendent and Colt's chief engineer. 1850 also marks the year that Colt was officially commis-

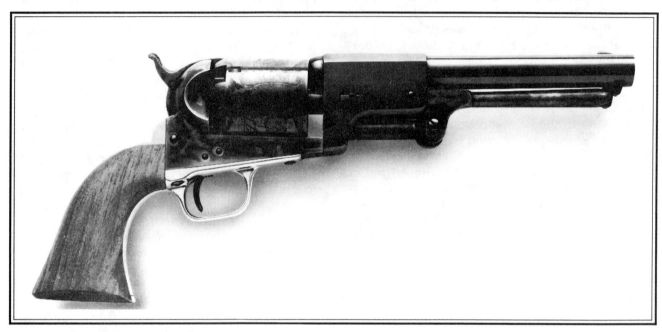

The Colt Walker and the Dragoon series that evolved in the late 1840s and 1850s put Sam Colt on the map as a successful firearms manufacturer. The Third Dragoon (above) from the blackpowder era was largely used by the cavalry. The 1860 Colt Army Revolver (below) marked the beginning of a new, stream-lined series of Colt revolvers. One of the famous Colts that literally made history, this 44-caliber repeater saw heavy action in the American Civil War.

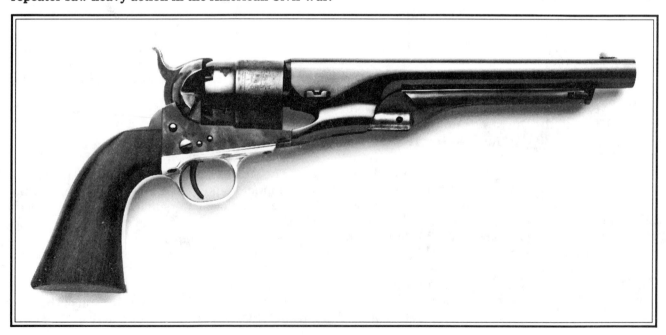

sioned into the Connecticut State Militia as a lieutenant-colonel, a rank he used well in promoting his weapons to government and military officials.

Colt put his promotional skills to work and traveled to Europe several times to establish new markets. He was particularly fond of England and eventually founded a plant in London to manufacture guns there. In 1851 at London's Great Exhibition, he was the star attraction of the American section. There he presented Prince Albert with a deluxe set of specially made Colt revolvers.

Prince Albert was only one of many notables who would receive beautifully engraved Colt presentation models. Inscribed, with gold or silver inlaid, hand-engraved scenes, ivory stocks in elegant velvet cases, these firearms were given to important dignitaries, royalty and high-ranking officers. They were often intended as thank-you's for favors done, or favors hopefully to come. Franklin Pierce, Zachary Taylor and Jefferson Davis received theirs. So did Commodore Peary and the Prince of Wales (later King Edward VII), as well as Czar Nicholas I and the Kings of Siam. Today, they are treasures and command premium prices. Then, they were considered gracious gifts—creating oohs and aahs that carried the name of Sam Colt clear around the world.

The Walker was followed by an improved model, then the Dragoons, which replaced the earlier horse pistols used by the cavalry. Then the Pocket and Navy models—thousands of them. Worldwide demand for guns began to soar. In 1855, Colt introduced the Sidehammer series in celebration of the opening of large new facilities in Hartford along the Connecticut River. Within a short walk of the State House, the new facilities were a model of 19th-century manufacturing and "enlightened" business operations. One of the buildings was Charter Oak Hall, which served as a cultural center for Colt's workers. The Armory Band played at dances and parades. Meanwhile, the Crimean War broke out in Europe, with fresh requirements for weapons.

Sam became a wealthy tycoon. But his reputation as a hard-drinking bachelor was an embarrassment to the man who wanted to join the upper crust of Hartford society. He needed a good wife. He was fortunate in his choice of a bride, a lady whom all considered gracious and fine. At 42 he married Elizabeth Hart Jarvis, the 30-year-old daughter of Reverend William Jarvis. The couple had a grand wedding on June 5, 1856, with all manner of fanfare, pomp and circumstance. The couple enjoyed a six-month honeymoon, during which they attended the coronation of Czar Alexander II of Russia. (Yes, he received a set of exquisitely engraved Sidehammers.) The marriage was a good one and Sam's treatment of his wife was golden. He built her a palatial villa, Armsmear, complete with picture-gallery ballroom and lush gardens and greenhouses surrounding it. Elizabeth, in turn, brought respectability to Sam's life—and children.

Unlike their father, the Colt children were not destined for greatness. The mansion in Hartford was visited by grief. The first child, a premature boy, survived only 10 months, dying on February 24, 1857. A daughter, born early in 1860, also died. Another daughter born in 1861 suffered the same fate. Only one son survived to manhood, Caldwell Colt—the playboy who exhibited no interest in furthering his father's business. He was not a chip off the old block, rather a speck of sawdust.

With the development of "silver steel," Colt was again able to upgrade his guns. In 1860, he introduced a whole new line beginning with the 1860 Army Revolver. A stream-lined 44-caliber sixshooter, it weighed about half of the Walker, and had plenty of impact and accuracy. For military use, it could also be fitted with a detachable shoulder stock. Ballistics tests by U.S. Ordnance officers concluded ". . . the Board are satisfied that the New Model Revolver, with the 8 inch barrel, will make the most superior cavalry arm we have ever had, and they recommend the adoption of this . . . , and its issue to all the mounted troops." Conflict was brewing over the slavery issue. Sam smelled gunsmoke. Finally shots at Fort Sumter ignited one of the bloodiest wars in history.

With typical opportunistic acumen, Colt had ordered his Armory to increase production early on to fulfill anticipated orders later. How right he was. Thousands of Colts were used during the Civil War and they were well-liked. The Colt had neither the topstrap design of the popular Remington, nor the in-between safety notches at the rear of the cylinder, but the Colt could be field-cleaned in no time and it proved entirely functional without the top strap.

Colonel Colt lived like a prince in his palatial villa, Armsmear. Grand, yet tasteful, the mansion was the embodiment of all of Colt's world traveling: Italian in its overall design, with touches of Oriental ornamentation, English gardens and Swiss views. Elizabeth, whom Colt adored, had an elegant, octagonal boudoir surrounded by a veranda, which served as her "morning room." (from *Armsmear*)

Perhaps the most famous Colt of all was the Single Action Army, this one in caliber 45 Colt. Produced after Sam's death, this sixshooter made its fame in the Early West.

The last models Colt actually worked on before his death were the 1861 Navy and the 1862 Police and Pocket Navy revolvers. The war dragged on; the factory machinery pushed night and day. And so did Sam Colt. He was the original 19th-century workaholic, up at 6 A.M. and going till the wee hours. It took its toll, as did the effects of rheumatic fever from an earlier age.

Elizabeth recounts Sam's last days in *Armsmear*, a memorial to Colt and his genius, written by Henry Barnard. One day in January 1862, Elizabeth said Sam was "looking very weary and soon went to bed." She "bathed his face and brushed his beautiful curls." The next morning Sam seemed better. He had a long conversation with Elizabeth. He was cheerful. At one o'clock he rose from his bed to dress, but his mind began to wander. He was unsure of himself. "Then he bade me a last farewell, calling me his faithful, loving wife, asking me to carry out all his plans so far as I might; and with his last kiss whispered that when God willed, I should go to him beyond the grave." Friday morning, January 10, 1862, at age 47, Sam Colt died.

Samuel Colt had amassed a fortune of at least 11 million dollars in his lifetime, which in the period made him one of the wealthiest men in America. He lived like a prince and hobnobbed with princes. Through ingenuity and perseverance, he produced hundreds of thousands of firearms in a way that helped revolutionize U.S. manufacturing. More important to us, by successfully inventing a repeater that eliminated time-consuming reloading, he transformed the way shooters shoot—forever.

11

PAUL CURTIS: LEGENDARY GUNNER

Paul Curtis was regarded as the premier arms authority of his era by some of his readers. By others he was considered too tame a gentleman to get out and hunt with the best of 'em. That he was eccentric, both fans and detractors agreed. Curtis was different.

Paul Alan Mackenzie Curtis was a would-be Britisher. Even though he was born in 1889 in New York, he often expressed the opinion that the British Isles were his mother country more than America. His regard for Scotland was almost fanatical. So much so, in fact, that he was known to promenade down New York City's Madison Avenue wearing Mackenzie kilts and other Scottish adornments. More than one patriotic American felt that Curtis was overly zealous about Scotland and its customs. But, after all, he was trained in Glasgow (as well as being educated in church schools in New York City and Long Island). He remained for life a student and admirer of Scotland. He shot grouse in that country whenever possible, and found that sort of shotgunning interesting and worthwhile.

Curtis's studies had leaned toward engineering and business and the young man worked for both types of firms for 15 years. But those who knew him saw Paul Curtis as out of place in the business world. A workaday life did not interest him.

Curtis's life was not laid out in a set of orderly chronological events by any biographer of his time. His story is a patchwork quilt, with events sewn together to form a pattern. We don't have everything. But what we do have is worth knowing. Two popular outdoor writers, who occasionally authored articles for *Field and Stream Magazine*, were interested in the Curtis mystique and wrote of it. One was Nash Buckingham, who hunted with Curtis and wrote of Curtis, the friend. "I knew Paul Curtis better than well," said Buckingham. "We visited each other's homes in New York state and Memphis, Tennessee, respectively. We gunned our own and other heaths."

The other Curtis biographer was the talented outdoor writer George Bird Evans. Evans's fascination with Curtis prompted his search into the man's life, a study the biographer called a compulsion. While Buckingham writes from a friend's point of view, Evans is more the sleuth, interested in sorting out the clues of unvarnished truth. Said Evans, "Few could tell me more than one or two things about him—images like snippets of movie film offering short bursts of motion, vivid but gone in little more than the time it takes to focus." Along with the two biographers, there is Curtis's own writing from which to draw. And from the combination of these sources, the man emerges as a real-life figure.

His photograph portrays a handsome man with clipped moustache who looks like an actor. And he was an actor, one of the top-ranking thespians in the Player's Club of New York. Some felt he had a career opportunity in acting, but Curtis did not pursue it.

Captain Curtis was an outdoorsman, a "rugged woodsman," but "in his peculiar way," assessed Buckingham. Curtis could ride a polo pony and he was an able cowboy. Buckingham said he was about as good as the average wrangler in staying aboard a bucking bronco. Curtis was a top-ranking game shot. He was sometimes selected to be the wingshooter at dog trials, where he might fire all day without a miss. In addition to his fine shooting ability with shotgun, small-bore and big-bore rifles, Curtis was an expert swordsman with foil or saber.

Curtis was accomplished and "utterly self-confident." Not everyone appreciated that attitude. But he was not a know-it-all, except, perhaps, on his own turf. Once he made up his mind about a gun or ammo, few could bend the man's opinion. He learned from others at every opportunity, however. At a time when conversing with "the servants" was not quite cricket, Paul did it. He strolled with the black men who worked the game fields and talked with them about their ideas on hunting. When those ideas struck Paul as new, unusual or especially worthwhile, he wrote them down in detail to be shared later in print.

On the personal side, Curtis was married three times. His first wife, Sarah Floyd of Virginia, apparently did not hunt. Her name is not in the Curtis "Game Register," Curtis's diary of sorts. Alice, the second Mrs. Curtis, appears in the register from 1924 to 1932. Mabel Curtis's name is entered in 1933, the year the couple was married. In 1934, when Curtis's 15-year tenure with *Field and Stream Magazine* came to an end, he and his bride moved to her home in Bermuda. Captain Curtis, incidentally, was listed in *Who's Who* for some time as a figure of general importance in society.

The first Mr. and Mrs. Curtis had one son, Paul Jr., who ended up in possession of *The Game Register of Capt. Paul A. Curtis*, a compilation of the man's game shooting from the years 1905 to 1938. The *Register*, bound in brown grain leather in a small book format, was loaned to George Evans. Little notation is made in it of Paul's first wife because, Evans believes, she did not hunt. But of Mabel Curtis, Paul's third wife and mother of Colin Mackenzie Curtis, there is ample notice. "Mabs" accompanied her husband on hunting trips and thereby was written into the accounts.

In one entry, the couple was on a hunting expedition in British Columbia in 1935, a packtrip to Mt. Robson in the Rocky Mountains of that region. Paul and Mabs were accompanied by a man noted as guide, along with another person whose duties were not recorded. On a freezing cold day in September, she awoke early and had a premonition of trouble. There seemed no reason for her fears, but she could not allay them. Her luck had been good—she had gotten her first moose only the day before—but her previous good fortune could not overcome her present feeling of doom. She woke Captain Curtis, explaining that she had an uneasy feeling about the coming day. He tried to console her, but could not. Mabs decided to stay in camp, thinking it a wise decision in respect for her bad feelings. However, after the guide and Paul rode off, she changed her mind, saddled her horse, and struck out after them. She caught up with the two men on the trail in a cold fog that had settled on the mountain.

With the exception of a wolverine that crossed the trail—a bad omen in Indian legend—no game was sighted. The trio decided to return to camp, especially since Mrs. Curtis's feeling of insecurity continued, and she remained mentally uncomfortable. On the way in, the guide spotted a mountain goat. He studied the animal through binoculars and decided it was a good specimen, worth going for. Paul suggested that Mabs take a crack at the goat. This might ease her anxiety. The lady said all right. She would try for the trophy mountain goat. Mabs worked the action to bring a cartridge up from the magazine into the chamber of her Savage lever-action. Then she took steady aim with the rifle from a prone position. Overcoming an urge not to shoot, she fired with what turned out to be a perfect hold. The prize goat was hers. However, in firing from the prone posture, the tang aperture sight, which was too close to her face, was deeply driven back into her shooting eye. Paul Curtis wrote of the event in the *Register*, saying:

Sept. 5, 1935/Mt. Robson, Colonel Creek, B.C./Mabs, Bill Blackman, Joe La H. & Self/1 gun/1 goat/Mabs got her Billy, 200 yds. But horror! at what a price! Her lovely eye. I shall love her all the more—adorable

Paul Curtis was zealous as a hunter and kept a *Game Register* in which he listed, over a 33-year period, the different species he bagged, where and how many. And there were *many*. Here he is with rucksack and sporting rifle on a hunt in Canada, where he lived for two years and took a record-class sheep.

one, for the unfailing smile on that terrible trail—. 'Stout feller.' My adorable Mabs.

Paul started the *Game Register* when he was 16 years old. It is not complete, for he did not keep a careful account from beginning to end. The first entry is dated November 1, 1905—hunting alone, he got one rabbit. He would eventually list 36 species of game, as well as a few varmints before the last scrawl draws to a close 33 years later. The first big game animal noted, a bull moose with a 42-inch spread, was taken in 1919 in Nova Scotia.

Curtis considered grouse driving in the hills of Scotland the most difficult wingshooting. But he excelled at that. "I watched him rake mallards out of the air high above the tallest timber, with a skill no other man has shown me in my lifetime of wandering for sport," attested John Bailey, one of Nash Buckingham's hunting chums.

In the early pages of the diary, Paul mentions another near-tragedy. It goes simply, "Was shot today, #8 shot—30 yards, hit by 68 pellets. A narrow escape." Nothing more on the matter was penned.

The *Register* eludes to how he derived the "Captain" in his name: there is only one entry for 1917—"No shooting. Commissioned in the Army, Nov. 16th." About a year later, Paul notes, "I killed three turkeys, 7 lbs., 8½ lbs., and 9½ lbs., 2 partridges & 3 rabbits. Still in Army, only got two days leave to hunt." That was written for

November 13 and 14, 1918, shortly after the armistice was declared. Buckingham says that Curtis was a gallant soldier in World War I, and *Who's Who* shows him fighting in France during that period.

THE ULTIMATE GUNNER

It is dangerous to criticize shooters from another era. What was right for them is not necessarily right for us. Today's judgments don't always fit yesterday's situations. However, in Curtis's case, there can be no doubt that his eagerness to

Paul A. Mackenzie Curtis hunted often on the Highlands of Scotland in the country he wanted to call home. He loved the land of the Scots so much that he would even stroll down New York avenues dressed in a Mackenzie kilt.

fill the bag surpassed the usual zeal of hunters from his time or ours. "Curtis had an appetite for killing that is beyond my comprehension," said Evans. Buckingham noted that Paul wanted to take all of the game allowed by law. He was not a lawbreaker by any means. But his tallies were more than bountiful. Curtis seemed to have a passion for compiling long lists of downed game more than a passion for savoring the incidentals of the hunt. As a valuable reflection of the man's feelings, his *Game Register* is revealing; as a storehouse of numbers, it is startling.

Entry: "Sept. 15, 1930/Blackhouse Moor, Peebleshire/5 guns/2 hares/1 snipe/168 grouse/self 30/total bag 171/A splendid day—did pretty well." Obviously, Paul did not drop all of that game himself, but he certainly helped fill the bag with his 30 grouse. All of the game was used for food. But that's still a lot of game.

Entry: "Aug. 29, 1933/Broderick Castle, Isle of Arran/Duke & Duchess of Montrose, Mabs & self/4 guns/88 grouse/46 self/Mabs killed 12 grouse & did well." A fold-out sheet in the *Register* contained a tally through 1938 which listed 6,754 bagged, including 537 ducks, 834 pheasants, 500 rabbits, and 983 Scottish grouse!

"I watched him rake mallards out of the air high above the tallest timber, with a skill no other man has shown me in my lifetime of wandering for sport," attested John Bailey. Bailey was one of Nash Buckingham's best friends, and saw Nash do some pretty fancy duck-shooting. There is simply no doubt that Captain Curtis was a fantastic wingshot.

Needless to say, Curtis's shooting brought notice from many in the sporting community. It was no doubt his ability with the gun that also drew him to the attention of editors and publishers and eventually earned him the esteemed position as arms editor for *Field and Stream Magazine*. From 1919 to 1934, Curtis wrote about his shooting ideas, which a large, eager audience digested monthly. And he wrote a number of books:

Guns and Gunning in 1934, a favorite Curtis title; *The Highlander* in 1937; and *Sportsmen All* in 1938 (Derrydale Press), which was highly praised.

Curtis became a great force in American shooting. "No American writer on shotguns, rifles, pistols, and revolver, together with their ammunitions, powders, scientific angles, applications, and ballistic variants, has been better equipped than was Curtis to depict and analyze that field, clearly and critically." That's how Buckingham felt, and he knew all the arms authors of the day. Buckingham also believed that *Field and Stream's* fine reputation for disseminating useful shooting facts was due to the work of Paul Curtis. "He never merely glamorized some new-fangled weapon or cartridge in order to boost its advertising appeal," said Nash. Instead, Paul used his indoor laboratory and outdoor range, which included a bullet penetration testing de-

As arms editor of *Field and Stream Magazine* from 1919 to 1934, Curtis imparted his shooting wisdom to a large audience of eager readers. Here, circa 1933, he demonstrates the proper stance for skeet shooting—easy, relaxed, yet alert.

vice, to discover what he could about arms and pass the information on to the reader.

In a letter to George Evans, Tap Tapply, another well-known shooter, remembered, "He [Curtis] took over the gun department of *National Sportsman* in July, 1937, and continued through January, 1939." Tapply also recalled that he had introduced Curtis to the readership of the magazine as a man who had lived for two years, 1926 to 1928, in northern Alberta, Canada, and who had taken a record-class sheep there. "He told me he shot a great deal in Europe as a guest of the upper classes, and I suspect he was a bit of a snob, although not obnoxiously so," concluded Tap.

The son of Ray Holland, who was Curtis's editor at *Field and Stream* for 10 of Paul's 15 years with the magazine, recalled that Captain Curtis taught him a great deal about shooting and swordsmanship. Mr. Holland said, "I am sure his favorite shotgun was a Grant, one of the lesser known English guns. He had rapid coordination, shot fast. I think this irked some of the people who hunted with him, believing he took shots they may have been entitled to. However, that was his way of shooting."

Shooters who live for the sport find each other. Curtis was often in the company of well-known marksmen of his day. Charles Wicks, who spent 48 years with Abercrombie & Fitch in the shooting room of that famous New York company for sportsmen, knew Curtis well. "Paul was eccentric," said Charlie. "He used to come to the gun room of A&F wearing Highland kilts and carrying a blackthorn stick. He was that kind of fellow. Dressed with style. He went with a wealthy crowd; shot grouse with Ira Richards. He was a friend of Bob Owen." The latter, by the way, who came to America from England to work on Winchester Model 21 shotguns, built some of the finest classic style bolt-action rifles ever made in this country. "Paul Curtis was a good rifle shot and he had an Owen rifle," concluded Wicks. Curtis had other shooting associates who were well-known in their time, and whose names are not entirely lost to history today—Robert Churchill, Lord Gough, Colonel Harold Sheldon, and others mentioned in this chapter.

Curtis was much like Jack O'Connor in his approach—or Jack O'Connor (see separate chapter), to put things into proper chronology, was much like Curtis. Although Curtis had an ana-

lytical mind, and in spite of his engineering background, he did not dissect. He studied shooting holistically and he spoke to the "average" sportsman from a platform of truth as he, Captain Curtis, saw it. He was, at the same time, adamant in his findings. He was not a student of field autopsy, Buckingham states with satisfaction. This is one credit deduced from the otherwise superior Curtis approach. He did not study the effects of terminal ballistics, which is a vital aspect of bullet construction or cartridge superiority or inferiority. Nonetheless, his general pronouncements were accurate; he used his powers of observation (without going into the details of spent bullet recovery or wound channel definition) to determine the effect of gun and ammo.

Each reader must determine the worth of an arms writer based on that reader's interests. *Guns and Gunning*, to my mind, is an absorbing book. The voice of Curtis is that of a Pilgrim pastor—all law with no room for dissent. However, the courage of his convictions comes through so clearly that we forgive his tone. "Incidentally," says Curtis, "it might be well to say here that there is little if any use for a double barrel rifle in America." The man's meaning is clear. He goes on to say, "they lack the accuracy requisite in a rifle for long range shooting. In fact, they are of advantage only when designed for cartridges larger than we require for our heaviest game. They have never been and never will be popular in America, and should be confined to the jungle." Amen. The sermon is over. However, every word of it is true, as history has born out. Double rifles have not gained a toehold, let alone a foothold, in America, as Curtis prophesied.

"FATHER" OF THE MODERN TELESCOPIC SIGHT

Paul Curtis's explanation of rifle sights and sighting, a chapter in his *Guns and Gunning* book, remains today useful and complete, with the exception of certain remarks on telescopic rifle sights, which do not bear up under present scrutiny. The peep sight as explained by Curtis can be covered no better than he did. He carried the reader back in time to the inception of the aperture sight, as it appeared on the crossbow, then swept forward with the history of the aperture sight to the present, explaining its function with icicle-point sharpness. "It is an optical fact that the human eye automatically seeks the center of any circle. Look through a finger ring or down a funnel and your eye will instinctively seek its exact center." Words of wisdom. "The shooter should make no attempt to place the bead or blade of the front sight accurately in the center of the aperture." So correct. A shooter of the aperture sight could never go wrong with Paul Curtis's advice.

Curtis, surprisingly, fell into the trap that the scope sight set for shooters of his era. The most intelligent men failed to understand that scope magnification had nothing to do with rifle steadiness. However, many otherwise erudite fellows warned that high-power scopes escalated shake. "The average man will assume that because the 2¾ power glass makes it easier to kill game, the four power will make it still easier. This is not the case, for as we increase the power, we proportionally increase vibration." I've tried to read into that, "we proportionally increase *apparent* vibration," but unfortunately Captain Curtis does not say that. We know that increased magnifi-

cation has nothing to do with the steadiness of rifle-hold. Furthermore, higher power allows better bullet placement. You won't see a 4X scope at a benchrest match where close clustering of bullet holes is essential to winning. And in the hunting field, the variable is king today because it offers both low magnification for wide field of view and higher power for greater discernment of target. A variable scope dresses all of my big game rifles, and the highest power setting is employed whenever appropriate. Variables were around in Paul's day, but they were not popular.

Captain Curtis did much to promote the use of the scope sight on the big game rifle in the first part of this century. He proclaimed himself the father of the rifle scope in America because of his early testimony to the value of the glass sight. Nash Buckingham confessed that he never bagged one big game animal with a scope-sighted rifle. Nevertheless, he was forced by logic to admit that the scope is the best sight for putting the bullet on target. Curtis wrote in *Guns and Gunning*: "Between 1920 and 1925 I experimented with

Curtis considered himself "father" of the modern sporting telescope sight in America. Here he takes aim through a Zeiss Zielklein telescopic rifle sight on a Springfield Sporter, custom built by Bob Owen. After Curtis experimented with the sight and wrote about it, Zeiss sales took off.

several foreign rifles fitted with scopes, all of which had some drawbacks, but of which the best was the Mannlicher-Schoenauer with a four-power Kales glass." He continued, "I experimented with it [a scoped Springfield] for several months and then launched my sporting scope campaign. That autumn when I returned from a protracted expedition into northwestern Alberta, where I killed thirteen head of big game of seven different varieties under all sorts of conditions, I wrote a magazine article describing my experiences with it and the scope became popular overnight. The Zeiss Company told me that they had but six in stock when I purchased it and that they sold over three hundred before the end of the year. In consequence, I feel justified in considering myself the father of the modern sporting telescope sight in America."

Paul and Mabs Curtis were in Scotland in 1939, grouse shooting of course, when they learned of the outbreak of the war in Europe. Paul immediately joined the Seaforth Highlanders and Mabs returned to Bermuda to be with Colin. Curtis was, Evans notes, "the first American to be commissioned in World War II." Buckingham relates that Curtis worked faithfully as a firearms instructor for the war effort "until his health broke under hard years of strain and he was forced to return to this country and seek warmer climates." Evans says that "Curtis was sent to the south of England as an instructor in small arms. During maneuvers there he received serious lung damage from poison gas, was hospitalized for a time in Scotland, and then seconded to the Cameron Highlanders who were assigned in Bermuda." He served as a liaison officer with American forces, a job that included many trips to Washington.

In 1943 Captain Paul Alan Mackenzie Curtis shot himself to death with his 38-caliber revolver. He was 54 years old. His marriage seemed to be going well, and he had little six-year-old Colin to live for. But Captain Curtis chose not to go on. The attack of poison gas on his lungs had reduced his ability to prevail in the outdoors. He was on an official trip to the United States that February. He had gone from Washington to New York City to be with friends. His trunk had been sent over from the Player's Club. Evidently, he opened the trunk and there, lying on top, was his revolver. Depressed, especially over the condition of his health and a tenuous future in the world he loved—the outdoors—he decided to take his life. At the sound of the shot, his friends rushed to his room—but it was too late.

12

HARVEY DONALDSON: PIONEER BENCHRESTER

"Harvey A. Donaldson, had it not been for your efforts, there would not have been any bench rest shooting." That's what Colonel Townsend Whelen said about this great shooter in 1954. Donaldson devoted his life to improving rifle accuracy through study, experimentation, handloading, equipment design and persistence. Although he was not the first benchrest shooter in the land, he was pivotal in promoting precision shooting in the early days of modern American marksmanship. He was always interested in the best accuracy obtainable. He shot for 80 years.

Donaldson was into the game of Schuetzen target shooting in 1895, producing witnessed groups that would be the envy of many modern accuracy enthusiasts. "My own hand loading started back around 1900," said Harvey. "I got my start through correspondence with Col. Whelen, Dr. Mann, and Niedner. From Niedner I got data, not only about hand loading, but he gave me drawings and information from which I made up a small arbor press loading tool. I might add this same tool is still in use on my loading table. At that time Niedner had his shop in Malden, Mass., and he was busy doing experimental machine work, for Dr. Mann." By the way, later rumor had it that it was Donaldson who got Whelen started in handloading, even before the Colonel joined the Army.

Harve, as many of his friends called him, had a keen mind and a good memory for data. He sped the learning process by inquiry. Early in his shooting life, Donaldson began asking questions of veteran marksmen. Those he couldn't reach in person, he wrote to. The U.S. Mails provided Harvey with a great deal of knowledge. Harvey repaid the kindness. He answered numerous letters after he became the expert. As a good recordkeeper, he retained not only the letters mailed to him, but filed with each a carbon copy of his reply. This author is fortunate to own a few of these letters with carbon copy answers. Harve corresponded often with shooting friends, and exchanged ideas with many peers, including those mentioned above, plus Roberts, Sharpe and Pope. While Harvey was a pretty good scientist, he was also quite subjective at times. He could be opinionated, too, concerning some of his shooting experiences. While you can't agree with every word that ushered from Donaldson's pen, his stature as teacher of thousands is irreproachable. Harvey had harsh criticism for arms authors, saying, "Those that can shoot, SHOOT, and those that can't, write about it." He was himself an arms writer, his first works on shooting published prior to 1900. His articles appeared in *American Rifleman* magazine in the 1930s and he regularly contributed to *Handloader Magazine*, writing 40 pieces for his column, "Yours truly, Harvey A. Donaldson."

Harvey lived a long life—89 years. He was born on April 6, 1883, in Fultonville, New York, and he left the shooting range for good on November 6, 1972. His biography may not read as interestingly as Selous's or Teddy Roosevelt's, but

Harve was a person of great energy and wide interests. He attended public school in Fultonville, as well as Peekskill Military Academy and the Al-

Harvey Donaldson was a true expert in the world of shooting. He wildcatted as many as 15 cartridges and made great strides in the pursuit of accuracy.

bany Business College. He played basketball, football and tennis, and was a good runner. At 18, he made the 100 yard dash in 11 seconds.

Harvey Donaldson's ancestors came from the Highlands of Scotland. The Donaldson clan had left Scotland to settle around Albany, New York. From there, many of them moved to Washington County to join a Scottish community at Argyle. They were a warrior brood. Many of Donaldson's relatives fought for early American independence, six of them in the American Revolution. One relative, John Barkley, served at the Battle of Oriskany, which took place 10 miles from Fort Stanwix on August 6, 1777. The Americans won the field, but each side lost about a third of its men. The battle was noted as one of the bloodiest of the era. Barkley was honored with his name inscribed on a battle monument. Three more "uncles" fought in the War of 1812, and five uncles saw duty in the Civil War.

Uncle A.B. Jones, the older brother of Harvey's mother, started Harvey in shooting. As with Ned Robert's Uncle Alvaro, Donaldson's shooting uncle was also a member of Berdan's famous Civil War Sharpshooters. Uncle A.B's experience dated back to 1840, and Harve was irate over what he called erroneous data on slug gun shooting, as presented in modern arms magazines from time to time. Harvey also defended the proper way to handle the Schuetzen rifle. Donaldson was into Schuetzen rifle shooting up to 1915, interested mainly in 200-yard offhand targets. Donaldson (and Pope) did much to remind the modern shooting public of the high level of accuracy achieved by the Schuetzen rifle. He spoke of C.W. Roland firing a .75-inch group when Roland was 75 years of age. Remember that this is a 10-shot group. While I own three 7mm Magnums capable of shooting sub-inch-sized 200-yard groups, I'm content when these rifles achieve such clusters with three-, not 10-shot strings. Of course, these are hunting, not benchrest rifles.

Uncle A.B. was not Harve's only shooting tutor. His mother was, too. Mrs. Donaldson taught her son the basics—in reading and writing, and how to shoot as well. She shot her own muzzleloader and she showed Harvey how to cast projectiles on the kitchen stove. In those days, you didn't drop in at the local gunshop for a box of bullets—you made your own. Donaldson retained as keepsakes a few missiles that his mother cast

on that stove. Harvey's father, Charles A. Donaldson, was not a shooter, however. He ran a drug store and a hotel in Fultonville. Harve had a brother who died at the age of 82 in 1967. When Harve was 22, he married May Gilbreth. That was 1905 and Teddy Roosevelt was in charge of the country.

Harvey Donaldson loved to hunt birds with a shotgun, and fish when the trout were jumping. He excused himself for being out of touch a while by reminding one correspondent that "Our trout season opened on April first, and for the next couple of months fishing will take all my attention." He never lost interest in woodchuck hunting, and there is no doubt that varminting had something to do with Harve's strong desire to create a flat-shooting smallbore cartridge capable of good long-range accuracy. He collected fine firearms, concentrating on the Schuetzen rifle. He owned examples by Pope, Schoyen, Zischang, Bremer and others.

While shooting was his life, he worked as a machinest many of his years. Donaldson noted in 1966, six years before his death, that he was putting in 10 hours a day working in a machine shop as a toolmaker. He claimed that he was still able to see a micrometer without the aid of reading glasses. Although his eyes were sharp, his hearing was not, which is a common ailment among marksmen who fired thousands of rounds prior to proper hearing protection.

One of Donaldson's keen interests was sports car driving. Harvey owned several outstanding automobiles, including a Stutz Bearcat, but the Corvette he owned became a symbol of the man himself. He was singled out by General Motors as the oldest sports car driver in America. An article in a 1961 *Corvette Magazine* applauded not only Donaldson's stature as oldest man behind the wheel, but said that Harvey had the most sports car driving experience. Harve had begun driving in 1900 with the purchase of a Stanley Steamer and a two-dollar registration license. Donaldson also competed in motorcycle racing, and suffered an 80-mile-an-hour crash that left him with a fractured skull and a burned leather jacket.

Most of all, Harve was a shooter, enjoying the sport for its own sake, and seeking greater precision. Donaldson was not one for proclaiming knowledge based upon firing a few rounds. He shot tons of lead downrange in his time. He began his shooting career with a muzzleloading squirrel rifle. As a lad, he dropped his first woodchuck with a 40-caliber blackpowder slug gun. He entered the domain of cartridge shooting with a Flobert single-shot 22-rimfire rifle, but it was not sufficiently accurate for Harvey, so he replaced it with a Stevens Expert Model 22 presented to him by a shooting uncle in 1892.

THE DEDICATED SHOOTER

We have to tip our hats to Harvey's raw shooting ability. Not every firearms experimenter of note was a fine marksman. Donaldson was. He did most of his shooting at a gun club range; therefore, a bulk of witnessed targets resulted. For example, we have a Donaldson five-shot group witnessed on February 12, 1931, with all bullet holes touching. He fired this group at 100 yards with a rifle carrying iron aperture sights, no scope. Another group at 100 yards he shot with the same rifle fitted with a scope. If you didn't know five rounds had been fired, you'd say that only three bullets made the ragged hole in the paper. The cartridge in both cases was a 32-40 chambered in a Schoyen-Ballard single-shot rifle, set triggers, target stock, heavy barrel. All shooting was done with "breech-seated" loads, cartridge and bullet introduced to the rifle separately. On February 13, 1966, Harvey's marksmanship, good rifle and careful loads produced a five-shot, 100-yard group of only three-sixteenths of an inch center to center. That's close shooting.

Dedicated. That was Harvey—dedicated to shooting. He commented about shooters.

The present-day bench rest shooter may think he does a lot of practice in getting ready

One of Donaldson's keen interests was sports car driving. Harvey owned several outstanding automobiles, including a Stutz Bearcat. But the Corvette he owned became a symbol of the man himself. In 1961 *Corvette Magazine* applauded Donaldson as the oldest man behind the wheel, and said he had the most sports car driving experience of anybody.

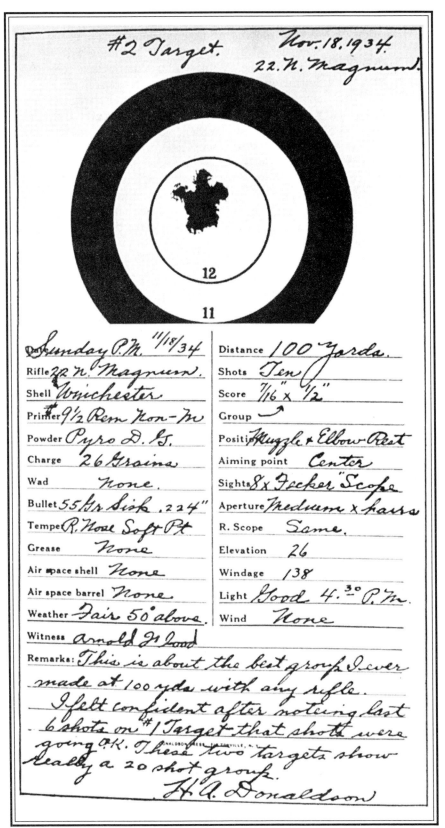

Donaldson devoted his life to rifle accuracy. This is one of his targets, fired at 100 yards in 1934. Note the variables that he kept record of in his shooting, from the powder used to the light conditions.

for a match. I wonder what he would think if he knew it was common practice for a rifleman of the old school to shoot say fifty shots off-hand almost every night during the summer months, as the light permitted, before he even ate his supper. This is what it takes, and such constant practice made holding and shooting in the off-hand position automatic.

Harvey's shooting ability coupled with his talent at a lathe brought Harvey to the attention of Dr. F.W. Mann, the great empiricist who was striving toward a better understanding of bullets in flight. Donaldson aided both Mann and Niedner with certain aspects of their shooting study. The result was further learning for all parties. What Dr. Mann called "X-Errors," Donaldson called "Off-Shots." We call them fliers. It was Donaldson who discovered that one possible cause of unexplained fliers—bullets that depart from the group for no apparent reason—was the possible unevenness of caseneck thickness. It was a discovery of significance, although, as usual, one would be at risk to claim that Harve was the first shooter on planet earth to think of it.

Harvey sorted cases by shooting, not by cartridge-case analysis. He learned that certain cases were responsible for fliers and that these cases suffered unevenness of neck thickness. He singled out these cases, retaining only the brass that produced the best groups. Fliers decreased significantly. Today, serious benchrest shooters outside neck-turn their brass to guarantee uniform neck thickness, accomplishing essentially the same task Harvey performed through sorting. In this, and other precision-shooting aspects, such as wildcatting for accuracy, Donaldson was ahead of his time. Harvey believed in case design as promotional to accuracy. Not that this factor was unheard of before Donaldson's time. Many shooters considered the 32-40 cartridge case in its various configurations inherently accurate, while these same marksmen thought of certain other case configurations as inherently *inaccurate*.

Donaldson's cartridge-case design research was responsible for the premier benchrest cartridge of his time. That cartridge was the 219 Donaldson Wasp. Today, the Wasp has been surpassed by the 6 PPC USA, the Palmisano/Pindell cartridge factory-loaded by Sako and brought into

the country by Stoeger Industries. More on the Wasp in a moment. First, it must be recognized that Donaldson's studies in wildcatting were not confined to cartridge-case design. Harvey worked with bullets, too. He was swaging jacketed bullets around 1906, although evidence suggests that Harve may have been making jacketed bullets in 1903. The dates matter because they indicate how early Donaldson was interested in striving toward a better missile to promote gilt-edged accuracy. Donaldson's bullet-forming dies were made by Niedner, incidentally. Harve knew long before making his own jacketed missiles that as the bullet went, so went accuracy. He had long ago cast lead alloy bullets of sterling accuracy for his Schuetzen rifles. Donaldson's own words on the subject of lead bullet casting reveal his quest for precision:

When casting bullets to use in these Pope barrels, the mixture of lead to tin had to be just right, and this was determined only by experimenting. The usual mixture was around one to thirty of tin and lead. Some used one to thirty-five. One reason, I believe, that the present-day shooter cannot seem to make the old rifles perform is because they cast their bullets too hard.

Back in the days before World War I, we shot our bullets in the same order as they came from the mould. In this way we figured we had better control of the mixture of lead and tin. More uniform, if you will. My own method was to use a board with a hundred holes bored in the top. When our mixture was the correct temperature and the mould working right, we placed each bullet as cast into the board. The holes in the board were numbered 1 to 100, and the first good bullet cast went into the hole marked "1" and the others in the proper order as cast.

Handloading consumed Donaldson. He worked up his own methods and built some of his own hardware. He was ever concerned with improving cartridges not only through specific reloads, but also through design—wildcatting. There were at least 15 Donaldson wildcats, among them: the 22 Krag, 25 Krag (the Donaldson design of this case), the 2-R Don., 6mm Don. Ace, 6.5mm Don., 220 Don. Ace, 250 Don., 270 Don., a 300

Don. Ace and of course the 219 Donaldson Wasp. The 22 Krag was also known as the Donaldson-Smith 220 Krag and the .226 Donaldson-Smith Krag; it was praised as a well-balanced, high-performance long-range varminter.

The Wasp was on Donaldson's mind in 1935. He was not sure what the cartridge would eventually be, but he knew what he wanted—a 22-caliber centerfire of modest case capacity, high velocity and excellent accuracy, the latter really

being the first criterion. The case would be of comparatively small capacity; it would enjoy 100 percent loading density; hence, it would be very efficient. During the decade from 1935 through 1945, some of Donaldson's ideas were turned into reality by Vernor Gipson, who mechanically constructed Harvey's test brass.

Capsulizing the Wasp effort, we can say that there were two versions. One was built on a shortened 25 Remington case; the other was constructed on a modified 219 Zipper case. The concept of short-and-fat versus long-and-narrow in terms of supreme accuracy was adhered to in Donaldson's case design. The 219 case won over the 25 Remington because it was easier to convert, and final cases could be made from 25-35 brass, 30-30, 22 Hi Power or 219 Zipper ammo. Furthermore, the rimmed Zipper case was better suited to the single-shot action, but could also be used in a bolt-action rifle. Looking back, with the 6 PPC USA as a model of current peak accuracy, one might say that the 25 Remington case, shortened and necked to 22 caliber or 6mm, especially with conversion to a small rifle primer, may have been better than the Zipper case. Certainly, the

idea of using the 219 Wasp in a single-shot action fell into disfavor, because the bolt-action rifle produced better accuracy. Nonetheless, the 219 Donaldson Wasp did make history and it did urge other designers to work on further improvement of benchrest (and varmint rifle) accuracy.

Harvey's contribution ran much deeper than his 219 Wasp cartridge, as important as that round was to the development of accurate arms and ammo. Partly due to his longevity, Donaldson remained a living repository of shooting history in America, especially the important aspects of accuracy development. He also had first-hand knowledge of many great riflemen, from Pope to Newton. He admired them. He sometimes up-

Harvey Donaldson shot avidly at gun clubs and kept good company with other accomplished shooters. To his immediate right stands Colonel Whelen, another "great" shooter.

braided them, especially in his later years, when he was pretty rough on his pals.

He suggested that Phil Sharpe composed his well-known reloading manual by gathering up all notes and details from the Donaldson library of knowledge. In fact, Sharpe was more or less a secretary, while Harvey supplied the data. Donaldson was not a modest man. He said, "Neither Mann nor even Ned Roberts was what you might call a rifleman." He impugned Ned's eyesight and his ability to shoot straight. He even suggested that Roberts's title of Major was unearned, and that Ned was not associated with the military organizations he had claimed to be part of. He seemed to enjoy picking on Ned Roberts most, claiming that Ned was not merely a near-sighted school teacher who lacked shooting ability, but that the Major couldn't handload worth a hoot either. Furthermore, Harve did not credit Roberts with the 257 Roberts cartridge. "Col. Townsend Whelen was largely responsible for the design of the .257 Roberts cartridge," claimed Harvey. Of course, Roberts wrote more than once that several shooters were involved in the design of that round.

Harve had plenty of valuable knowledge about the old shooters and their hardware. He discussed the Mann-Niedner Hamburg rifle in a 1967 *Handloader* column. Harvey called this an early bolt-action single-shot Schuetzen rifle. Donaldson credits Niedner with an entirely new bolt design for the Hamburg rifle, and states that the result was the strongest action of its type made to date. He spoke of tests that destroyed barrels, while doing no harm to the action, which is what we see today with the experimental Poff/Palmisano 45-degree locking-lug action. The Hamburg bolt carried seven locking lugs. The Hamburg rifle was chambered for the 25 Krag wildcat cartridge, Harve noted. The cartridge casehead was enshrouded, as seen with current Winchester and Remington bolts.

Donaldson was on the scene for a great deal of gun history. Many of his articles on arms history are valuable to students of the sport. For example, the February 1936 issue of *American Rifleman* magazine carried an article entitled, "The Original .22 High Power," by Harvey Donaldson. And while he wrote caustically to many of his readers, he also helped thousands of shooters with his excellent shooting tips.

We learned from Harve that Schuetzen rifles are a law unto themselves, requiring special care, feeding and handling. Donaldson noted that resting the Schuetzen by the fore-barrel did not harm its ability to group bullets. He spoke of specific benchrest methods conducive to best results. Harvey handed out some good information on dressing the bore of the rifle for greatest accuracy (also called fouling the bore), and he did quite a bit of work on primers and ignition. He also made supremely good sense about targets, that going for best groups required a very small aimpoint. He showed reloaders how to get more powder into the case using a funnel with a long stem. He also gave good advice about selling good rifles—don't do it. You'll be sorry.

Harvey Donaldson was a great shooter. He knew how to learn from others, how to modify their information and improve upon it, and how to impart new ideas to shooters. He attended most of the important benchrest shoots within his geographical reach, and he only stopped shooting when he could no longer sit at the bench for long hours, concentrating upon the bull's-eye. His own fine marksmanship and knowledge of firearms he credited to "the help and assistance of the best shooters in this country."

The fact that Harvey A. Donaldson made a great impact upon the world of shooting is undeniable. But perhaps more remarkable is the fact that so many of Donaldson's tenets of accuracy—having weathered the test of time—remain of paramount importance to shooters today.

13

FRED HUNTINGTON: CHAMPION OF RELOADING

Born to shoot. Fred Huntington couldn't remember when his interest in firearms began. "I have always loved guns and gun collecting," he said when asked about his early shooting career. Huntington is the champion of reloading. He made his mark in the industry when he designed and constructed a better reloading press. Fred concocted numerous other innovations that promoted the art of handrolling ammunition. But Fred Huntington was not always involved in providing reliable reloading tools. He spent more than half his life in another trade.

Fred Huntington's father, also named Fred, was born in Bloomington, Illinois. He was a salesman who moved west in 1906—way west, all the way to Oroville in northern California, with Mrs. Huntington, who was born about 100 miles from St. Louis, Missouri. In Oroville, the elder Huntington opened a laundry and dry-cleaning plant. He was no laundryman, but he took possession of the plant in lieu of a $5000 loan. It seemed the only way to collect on the debt. Huntington Sr. learned the business and turned the establishment into a thriving operation.

Young Fred, born 20 days before Christmas in 1912, enjoyed his early years in Oroville. Although his father preferred fishing over hunting—and although "He was usually too busy with the laundry to take me out shooting," Fred Junior found the opportunity to push hundreds of bullets downbore. Shooting was his passion. When Fred

finished high school, he attended laundry and dry-cleaning school for one year and went straight into his father's business. Fred liked Oroville and planned to live his life there. The most direct route to success and to remaining in the California town was to continue with the laundry business. And that's what our reloading captain did—for quite some time.

Fred recalls beginning with serious shooting in 1937. His endearment to firearms, reloading and hunting was a continuous involvement. Fred Huntington Jr. was pulled like metal fragments to a magnet by "the back room," where his deepest interest rested—the nucleus of a tool-and-die empire was maturing.

Fortune sometimes wears a crooked smile. Fred Huntington had a terrible time getting all of the ammunition he wanted in the early 1940s. Had this dearth of ammunition not prevailed, our man may never have embarked on a new career. At this juncture, in 1941, Fred came across a book written by W. F. Vickery, a well-known gunsmith of the era. The book, *Advanced Gunsmithing,* changed Fred's life. Between its covers was an explanation of how to make both a press and dies for the creation of 22-caliber bullets. In the rear of the laundry was an old Seneca Falls lathe. Fred Huntington went to work with the lathe, and when he was finished, he was in the bullet-making business. He contacted W. F. Vickery, who took an interest in Fred, shipping him a set of

Fred Huntington, the man who made RCBS synonymous with reloading.

Vickery-made 22-bullet dies so that the young man could compare them with his own creations. From a study of the Vickery dies, Huntington knew he was on the right track. He was happier in the work of making bullets than he had ever been in getting clothes clean.

THE LEGEND OF RCBS

A year later, Fred's die-building prowess had expanded not only in units produced, but also in quality through experimentation. Huntington was working on a set of bullet-forming dies that would function with the original Pacific press made in San Francisco. When he had completed his work, he brought the resulting product to Frank Stratinsky, who was then the chief tool-and-die man for Pacific. Stratinsky played a major role in the Huntington saga by introducing the young inventor to Captain Grosvenor Wotkyns. Wotkyns' name is today linked with the development of the 22 Hornet, among other shooting accomplishments. Wotkyns engendered an immediate appreciation for the Huntington die. He wanted a set. He also wanted to buy a set for a shooting friend. Huntington complied. He made the two sets of dies and delivered them to San Francisco. A truly good product will, in part, promote itself. Soon, Huntington was driving to San Francisco on a regular basis delivering his wares. Now his dies needed a name. Wotkyns said why not call them the "Rock Chuck Bullet Swages?" After all, Fred's dies were for the 22-caliber bullet that was used mainly in the varmint rifle. The name, albeit unwieldy, stuck. Fred decided to reduce the title to its initials, RCBS. If you haven't heard of RCBS, you don't reload.

Papa Huntington was a reasonable man who wanted his boy to be content. But, after all, Fred was supposed to be in the laundry business, not the tool-and-die trade. The young man spent much of his workday in the back room of the plant, grinding away on one piece of metal or another. Furthermore, the back door was almost as busy as the front door, with shooting enthusiasts coming and going. After trying to convince his son to continue with the laundry plant, Mr. Huntington decided it would be good if Fred moved his enterprise to a new location.

So in 1948, Fred had his own shop. It was very small—only 20 feet by 20 feet in dimension, but in it wondrous things were happening. In my

A young Fred Huntington poses with a fine Dall sheep. Huntington stalked game with Jack O'Connor, as well as many other notables.

opinion, there's not a great businessman who hasn't an affinity for attracting intelligent people to help promote his ideas. Fred Huntington gathered such men around him: Jack Ellis and Al Swift, to name two. These fine technicians helped Fred with his die work, as the shop expanded to offer gunsmithing. Although neither man remained with the Huntington operation, both contributed to the Huntington story. Frank Stratinsky wrote his chapter in the Huntington biography as well.

With Jack Ellis doing firearm repairs and working on special die-making problems, and Al Swift machining dies, Huntington's shop flourished. Next Stratinsky came on board, making a full line of reloading dies. Huntington had already earned a patent for his bullet-forming die invention of 1940. He soon received a second patent. Working with Swift, Huntington designed a new press. Initially called the New Leverage System Model A RCBS Reloading Press, it would change all major machines in the future. Fred stated recently, "Quite a few of the reloading firms at the time badmouthed the Leverage System, but when the patent ran out, I had two firms paying me royalty and two or three more jumped on the bandwagon, copying what I had invented and furthered." The most popular reloading press design of the hour stems from the Huntington style, which speaks for Fred's tremendous impact on reloading.

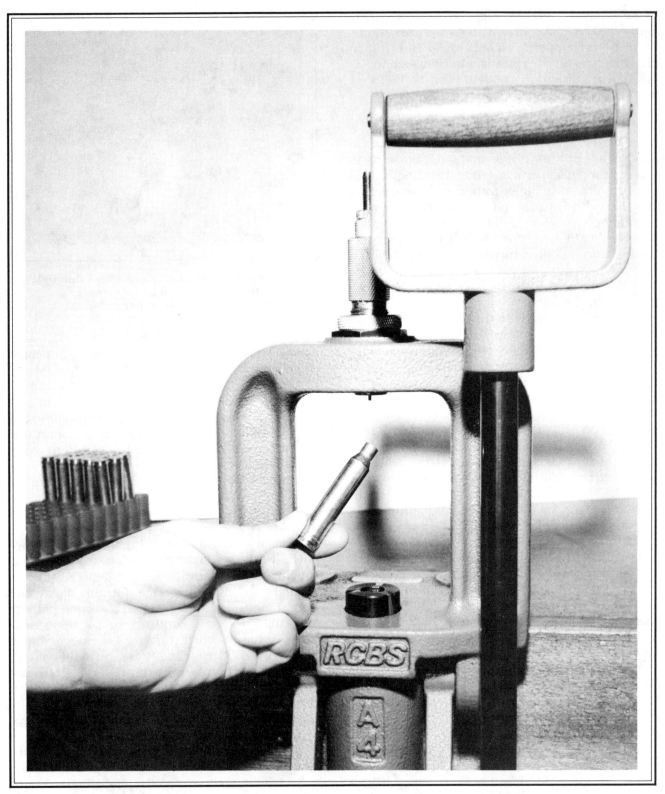

The fine RCBS Big Max press is one of a long line of reloading tools. High quality is the byword of an RCBS product.

Jack Ellis wanted to return to San Francisco, which he eventually did. Standing by to take his place was Don Tucker. "Don told me that he could learn how to grind a reamer in a month if Jack Ellis would teach him. I had reservations, but I gave him a chance. He did it. His reamers were excellent," praised Huntington.

At about the same time, Huntington inherited another man in the shop. If it was unlikely that Don Tucker could grind a beautiful reamer in only 30 days of training, what were the odds of this new worker learning the tool-and-die trade? After all, Bill Keyes came out of the lumber business, where he had worked for a sawmill. But Bill wanted to do the work, and although he had never touched a lathe in his life, he took to it like a bear to honey. Fred has said more than once that in his opinion Bill Keyes is one of the finest special die makers of all time. The RCBS operation was on a roll. The popular—famous would not be too strong a term—"Reloader's Special" came to life. Anyone doubting Fred Huntington's impact on the world of shooting need only remind himself that thousands of prospective reloading fans moved from the shadows of, "I would sure like to handload," to the sunshine of, "I'm reloading my own ammo," on an RCBS "Reloader's Special" kit. There was no doubt—RCBS was for real. The Rock Chucker Press, along with the "Reloader's Special" added to the fame of the company. Here was innovative, high-quality reloading machinery built by people who loved what they were doing.

Fred's father could see the future now. In 1952 he told his son that should the handloading enterprise fade out, he, Mr. Huntington, would help Fred establish a dry-cleaning business. The senior Huntington was in the process of selling the laundry at that time. But Fred was finished with laundry. He was a businessman in his own right. And his business was reloading, not redoing collars. Furthermore, he would make the greatest impact on handloading that the general public of shooters had ever seen. Fred's story is one of continual success. He never backtracked. He suffered no major setbacks. His is not a tale of toil and failure, followed by glory. It was simply one success after another. How successful? Not everyone drives a Rolls Royce. Fred does. His second love, following shooting/hunting, is the automobile, and resting behind his reloading tool plant are about 50 collector's cars. The last time I counted

my vintage Mercedes autos, I came up with exactly—zero. Fred's not sure how many he has.

Fred's small shop could not accommodate the great demand for his products. He had to impound his own garage for more shop space. That move helped for only a short while. In 1954, Fred built a larger shop, 30 by 60 feet, right next to the old one. Since he owned the adjacent land anyway, he figured he might as well use it. "This plant, I felt, would serve our needs for many years," he predicted. But it didn't. While Huntington's RCBS company needed a larger facility within two years, Fred waited until 1958 to build his full-scale RCBS operation. The new establishment began as a 7500-square-foot factory, soon

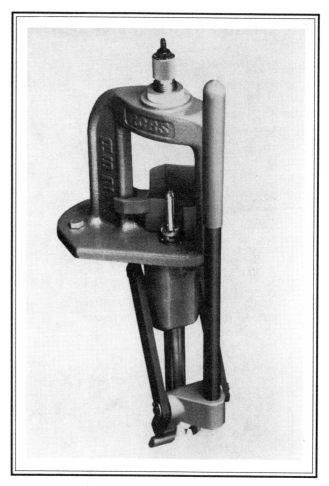

Another RCBS press. Fred Huntington's basic model has been repeated over and over again in scores of individual models. It has meant success after success for the innovative champion of reloading.

The symbol of RCBS, the rockchuck, is essentially a western woodchuck. This mount of a rockchuck presided over the front counter at Omark Industries, who bought RCBS in 1976.

expanding to 50,000 square feet.

In 1976, Fred sold the RCBS interest to Omark Industries. "I had hired 250 people by then," Huntington said. "From about 1965 to 1976, my company had the largest payroll in Butte County." Today, Fred's two sons, both of whom have deserved reputations as sterling as their father's, have followed him in the reloading business. Fred Huntington Jr. supervises production in the RCBS plant, while Charles "Buzz" Huntington serves as general manager for Huntington Die Specialties.

In the time frame from the late 1940s to the present, Huntington proliferated many innovations in reloading tools. He isn't finished yet. His new Huntington Compac Press is witness to the man's continued interest in the reloading game. This is a compact, portable reloader's press "designed for the back packer, benchrest shooter and those that require a small portable tool."

HUNTING AND SHOOTING MAKE A DIFFERENCE

"Everyone should be taught to hunt and shoot," Fred contends. He believes that shooting is a skill-sport that builds character, and that hunting lends tremendous self-confidence and self-esteem. Fred ought to know. He has been a hunter all of his life. Varmint hunting undoubtedly helped to further Huntington's interest in the bullet-making business when he was a young man. Hunting also made a traveler of Fred. He would eagerly drive hundreds of miles for a rockchuck or prairie dog shoot. He hunted for many years with the great gunsmith, Vickery, looking for rockchucks in the Boise, Idaho, area. He happily drove all the way from California to Wyoming for prairie dogs. "I started prairie dog hunting in the early 1950s with Bill Matheney of Recluse, Wyoming," said Huntington. "I also hunted deer and antelope with him. I. . . took several nice hunts with Jack O'Connor, including a great trip into Moose Creek Lodge, and then to the Yukon in 1956 for 30 days with Jack." These two trips were the subjects of *Outdoor Life* articles penned by O'Connor (see separate chapter). Fred hunted with Warren Page as well, with Pete Brown and other firearms authors, too. His hunting adventures led Fred to many other parts of the world—to Iran and Africa, too. Although he has never claimed to be a "mountain man," Fred Hunting-

The word "hunt" belongs in Huntington's name. Fred always loved to hunt not only big game, but varmints as well. Above he poses with a pronghorn antelope buck that he bagged in Wyoming. Below he is pictured with a mule deer buck.

ton has always stayed on the trail until the last rays of sunset visually announced that the hunt was over. Today, the Huntington game collection consists of almost 100 trophy big-game specimens that are honored in the Oroville store.

My guess is that Fred Huntington would have been a starburst success had he remained in the laundry and dry-cleaning business. He's the kind of guy who probably would have come up with a way to bleach raspberry stains out of white shirts. Fred is inventive, energetic and willing to take a chance. He would have made it in any business because of his talent and tenacity. He could have been a success had he opened an ice cube factory in the Arctic Circle. His abilities all furthered his efforts. The ability to design ingenious tools, the ability to organize people, a knowledge of the manufacturing process, and the art of selling combined to make Fred Huntington the leader of the reloading industry. People like the Huntington product, and Huntington, the man. "I made not only customers for our products but many friends!" Fred reflected one day.

When this author was in South Africa, an enthusiastic big game hunter and shooter by the name of Elroy French showed me his reloading room. Myriad well-located tools and components graced the inner sanctum of his handloading chambers. Two presses occupied proud positions, well-fastened to a rigid handmade bench. I was not surprised to see the brand name showing on these tools. The name read RCBS. "Know what RCBS means?" I asked the owner of the room. He said he did. It meant some of the best reloading equipment you could buy, anywhere. "No. It means Rock Chuck Bullet Swages," I was going to say, just to show how erudite we American handloaders were. But before the words left my lips, I canceled them. "That's right," I said. "It means some of the best reloading equipment anywhere."

Many thousands of shooters are happy because Fred Huntington decided to court his true love from a youthful dream to a lifelong reality. His industry and genius have provided high-quality reloading tools at affordable prices, promoting not only a lot more shooting, but also more accurate shooting for marksmen all over the globe.

14

ELMER KEITH: BIG BORE ADVOCATE

Keith sat on his sofa across from me. Frank Wells sat in the chair across from both of us. The renowned shooter rested my 458 Winchester custom rifle across his lap, but he pointed to my 7mm rifle when he spoke. "That's fine workmanship on your 7mm Magnum, Sam," he said, nodding toward the Frank Wells custom rifle lying on the carpet. "Good deer cartridge," he added. As Elmer spoke, he continued to examine the 458.

After our visit, Wells and I hit the highway and headed back to my home, which was then in southeastern Idaho. We didn't say anything for the first 20 minutes. Then Frank spoke up. "Notice how he hung onto that 458, but he lost interest in the 7mm pretty fast, didn't he?" Frank continued, "He's the same guy in real life that he is in print." I agreed. Keith readers have long maintained that Elmer told it straight. He related the truth as he saw it. He was consistent. You didn't get any bunk. I saw Elmer Keith twice more. He had invited me back to his home, and I wanted my eldest son to meet the man, to listen to him, to admire his trophies and rifles. Elmer's hospitality was noteworthy. He came to the door wearing one of his traditional outfits—a white shirt, gold Cape buffalo head bolo tie, 10-gallon hat, cigar in hand. He had an S&W 44 Magnum handgun strapped to each hip as well. He wasn't trying to impress anybody. That's why Keith was impressive. He was just being himself.

Elmer Keith was born in Hardin, Missouri,

March 8, 1899. He is usually associated with Montana and Salmon, Idaho, however. On my first trip to Salmon, I had no tangible address for Keith. He'd said, "Just ask somebody. They'll tell you where I'm at." I asked in town, and the very first person I ran across gave me accurate directions to the Keith home. He was never a cosmopolitan man. He briefly lived in cities when he had to, but home for him was in the outback. He worked on ranches, also ran them, broke broncs, rounded up cattle, and hunted. He hunted a lot.

Keith lived a life of adventure, especially during his early years. He had more than his share of close scrapes with man, beast and fire, when in 1911 a boarding house he and his family were staying in broke into flames. Twelve-year-old Elmer was upstairs. He could not readily escape, and was so viciously burned that he almost died. One could still see the scars from that fire on Keith's person throughout his life. A badly damaged hand, which most people thought would remain impaired for life, healed well.

Elmer continued with an active career. From the beginning, he tested firearms, ordering a new rifle whenever he could afford to, and "wringing it out." Early on, Keith decided upon what he really wanted in a rifle, ballistically. He wanted a bullet with plenty of mass fired from a rifle of considerable accuracy. Throughout his hunting and writing career, Keith would remain true to his big-bore conviction.

Elmer Keith was one of the great shooters of any era. In 1973 he received the first Outstanding American Handgun trophy in honor of his great contribution in the advent of the 41 Magnum and 44 Magnum rounds, and to big-bore handgunning in general.

Keith was a gifted marksman. A fellow writer saw him shoot a 44 Magnum handgun at 200 yards. The observer reported that Keith hit a foot-square target with uncanny regularity at that distance. His long-range shooting ability would have been deemed fictional had it not been for witnesses. Keith was as fine a rifleman and shotgunner as he was an expert with a handgun. His 334 O.K.H. rifle was sighted in dead on at 300 yards, which meant that the bullets grouped several inches high at 200. But Keith was a master of compensation and he felt he could hit big game regularly with his 334 O.K.H. out to 400 yards and farther. Keith's 10-gauge magnum could be counted on to drop geese cleanly at long range using large shot pellets. Even for the shotgun, the man preferred projectile mass for energy retention. He shot competitively, placing high in many important matches. He probably could have made a big name for himself in target shooting—he was that good.

But his deepest firearm interest—whether rifle, handgun or shotgun—was in the hunting field. Keith's wife, Lorraine, loved the outdoor/ranch life, too. She hunted big game with Elmer from early on in their marriage and they raised their children in appreciation of the outdoor life. The Keith youngsters were always at home in the hinterlands. Tragically, Elmer and Lorraine lost a child following a car accident. The little girl was more seriously injured than she at first appeared to be. The child continued to fail little by little and finally succumbed to her injuries.

Keith continued as a rancher. He also drew income from hunting. Rather than being a guided hunter, Keith was himself a guide, showing the outback to many men, including Zane Grey. Keith hunted all over—he made trips into Canada in the late 1920s, down Mexico way, many different western states, and he also beat many paths through the bush of Africa, amassing a huge storehouse of know-how and hunting experience. From this warehouse of experience, Keith drew up his many hunting stories for books and articles.

BIG BORES ALL THE WAY

Elmer Keith became famous as a big-bore enthusiast. He distrusted small-bullet/high-velocity rifles for big game. Most riflemen change perspective over the years. I thought the 270 wore a halo early in my hunting career; I still like the round, but haven't taken a big game animal with a 270 for years. Other riflemen start with a ballistic concept, then switch later on. Colonel Whelen once pointed out that the 30-30 was the ideal deer cartridge, while the 30-06 was too much firearm for most American big game. Keith did not swerve from the big-bore trail. He began his love for firearms believing that a Sharps buffalo rifle was far more potent as an elk-taker than any 30-06. He ended his shooting career feeling exactly the same way. Nobody ever convinced Keith otherwise. The only slack he ever cut for the smallbore fan was an admission that the partition bullet gave more impetus to lesser calibers. He did not use his love of heavy bullets as a trademark or a gimmick to sell controversial magazine articles. He believed in big holes in the barrel, with big bullets coming out of their muzzles.

In his *American Rifleman* article of January 1936, "The .400 Whelen on Elk and Mule Deer," Keith voiced his admiration for the big-bore rifle. In this instance, it was a 30-06 Springfield cartridge necked up to accept a 40-caliber bullet. "Over twenty years of hunting American big game, especially our heavier species, has convinced me that for reliable results under all conditions in timber and brush, with raking and running shots, only long, heavy bullets with thick jackets, and at velocities of from 2,000 to 2,400 feet, will surely produce reliable results." That conviction created two camps of readers: the Keith fans, who believed that big bullets were worth more than ultra-high velocity; and the anti-Keith readers, who preached, "It's where you hit 'em that counts, not what you hit 'em with." Elmer got his share of mail from both factions.

Keith gave no quarter. He never backtracked. He did not, for example, recommend the big bore for brush and timber hunting only. He felt that the big bullet was the right one no matter what the ecological niche of encounter. For example, Elmer considered the 400 Whelen a proper choice for long-range hunting, citing its use on antelope out to 400 yards. He tolerated the 6.5 Mannlicher-Schoenauer because of the long 160-grain bullet, allowing that a careful hunter could do all right on big game with such a cartridge because the long projectile might reach the vitals. He believed in the Nosler Partition bullet. Keith promoted any projectile that retained jacket and core as a unit.

Such a bullet, he felt, expanded to a large caliber during penetration, while retaining much of its original mass, thus improving smallbore performance. "The Nosler bullet, or any other bullet that will expand, but stay together, helps make the smallbores, like the 7mm, into better performers," said Keith. But big bores were Elmer's choice.

He considered the 25-35, which he used for a while, not much better than a spear, and inadequate even for deer at modest ranges. He of course did not like the 30-30 either. He felt that of the 30-30-type rounds, he could abide the 303 Savage, mainly because of the latter's 180- to 190-grain bullets. But even with heavier projectiles, he didn't consider the 30-06 a cartridge best-suited for game beyond the deer ranks. Certainly, it was no elk or big bear rifle. The 270 Winchester was all right for deer, better than the 250 Savage, Keith declared, but again no elk rifle. Before he could study the cartridge and use it in the field, Keith did remark glowingly about the 270. But

A young Elmer Keith on his ranch house doorstep with a "pet" coyote. Keith was a good horsemen, broke broncs, rounded up cattle and did a lot of hunting.

Keith was a rugged outdoorsman. He and his wife, Lorraine, hunted year round and raised their children to appreciate the outdoor life. This was their cold-weather camp on Snow Creek, aptly named.

those feelings were quickly replaced with disregard for the cartridge as a big game harvester. The 7mm Remington Magnum with the 175-grain bullet Keith considered an excellent deer round. When he looked at mine, though, he categorized it as a fine rifle, and a good deer cartridge with the 175-grain bullet, but, thank you, he'd like more bullet weight for elk.

Keith's penchant for big bores raised the hackles of some readers, and ired many fellow arms authorities as well. But Elmer spoke from vast experience, and you had to listen to what he had to say, whether or not you always agreed with every nuance of his ideology. In a conversation with a SE Idaho resident who claimed to have known Keith in the late 1920s, the more the fellow talked, the more irate he became about Keith's love for big bullets: "I killed an elk with a 25-35 one year just to show Keith it could be done," the old gentleman assured me, color rising in his cheeks. But Keith recited many tales of game wounded with light bullets. His stories made some people angry. They made a few people *very* angry.

Keith wrote more broadly on firearms topics than he is often credited. He is remembered for his role as the torchbearer for big-bore rifles (and handguns), and for his 10-gauge shotgun loaded with big shot. However, few shooting subjects were ignored by the prolific arms author in his career. He authored 10 books and numerous magazine articles. He was a good writer who wrote with authority, but not audacity. Elmer, however, did not consider himself a wizard with the English language, because he was not "trained." He was more at home testing a double rifle than banging the keys of his typewriter. He believed that the editor should take command of commas and semicolons, while he, the author, ensured that the material was accurate and innovative. Keith was neither a trained scientist nor an engineer or ballistician. He was a pragmatic arms-tester and an excellent reporter who brought useful information and hundreds of good ideas to the attention of arms readers.

He wrote carefully and well about many different rifles and events. "The Officer's Model 1873 Springfield," a piece Keith wrote for the October 1936 *American Rifleman* is a good example of his research and testing of various firearms. Of course, he fired the rifle as part of the report. At 500 yards, Keith did quite well on a "rock about two feet in diameter" with this test rifle. He also hit a rock with regularity at 350 yards, this target reported as being about a foot in diameter. If someone else said that, you might squint an eye. But Keith could do it. He wrote on "The Blake Bolt-Action Magazine Rifle," again in *American Rifleman* of June 1936. He reported on the natural history of the bull elk in a 1951 issue, being sure to warn hunters against smallbores for these big game animals. He said, "I personally do not care for any bullet under 250 grains in weight—300 grains is much better—nor calibers under .33."

He penned a story on gunstock making for production rifles, "Gunstocks and Stock Blanks,"

Elmer Keith excelled with firearms of all types. Noted for his fine marksmanship with both rifle and sidearm—he was in part responsible for the advent and success of the 44 Magnum cartridge—he was also a fine shotgunner.

that appeared in the May 1949 *American Rifleman*. He even wrote on blackpowder shooting. "If your finances happen to be a few steps behind your enthusiasm (and whose hasn't been at one time or another?), you're a prime candidate for the ranks of the blackpowder burners," Keith said in a September 1944 *American Rifleman*. He progressed from this well-written lead into an explanation of blackpowder basics. The article would be as timely today as it was in 1944.

In his book, *Big Game Rifles & Cartridges*, a 1936 title now reprinted by Wolfe Publishing Company, Keith listed 74 big game harvests at the time. "I am a firm believer in the use of more powerful rifles than are usually recommended for our big game. . . ," he proposed in the Foreword of the book. He went on to discuss a formula for energy, one that paid more respect to bullet weight than Newton's kinetic energy construct.

OUTSTANDING AMERICAN HANDGUNNER

What was Keith's legacy to American shooting? Although he was, without a doubt, one of the most influential writers of rifle-shooting we've had in our history, we would probably have to place his largest contribution to shooters in the arena of the big-bore handgun rather than the rifle. Keith was truly a moving force in this area. He advocated large-bore handguns from the start, never swaying from his conviction that a bullet of decent weight fired from a handgun, even at modest velocity, was powerful medicine at close range. In September 1944, Keith said in "Sixguns for Defense," an *American Rifleman* article, "My own choice for such use is the four-inch barrel Model 1926 Smith & Wesson .44 Special, with heavy handloads. . . ." He wore a couple of four-inch barreled 44 Magnums on his belt when I saw him last in the 1970s.

Keith's desire for a powerful 44-caliber handgun inspired the 44 Magnum cartridge, one of the most widely used handgun rounds in existence today. He began work with the 44 Special, using top-end loads. He later worked with Remington to promote the production of the 44 Magnum. Indirectly or directly, he also spurred much of today's strong interest in hunting big game with the handgun. Keith was even awarded the first Outstanding American Handgun trophy given in 1973 in honor of his great contribution in the advent of the 41 Magnum and 44 Magnum rounds,

and to big-bore handgunning in general.

This is not to say that Keith had no impact on rifles or rifle cartridges. Whenever you look at a 338 Winchester round, consider that Keith was a proponent of that caliber many, many years ago. His 333 O.K.H. and 334 O.K.H. are examples of 33 calibers Keith had something to do with well over a half century back. However, Elmer did not convince the riflemen of America to abandon the smaller bores in favor of the larger ones. The 30-06 still accounts for far more elk than any 33- or 40-caliber cartridge. Therefore, to say that Elmer persuaded riflemen away from smaller calibers is inaccurate.

Keith was also a proponent of the telescopic rifle sight before "scope" became a household word. Taking that one step further, he touted the American-made scope as being every bit as good as the imports of the hour. "For most types of big-game hunting, the hunting-type telescope sight is a very great advantage. For all long-range shooting at such game as antelope, mule deer, sheep, goat, and caribou, as well as wolves and coyotes, it is almost a necessity." (*American Rifleman*, December 1944) Keith's admiration for the scope and his recommendation of its use in the big game field had certain impact on the broadened use of the glass sight. He credited Rudolph Noske, American scopemaker, with making the first truly practical glass hunting sight for big game rifles.

Elmer Keith also left his mark in an area he probably never dreamed to conquer when he was a young man—the world of writing. His books and articles are as well-received today as ever. Elmer knew more of cowponies and elk than he did of punctuation and syntax in those early days, but he was an intelligent man and he had a natural bent for accurate reporting, as well as a flair for telling a story. He *did* what he wrote about. And he did it about as well as anyone. He had perseverance for his work and a tenacity for life. He stayed with his work throughout his days. "I have no intention of retiring," said Keith. "You retire, you become a vegetable. . . ."

His last tour of writing duty was with the Petersen Publishing Company as Executive Editor of *Guns and Ammo* magazine. It's safe to say that many of us turned first to Keith to see what he had to say before reading the rest of the magazine. When O'Connor's work appeared in the same

Cowboy hat and cigar were Keith's trademarks, but more so were the sixshooters, usually 44 caliber, he wore on either side of his belt.

magazine, many shooters felt that the two best arms authors in the business were on one masthead. Elmer died on Valentine's Day, 1883, in Boise, Idaho. He had lived 84 years.

In his lifetime, Elmer Keith hunted practically all American big game, and he made two good safaris to Africa, as well as one Asian hunt.

But most of all, he will be remembered by shooters as the man who loved the big bore, who believed in bullets of mass to get the job done, and who backed up his belief with his shooting credits, not with lip service. Keith was one of the greatest of the "gunwriters." His work will be around for a long time.

15

BEN LILLY: ROCKY MOUNTAIN RIFLEMAN

As romantic a figure as ever walked the West, Benjamin Vernon Lilly was known by hunters and ranchers as simply "Ben." His life was so fictional in nature that he a became a legend long before his death. But Ben was no myth—he simply lived a mythical life. Next to Davy Crockett, Lilly was the greatest bear hunter of modern times. He piques the imagination, for even though this bearded tracker was scarcely more familiar with roof and bed than the caveman, Ben was no barbarian bent over a wilderness campfire, living on wild herbs and half-cooked meat. The problem with legends is defining where fiction ends and fact begins.

Thanks to J. Frank Dobie, the well-known American author, we have reliable biographical knowledge concerning this giant among American hunters. Dobie notwithstanding, the Ben Lilly legend would be no more than that, an interesting story about a man of modern times who knew more about mountain lions, black bears and grizzlies than he knew of civilization. Dobie met "The Nestor of the Mountains," as Ben was called, in January 1928. The writer was in El Paso, Texas, seeking information on gold mines and western lore, making ready with a packtrain to cross the Sierra Madres of Mexico. There was to be a talk by a great modern mountain man, B.V. Lilly, on the subject of hunting bears and lions. Lilly was no lecturer. He said afterwards that the only other speech he gave was in Sunday School when he

was a child. Lilly was 71 years old at the time.

After the talk, Dobie took the opportunity of visiting with the grand old hunter. "I have heard of you many times, Mr. Lilly," Frank said. Ben replied that his reputation had grown larger than his person, being like his shadow in front of a late afternoon sun. Lilly revealed himself as a Thoreau or Emerson, saying that property was a handicap to a man, for a man was rich in proportion to the things he could do without, not by measure of the hardware he had to own in order to survive. "Every man and woman ought to get out and be alone with the elements a while every day, even if only for five minutes," said Lilly. "I can't think at all except when I am out. I like to think of the past. I can think of myself as a barefooted boy standing before the fireplace with my hands spread out, and of my mother close by me, and I am happy."

Ben continued to speak with James Frank. Then he invited the writer to look at a manuscript, actually two manuscripts, that he hoped would someday be the opening chapters of a book on hunting and his life. Dobie went to the Shelton Hotel with Lilly. Ben was quartered in one of the rooms, but would not sleep inside the building—the air was too "rancid." From the hotel safe, the innkeeper withdrew a bundle of papers at Lilly's request. They contained "What I Know about Bears" and "What I Know about Panthers." That night Dobie read the first manuscript. It was to be the first chapter of the Lilly book, a work that

Ben Lilly: Nestor of the Mountains, at age 50. At home only in the wilderness, the tracker became a legend in his lifetime. He hunted bear and "panthers" and would winter in the hills, learning about the creatures' ways.

Bears like this Blackie were almost an obsession with Lilly, although grizzlies held equal, if not more, fascination. In 1913, Ben skirted death with a nine-foot bruin after tracking it for three days, then wounding it.

never materialized.

The next afternoon, Dobie again met with Lilly, and this time the author had a chance to read about panthers. He was drawn into Lilly's world of the hunter. Since he would be reading instead of talking with Ben, Dobie offered the old woodsman copies of the *El Paso Times* and *Saturday Evening Post*, which were in his coat pocket. Ben refused, saying, "No, I thank you. I find this very in-ter-est-ing." Dobie looked up. Ben was totally absorbed in "What I Know about Bears." After the session, the two men parted company.

But Dobie could not forget the Nestor of the Mountains. In 1940, four years after Lilly's death, J. Frank wrote an article about Lilly in which he mentioned Ben's writings. They apparently had not been located after Lilly's death. In response, Dr. L.A. Jessen, a dentist from Bayard, New Mexico, wrote saying he had, somewhere, two articles by Lilly—one on hunting bears, the other on hunting mountain lions. Dobie heard no more from Jessen. Finally, he went to the New Mexico dentist's office. Through diligent searching, Dobie found the panther manuscript and also Lilly's diary for 1916. Later on, Dobie recovered much more of the diary. With reliable written information and testimonies by many people, J. Frank Dobie penned *The Ben Lilly Legend*, which was published by Little, Brown and Company in 1950. (All quotations used here are from that book.)

IN THE BEGINNING

Lilly was born on the last day of the year 1856 in Wilcox County, Alabama. His father, Albert, and his mother, Margaret Anna McKay, had married on November 7, 1855. I suspect that Ben's literacy was a product of his mother's education. A graduate of Nicholson Female College of Mississippi, she became an instructor, teaching astronomy in finishing school. These facts do not make Ben's mother a scholar, but she was a reader. No doubt it was her influence that gave Ben a solid background in Bible reading and sound belief in its Word. Ben would not work on the Sabbath. It is said that if he and his dogs were on a hot trail, the man would give it up in favor of resting on the Seventh Day, at which time he read his Bible and contemplated matters of the universe and the hereafter. Albert Lilly was a blacksmith and a wheelwright, from a family that seemed bent toward metalworking. There was a gunmaker in the clan, Benjamin Franklin Lilly, Ben's namesake, whose firearms were coveted for the turkey shoot because of their accuracy.

Life in Alabama and Mississippi was one of quiet treks in a land yet unsettled. In his youth, Ben worked on a farm, but his real interest—he considered it a patriotic duty and birthright—was hunting. Not for trophies, but for stock-killing bears and mountain lions, which Ben insisted on calling panthers. While the trade seems foreign to a modern point of view, it is still carried on to this hour. I have had the experience of taking the trail with a government hunter, who lives part of his life in Ben Lilly fashion. A few years ago, a stock-killing bear was working a territory in the high mountains of Colorado when my friend was called in to locate and dispatch the animal. John lived in a pup tent for a month as he pursued the bruin, finally catching up with it. Young Ben Lilly was well-suited to the occupation that would pervade his life. He was a superior tracker and a woodsman without peer. He could live off the land like a bear. And he was an explorer. While we feel at home on our city streets, Ben Lilly enjoyed the same sense of security only in the outback, away from signs of human development.

Eventually Ben inherited a farm. He stayed with it for a while, but he didn't like the work. It was boring. A friend of Lilly reported that he saw the man furrowing the earth with his horses at full gallop so he could finish the distasteful deed as quickly as possible. Ben was a natural athlete and a powerful man. He had "springs in his legs," always broad jumping to show his ability. Local records were supposedly kept, proving that Lilly's athletic prowess could have qualified him for the Olympics. On a hunt with Theodore Roosevelt, Lilly demonstrated his physical adroitness by standing in a barrel and then jumping straight up out of it without touching the rim. He was also a fast runner, and as for hiking, days on end without rest did not slow the great tracker of the Rocky Mountains. His hunting was accomplished first on foot, then by horse, later on foot again, hiking miles and miles without cessation. With all these physical merits, Ben could not swim. In spite of this, he would dive into the water, and if his feet didn't touch bottom with his head above the surface, he would walk the bottom anyway, with head submerged. If his rifle got swamped in the process, I suppose he found a way to dry it out.

Young Ben made a mistake in 1880—at least for him. He got married in the fall of the year to Lelia, a lady reported as crazy. Following the marriage, his hunting trips lengthened. A hike of half a hundred miles was nothing special. Mrs. Lilly was supposed to have upbraided her husband regularly, sometimes with good cause. Ben was not much for taking care of things. He'd flop a muddy saddle on the porch, or bring his equally muddy body into the house, saying that for health's sake one should allow wet clothes to dry without taking them off. The best-known story about Ben Lilly, be it fact or fiction, was the chicken hawk tale. It seems that Mrs. Lilly complained that her chickens were being repeatedly raided by the raptor. She challenged that if Ben liked to hunt so much, why didn't he get busy and end that hawk's career? Ben complied. He was gone for over a year. When asked why he was away for so long, he replied, "The hawk just kept on flying." So goes the tale. . . . Ben returned home only to see his children, especially Vernon, called Dick, who was a "frail child."

Lilly became a cattle buyer. Buy and sell was his trade, and he plied it well. He did so well that

As mountain lions and bears became his trademarks, Lilly even drew them on envelopes of the correspondence he wrote to friends. Note the postmark on the upper envelope—Silver City, New Mexico, 1928, and also his rendition of "bee V." Lilly.

he accumulated a fat wad of money. This roll he gave to Lelia as a going-away present. Ben wanted, and obtained, a divorce after returning home from a cattle-buying venture only to find Dick lying dead on the floor. Ben knelt by the little lad, and when he got up, he bade his wife good-by. Lelia left, too, and she remarried. But she did not get well. Much of the 30 remaining years of her life she spent in an insane asylum.

Lilly went from cattle trading to finding and selling wild honey. In 1890, he remarried. He and his second wife, Mary, had three children. Their two daughters were survivors in Dobie's time, but the son died of tuberculosis. Wanderlust continued to rule Ben's life. He hunted bears and cougars for the adventure of it. Mary said that if he went out hunting again, he might just as well stay gone. So Ben turned his money, except for five dollars, over to her, bade his offspring ''so long,'' and departed for good. He didn't need a house. Oat meal, dry corn out of season and fresh corn in season were enough grub to carry the hunter into the deepest wood.

THE HUNTER AS MARKSMAN

You don't have to be a great marksman to be a great hunter. But Ben Lilly was both. One thing that all of Lilly's associates agreed upon was that the man could have made a living as an exhibition shooter. Some of Ben's shooting feats seemed to be cast in the die of fiction. However, knowing that Ad Toepperwein performed uncanny shooting tricks before the eyes of multitudes and that Miss Sure-Shot Annie Oakley (see separate chapters) did the same, Ben Lilly's shooting seems more plausible.

He was known to wingshoot bumblebees and yellowjackets. Witnesses claimed he could bring a buzzard down (remember that hawk and buzzard shooting was condoned into the middle of the 20th century) with riflefire. Moreover, as the hapless bird was wheeling groundward, Ben could hit it again and again. Some folks said Ben could down mosquitoes, too. Maybe. Today, we are more inclined to disbelieve great shooting than to believe it because we have ceased rifle-firing at aerial targets. In my youth, a buddy and I often shot against a huge dirt bluff along the All American Canal near Yuma, Arizona. We lived to shoot. Not a day passed without 22 bullets whizzing into the dirt cliff, especially after we both had jobs, and

Lilly pursued lions and bears all over the West, including Mexico. He needed the skills and local knowledge of men such as this old vaquero, Don Pancho, who lived in the border country at the time.

even before that because we sold game and fish for 22 ammo. What we could do with our 22 rifles would be scoffed at now. Nor could either of us come close to repeating those aerial rifle tricks of the past because we never practice them. I believe most of the Ben Lilly shooting legend—maybe leaving off the mosquitoes.

Ben owned several different firearms, one of which was a 32 rimfire rifle. The 32 was a perfectly useful cartridge that did not weather the test of time. A good close-range round with ample power to bag a wild turkey, it was so mild-mannered that learning to shoot straight with it was easy using an accurate rifle. Frank C. Hibben, who also met the mountain man, verified his shooting skill with various firearms. Lilly owned, according to Hibben, a 22 rimfire, a 30 Winchester (I am unfamiliar with this cartridge, although there were a few 30-caliber rimfire cartridges in limited use during the 1800s), a 303 Savage, the 30-30 Winchester and, of course, a 33 Winchester. Introduced in 1902, the 33 was a 33 caliber that fired 200-grain bullets of .338-inch diameter at about 2000-2200 feet per second muzzle velocity. I never think of the great B.V. Lilly without picturing the woodsman walking along with his Winchester Model 1886 lever-action rifle chambered for the excellent 33 Winchester cartridge.

Hibben, whose work on Lilly was not admired by J. Frank Dobie, does not depart from the marksmanship glory usually bestowed upon the famous bear hunter. Many of the feats sound reasonable in light of other verified shooting accomplishments witnessed by thousands of onlookers. Saying that Ben Lilly could not shoot a fast-moving animal through the heart in spite of a brush screen partially obscuring the target is to suggest that Ad Topperwein could not hit a two by two block of wood with a 44 revolver. About shooting both antlers from a running buck and then dropping the deer with a third shot, I don't know. We shall have to give Lilly the benefit of the doubt. Hibben reported that the cowboys of the Heart Bar Ranch on the Gila River maneuvered Ben into occasional shooting contests, not because they thought they could win, but to watch the man shoot. Hibben says Ben fired only a rifle, never a sidearm. As for shooting a mourning dove out of the air with a 30-30, that's possible, especially if the bird is coming into a waterhole. But how about shooting the avian and then hitting it twice more before it touches ground—with a 30-30? Ben, no doubt, had nerves of steel. He was a steady man. Perhaps his lifestyle aided his marksmanship. Lilly did not drink alcohol, nor did he smoke tobacco. He did, according to Hibben, stir up a brew from wild cherry leaves, however, which, says Hibben, had the potency of fuel oil.

To keep in practice for big game, Ben sharpened his eye on smaller animals and birds. In this respect, we modern hunters do not admire Lilly's lack of regard for wildlife. He was reported to have slain 11 deer. I found no mention of their being put to use. As Dobie pointed out, Lilly was somewhat like John James Audubon, who copped a closer look at birds by shotgunning them down in large numbers. Said Audubon, "I call birds few when I shoot less than one hundred per day." Lilly went on to decimate the ursine population of Louisiana. The verb is carefully chosen. When Ben was done, finding a bear in the state was not likely. He was a predator hunting by profession, and as such was paid for his services. Lilly trusted banks and kept his money in them, and failing banks gobbled up his savings. But the man's needs were few. If he did require something that cost money, his credit was good. He was assumed entirely trustworthy in a debt.

Another thing about Lilly's shooting. Now and again, he displayed his prowess on inanimate objects. He was known to shoot the pith out of a corn cob center, the bullet boring out the center of the cob lengthwise. More often, though, the target wore fur or feathers. On a turkey hunt with L.L. Davidson, Ben lured three birds—he mastered calling with his mouth and did not use an artificial instrument. When the birds bolted out of shotgun range, Lilly dropped all three on the run with his rifle, apologizing to Davidson while explaining that the shotgun could not have

Lilly considered his hunt with Teddy Roosevelt in 1907 as the greatest honor of his life. Commissioned to "get the President a bear," he looked for sign such as this track.

Mounted and ready to ride, about 1917, Lilly traveled simply. His steed may not be a show piece, but it served the needs of this modern-day mountain man.

reached the target. Lilly wrote in a letter dated 1928, "If a bear or lion ever jumps out of a tree and I am in sight, I will get three balls in it before it hits the ground. I never saw a lion that I did not kill or wound. I shoot well at ranges up to 400 yards, running or standing, with a .30-30 or .33 or .303 caliber. At long range I kill by holding the sight high over the animal." We can label that brag, or go along with Dobie in saying that men who are good at something know it.

Ben considered his hunt with Theodore Roosevelt the greatest honor of his life. He arrived at the presidential hunting camp on Sunday, October 5, 1907, having been summoned by telegram to make the trip. Appointed Chief Huntsman of the camp, Old Ben could get the President a bear, you bet. But Monday was a failure. The hunt was overburdened with superfluous dogs, noise and men. It was more circus than serious. Tuesday brought rain. Ben left camp and located fresh

bear sign. The entire week passed without Roosevelt getting so much as a look at Mr. Bruin. The newspapers carried many stories of Lilly, the "wonder of the woods." Reportedly, the President got up on the morning of October 15, Tuesday, and went for a swim in Bear Lake, 100 yards out and back. The air temperature was 40 degrees. The water had to be cold enough for a polar bear. By Friday, the President got a small bear, no thanks to Ben, who was off in the woods cutting sign. The hunt ended. Everybody went home, except for Lilly. It was Sunday. Ben waited until Monday to travel. Teddy had little good to say about Lilly, considering the huntsman a religious fanatic.

The Rocky Mountains proved to be Lilly's choice realm of contentment. The huge blue ranges that extended along the Arizona-Mexico border, still wild even today, lured and held the man captive. Ben met the grizzly bear in these reaches, an animal far more ferocious than the smaller black bear, with all respect to the latter. In the White Mountains of Arizona, that tall and beautiful wilderness country, Ben had his closest call with a bear. A Silvertip grizzly hunt commenced on April 13, 1913. Ben followed the bear for three days in the snow, his diary reports. He had no food to eat as he traveled. He was meagerly dressed for the cold mountains and survived the nights only by keeping vigil in front of the campfire. Lilly wounded the bear. He trailed it. The grizzly charged from 15 feet. Ben fired twice, the first shot striking the animal's chest, the second entering under an eye. The grizzly fell forward against the hunter. Ben shot again. Then he drove a hunting knife with an 18-inch blade into the animal. "I took careful measurements of this bear, according to government standards. He measured nine foot from the tip of his nose to the end of his tail."

Ben was in his element. He did not leave the mountains in winter on a regular basis. He holed up like a bear himself. Earlier in his hunting career, he had relied on horse power to convey him along the trail. But he was no horse-lover. As a tracker, he liked to rely on his own energy and leg power. When he had had a horse, he'd often stake it for days, returning to water and feed the animal when the hunting was done. Finally, he decided a steed was more anchor than engine, so he resorted to his own mighty limbs to move over the land. From 1912 to 1927 he lived in the mountains, learning a great deal about bears. His contact with ranchers in the area provided much information about the man. His supplies were few. He carried two rifles at this time, a 30-30 for lions and food, and a 33 Winchester if he knew he was going to be in pursuit of a bear. He lived off the land now with neither oatmeal nor corn as staples. Instead, he boiled meat. He jerked meat. He fried meat in lion fat. In season, he had squash to cook. If he could get milk at a ranch, he would drink great quantities. He sometimes baked ash

cakes and made custard with eggs and milk when he could get the ingredients. His aversion to hot drink was set aside at times when he brewed up an Oriental tea, or made drinks from pinon leaves or other native plants.

Lilly emerged from seclusion to guide an elaborate hunt for an Oklahoma oil man, W.H. McFadden. The hunt was outfitted with luxuries brought in by wagon and pack mule. Ben was hired on as the main sign-reader. Tents. Servants. Wine. And no limit on time nor money. Ben's job: get McFadden a grizzly bear. McFadden stayed in camp, then left on business. While he was away, Lilly found bears and tried to keep track of them until McFadden returned. The oil man was never on hand to get his bear. Ben later guided for other hunters. But his main work was "predator control" in a land where ranchers were looking forward to raising cattle without fear of losing half of their stock to cougars, grizzlies and black bears. Asked to be a guide on a special hunt, he refused. The party in question said that Ben Lilly apparently did not know who he, the client, was. No, he was told. You don't know who Ben Lilly is.

B.V. Lilly died in Silver City, New Mexico, December 17, 1936, two weeks shy of his 80th birthday. His daughters attended the funeral. Hardly recognizable without his beard, he was clean-shaven for the first time in decades. A Methodist minister who did not know the old hunter presided over the services.

In 1947 Lilly was honored with a plaque arranged by J. Stokely Ligon and other friends. A bronze was imbedded in a huge granite boulder. One side bore the head of a lion; the other, the head of a bear. In the center was a likeness of Ben. The plaque rests fifty miles from the Mogollon Mountain Range in the Gila National Forest, Ben's favorite hunting place. Had Lilly been born earlier, he would have taken the trail with Jim Bridger, Jedediah Smith and John Colter. In the end, Ben Lilly became the last, legendary mountain man.

16

DR. F.W. MANN: RX FOR ACCURACY

F.W. Mann relied upon observation during his long, arduous study of the bullet in flight. His investigation culminated in a book named *The Bullet's Flight from Powder to Target*, with sub-title, "The Internal and External Ballistics of Small Arms." Dr. Mann called his book "A study of rifle shooting with the personal element excluded, disclosing the cause of the error at the target." The byline read, "F.W. Mann, B.S., M.D.," for Mann was a physician by vocation. In his own credits, Mann lists himself as a member of the Cornell University alumni, Boston University alumni, and "Life Member of the Massachusetts Rifle Association."

How did the good doctor become a ballistics expert?

Levi and Lydia Lurana Ware Mann were living at the old homestead in Norfolk, Massachusetts, when they were blessed with their son, Franklin Weston, on July 24, 1856. Franklin was eighth generation from William Mann of England. The family roots were deeply set in the soil of Massachusetts. The Reverend Samuel Mann, a graduate of Harvard, class of 1665, was the son of William. From the beginning, the Manns were solid citizens of the community. Frank's father was a farmer and owned a mill. He also served as church deacon, choir leader and Sunday School superintendent, as well as Chairman of the Board of Selectmen and a member of the legislature. Young Frank Mann was raised in a healthy en-

vironment of honest labor. While a rather small person, he was "wiry," tough, resilient. He was stronger than he looked, a reward earned as a farmhand.

Mann attended his village primary school, then graduated to Walpole High School. He was a thinker, enjoying debates on matters of religion, history, politics, law and economics. As a religious person, he shunned foul language and strong drink. Mann had an early opportunity to indulge in the sport of shooting. A building on the farm grounds was replete with window for marksmanship practice on foul weather days. He took advantage of the situation, firing a rifle as frequently as his duties would allow. In the old building, a vice was so stationed as to allow a rifle to be held in its jaws. The lad had an opportunity to learn what happened when bullets were sent downrange from a rifle in a fixed position. Little did he know that he was already becoming a student of ballistics. He furthered that interest as part of his formal education at Cornell University, where he attended and earned, in 1878, a Bachelor of Science degree.

It was in college that Frank got the idea of building a perfect top which, after becoming exhausted of its original thrust, would come to rest in a standing position, entirely stable. His friends laughed. Of course, Mann knew that in theory, at least, his top was a possibility. While there is no evidence that Frank's tops ever came to a point-

Dr. F.W. Mann, student of the bullet's flight. With the assistance of other dedicated shooters, such as Harry Pope and Adolph Niedner, Dr. Mann spent years investigating one single question: Why do bullets disperse, even when the rifle is placed in a machine rest?

on standstill, there is data to support that one of his tops spun for three-fourths of an hour. In the laboratory of a Professor Anthony, Mann beat his own record by a mile. By placing his best-balanced top under glass to remove it from atmospheric disturbance, the device spun for two hours and 57 minutes.

While Franklin was greatly interested in the laws of physics, he channeled his efforts in an-other direction—medicine. For this work he at-tended the Medical School of Boston. He served as intern at the Massachusetts Homeopathic Hospital, where he began to make tracings of heart beats for various patients. Mann kept rec-ords, case histories of various persons with heart trouble. He noticed emerging patterns that showed characteristic signs of different heart problems. He used these recorded patterns as guides in diagnosing various cardiac diseases. He was granted his degree in 1883.

A year out of graduate school, Franklin married Frances Gertrude Backus of Ashford, Connecticut. Dr. Mann practiced for four years, but he realized that medicine did not satisfy him. In 1887 he ventured into the machine business at Milford, Massachusetts. Dr. Mann's future years of experimentation would be funded not by dispensing prescriptions to the ill, but through an invention that served as a prescription for the poultry business. Mann began studying the food value of fresh bones for the raising of poultry. He saw the enormous waste of this resource because of the inability to process the bones and attached tissues. In 1889, Dr. Mann gave the world the Mann Bone Cutter, an entirely new machine intended for the reduction of bone into a useful food

for poultry. Two years into it, demand far outran supply. Mann had to move his operation to larger quarters. Soon, he was financially secure for life. He could do what he wanted to do.

His thoughts returned to some of the questions of his youth, his reflections on bullets flying through the air. What affected that flight?

Adolph Niedner worked closely with Dr. Mann, as did Harry Pope. Niedner said of Mann, "Dr. Mann was a genius. He was fifty years ahead of his time. His book was the best thing of its kind ever written. . . ." Niedner was most impressed with the way Dr. Mann operated. He insisted on writing things down, rather than dismissing them to memory. Adolph asked Frank a question one day. The doctor did not respond. Some time later, Niedner received a letter from Mann, which contained the answer to his question. Mann had re-

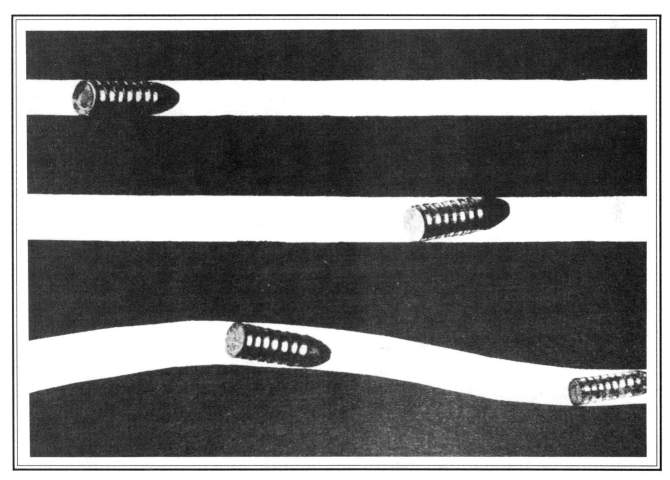

An artist's rendition of Mann's "phantom flight of the bullet." The top bullet is flying "point on," while the rest of the 32-caliber projectiles are tipping on their axes by degrees.

corded the question with a note. Then he tested for the answer. Only when he was satisfied with the results did Mann write Niedner. But he had not forgotten. "He had too much information stored in his head," said Niedner, "and he was afraid of giving the wrong answer." After many years of working together, Niedner said, "He was the best friend I ever had."

PIONEER OF MODERN BALLISTICS

Mann was called by some the father of modern ballistics, not because he invented the concepts that pertained to that branch of physics— others did that—but because he devoted his mind to answering one looming question: "What are the actual causes of bullet deviation?" Why couldn't you count on each bullet driving through the same hole in the paper created by the preceding bullet, especially if the firearm were machine-rested? Mann knew, as do all shooters, that no matter how well-rested the rifle, bullets deviate from their intended path.

Why do they? Mann asked. He could not accept the answer, "It's just that way because. . . ."

Niedner and Pope were put to work building the rifles and test machinery Mann needed to conduct his experiments. They offered him the best test equipment possible. "Niedner, all I have to do is give you the idea and you can work it out," Mann praised. Often, when Adolph was finished with a test device, Dr. Mann would look it over and ask if any immediate improvements were possible. If Niedner said yes, the doctor would then tell him, "Now go ahead and build me an improved model and keep this one for yourself."

"We made and fired bullets that cost a dollar-and-a-half apiece," said Niedner. "Some we turned out of steel or bronze, making them by hand on the lathe." Mann and Niedner made 25-caliber bullets of steel with a base band one-sixteenth of an inch thick. This band was made of German silver (the same as Nickel silver—a white alloy of copper, nickel and zinc). The bullets were hardened at the shank, but soft-nosed because they were made to test penetration. Hard-nosed bullets, Mann found, would deflect against the target, which was a plate of steel three-fourths of an inch thick.

One of the many interesting phenomena of shooting occurred in these penetration tests. Niedner explained: "We. . . found that if a bullet fails to penetrate it will sometimes follow straight back along the line of flight. We had bullets come back and strike the muzzle of the rifle in the V-rest. After one or two near accidents we always covered the man at the V-rest with a heavy horse blanket for protection in case a bullet came back."

Mann had to make his own test bullets. He had a bullet press constructed for the purpose. It worked well, but Frank wanted more force. He had Niedner build two special bullet presses, one for himself and one for the craftsman. "They were very powerful presses and had a flywheel and lever for applying pressure," Niedner reported.

Work was conducted at an experimental range constructed at the homestead farm where Franklin was raised. Dr. Mann, Mann's brother William, and Niedner built the range with attached shooting house. It was stocked with provisions and a couple of swing-away beds to allow for continuous testing. The experimenters could live at the range while their work progressed. It was a covered range with ventilator and windows. There was also a swinging bulkhead in the middle to stop bullets at the 100-yard mark. A V-rest set in a concrete base comprised the shooting platform. Niedner hand-finished the V-rest. It had to be right. But when it came to laying a base line,

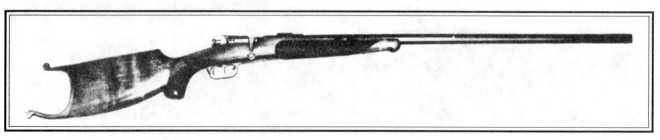

Dr. Mann commissioned men like Niedner and Pope to build many interesting firearms for him. This one is the Mann-Niedner bolt-action rifle.

One of Dr. Mann's machine rests with sheltered conditions for the bullet. Mann attempted to remove as many extraneous variables as possible from his work.

there was trouble. "Dr. Mann had several professors try their hand at laying out a base line for the V-rest, and his brother tried, but all of them failed. They couldn't lay out a base line that would remain constant. Harry Pope and I went down one night and laid out the base line after midnight, and after that we had no trouble with it."

The all-important V-rest was non-adjustable. It was by definition a machine rest. However, it was in reality a solid rest so situated that when a barrel was laid in it, the center of the bore was aimed at the target butt downrange. The test guns were not finished rifles, but rather breeched systems. The ones Niedner made for Mann were fired by turning the bolt slightly with a screwdriver. Much testing ensued. Niedner would arrive by train and walk from the Highland depot to the range. The key was left out for him. Mann allowed others the use of the range when experimentation was not in progress. "I did a lot of unusual work for Dr. Mann," Adolph said, "experimental work in order to find out things about the flight of bul-

lets." Niedner made barrels that were six feet long, and barrels that were so short the bullet protruded from the muzzle before firing. The extra-long barrels were built by screwing two barrels together. The long barrels were used in muzzle blast experiments. However, even barrels of six feet produced muzzle blast with high-intensity big game cartridges.

Some of Mann's findings seem somewhat pedestrian today; however, they had impact at the time and remain ever true and valuable. Mann concluded, for example, that the major cause of a bullet deviating from its intended flight pattern was lack of projectile uniformity. Today's bullets are built with uniformity in mind. In scale-weighing at random 10 bullets from a box of 100, deviation from the average was less than a half-grain—remember that there are 7,000 grains to the pound, so that's a tiny degree of difference. The jacketed projectiles that a friend of mine and I make with a Corbin press are even closer to perfection.

Mann also concluded that uniformity in all loading components—powder, brass and primer as well as bullet—affected accuracy. "Like conditions get like results," said Mann. Niedner made many test units, including one built on the Hamburg action, which had the strength to withstand high-pressure loads. Mann's Hamburg was a screw-bolt design, single-shot, chambered for the 25 Krag. Niedner also stated that he built a bolt-lever rifle for Dr. Mann.

Experimentation was not without its hazards. Mann instructed Niedner to install a new-style firing pin on a single-shot rifle. Niedner warned that this might not be a good idea, but the doctor said go ahead with it. Dr. Mann, Niedner and Harry Pope attended a shoot at Walnut Hill shortly thereafter. Mann used the rifle with the new firing pin design. Suddenly, Niedner was summoned with great urgency. Dr. Mann's rifle had blown up. "I ran over to the shooting house," Niedner reports, "and Frank was leaning against the side of the building with both hands and had his head down. The blood was streaming from his nose. I led him over to the pump, washed the blood off his face, and got his nosebleed stopped. I could see he wasn't hurt bad. I asked him what had happened and he said: 'The gun blew up.'. . . The breechblock had been wrecked but had held and the firing pin hadn't blown out. Putting in that new firing pin had weakened the breechblock, as I had told Dr. Mann it would, and the cocking knob had blown back and struck him on the nose. It made a little round mark right on the end of his nose which he carried to the grave with him."

The Mann story, of course, ties in with the lives of Niedner and Pope. However, the entire "Walnut Hill Gang" pertains, because Mann was one of the fellows who joined in with the bunch on woodchuck hunts as well as target shoots. The farmers around Shushan, New York, looked forward to a thinning of the big rodents that were burrowing in their fields and eating away at the profits. Dr. Mann, Niedner and Pope made this hunt along with Ed Leopold and Dr. Henry Baker, influential shooters of the era. Charles Newton once joined the regulars for a week of chucking. Dr. Mann was not terribly interested in woodchuck hunting, but he was deeply intrigued by the rifles used in the sport, and he did shoot a few rodents himself. Here enters the comical story of Niedner and the Mann rifle that would not sight

in. The rifle shot high in spite of all adjustments. Mann was ready to give up and go home, as Adolph put it. But Niedner said he'd take a look at the errant rifle. That evening he located two birch trees growing together. "I stuck the barrel of Dr. Mann's rifle between the two trees and bent it down a little, just about what I figured was needed to make it shoot lower." The rifle sighted perfectly at 200 yards and Frank was happy. He wanted to know what Niedner had done to correct the problem. Adolph was silent on the matter at first. That winter, however, Mann was in Niedner's shop when the subject of the rifle surfaced again. This time Adolph admitted to the barrel-bending. Dr. Mann jumped to his feet shouting, "You spoiled the barrel!"

"I just laughed and told him, 'Frank, you always claimed that was the best shooting gun you ever had.' "

Mann and his associates were doing some fairly remarkable things, considering the time frame of their experimentation. For example, the 25 Krag cartridge, chambered in the Hamburg rifle, was chronographed at 3,400 feet per second muzzle velocity with a 103-grain bullet—pretty fast for 1912.

Niedner's association with Dr. Mann was curtailed during the last two months of Mann's life because Adolph was on jury duty and unable to get free to work on firearms. Furthermore, the doctor was not well, although he did hunt with Pope in August of 1916. He wrote a letter to Niedner from the old woodchuck hunting area. "This morning I put three shots over your old range and then sat down under the trees. Shot three chucks back of Dempsy's and over on the hillside toward the 200-yard butt to the left. It was lonesome and it made me homesick." The latter part of Dr. Mann's life was spent testing for high velocity. He wanted to break the 8,000 foot-per-second barrier. He had achieved 4,000 feet per second. But Mann was concerned that his methods were not safe; therefore, he would not share his data because someone could be injured trying to duplicate his tests.

Mann tried the loads of other experimenters of the day. None proved worthy of further scrutiny, although a particular rifle and cartridge did quite well in velocity. However its bullets exploded between muzzle and target, not one of them reaching the butts. Duplex loads were tested.

According to Mann, these bullets illustrate "the action of high-pressure, smokeless powder in low-pressure rifles."

Front ignition was also under study; Mann apparently had cartridge cases made with interior tubes extending from the primer pocket forward toward the shoulder of the case. The idea was to direct the flame from the primer toward the upper end of the powder charge, beginning ignition there instead of at the head of the case. Mann had a million and one shooting ideas, all pushing like a solid wall of thought trying to escape his fertile mind. He had a penetrating imagination, the sort of imagination associated with a Jules Verne or Issac Asimov. I have always believed that whatever man could imagine, man could eventually achieve. Mann seemed to apply that fanciful thought as a dictum. He was an empirical scientist, not a paper-and-pencil wizard. Not all of his experiments were trapped between the rigid walls of the scientific method. But that wasn't so bad, because the raw data spoke loudly enough. Had he reached 8,000 feet per second, that achievement would have served well enough for any scientist.

Dr. Mann made numerous tests. Not all of them appeared in his book, *The Bullet's Flight*. There would have been a second edition to this text had the doctor lived, or so we may surmise. We know Mann was collecting data for another work. A full understanding of the doctor and his efforts calls for a reading of his book, though. While original copies are expensive and difficult to find, Wolfe Publishing Company has reprinted it, with marginal notes by Harry Pope and Mann.

Some of Mann's conclusions verified previous information, incidentally. These proved almost as important as his original labors. For example, he tested the theory that in blackpowder firearms, greater accuracy was achieved when the projectile closely matched the bore diameter of the rifle. "Through all the tests and experiments made at the homestead range the bore-diameter bullet as before mentioned has shown its superiority," Mann stated in his book. Franklin's tests of "Unbalanced or Mutilated Bullets" was from the realm of originality. He fired hundreds of bullets that were purposely and precisely altered to see if he could find a predictable response from these unbalanced or mutilated missiles. In his book, Mann revealed six tests associated with the unbalanced or mutilated bullet study.

However, the six tests were only part of the overall investigation. Read from Test 130: "Aug. 11, 1903, 5:30 P.M., dead calm affording perfect weather conditions, with Pope 1902 rifle, 187-grain soft-lead bullets, some with cut points and others with plugged holes, but all swaged bore diameter after plugs were inserted." He even noted how the bullet was loaded into the cartridge case so that he could study the effect of bullet damage in accord with how the damaged section was presented to the rifling. "Bullets heavily mutilated, as shown at lower corner of Plate (21), by cutting their points, and emerging from muzzle with their light side up, printed at 12, 9, and 3a at 10 o'clock instead of 4, where they would have printed if lightened at bases instead of points." Dr. Mann's method of operation was simple, yet effective. He designed a test plan. Then he had the appropriate test equipment made. Finally, he engaged in his empirical review, looking at the results of his examinations until he found a pattern. After a pattern was firmly established, he pronounced a solution to the problem.

Harry Pope, by the way, was not entirely entranced by Mann's book. The Wolfe edition with marginal notes reveals a subtle, and sometimes not so subtle, ire in Harry's written words. However, it seems that the professional disagreement was set aside and that the men remained friends in spite of Pope's remarks. Pope says, for example, "Mr. M seems to have been ignorant of the great difference in accuracy caused solely by changes of primer, nitro priming, grain and make of powder, temper of bullets and grease. The oleo wad is often a decided source of inaccuracy." Mann did not always appreciate Pope's remarks, although at times he did. "I suggested with sawdust to Mr. M in Hfd. O.K. Mann." The initial pencil note was presumably Pope's, stating that he was responsible for the sawdust suggestion. Mann agreed with it by making an O.K. notation next to Pope's remark. I may stand corrected on this matter. Either way, there was not, by any measure, total agreement between Mann and Pope concerning the former's findings.

Purely scientific ballistic minds will not en-

tirely agree with the Mann approach, either, believing that the extraneous variable might crop up, confusing the real cause of the tested condition. However, from a practical point of view, it's difficult to fault Mann's work. Although the word "proof" cannot be attached to every finding, the evidence presented is often overwhelming. In the final analysis, one must ask if Dr. Mann's labor provided a true value for the shooter. It did. Anyone who reads his work carefully will learn from it. If the reader weighs the findings with care and he applies those findings to his own firearms, the result will usually be improved scores at the target—better accuracy, in other words.

Dr. Mann was on a quest for truth. He was devoted to finding out all he could about the bullet's flight, within the framework of his technical capability and his testing apparatus. Nathaniel Emmons Paine, MD, said this of Mann, his words a preface to The Bullet's Flight: "I conclude that when Frank was groping in the dark vaults of the unknown for science's sake, that he truly found his lamp of Aladdin. And the Genie of that discovery had made possible the contribution of the riches of knowledge and achievement which he so generously imparts to others in this volume."

Franklin W. Mann was an interesting figure in the world of shooting, a person who spared no amount of time or funds to satisfy his curiosity. Dr. Mann's daughter, Mrs. Willard Lewis, offered her biographical comments in the beginning of the Wolfe reprint of The Bullet's Flight. They reveal something of the man that all of his notes and studies cannot. "Father did the work of three men," she said. Sometimes he would lose his temper, having no doubt worked very hard toward a futile solution to a problem. "Perhaps we children heard a dish smashing against the wall. 'Hadn't Mother been told to put all cracked and nicked dishes in the trash?' he would complain. 'Surely she realizes that cracks are filled with germs and that nicks can cut the children's fingers. What are a person's nerves made of, anyway?'"

Mann was a lover of animals, especially cats. And he was also a lover of fairy tales, which he read to the children, marking the date neatly. Snow White had six dates by its title. He often skipped coming home at midday. When questioned about it, Frank told his wife that when he came home at lunchtime he would eat, and when

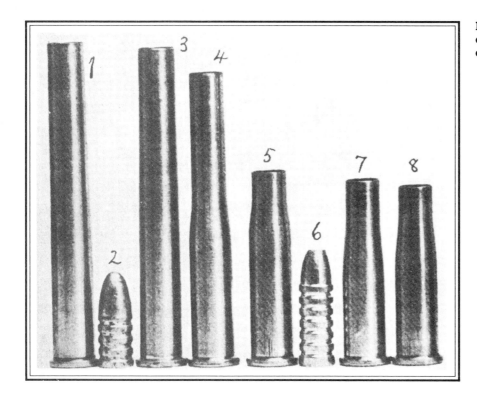

Eight of the many cartridge cases Mann used while he experimented with cast bullets.

he ate he got sleepy, and when he was sleepy he could not work. "Then I waste time." He might add that it was the seventh time he had to start an experiment all over again.

Dr. Franklin Mann died on November 14, 1916, only seven years after the publication of *The Bullet's Flight.* He was 60 years old. His daughter remarked that during the last six months of his life he did not pursue his shooting studies. He spent his time with his wife instead, as they used to in earlier days. He seemed to know, as a physician might, that the grains of sand in his hourglass of life were few. "In spite of his accomplishments, Father died a tired, worried, and disappointed man. After the shock of his death had passed, we realized that all his heartaches and worries were over." The man was gone, but his legacy to the world of shooting—his prescriptions for accuracy, if you will—as related in his book, grow more appreciated with the passing of time.

17

FRANK MAYER:
LAST of the BUFFALO RUNNERS

A serious issue that faced the Congress of 1870 was whether to give up on occupying the American West versus trying to conquer the fierce Plains Indians. Fighting these Indians was tantamount to guerrilla warfare. As soldiers learned then, and certainly since, the entrenched warrior has an advantage over the interloper. The resident fighter knows the ways of his world, its geography and its seasons. The Plains Indians were not inferior in the art of soldiering. Sure, their equipment was less sophisticated than the U.S. Army's, but their tactics were effective. Perhaps, some politicians thought, it's best to leave that rugged, inhospitable, vast and untamed terrain west of the Mississippi River to whomever wants it. Numerous thinkers felt otherwise. A plan was formulated, not a paper plan—more a mutual agreement. Attack on the oblique. Don't try to round up the Plains Indians—the Crows, Blackfeet, Sioux and other tribes of the Far West. Instead, go after their life source: the American bison. Remove the bison—which gave food, shelter, clothing and supplies to these people—and the Indian would follow.

Now add economy to the picture. A living sea of hides was there for the taking, each one worth between two and three dollars, occasionally more. They valued in the millions. Furthermore, a railroad was planned. Railroad tracks and bison don't mix. Buffalo—the common name given the largest quadruped on the North American continent—

bigger than a moose or Kodiak bear—would be entirely in the way of settling the land. You don't build farms in the midst of vast buffalo herds, and you don't raise cattle, either. A barbed-wire fence is but a momentary annoyance to a buffalo. Many problems would be eliminated if the shaggy animals were slaughtered. Therefore, it was not a matter of happy sports hunters riding to the plains for the sake of a good time, although there was some of that—it was good old American enterprise. Army wagons creaked westward carrying ammo. Need some shooting fodder? Let Uncle Sam supply you. It was, as Frank Mayer, the famous rifleman of this chapter called it, a gold rush—except this gold was on the hoof and it wasn't yellow.

A man could get as much as a whole American dollar for a single buffalo tongue, which would be salted and resold. Buffalo also provided meat for the railroad builders. Professional hunters, such as Buffalo Bill Cody and Billy Comstock, took care of that. Although the hides were valuable and most wanted, eventually the bones would be useful as fertilizer. As sad as it was, killing the buffalo proved somewhat necessary to an America that wanted to move west. There were millions of bison. Somebody had to do the job of culling them.

Frank Mayer was one, and he may have stayed at the game longer than any other "buffalo runner" ever. Mayer began hunting bison in Texas. The year was 1872. When he dropped his

Frank Mayer—the last of the great buffalo runners. The rifle meant everything to him, for only certain ones could compete for meat on the plains. Pictured here with his first rifle, Mayer kept the long-barreled muzzleloader until his death.

last shaggy in Wyoming, it was 1881. His nine years as a runner were uncommonly long in the trade. Most men gave up after the first experience. The ones who made it to the second year were few. Fewer still were chasing bison on the plains for more than three years. It was tough work. Mayer was more than a buffalo hunter, though. He was educated, a writer, a reloader, an expert marksman and a fellow with considerable firearms knowledge—of arms history in general and of the Sharps Rifle in particular.

Frank was born in the Lac du Chien region of Louisiana on May 28, 1850. He lived for over 100 years. His longevity gave modern shooters a valid view of the way buffalo were really hunted, and of the marksmanship and firearms required to do the job. Mayer proved to be the best link we have with the buffalo era, as far as shooting interest is concerned.

During the Civil War, his father served as an artillery officer for the Union Army. At 13, Frank lied about his age to gain entrance in the "Cause" and he became a drummer boy for the same side. His early encounter with war may have prompted Frank to drift and seek adventure. But he did attend school before he struck out on his own. After the War, Frank received a degree from the Columbia School of Mines in New York. Evidence indicates that he also attended two German universities; there is no record of sheepskins from these institutions, but his literacy shows clearly in his writing. Frank Mayer was definitely an educated man.

At the age of 20, with adventure in his heart, and "I didn't have anything better to do" in his head, Frank journeyed to Mexico. His education earned him a position as manager of a smelter. The owners of the smelter were interested in only the gold and silver processed at the establishment. Frank could have the lead as "waste." So the young man took the lead and sold it to Mexican insurrectos for 50 pesos a ton. This was the time of political turmoil prior to Porfirio Diaz's control. When the Mexican government got wind of the lead sale, Mayer left town. In fact, he departed the entire country "between sundown and sunup." He didn't even say "adios."

Frank's next job proved even more interesting. He would become a buffalo runner. The glamour and profit called to him. An enterprising man, Mayer started at the top. He did not enter-

tain becoming a skinner first, working his way up to runner. He looked at this new venture as a business, hiring a crew of men with whom he shared his profits. Frank was smart. The men worked harder in the profit-sharing plan than they would have under a low wage system. Frank kept 50 percent of the money, paying the overhead from his part of the income. The other 50 percent he shared with his men.

Mayer learned everything about his new trade from Brazos Bob McRae, the best buffalo slayer of them all, according to Frank. Whether Mayer went on to better the abilities of his teacher is tough to say. But it's certain that the young hunter did hone his skills to become one of the most proficient buff runners on any range. Thirty buffalo per day was the goal. That brought 60 to 90 dollars. Even with over half going to his crew and expenses, it was good money. A carpenter of the 1870s earned about three dollars per diem; that was for 12 hours of labor. Sometimes hides brought as high as $3.50 each. One buffalo could be worth more than a day's effort at a trade. After a good day of shooting, Frank would have 20 dollars profit in 19th-century silver certificates and no income tax to pay.

Frank was first rate at what he did. One day he dropped 59 bison with 62 shots. On the plains, they worked according to the axiom: "One cartridge equals one hide." Of course, that was a goal, not a fact. The bison was no pushover. A mature bull weighed 1,500 pounds. A 2,000-pound male was common. And some were bigger, too. Recently, a rancher near Savageton Route, Wyoming, harvested a herd sire that weighed over 2,500 pounds. A powerful blow had to be delivered to a vulnerable spot. As Mayer put it in a 1934 *American Rifleman* article, "Of course, to live this axiom we had to have rifles that would kill at one shot, not occasionally, but invariably, and also the skill it took to make one-shot kills—not occasionally, but invariably." Good shooting meant profit. Mayer once peddled 500 salted buffalo tongues to an English club for the sum of $250.00. "Those of us who stayed developed a deadly technique. We had to. In the beginning, any amateur could kill buff. But as the beasts became scarcer and more shot at, they became warier, harder to find, harder to kill, so that only the competent, with the best of equipment, could make the game pay. Since this was a rifle proposition almost en-

"... In the beginning, any amateur could kill buff. But as the beasts became scarcer and more shot at, they became. . . harder to find, harder to kill, so that only the competent, with the best of equipment, could make the game pay." Mayer stayed with buffalo running nine years—longer than most, and he made it pay.

tirely, the deadly technique I just mentioned consisted of getting the right rifle and learning how to use it."

Mayer was astute. He knew that politics played a role in the buffalo slaughter. He also knew that the bison was doomed. A few citizens voiced alarm over the numbers of animals slain. The terrible waste of meat concerned conservative thinkers. The Territory of Wyoming was almost closed to buffalo hunting to stave the waste, but General Sheridan made a powerful speech relating the fact that more had been done to displace and damage the Plains Indian through bison hunting than through the Army fighting these

warriors for years. The hunt went on. The Army continued to give away free ammunition as incentive to the less professional bison slayers. But it was the professionals whose methods brought the results sought after. Mayer said, "In the first years all kinds of rifles were used. If one were to attempt to list all of the smokesticks used against the poor brutes, the result would practically be an enumeration of every kind of rifle, and smoothbore as well, used in the United States up to that time." Kentucky Rifles. Fine Billinghursts. Golchers. Hawkens. Henrys (the muzzleloaders, not the later lever-action Henry rifle). And of course the Civil War breechloaders. All were used against the shaggy. However, these were not chosen by the professional runner.

GOOD GEAR GETS THE BUFF

Unlike Teddy Roosevelt's hunting companion, who was killed by a bison when the bull impaled the man in a close-up encounter of the horse-and-rider kind, the true runner did his work from a distance. Few buffalo hunters were trampled by bison, which gave many men an absolutely false impression of the beast. After all, nothing, not even the fierce Cape buffalo of Africa, is dangerous to man from a distance of 300 yards. And 300 yards was no trick shot for the practiced buffalo hunter. A piece of long-range shooting history was born on the buffalo plains. In Mayer's book, *The Buffalo Harvest,* he says, "Most of our shots were from 300 yards and beyond." The idea was born that the American bison was big, but rather harmless to man. Not so. While the professional runners did not always respect their quarry, they did learn to respect their rifles. They should have. They were using the deadliest long-range shoulder artillery yet developed.

Mayer invented his own bipod for long-range shooting. The common rest was the crossed sticks device, two dowels held loosely together so that a man could sit or kneel, resting the rifle's forearm at their intersection. The crotch provided by the sticks allowed a fairly solid shooting platform. But Mayer commissioned a Houston, Texas, gunsmith to build a bipod that attached to the barrel of his rifle. The legs collapsed along the length of the barrel for carrying, then snapped into position for shooting. Today's excellent Harris bipod is remindful of Mayer's invention. Distant shooting was the byword. More buffs could be taken before the herd bolted if the animals were fired on from a distance. It took a few moments for the shaggies to locate the source of trouble.

Far shooting was accomplished on other forms of life as well. In his book Mayer notes, "Again, on the Staked Plains (Llano Estacado) in Texas, I stood off a band of young Comanche bucks. I opened fire at long range with my .40-90 to discourage their coming too close. In three shots at a distance afterward paced by my skinners at 759 yards, I got one buck and two horses." Presumably, Mayer accomplished this shooting with the rifle he purchased from Colonel Richard I. Dodge. In the 1934 *American Rifleman* article, which saw print when Mayer was 84 years old, the hunter said, "My first Sharps, in fact, was a .40-90 which I bought from Colonel Dodge. I paid him $125 for it. It had a 32-inch barrel, weighed 11 pounds. On it I mounted a full-length one-inch tube telescope, made by A. Vollmer of Jena, Germany. This scope, a 20 power, came originally with plain cross-hairs. To these I added stadia hairs, set to cut a height of 30 inches at 300 yards." Obviously, Frank knew what he was doing in the long-range shooting department.

The stadia wires, or stadia hairs as Mayer referred to them, are multiple horizontal wires that subtend an optical number of inches at a given distance. They are used for judging range. The two wires are compared with the target. By knowing the approximate size of the target, the

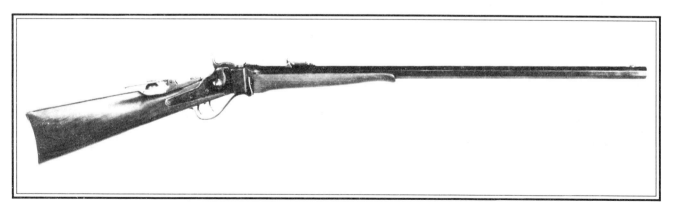

Mayer's favorite rifle for taking buffs was the Sharps "Special Old Reliable," the famous 45-120. To ensure a hit at long distances, he devised his own bipod as well as a clever way to use stadia hairs on the scope he mounted on his Sharps. This Shiloh replica of the Sharps 1874 No. 3 Sporting Rifle, similar to what Frank used, has optional tang sight.

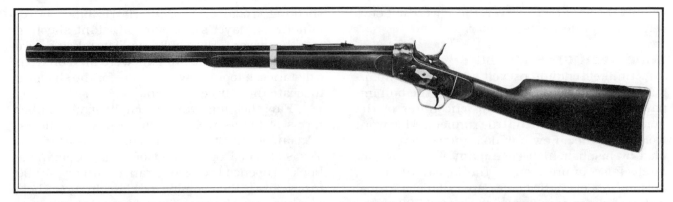

The Remington Rolling Block was another famous buffalo rifle, although not as well-liked by Mayer as his Sharps. This Remington replica from Navy Arms Company has original-style octagonal barrel.

shooter also knows the approximate distance. Using stadia wires, Mayer's range guesstimation no doubt became more science than art. He could determine the distance of a bison with considerable accuracy. While buffalo rifles were not flat-shooting by today's standards, their big bullets "carried up" well. That is, they retained good velocity and power. Their accuracy did the rest.

"With this old .40-90 of mine I could kill any buffalo that walked, up to 400, 500, or 600 yards; kill it with one clean shot, provided I hit in neck or heart." The 40-90-370, as it was known, was so called because it was a 40-caliber cartridge that usually held about 90 grains of black powder, firing a bullet of 370 grains weight. Mayer went to a heavier bullet in his 40-90, a 420-grain projectile which, at long range, brought more satisfying results. At the time, English black powder was, according to Frank, of higher grade than the American propellant he could obtain. An English sportsman gave Mayer two kinds of British powder, Curtis & Harvey and Pigou, Laurence & Wilkes brands. Mayer found that the residue left by these powders was easier to remove than the fouling of American black powder. He continued to buy English powder from the Tryon Company of Philadelphia, in spite of its price—50 percent more than American. Frank later discovered American Dead Shot black powder, which he found as good as English propellants.

In those days, Remington made worthwhile buffalo rifles, but Mayer was a Sharps man. In addition to his 40-90-370, he bought at least three more Sharps single-shot cartridge rifles. One was a 40-70-330, another a 40-90-420. These two

were good rifles and cartridges, but with repeated fire, the reloaded blackpowder cases of bottleneck design tended to stick in the chamber. Frank left these rifles for what he felt was the finest "buffalo gun" of them all: the Sharps "Special Old Reliable," the famous 45-120-550. The professional bison slayers called it the "Sharps Buffalo" or "Buffalo Sharps" model. It fired a 45-caliber cartridge with a capacity of about 120 grains of black powder behind a bullet of 550 grains weight. My own testing revealed a chronographed muzzle velocity of 1500 feet per second with 120 grains of GOEX black powder. Pigou, Laurence & Wilkes guaranteed Frank a muzzle velocity of 1400 fps, using 120 grains of their powder in a 45-120-500 Sharps round. In 1875, Mayer paid $237.60 for his special order 16-pound Sharps 45-120 rifle

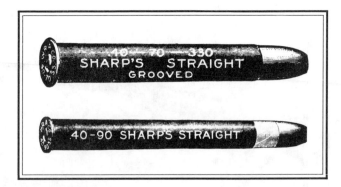

The 40-70-330 Sharps and the 40-90-370 Sharps were two favorite Mayer cartridges for getting buffs. Mayer handloaded his own ammo and preferred English black powder because of its low fouling properties.

with 32-inch barrel, 1:16 rate of twist. He said it was worth every penny. After a 10-power German scope was mounted, again with stadia wires, Frank owned "The deadliest rifle ever made in America—including rifles made up to 1934."

Mayer was a handloader, who developed his own methods of reloading ammunition. The new Sharps rifle came with bullet mould, decapping/recapping tool, cartridge case resizer die and bullet seater. Frank reloaded his 45-120 by decapping and repriming in the normal fashion. But instead of the regular powder charge, he first installed five grains of finely granulated black powder (probably FFFFg) to help consume the total powder charge. He then placed a full 120 grains of Fg black powder on top of the fine-grain fuel, giving a powder charge of 125 grains, which the case readily digested. On top of the powder charge, Frank inserted a thin grease-proof wad followed

by a disc of lubricant 3/32nds of an inch thick made from alum-hardened antelope tallow. He seated a paper-patched bullet, but not before he anointed the front of the patch with a trace of graphite distributed with a piece of impregnated buckskin. The graphite, Mayer believed, aided the bullet's passage through the bore. Frank did not cast his own projectiles. He bought them ready-made (1:16 alloy, tin/lead) from a caster in St. Joseph, Missouri.

Patching, however, was not trusted to a commercial house. Mayer used thin patches in winter, increasing patch thickness with higher ambient temperature. Proper patching paper was used. When Frank ran out of commercial patching material, he turned to specially treated antelope fawn skin or cleaned and sun-dried pieces of antelope intestine. When using these homespun bullet patches, Mayer applied extra graphite.

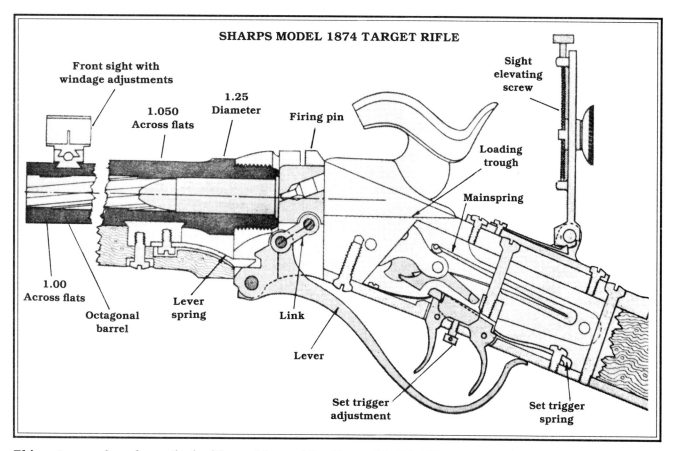

SHARPS MODEL 1874 TARGET RIFLE

This cutaway view shows the inside workings of the Sharps Model 1874 Target Rifle. Essentially the same as Mayer's Sharps "Old Reliable," it was the preferred weapon to use against buffalo because it delivered the power and accuracy needed at long distances.

Paying strict attention to each detail provided the buffalo runner with the finest in contemporary accuracy.

Accuracy and power were essential to success. One was worthless without the other. The enterprise depended upon keen rifle knowledge and marksmanship. A tale of the plains says that during the time of buffalo hunting an Indian medicine man was operating his own flimflam. The medicine man had a neat trick he used to convince his fellow warriors of his great and extraordinary powers. He would leap from his horse and prance around in mockery of white soldiers in the distance, too far for a telling shot. A soldier would try his luck, firing a bullet in the direction of the medicine man, who would then jump into the air, coming down with a pre-placed lead projectile in his mouth, supposedly caught with his teeth. This awed the braves, who thought their medicine man a mighty fellow to catch bullets from the rifles of the White Eyes.

One day the medicine man pulled his trick on a buffalo hunter. He was up against a precision marksman armed with a Remington or Sharps rifle, probably fitted with a telescopic rifle sight—carefully sighted in. The buff runner knew his firearm and how to employ it. The medicine man slipped the bullet into his mouth, ready to dance into the air to show what an amazing creature he was. Only he didn't have a chance to spit the bullet out into his hand. Instead, he caught a lead projectile from a buffalo rifle. So the story goes. The tale may be fiction, but it is accurate in substance—the buffalo hunter could shoot.

And his rifle matched his marksmanship. "I have seen one full magazine (16 shots) expended on the final bagging of only five buffalo," said Mayer of the 56 Spencer rifle. He had no faith in such arms. He also had little faith in the modern rifle as compared with the older Sharps. Mayer liked to tell a story that originated in the Rocky Mountain News of December 20, 1932. Eight renegade buffalo had to be destroyed by officials. The men fired 15 shots to kill one animal. Another required two hits. Another five. Ten shots were necessary to drop another. The rifles used were noted as a 35 automatic, 30-30 and 30-06. The disgusted Mayor of Denver, who witnessed the shooting, said at one point, "Get an Indian." Mayer agreed, saying, "Get an Indian is right. An Indian or an old plains buffalo runner!" More than 50 cartridges were fired to dispatch the eight bison. No self-respecting buffalo hunter could have made a living that way. In the *American Rifleman* magazine, April 1936, Mayer commented:

I suppose that these modern conditions are really indicative of progress, in a theoretical sense, and that I am only a pre-Victorian fogy whose old-fashioned ideas have been long outdated. However, I am stubborn enough to insist that I liked much better those obsolete old slow-pokes who not only knew how to shoot their rifles with consummate skill, but knew how to make them as well. In those days [early America], the rifle was a tool used in the making of a nation; today it is a toy which changes with every freakish fad.

Frank Mayer was an accurate reporter and a good writer. When his buffalo running days ended, he wrote of buffalo hunting, of rifle history, of cartridges, muzzleloading, reloading, marksmanship and other topics pertinent to shooting. He cherished fine firearms, including his first long arm, a percussion rifle that remained in his possession until his death in the 1960s. He also loved to hunt. Frank was 101 years old when he dropped a Colorado mule deer buck. He was a great marksman, a knowledgeable shooter, and he lived by the courage of his convictions.

18

CHARLES NEWTON: FATHER of HIGH VELOCITY

Charles Newton's story is more technology than biography. He is the undisputed father of high velocity—he looked to super speeds and flat trajectories years before anyone else—at least anyone whose work became public. Unlike Annie Oakley, Buffalo Bill, even Jack O'Connor or Elmer Keith, Charles Newton's personal life did not attract many biographers. We gather from his own writing that Newton was colorful, caustic and abrupt. He suffered the same problems of maturity and adjustment that all of our great shooters experienced, but perhaps, unfairly, he did not achieve the fame that the others enjoyed. Today's shooters know O'Connor, Keith, even Selous and Bell better than they know Charles Newton. The modern rifleman wouldn't recognize Newton from Methuselah. Yet, every shooter who fires a bolt-action sporting rifle with high-velocity cartridges has felt the impact of this great inventor.

Charles Newton was a Jules Verne in his thinking, with an important difference. Verne's imaginative submarine was built out of words, only a paper forerunner of the modern atomic vessel. Several of Newton's drawing board cartridges and rifles arose from the page to become reality in the man's own time. The futuristic accomplishments of Mr. Newton took place in the broad daylight of invention. His claim to the "Father of High Velocity" is backed by the hardware that the man created.

Before there was a Cutts Compensator, New-ton was experimenting with the effect of putting holes in the muzzles of longarms. He had a three-position wing-type safety before it was seen on a factory rifle. It was Newton's floorplate design that was installed on the famous Model 70 Winchester rifle. Newton had a plunger-type ejector light years before they were used on commercial rifles such as the Model 700 Remington, and his ejector was more elaborate in that it protruded beyond the face of the bolt *only* when the bolt was drawn back to its full rearward position. Remember that all of these inventions and many more arose in the dawn of this century, and not from a gun designer, but from a lawyer.

Newton was born in the small town of Delevan in western New York state, January 8, 1870. His father, Henry, was a farmer who lived an apparently uneventful life, married to Charles's mother Esther Fuller Newton. It is said that Chas. Newton taught school during his 16th and 17th years. He was married in 1894, and at age 25 went to law school. He was admitted to the bar in 1896. Law school in one year? But the dates are not germane to our interests. That Newton was an arms manufacturer by 1915 is.

Newton's early involvement with firearms is not clear. But six years in the New York National Guard, where Newton attained the rank of sergeant, may have precipitated his desire to build firearms. Chas. Newton (he preferred Chas. to Charles and never signed the latter) originally fa-

Charles Newton, proponent of high-velocity cartridges and inventor of many high-power rounds, such as the ''Imp'' and the 250-3000 Savage. (Original line drawing by Jackie Wagner from *Charles Newton, Father of High Velocity*).

vored the lever-action rifle style. In the early 1900s, a bolt-action versus lever-action controversy raged. Newton considered the bolt-action rifle OK for the army, but certainly not appropriate for sporting use.

The genius was there. People have all kinds of "handles" attached to them—sometimes deserved, sometimes not. Newton's "father of high velocity" title is more than deserved. That he was a firearms genius and one of the most innovative, ahead-of-his-time shooter of this or any other century is without question. When simultaneous inventions occur, it is often difficult to assign proper credit to the inventor. Occasionally, a later party who may have perfected, or made more practical, an original idea, receives the major credit. Not so Newton. His cartridges, arms designs and bullets were well ahead of their time and were not imitations. This is not to say that others were not tuned in to high velocity. The existence of the 280 Ross cartridge proves that high velocity was no stranger to contemporary thought.

NEWTON'S CARTRIDGES: REAL HUMDINGERS

Newton's cartridges were, to say it straight, real humdingers. They were of such far-reaching design that all of them have either surfaced today as factory cartridges in altered form, or they have been ballistically duplicated by a loading company. We know of 10 Newton rounds. One was called "The Imp" by Savage. Charles Newton's desire for high velocity gave rise to this "necked-down" cartridge known by today's shooters as the 22 Savage Hi-Power (the 5.6X52R in Europe). The Imp was the 25-35 Winchester squeezed to 22 caliber. It appeared in a 1911–12 version of the Model 99 Featherweight. Newton designed the round as a woodchucker. Of course, shooters just had to try the little 22 centerfire with its 70-grain bullet on larger beasties.

Newton also necked the 6mm Lee Navy cartridge down to 22 caliber—if that's not the 220 Swift, then what is it? Furthermore, he necked the 7X57mm Mauser to 22 caliber to fire bullets of .228-inch diameter. Today we have the similar 5.6X57mm RWS, a cartridge produced by the famous West German RWS company. With current powders, the 5.6X57mm is capable of achieving 3800 feet per second (fps) muzzle velocity (mv) with a 60-grain 22-caliber (.224-inch) bullet.

"Doubtless the .22 high power has by this time," said Newton in a June 1913 *Outdoor Life* article, "demonstrated its inability to invariably and promptly kill not only moose but walrus and polar bears as well, while another season will witness like disappointment in the line of rhinoceros and Cape Buffalo. It is neither poisonous or super-natural, nor is it a Martian ray [gun]."

Because Newton knew that people would continue firing his 22-centerfire creation at everything from sod poodles to the abominable snowman, the inventor went back to the drawing board. When he was finished, a new round was born: to be called the 250-3000 Savage. If the average shooter knows anything about Newton, he knows of him through this round because cartridge data will often tell the story of Newton conceiving a 25-caliber number capable of firing a 100-grain bullet at 2800 fps mv, while the Savage minds applied a good dose of Madison Avenue to the creation, dropping bullet weight to 87 grains in order to achieve 3000 fps. It was an excellent advertising maneuver. Savage even added the 3000 to the cartridge title. Furthermore, it is believed that Newton's original idea centered around a 117-grain bullet at 3015 fps mv from a longer cartridge case. However, the 250 Savage was chambered in the Model 99 lever-action rifle in 1912.

Incidentally, Harvey Donaldson (see separate chapter) wrote that Newton did not invent the 250 Savage cartridge, claiming that Newton's 25 was based on the Krag case cut to 30-30 length and necked to 25 caliber. The Savage people may have gotten the idea for a short 25-caliber round from Newton, says Donaldson, but Savage did not use Newton's original concept for the round.

Donaldson believed that Newton was the first to experiment with the varmint cartridge as we know it today, working with Mann and Niedner in the winters of 1905 and 1906 on a 25-25 Stevens straight case tapered to 22 caliber and firing jacketed bullets of 50, 66 and 87 grains weight. Niedner made the bullet dies. Newton developed several new cartridge designs from 1909 through 1912. Two of the better ones left the drawing board as the 25 Newton Special and the 7mm Special or 280 Newton. Today, we'd call these cartridges the 25-06 Remington and the 280 Remington, according to Bruce Jennings Jr.

Jennings wrote the biography, *Charles*

Newton, Father of High Velocity (available through Bruce M. Jennings Jr., 70 Metz Road, Sheridan, WY 82801). "The object of compiling this book," said Jennings, "is to bring out of the cobwebs of the libraries, collectors' files, etc., the great ballistic, experimental and design accomplishments of Charles Newton." Indeed, it is a well-written, highly recommended story about Newton and his genius. Ballistically speaking, Jennings is correct, of course. The Newton 25 Special is the 25-06. The 7mm Special is ballistically a 280 Remington, but the latter's case is longer than the 30-06 case. Great confusion exists concerning the actual development of the 25-06. When I prepared an article entitled "A Short History of the Hot 25s," I could not truly sort the wheat from the chaff. The 25-06 was known as the 25 Niedner for decades, and it probably appeared first in a Niedner-made rifle circa 1920.

Feel free to select your own 25-06 inventor. Gun history is viewed through the veil of time and interpretation. *Speer's Tenth* says: "Available information indicates that the 25-'06 was first offered by the A.O. Niedner custom gunmaking firm about 1920, and over the years the cartridge has often been listed as the 25 Niedner." *Hornady's Third* says: "In 1969, forty-nine years after A.O. Niedner introduced this wildcat, Remington adopted the round. . . ." Jennings says Niedner did offer the 25-06 first, but Newton invented it. M.D. Waite, technical editor of *American Rifleman* magazine in the 1970s, concurs. In an article entitled "Charles Newton, Father of the .25-06," Waite said, "In 1912, Newton designed a new cal.

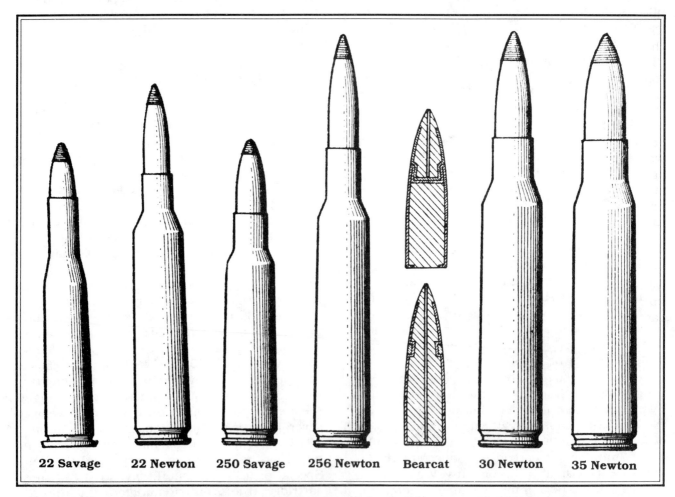

22 Savage   22 Newton   250 Savage   256 Newton   Bearcat   30 Newton   35 Newton

A lineup of the amazing Newton cartridges/bullet: (from left) the 22 Savage, 22 Newton, 250 Savage, 256 Newton, the Bearcat bullet (which stayed at the blueprint stage), 30 Newton and 35 Newton. There was even a 400 Newton, a necked-up 35.

.25 high-velocity cartridge, the .25 Newton Special, known today as the .25-06. The case for this cartridge was modified from .30-'06 brass by necking it down for a cal. .25 (.257″) bullet.''

If you wish to give Newton credit for the 25-06 Remington and 280 Remington cartridges, good. If you wish to give Newton credit for neither round, that's all right, too. The 25 Special was, in principle if not every aspect of case dimension, a 25-06. But the 280 Newton was, according to Phil Sharpe who wrote *The Rifle In America*, built on a case larger in diameter than the 30-06. The literature states that Western Cartridge Company factory-loaded the 280 Newton. The cartridge was supposed to have fired a 145-grain bullet at 3050 fps mv. However, a November 1939 letter from Western Cartridge says nothing of the 280 Newton round. "In the past we have loaded three calibers of the cartridges designed by Mr. Newton. These are the .256, the .30 and .35 calibers. At the moment, we include only the .256 Newton and .30 Newton in our line of cartridges, the .35 Newton having been obsoleted. We have never loaded the .33 or .250 calibers." Or the 280.

Newton lays claim to other cartridges that are more exciting and without question his inventions. One is the 22 Newton. This cartridge was of much larger dimension than the 22 Savage, built on a 7×57 case. However, unlike the current 5.6×57mm RWS that fires 22-caliber projectiles, the 22 Newton launched bullets of .228-inch diameter, not .224-inch. The 90-grain 22 bullet was Newton's way of increasing ballistic coefficient, as well as giving his hot 22 sufficient bullet weight for larger-than-varmint-sized game. Newton claimed 3100 fps mv for the 90-grain bullet. In his study of the cartridge, P.O. Ackley casts no doubt on Newton's ballistic figures. Newton thought his 22 cartridge fine for deer and "ample" for larger game. But the 22 Newton made no headway, although it was apparently factory-loaded by the Newton plant for a while.

While the cartridge did not succeed, it must have furthered interest in similar rounds, such as the excellent 226 Barnes, a wildcat firing a long .226-inch bullet of 125 grains weight—the 226 Barnes compiled a fine record on big game. While the 22 Newton found no great sympathy among shooters of the day, the factory-loaded 256 Newton did make headway. The cartridge launched a 123-grain bullet at 3100 fps mv. It was built from shortened 30-06 brass and along with the lighter bullet, the 256 was supposed to have propelled a 6.5mm 140-grain missile at 2900 fps mv. Ackley's *Handbook* shows a 160-grain bullet at 2550 fps mv. The 256 was powerful, but light-recoiling, a good cartridge for most American big game. But it perished all the same. American shooters have never been mesmerized by 26-caliber rounds. This has been proved by the ho-hum sales of the 264 Winchester Magnum and the never-made-it-big stature of the fine 6.5mm Remington Magnum round. Regardless, the 256 Newton was a good cartridge.

The 30 Newton didn't last long, either. This is not the 30 Newton Express, by the way, which was built on necked-down 40-90 brass. Newton was a single-shot fan, and his 30-40-90 was an attempt to put high velocity into a single-shot rifle. The 30 Newton was a "beltless magnum," longer than the 30-06 with a "fat" rimless case. It held more powder than the 30-06 case by a good measure. Furthermore, the 30 Newton's case design corresponded with the style modern benchrest shooters believe most conducive to accuracy—straight walls, short for its caliber, with sharp, but not overly sharp, shoulder.

The round was supposed to have been designed at the request of Fred Adolph. First chambered in the Adolph custom rifle as the 30 Adolph Express, by 1915 it was named the 30 Newton. It was loaded by the Western Cartridge Company until about 1938, with ammo remaining for sale well after that date. The non-belted case made sense. A belt on the slope-shouldered 300 H&H Magnum offered a good headspacing device; the same can be said for the 375 H&H, but a belt on cartridges such as the 7mm Remington Magnum, 300 Winchester Magnum, 338 Winchester and a whole corral full of similar rounds continued only because these numbers were originally created from redesigned 300 H&H brass. The belt is not necessary on these modern rounds. The 30 Newton did not suffer in the least for lack of a belt.

Adolph supposedly requested a big 30-caliber cartridge capable of high velocity and energy, with flat trajectory. Newton gave it to him. Original loads included, according to Sharpe, a 170-grain spitzer bullet at about 3000 fps mv. Newton claimed a mv of 2600 fps with a 225-grain bullet. About the recoil of the 30 Newton there is disagreement. Newton stated that felt recoil was no

Charles Newton's first rifle, chambered for the 22 Krag. Newton—the gun genius—tried numerous wildcats in his quest for the most accurate, flat-shooting, powerful cartridges.

worse than the 30-06, and Colonel Whelen backed this up. Sharpe summed up the recoil as "... unpleasant." So much energy in so light a rifle would no doubt have kicked like a rodeo bucking bronco.

A 33 Newton followed, but only on paper. This round was to develop 3000 fps mv with a 200-grain bullet, but the idea of a big 33 was soon abandoned. It found no market. Consider, however, that the very popular 338 Winchester Magnum is ballistically a 33 Newton and that the failure of the round was probably due to timing. In the days of Newton's cartridges, true high velocity was not yet the watchword. Remember that the first loads for the famous 30-06 Springfield were nothing like today's. A 220-grain bullet at around 2200 fps mv was the rule. A 150-grain bullet at 2700 fps mv was a common 30-06 load early on. Newton's ammo was well ahead of these figures.

When Newton opened the 30 case, the 35 Newton was born. Original claims gave a 250-grain bullet a mv of 3000 fps, which would earn a muzzle energy of almost 5,000 foot-pounds, on a par energy-wise with the modern 458 Winchester. One load I found used 81.0 grains of IMR-4350 powder for a mv of 2800 fps, not 5,000 foot-pounds, but sufficient force to drop all fauna on this continent. The necked-up 30 Newton did not charm the shooting world, either, although the famous professional hunter, Charles Cottar, used it in Africa on rhino. He mentioned that the rifle was defective, recoil having split the stock so that upon firing, the cargo of cartridges dropped out on the ground. Cottar was killed later by a rhino. My source did not make note of the rifle he was carrying at the time.

Other Newton rounds failed, such as the 276 Newton, a modification of the 276 British. In *Stoeger's Catalog and Handbook* for 1939, the 256 Newton was listed with a 129-grain OPE (Open Point Expanding) bullet of 129 grains weight. The 30 Newton was in the same catalog, showing a bullet weight of 180 grains, again OPE style. The 35 Newton was also represented, with a 250-grain OPE bullet, all three rounds carrying the Western brand name, and all listed as waning in popularity. A 400 Newton was also created by necking up the 35. Only four rifles were ever chambered for this cartridge. The 400 Newton was loaded with the 405 Winchester 300-grain bullet. Velocity from a 24-inch barrel was noted as 3042 fps for a muzzle energy of 6166 foot-pounds.

NEWTON'S CONTROVERSIAL RIFLES

Newton's factory rifles had clean classic lines. They were a lot easier to caress than many of the bulky factory stocks we have today that carry excess wood (or fiberglass). Barrels were generally 24 inches long, although a 26-inch version could be ordered. The rifles weighed over seven pounds and under eight—quite light for a 30 or 35 Newton cartridge. Trigger: double set. Price: 50 dollars each.

Newton's genius readily shows in many of the features. The rifling system was innovative, although no doubt based on earlier English concepts. Newton's "oval rifling" pattern did not engrave the bullet in the same manner as regular lands and grooves. Advantages were said to be somewhat higher mv and slightly improved accuracy. Harry Pope, who was hired as barrel production supervisor for the Newton plant, designed the rifling machinery (barrel-making equipment) for Newton's rifle.

The short-lived Newton factory rifle was of the one-piece turnbolt design with a blade ejector, spring-activated (common nowadays). The bolt had interrupted multiple locking lugs—front-locking. Box magazine, with rounds staggered. The one-piece forged receiver was quite like a Model 98 Mauser in design with Mauser extractor. Recessed bolt face for cartridge head containment. And numerous other features of interest to gunsmiths and firearms engineers.

While P.O. Ackley called Newton's rifles "very fine," Sharpe found them unreliable. He put it this way: "One of our most brilliant and advanced firearms engineers of the twentieth century was the late Charles Newton." But Newton's rifles, Sharpe said, were untrustworthy and "On paper his guns were excellent. Properly built, they lived up to the original calculations." However, "Some of the poorest rifles this author has ever examined . . . were Newton rifles." Complaints came in about delivery. E.C. Crossman, a Newton opponent when Chas. was defending the lever-action rifle against the bolt-action rifle, called Newton's catalogue "The Pipe Dream Gazette" in the February 1, 1917 issue of *Arms and the Man*.

Newton had to abandon his early admiration for the lever-action. His cartridges were designed for high velocity and that meant comparatively high pressures as well. The lever-action rifle of the day would not contain them. Earlier, Newton had fought for the lever-action system. In one of his rebukes, Chas. had put a verbal noose around then Lt. Whelen's neck when the latter listed the many advantages of the bolt-action rifle versus the lever-action. Newton throttled each claim in his acerbic style, stating that levers were strong enough for any reasonable cartridge, and quite capable of clean feeding and reliable extraction. In concluding his rain of barbed word-darts at Whelen, Newton proclaimed, "The lieutenant's experience has indeed grown, but it has grown solely along the lines of using a military rifle and not one sportsman in one hundred thousand has his experience grow so thoroughly along that line."

Newton said the bolt action was "awkward." Pressures in the 40,000 pound per square inch (psi) range were generated by the 30-30 and similar cartridges of late 19th-century/early 20th-century fame. Newton's cartridges had to develop *over* 50,000 psi in order to generate their ballistic claims. The bolt-action rifle would have to be chosen for Newton's rifle, and it was. Chas. never built a lever-action rifle in his plant.

Newton did, however, try to upgrade the strength of the lever-action design with his LeverBolt rifle. The particulars are somewhat unwieldy and ill-suited to our purposes, but the rifle was to incorporate the speed of the lever action with the camming power of the bolt action. It was never produced, although Marlin seems to have been drawn for a while to a 50/50 split of profits

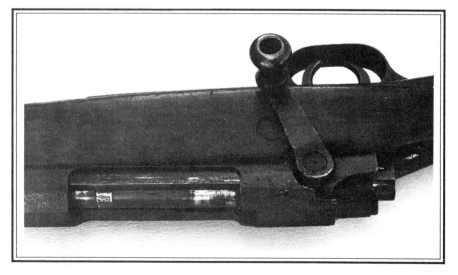

Newton's rifle of choice was initially the lever-action, but he realized that only the bolt-action would accommodate his high-velocity rounds. In an effort to compromise, he tried to upgrade the strength of the lever-action design with his LeverBolt rifle (left). This design lends itself to an alteration of any Mauser-type bolt-action rifle.

on a LeverBolt rifle.

Newton's bolt-action rifles incorporated many interesting features, however. His bolt design was unique, with an interrupted screw-type locking lug system. Newton experimented with a vented muzzle. The Charles Newton take-down feature claimed total rigidness of design in that the rifle remained sighted in no matter the number of times disassembled and reassembled. Furthermore, the take-down rifle incorporated an exceptional take-up adjustment so that the rifle never "shot loose," as the earlier Winchester take-down models had. Many sportsmen who owned them gave considerable positive testimony to Newton's rifles.

OF BULLETS AND BARBS

Chas. Newton also studied bullets, and in 1914 a patent was granted for a bullet with a copper wire embedded in the center of its point. The tip of wire helped to maintain the form of the nose by stiffening that part of the projectile. It was Whelen who said many good things about Newton's bullets. Of one of Newton's 30-caliber offerings Whelen remarked in a letter, "Those 170-grain protected-point copper-jacketed spitzer .30 caliber bullets are so good that I cannot do without them. They have become the standard .30 caliber hunting bullets with me now. I must have 500 of them right away. . . ."

Newton also received a patent for a "compartmentalized" bullet. That it was unique unto itself is probably taking things too far. The H-Mantle bullet of Germany is also very old, but the fact remains that Newton did have a partition-type bullet in 1915. A patent was granted to Newton for a protected spitzer bullet design on May 12, 1914.

Newton knew that his cartridges could never get by with the earlier smokeless powders offered around 1900. In 1913 he received a patent for progressive burning smokeless rifle powder. Fortunately, many worthwhile powders soon prevailed. These, such as IMR-4350, were suited to Newton cartridges.

Although Newton was a writer, he did not pen nearly as many articles as others. He did, however, write on numerous topics, such as the Kentucky Rifle, long-range rifles, boattail bullets, armor-piercing ammo, the Ross bolt-action and how to avoid wearing one as a decoration in your cheekbone, the limitations of the 22 Hi-Power, bullet/bore fit, scope mounts, trajectory versus bullet drop, and many other subjects of concern to shooters. He strongly promoted handloading, not only for economy and improved performance, but also for pure enjoyment. Of course he developed his own special handloading tool.

He used the printed media as a platform for feuding. He took Whelen on several times, but seemed to be more inclined to barb E.C. Crossman whenever possible, even though he, Newton, had actually answered Crossman's request for a "perfect hunting cartridge for America" by inventing the precise round, ballistically, that Crossman called for—the 256 Newton.

Shooters are often forced to relinquish their original ideas and opinions in favor of new proofs gained from further experience. Newton was no exception. He certainly ended up a bolt-action fan, for only in the bolt-action rifle were his cartridge designs and ballistics realized. He attempted, in fact, to create a better bolt-action design.

Sharpe doubted, however, that over 7,000 Newton rifles were ever built. Charles Newton died of a heart attack at his home on Howe Street in New Haven, Connecticut, on March 9, 1932. Sharpe felt that Newton had "died discouraged," and made little, if any, major profit from his designs or manufactured products. His Newton Arms Company of August 4, 1914 had a short life. His catalogs were filled with praiseworthy items that did not sell well. The rifle plant was closed by August 1, 1918, while the Newton cartridge plant went defunct the following January. The firm known as the Chas. Newton Rifle Corp., opened in April of 1919, didn't make it, either. His rifles have not continued. Gone, too, are the Newton reloading tool and the bullet designs.

Did Newton fail?

In his manufacturing ventures, perhaps. But in terms of future endowments to the world of shooting, his genius lives on. His ideas for high velocity, high-impact energy and flat trajectory have been incorporated into the arms and ammo modern shooters enjoy. He was a true pioneer in the realm of riflemaking and bullet design. He promoted the style of cartridge that is widely used over much of America today. We can rightly remember Charles Newton as the successful "Father of High Velocity."

19

JACK O'CONNOR: THE RIFLEMAN'S RIFLEMAN

Tempe, Arizona, O'Connor's boyhood paradise, was a town of distinctive frontier flavor. The Old West had not yet faded into a distant past. Its wildness still existed in fact as well as in the imagination, painted against a deep blue sky—open and free, with sweeping land on all sides. Here John Woolf "Jack" O'Connor grew up. Here he learned to hunt, to shoot and to relish the gifts of nature.

O'Connor was born in Nogales, Arizona, on January 22 two years into the 20th century. In 1902 the horse was still a major mode of transportation; a person read by gas light and cranked a phonograph handle to listen to music coming out of a cylindrical "record." Jack and his parents, Andy and Ida Woolf O'Connor, lived for a short time in a small apartment in San Francisco. But after they moved to Tempe, Jack's life changed when his mother announced that she and Jack's father had, that very day, divorced. The boy was five years old; he continued to live in Tempe with his mother and his sister, Helen. Mrs. O'Connor had been born in 1873 in Kentucky (she died in 1962), her father moving westward to ranch on the New Mexico/Arizona border for a while, and then on to the Tempe area. She taught at Tempe Normal School, which was later to become Tempe State Teacher's College, and eventually Arizona State University, one of the largest educational institutions in the world. Jack would later teach at the University of

Arizona, too.

Jack's father, Andy, had loved baseball and played catcher, his gnarled fingers bearing testimony to the days when a catcher's mitt was no more than a pad of leather tied around the hand. He taught school for a while, but mostly Mr. O'Connor swayed back and forth from one enterprise to another. A well-read, intelligent man, his father, Jack believed, was a dreamer who expected "one big deal" to make his fortune. Jack saw his dad several times in later years, but the relationship was distant. The two were never fast friends, nor did they see each other regularly.

Jack O'Connor loved to hunt. He hunted the Salt River valley area for ducks at an early age, and at 12 he shot his first "big game" in the remoteness of his Arizona home. He dropped the mule deer buck out of season with a 30/40 Krag at a time when game laws were words on paper, not strictly adhered to or stringently enforced. His proficiency with a rifle led him to serve in the 158th Infantry of the U.S. Army for a short time in World War I.

But Jack was a reader, too. He loved books. And later on he was able to merge his hunting and writing interests into a career. He was educated as a teacher and attended Arizona State Teachers College from 1921 to 1923. He studied at the University of Arizona for one year, but he finished his requirements for a bachelor's degree at the University of Arkansas in 1925. From there, he earned a Master of Arts degree in English from the University of Missouri. That was 1927. Just before attaining that degree, Jack married Eleanor Bradford Barry.

After graduation, O'Connor taught and began freelance writing. By 1930, he had published his first novel, *Conquest,* which was not a big seller. Jack had returned to Arizona with his wife, Eleanor, light of his life, mother of his four children, hunting partner, and lifelong friend. In 1931 he taught in Flagstaff at what was then a small teacher's college in that mountain town. Three

An artist's rendition of Jack O'Connor. His face became familiar to millions of shooters as the gun editor of *Outdoor Life* magazine.

years later, he accepted a teaching position in Tucson at the University of Arizona, where he remained on the faculty for 11 years. Apparently, he was a pretty animated instructor. He once leaped over a series of desks during a classroom lesson in order to pound the butter out of a kid who had thrown a baseball glove at him, hitting him in the face with it.

"I started peddling stuff in 1929," Jack said in a letter to this author dated 11-8-1971, "the year the Depression hit. Between 1930 and 1933, when the magazines ran out of old manuscripts, Dante couldn't have peddled *The Inferno*." Jack's second novel, *Boom Town*, came in 1938. It sold much better. In 1937–1938, during his new association with *Outdoor Life* magazine, Jack freelanced again. "I made $10,000 the first six months—about $600 the second," he said. (letter to author, 8-20-73)

O'Connor became a prolific writer. His career was taking form. Captain E.C. Crossman, excellent *Outdoor Life* staff writer, had committed suicide in 1939. Ray Brown, Editor-in-Chief of the magazine, liked O'Connor's writing. By 1941 Jack was the Arms Editor for *Outdoor Life*, his work being read by avid shooters every month. His columns, "Getting the Range" and "Shooting," were main course meals for hungry shooters seeking food for thought. However, he was adding many book titles to his list of credits as well. *The Rifle Book, The Hunting Rifle, The Complete Book of Rifles and Shotguns, Jack O'Connor's Big Game Hunts,* and *The Big Game Animals of North America* are only a few of his works. An early book, *Game in the Desert,* is recognized as a classic and will often fetch $300 and more per copy from used book dealers. It was *Game in the Desert* that may have furthered Jack to national fame as an outdoor writer. I read the book over and over again as a high school student, almost lifting the words from the page with my eyes.

Jack's 1969 title, *Horse and Buggy West, A Boyhood on the last Frontier* remains, at least to my thinking, one of his more important works. Although it never ranked with Steinbeck's *Travels with Charley,* it contains fascinating information on the transition period when the Old West was behind us, the New West in front of us. O'Connor fans will want to read *Horse and Buggy* for a solid inside look at the firearms author who penned it, for it reveals many of Jack's feelings concerning change in the structure of America. It is a much more important book than the literary moguls have allowed it to be, and now that Jack is gone, a copy can often bring a tidy little wad of greenbacks.

O'Connor hunted five continents and was a recipient of the coveted Weatherby Award. He was, more than anything else, a rifleman-hunter, doing very little with handguns. The hunts were usually guided, and Jack's deepest interest was making that one good shot at a fine, mature big game specimen. He was a crack shot in the field, although he was not the freelance hunter that Elmer Keith was. His favorite big game animal of all time, in spite of a trophy room replete with tigers, kudus, bighorn sheep and other exotics, remained the little Coues deer of Southern Arizona. Jack described this tiny fellow as the wittiest of big game, ranking only a mature, hunter-wise kudu on the same plain.

ABOUT RIFLES AND COMMON SENSE CARTRIDGES

O'Connor's love for the shotgun is obvious by his work. Jack enjoyed bird hunting immensely. But the great bulk of his writing centered on the rifle. He made a decided impact upon American shooting by writing mostly to the grassroots rifleman. Many contemporary ideas harbored by modern riflemen sailed first upon the literary oceans of Jack O'Connor's writing.

A major concept Jack promoted was the middle-ground cartridge, firing bullets of modest weight at high velocity. He was neither a big-bore fan, nor a small-bullet, super high-velocity devotee. He believed in caliber/cartridge appropriateness, and his platform made a telling impact on American shooters. Jack was for common sense among cartridges and he was a conservative not only in his political ideas, but also in hunting—he often said that long-range big game shooting was not for the unpracticed. He felt that most hunters should limit themselves to 200 yard shots, maximum.

Few arms writers can claim responsibility for making or breaking a rifle cartridge single-handedly, but it's safe to say that the 270 Winchester's success is in great part owed to O'Connor's genuine love for the round and to his many stories devoted to it. In "The .270 in Africa," for example, a column in the March 1967 *Outdoor*

Life, Jack said, "I have read many times that the .270 is almost as worthless on African game as a fly-swatter." And then in typical O'Connor style, Jack denounced that notion with his usual approach—a solid structure of humor underladen with a foundation of hard facts. When I set forth to buy my first bolt-action big game rifle in 1958, it had to be two things—a Model 70 Winchester and a 270. I was so adamant on the latter that the gunstore proprietor had some fun when I came in to pick it up. "There weren't any more 270s, Sam," he said, "but I knew you'd settle for a 30-06 so that's what I ordered." I had waited a "lifetime" and had just spent a summer of labor as a dishwasher for that rifle. "Hey, just kidding," the man said, when he saw that I wasn't smiling.

But O'Connor remained objective in his approach to promoting the 270 Winchester as he did in the advancement of all his ideas. When asked if he would prefer a 270 or a 30-06 for big bears, Jack said he'd rather have a larger cartridge than either, but if limited to just those two, he'd take the '06. Furthermore, he hunted with the '06, and many other rounds extensively. He also liked the 7mm Remington Magnum very much. He wasn't in love with the 264 Winchester, thinking it nothing more than a 270 in a fat case that burned extra powder for nothing. He counted the 280 Remington as a clone of the 270 and saw no particular need for it, either. While thought of as anti-big bore in some circles, Jack admired heavy bullets and used them when he deemed them appropriate. He found the 458 Winchester a fine cartridge for heavy game in Africa, for example, and he considered the 470 equally at home on game that "shot back." He simply did not feel that large-bore rifles were necessary for most American big game.

O'Connor was instrumental in promoting good big game bullets. Again, his approach was from the sensible side. He based his commentary on field performance, data he had gathered himself, and input from other hunters, often received in correspondence. Jack certainly got the mail. He made it a point to answer the great majority of letters that he received. He dictated his responses to a secretary, which was a help, but answer letters he did. Sometimes he learned from these letters, to be sure. He was more open-minded than given credit for. He had a good memory and could recite instance after instance of bullet performance, good and bad, which were related to him by readers and friends, as well as through his own field experiences.

Jack was partially responsible for the wide acceptance of the telescopic riflesight. That may sound implausible, but not every rifleman, even of the 1950s, was in favor of the glass sight. O'Connor's straight talk on the value of magnification, the precision of a scope sight's reticle and its overall reliability convinced more than one fellow to try the scope. He was not a fan of the high-power scope, however, and insisted that a 3X or 4X scope was adequate even for mountain hunting. In addition, he did much to persuade his readers that careful sighting in of the rifle from a solid benchrest was paramount to good hunting results and ethics.

He made shooters aware of many concepts, including stock design, aspects of reloading, bul-

As other writers were bemoaning the changes made in the Model 70 Winchester (above), Jack commended the improvements.

Jack O'Connor had a quick wit—on the dais or at the desk. He influenced shooting by promoting the tenets of good marksmanship. He advocated rifles with common-sense cartridges, rifle sights and sighting-in from a benchrest, points other writers tended to overlook.

let performance, trajectories, rifle-handling, and other factors considered mundane today, but which were routinely overlooked by many firearms writers, even as late as the 1960s. He was "trigger-wise" and his demand for safe, but crisp triggers of light let-off taught many shooters the value of a good trigger. He advocated teaching hunters how to harvest game more reliably through better field marksmanship, especially by attaining a rest or at least assuming the sitting or prone position before firing. Many a new hunter incorporated Jack's theories concerning field marksmanship, to the betterment of their big game harvests. I was one of them.

O'Connor appealed to the vast majority of grassroots hunters who read his work, for he helped them become better at the activities they loved so well, hunting and shooting. "Bullets in the Breeze," a column that appeared in *Outdoor Life* of March 1957 is typical of an informational O'Connor piece. Jack could *explain* things. His teaching background was always working overtime. In the wind-drift piece, he carefully employed time of flight data without once bogging the reader down with difficult formulas or heavy-duty words from the world of physics.

Jack O'Connor was the most outspoken advocate of the 270 Winchester cartridge. Many shooters credit O'Connor with the current popularity of the cartridge—No. 2 in the West, just behind the 30-06.

Not that Jack was a slide-rule ballistician. He wasn't, nor did he consider himself such. His background in hard science was not deep. But Jack often researched a given proposition quite thoroughly before embarking on a discourse of the subject. In the main, however, he wrote from knowledge gained on the big game trail, and he was often on that trail, if not in the contiguous 48 states, then in Alaska; and if not Alaska, then the Yukon, or British Columbia, or perhaps India, Iran or Africa. He gained a good deal of rifle-hunting know-how by actually *hunting* for a wide variety of big game animals.

Jack had much to do with stock design, not directly, it can be argued, but indirectly. He preferred, for the most part, the classic style as seen in the work of Owens and Biesen and Linden. But he more than tolerated the California design, declaring that it was a stock of utility and worth. He hated frills, however, and was not prone to inletted diamonds and other figures, or stock carvings. You listened to O'Connor. You trusted what he said. You listened partly because he wrote exceedingly well, yet with a light hand. Of stock design he once said, ". . . some stocks. . . are handsome and efficient, some. . . are efficient but not so handsome, and some. . . not only are inefficient but so fantastically ugly as to cause a miscarriage in a lady crocodile." (*The Complete Book of Rifles and Shotguns*) Indirectly, it was O'Connor's stock savvy that helped promote the supremely graceful stocks of the hour, as seen on Wells, Zollinger and Fisher custom rifles.

Jack O'Connor was also instrumental in

promoting the custom rifle. He owned and shot several customs and he wrote glowingly of the handmade rifle. Many of us first contracted a fever for custom arms from turning the pages of Jack O'Connor's books and articles. He praised not only the custom rifle, but also the riflemaker. He clearly stood behind the efforts of certain gunmakers of his era, and he gave great credit to the craft of the individual artisan. I wonder how often O'Connor's custom rifle theories hovered over the heads of upcoming riflemakers, like the cartoon light bulb, provoking new ideas? Assuredly, he had an impact on custom arms designs.

He had a lot to say about *what* a big game hunting rifle should be. His prescription for its barrel length (22-inches for a 270 Winchester) and overall weight (8 pounds with scope and sling) was given more than lip service by many shooters. He spoke of slings and carrying straps, and their uses. And he talked about bedding rifle barrels. He strongly advocated handloading. There was, at one time, a campaign against handloading, and Jack helped in breeching the gap between handloader and factory ammo-crafter. And he did more. Much more. He was an interesting person. A man who could persuade. Rifle manufacturers

Born and raised in Arizona, O'Connor developed a love for hunting and the vast expanses of land he called home. In addition to his well-liked works on shooting, he wrote *Horse and Buggy West*, a biography of his early life and the history of an era in the Southwest.

were in touch with Jack. It is certain that the shooter/writer had much to say concerning rifle and cartridge designs that ended up on factory shelves.

Later in life, he'd have many friends in the arms-writing business, some of whom he admired greatly. He felt that the writing of John Jobsen, for example, was admirable, and he read Colonel Whelen with great respect. Some others he was genuinely unimpressed with and without mentioning names took them on in print from time to time, recounting tales they had told and then reciting why that writer's ideas were awash.

Jack and Eleanor finally moved to Idaho, where they spent the remainder of their days. Jack's beloved Arizona had changed too much for him. He wrote, "Today I am a stranger in my old home town. Phoenix has become a great city that has engulfed much of the pleasant Salt River valley countryside." (from *Horse and Buggy West*) They lived in Lewiston, Idaho, in a large two-story white home on a few acres of green grass landscape. "Hail and Farewell," he wrote in a July 1972 article. "This is my last appearance as shooting editor of *Outdoor Life*. I was 70 years old last January, and I am about five years overdue for the pasture. I have lived out my Biblical three score and ten, and my remaining years on this earth are gravy."

I believe that most reporters should air their views in private, rather than on paper, radio or television. News peddlers are often far from expert on many of the events they report on. And they should be content parroting public events rather than interpreting them. In my role as reporter of O'Connor, however, I breech that conviction by offering a personal note. I met the man. I visited in his home. And I compiled a thick file of letters he was kind enough to send me over the years.

He was a great writer and a fine teacher. Having consented to critique a few of my early manuscripts, I'll never forget Jack's first comment of my work. "Don't you know what a paragraph is?" he demanded. From then on, I made it a point to know what a paragraph was and how to use it. O'Connor taught us all a lot about rifles and rifle-shooting. And he offered plenty of good information on shotguns and shotgunning as well. We followed his writing because it was fun to read. Jack had something to say and he knew how to say it. He died on January 20, 1978 on the *S. Mariposa* as the ship was returning from Hawaii. A heart attack claimed his life.

Jack O'Connor's writing is still fun to read and is ever informative. His work is going to remain an important part of outdoor literature for as long as outdoor literature is read. O'Connor was one of the best of the great riflemen writers.

20

ANNIE OAKLEY: CELEBRATED MARKSWOMAN

The copper penny whirled into the air like a tiny satellite. Crack! At the rifle shot, the coin flew wildly out into a field and there lay still, deformed from the bullet's impact. Mrs. Frank Butler had scored another hit. "Throw!" the little white-haired woman of 62 said. She leaned against the table to support herself after dispensing with her crutches. Ping! Another penny flew off its appointed course at the crack of the rifle. Then another. And another. Annie Oakley was shooting again. It was 1922. She had not held a rifle in her hands since the previous year when an accident had rolled her car. She hit 25 pennies in a row. Then she blasted five eggs out of the air—all thrown at once—with five quick shots. Few marksmen, no matter their renown, could shoot like Annie Oakley.

Although this book concentrates largely on men shooters (there were so few women who made a name in the world of firearms), Annie Oakley breaks the mould. Chances are, there isn't a single person reading this chapter who could match Annie's ability with a firearm in exhibition shooting. Certainly the person at this keyboard could never do it. Annie's feats of marksmanship sound more fictional than factual. But Annie's amazing ability with firearms was not a talent hidden under a bushel. Her exhibitions of rifle, shotgun and revolver magic were witnessed by thousands of people at uncountable performances in her lifetime.

That lifetime began in a tiny log cabin in Darke County, Ohio, on August 13, 1860. The fifth child of Susan and Jacob Moses, Phoebe Ann Moses was called "Annie" by her four older sisters. The name stuck. She later changed her last name to Mozee, remembering being taunted by teasing children who chanted, "Moses Poses, Moses Poses."

Annie's father, badly crippled by exposure to a winter storm, died in 1866. Mrs. Moses tried to keep the family intact, but could not. At age nine, Annie was given over to another family, whom she later referred to as "The Wolves." She was starved by these people, overworked and often severely punished without warrant. Annie ran away, walking 40 miles to get home. But she was forced to return to "The Wolves." Finally, Annie's mother married Civil War veteran, Joseph Shaw, and the girl was able to return to her real home. Monetary dearth continued, but kindness from her stepfather made up for a lack of worldly possessions.

HUNTING HONES HER SKILLS

Annie always said she learned her shooting as a hunter. She began hunting for food as a youngster and with her rifle provided meat for the hungry family. "I was eight years old when I made my first shot, and I still consider it one of the best shots I ever made," she announced. "I saw a squirrel run down over the grass in front of the

Annie Oakley—Little Miss Sure-Shot—the pride of the Buffalo Bill Wild West Show and a lady who, with her crackshot shooting, entertained and endeared herself to the rich and famous from all over the world.

house, through the orchard and stop on the fence to get a hickory nut. I decided to shoot it. . . .," reports Don Russell in *The Lives and Legends of Buffalo Bill*. Annie got the loaded rifle down. She had to climb on a chair to do it. Chided by a brother who told her that only head shots counted on squirrels, little Annie proceeded to put a bullet squarely on target. Her mother forbid her to touch the rifle again. She obeyed—for about eight months.

Annie was so good a hunter that there was extra meat to sell as well as meat for the family table. Excess game was sent to Charles Ketzenberger, owner of the Greenville general store.

Ketzenberger passed the game on to a mailman who sold the meat to Cincinnati hotelkeeper, Jack Frost. Annie's marksmanship began to gain note in the region. Not satisfied with dropping a quail on the rise with her shotgun, she would whirl around in a complete circle after the bird flushed; then she would fire and hit the quail. Soon she was wingshooting with a rifle. She won prizes at local turkey shoots. That's how she met her husband-to-be, Frank Butler.

Butler was himself a popular marksman. He was a part of Butler & Company, a traveling theatrical troupe. It was common for Butler to accept challenges from local shooters as he was giving his exhibition of marksmanship. Jack Frost, the hotelkeeper, set Butler up—in the modern sense—to shoot against Annie in a Thanksgiving Day match. She was only 15 at the time. Butler, it is claimed, did not know his opponent was a girl. Contrary to the movie version of the story, Frost won his 50 dollar bet. Annie won the contest by nailing 25 targets with 25 shots. She found out from this match that there was much more to exhibition shooting than she thought. She watched with great interest as Mr. Butler performed his firearms tricks. A year later, at age 16, Annie was an even more practiced shot. She was also married to Frank Butler on June 22. No negative comments exist about this relationship. Annie and Frank were made for each other. Frank did not mind that Annie now stood in the limelight, moving him into her shadow. He knew she was the more gifted shooter.

Enter "Te Toncka Ua Tocka," better known as "Sitting Bull." The Battle of the Little Big Horn had raged on the plains not too long before. Sitting Bull and his sidekick, "Rain in the Face," were on their way to Washington, D.C., when both warriors had a chance to observe a lady shooter doing her work. Having just lost a daughter of his own, Sitting Bull took immediate fatherly interest in Annie. He gave her another name. Annie Moses, who had become Annie Mozee, who was now Mrs. Frank Butler, who had also given herself the stage name, Annie Oakley, was now given another sobriquet by Sitting Bull. He called her "Watanya cicilia," or "Little Sure-Shot." The stoic Indian, enthralled by the gifted marksmanship of the tiny woman, reputedly stood in the audience waving his arms and crying out the new name.

The Chief hung Annie's picture in his teepee. Solid resources insist that Sitting Bull was lured into remaining with the Buffalo Bill Show by the promise that if he did, he could see Little Sure-Shot every day. The Hunkpapa Sioux Indian indeed adopted Annie as his daughter in a formal ceremony. Annie Oakley was billed as the adopted daughter of the famous Indian Chief, Sitting Bull—which served to inflate her fame as well as Buffalo Bill's wallet.

At age 25, Annie and Frank had been a part of the Sells Brothers Circus. Neither of them apparently had enjoyed the association very much. When a chance to move on presented itself, the two sharpshooters took it. But the timing was all wrong. Buffalo Bill's show had recently absorbed a bitter loss. A Riverboat carrying the show had sunk. Guns, ammo, mules, buffaloes—all were lost. Saved were some horses, a band wagon and the Deadwood stage.

Captain A.H. Bogardus, the crack shot billed as "Champion Wingshot of the World," quit Buffalo Bill Cody at this time. There was an opening for a new shooter, but no funds to hire one after the riverboat accident. However, Annie put on an exhibition for Buffalo Bill and, a few months later, her shooting earned her a place with Cody's troupe. "She sighted with a hand mirror and shot backwards as Frank threw glass balls in the air. She hit them all," recounted Sell & Weybright in *Buffalo Bill and the Wild West*. Annie would go

After Chief Sitting Bull lost his own daughter, he adopted Annie Oakley into his tribe and into his heart. Some say he stayed with the Buffalo Bill Show so he could see Little Missie every day.

on to open the Buffalo Bill show for the next 17 years. Her famous mirror trick shot was, incidentally, duplicated using a shiny knife blade, with Annie firing at the image reflected on the blade's surface.

Many may wonder why Miss Oakley came on early in the show. Today, you'd save the best for last. But there was good reason. "She starts very gently, shooting with a pistol. Women and children see a harmless woman out there and do not get worried," said Major Burke, spokesman for the show, when asked why Annie was the first act. Buffalo Bill's Wild West and Congress of Rough Riders of the World opened with "The Star Spangled Banner" played by the Cowboy Band. Then the Rough Riders, horsemen from various armies of the world, passed in "Grand Review." Immediately following was the first act—"Miss Annie Oakley, Celebrated Shot, who will illustrate her dexterity in the use of Fire-arms." The profits from Buffalo Bill's show rose significantly after Annie joined the company.

People loved Annie. She was pretty and petite (she weighed about only 100 pounds) and presented a charming personality. Buffalo Bill was no exception in adoring Annie. "They told me about you, Missy. We're glad to have you," he said, according to Sell & Weybright. That name stuck, too. Afterwards, she was often called "Little Missie." Notables around the world felt the same about Annie as did her friends and countrymen. She was applauded by commoner and royalty alike. The Princess of Wales extended a right hand to Annie, as well as to a couple other ladies of the traveling Buffalo Bill show, and the two shook hands. Proper custom was an offering of the royal hand, the left one, to be lightly kissed, not "shook." But Annie did that to people. She broke down many barriers.

The German Crown Prince, who would later become Kaiser Wilhelm II, had witnessed Little Sure-Shot shooting a cigarette from Frank Butler's lips in a London exhibition. He wanted to have Annie shoot a cigarette from his lips, too. Naturally, these daredevil tricks were a part of show business and not encouraged for the general public. However, to have Miss Annie Oakley shoot a cigarette from your lips was an honor—and no one was worried about her missing the shot. The Crown Prince stood still. Annie fired. The bullet neatly separated the ash of the cigarette from its tobacco-filled paper cylinder. Annie allowed later, after World War I was in progress, that she wished she had missed that shot. She said she'd like another opportunity—only this time she'd shoot for the good of her country rather than the sake of marksmanship.

Annie Oakley may have done more for shooting in her time than any other single person. She was the inspiration for comic book characters, for the musical *Annie Get Your Gun*, and for many movies and even television stories. Her charm, of course, had much to do with her widespread fame, but it was the shooting that earned her reputation. With the exception of Mrs. Ad Topperwein, there is no equal for Annie Oakley in the annals of superior lady marksmanship. Unfortunately, some of the movies and stories were embellished erroneously through fictionalization—the fiction was far less interesting than the true story. Annie's innate character was quiet and sedate, not brash and tough. She was indeed a bit puritanical away from the stage lights and enjoyed working with her embroidery and needlework. She was definitely good with her hands—whether it was a needle or a gun.

THE GREATEST LADY TRICKSTER

In 1884 at an exhibition in Tiffin, Ohio, Annie broke 943 out of 1,000 glass balls that were thrown into the air. She was firing a Stevens 22 rimfire rifle. In 1885 she broke 4,772 glass balls out of 5,000 thrown. She accomplished this feat with shotguns, loading them herself in between shots. It took her nine hours of shooting time to fire upon the 5,000 targets. A bet of $5,000 was laid on the line—that Annie could not hit 40 out of 50 pigeons at 30 paces with the birds on the rise—she hit 49 of them. Miles Johnson, then New Jersey state shooting champion, challenged her to repeat the act against him the very next day. She beat him, again hitting 49 out of 50 birds. In another exhibition, Annie fired 5,000 shots from her rifles at 5,000 glass balls tossed into the air. She recorded a 95 percent score. She also split playing cards edge-wise. And she shot coins from Frank's fingers. Annie also hit small balls as they swung from the ends of cords. She "drew" designs with bullets in the same fashion Ad Topperwein did later.

One of her tricks was to shoot 25 times in 25 seconds, aiming at the center of a playing card.

The pretty, petite markswoman, here wearing many of her shooting medals, was renown for her tricks with guns. She could split playing cards edge-wise, shoot coins from her husband's fingers and cigarettes from his lips.

Annie Oakley's life cannot be told without mentioning Buffalo Bill Cody, the man who helped make her famous. His flair for publicity helped to promote Annie Oakley, as her outstanding skills in turn helped his enterprise. Her crowd-pleasing act opened the Buffalo Bill show for 17 years.

The center of the card would be chewed away by bullets. Another trick was to run 10 feet, vault over a table, run another 10 feet, grab a shotgun and break two clay birds that had been trap-thrown prior to her sprinting. Interestingly, Annie Oakley was never billed as a champion shooter or competitive marksman, even though Johnny Baker, who was called "Champion Exhibition Rifle and Shotgun Shot of the World" had competed with her and lost every time for 17 years in a row when both were employed with the Buffalo Bill show. "There never was a day I didn't try my damnedest to beat her! It would have been better for the show if I *had* beaten her sometimes. But she wouldn't throw a match, not even for the sake of the show. You had to *beat* her—and she wasn't beatable!" said Baker ("Little Sure-Shot," by E.B. Mann, the *American Rifleman,* April 1949).

A young Annie Oakley in a beautifully embroidered dress carries her favorite Marlin 22 rifle. She was one of the "great shooters" of all time.

While there is no indication of prejudice here, it does seem odd that Buffalo Bill would not have taken the advertising advantage by giving Annie a title, at least "World's Greatest Lady Shot."

Annie's luck had improved over her difficult and deplorable childhood days—but not completely. Her tenure with the Buffalo Bill show was, apparently, a happy one, although they parted ways for a short time. When asked about Buffalo Bill, Annie said he was a supremely fine gentleman, that he was a family man, and that she trusted his loyalty to such a degree that there was never a contract between them. "And the whole time we were one great family loyal to one man. His words were more than most contracts. Personally I never had a contract with the show after I started. It would have been superfluous." (*The Lives and Legends of Buffalo Bill*) However, Annie and Frank did leave Buffalo Bill to sign up with another show, Buckskin Joe's Wild West. They didn't like it. They helped promote a merger between the Buckskin Joe outfit and Pawnee Bill's troupe. "Annie Oakley, after failure of the Pawnee Bill show, appeared in a variety bill at the opening of Tony Pastor's Opera House in New York, scheduled a few shooting matches, and took the part of 'Sunbeam' in a melodrama, *Deadwood Dick.* Then she settled whatever disagreement she may have had with Cody in Salsbury and rejoined Buffalo Bill's Wild West for the season of 1889," says Don Russell. The tour that year included shows in France, Spain, Italy, Austria and Germany.

Accidents tarnished the stardom, though. The day before a big shooting match, Annie's hand was ripped open by a target trap spring. A physician had strictly forbidden Little Sure-Shot to compete. But she shot all the same with her "the-show-must-go-on" attitude. She fired one-handed against her opponent and broke 24 out of 25 birds, tying the match. Then the Buffalo Bill troupe suffered three train crashes in two years. In North Carolina in 1901, a collision that killed over 100 horses also badly injured Little Missie. She suffered internal injuries and was hospitalized for many months. But Annie did perform well over 1400 exhibitions after this unfortunate mishap. Her associates lamented, though, that she was never again the same person.

In 1902-1903, Annie performed in the melodrama, *The Western Girl.* Ten years later she toured with the Young Buffalo Wild West Show. During World War I, the Butlers toured the army camps, putting on exhibitions and giving shooting lessons. For a short time, they even taught and demonstrated their shooting skills at the Carolina Hotel in Pinehurst, North Carolina.

The last accident took its toll in November 1921 in Dayton, Florida. This was the auto accident that left her crippled. Five years later, on November 2, 1926, in Greenville, Ohio, in her home county of Darke, Little Miss Sure-Shot died. Twenty days later, Frank Butler, her husband and companion of 50 years, was dead, too.

Annie Oakley was perhaps the most talented lady marksman of all time. Although she was never officially granted the title of "Greatest Lady Trickshooter," without reservation we can say that she was one of the finest shooters—man or woman—any era has ever seen.

21

WILLIAM COTTON OSWELL: PIONEER OF CIVILISATION

"We shall never see his like again." Those worshipful words emanated from a man who himself was highly admired in his time, and well after, the great shooter, Sir Samuel Baker, whom we met in Chapter 4. Baker said of William Cotton Oswell, "His name will be remembered with tears of sorrow and profound respect." Baker, the rugged hunter of Ceylon and Africa, credited Oswell with salvaging for memory the very early days of African hunting adventure, when "the ground was untrodden by the European foot; the native unsuspicious of the guile of a white intruder." William Cotton Oswell was one of the earliest ivory hunters to travel in South Africa. He hunted there in the mid-1800s, before procuring ivory had gained a wide following. At the time of his death on May 1, 1893, he was considered the only remaining professional hunter who could personally relate the story of pre-settlement South Africa. Baker felt that Cotton Oswell would have gained even greater prominence had he been less modest. Modesty kept the old hunter's light hidden under a bushel, Sir Samuel believed.

Oswell had a legitimate claim to fame as friend of, and in some respects mentor to, Dr. David Livingstone. During the era when Livingstone was an unknown missionary working under Reverend Robert Moffat, whose daughter Livingstone married, Cotton Oswell was the explorer's advisor and confidant. Oswell, along with a friend by the name of Murray, Dr. Livingstone and the Living-

stone family, set out to discover an interior lake in Africa. Oswell and Murray financially backed the venture, but Dr. Livingstone was such a help in communicating with the natives and in his strategic planning for the trip that after the trek, Oswell gave Livingstone a new wagon and span of 16 oxen as a present, along with a complete personal outfit for travel. Dr. Livingstone applauded Oswell in his treatise, "Zambesi and its Tributaries," but the grand hunter insisted upon being edited out of the manuscript for the most part.

Nonetheless, recognition came to Oswell when he was awarded the medal of the French Geographical Society as party to Livingstone's "discovery" of important lake systems in Africa. Oswell, therefore, was both explorer and hunter. He suffered in later life by what I call "The Old Hunter's Syndrome," whereby it is easier to divorce oneself from previous exploits in the field by apologizing for being a hunter. The Old Hunter Syndrome is a malady that Roy Chapman Andrews, Arthur Godfrey, and many other hunters suffered in the twilight of their years. "I am sorry now for all the fine old beasts I have killed," lamented Oswell, ". . . [but] every animal, save three elephants, was eaten by man, and so put to good use." But make no mistake about it, Oswell loved every footprint he impressed upon African soil in pursuit of big game. Furthermore, he was like the famous old hunters, such as Sir Samuel,

Portrait of William Cotton Oswell—great 19th-century elephant hunter and "Pioneer of Civilisation." Oswell was the first white man to see many parts of Africa previously unknown to Europeans and knew South Africa in its pre-settlement days.

Captain James Forsyth and Major Shakespear, who not only loved to hunt, but who also revered the firearm and included data in their writings concerning rifles and loads for big game.

In the course of his adventures, the famous Briton was the first white man to enter many regions of South Africa. Two attributes seemed to mark Oswell, both highly admirable: gentleness and fearlessness. A good combination of traits. The natives of various regions were said to adulate Cotton Oswell, for they trusted him never to abandon a dangerous position for his own safety at the sake of his men's lives. Oswell said, "I never had occasion to raise a hand against a native. . . ." For better or worse, Oswell helped open many interiors of South Africa because he was so trusted that his successors were equally trusted when they arrived. Because of his early exploration of many previously unseen (by Europeans) areas, he was given the title "Pioneer of Civilisation" by the Government of England.

His physical attributes were a match for his personal nature and actions. Oswell was six feet tall, but not of the massive build owned by Samuel Baker. He was muscular and strong, but light of weight and enduring in the field. Baker noted that Oswell had a "handsome face, with an eagle glance, but full of kindness and fearlessness."

Oswell hunted from the saddle. He was known to fire with great accuracy from the back of his horse, or to dismount at the trot with immediate and accurate aim. His favorite rifle was a 10-bore double-barrel Purdey. This was a smoothbore, by the way, and therefore not accurately called a rifle; however, in deference to its firing a single projectile from each bore, and to the fact that it had rifle-like sights for aiming, we will refer to Oswell's favorite hunting instrument as a rifle.

Why smoothbore? Because of Oswell's hunting style. The object was to get close and shoot fast, very often from only 10 or 15 yards. A smoothbore had plenty of accuracy for this sort of work on big game. Oswell's load was six "drachms," or drams, of "fine grain powder," or about 164 grains weight for each charge. If we consider the 10-gauge "spherical balls" as 10 to the pound, each would have weighed roughly 1.6 ounces each, depending upon their exact diameter; these undersized lead balls were fitted with a linen patch to take up the windage in the bore.

The rifle weighed 10 pounds even. Baker borrowed Oswell's favorite rifle in 1861 for the former's expedition to locate the sources of the Nile. "This gun was a silent witness to what its owner had accomplished," said Baker.

The patching of the 10-gauge projectiles, not only with linen, but sometimes with waxed kid glove material, was total. The ball was rolled tightly in the patch, rather than the patch being set over the crown of the muzzle with the ball centered upon it. Excess patching material, whether leather or cloth, was cut away with scissors, leaving the lead ball fitted with a tightly wrapped covering. Then the ball was introduced to the muzzle and rammed home on the powder charge. No further wads of any kind were used. This method was fast in the field, especially due to the fact that the smoothbore had no rifling to detain the ramming of the patched ball.

Oswell's smoothbore was much easier to maintain than a rifled arm, for there were no grooves to fill up with blackpowder fouling. Premeasured powder charges were carried in paper "cartridges." When the hunter required a load, he nipped the end off of the paper tube and slipped the tube downbore with the open end toward the breech, paper and all, followed by a pre-patched round ball. This process meant very fast loading because the patched ball was not closely fit to the bore—the ball *and* the paper tube of powder were rammed downbore simultaneously, with one swift stroke of the ramrod. Then the rifle was capped— no easy matter on horseback—and thus ready to fire. This was Oswell's method of operation. It was reliable. He said of his percussion caps, "Let me here record my gratitude for the nearly absolute perfection of the copper caps I used—Joyce's."

To describe Oswell's favorite rifle is to describe the man as a hunter. Baker reported that the stock was eaten away in places by as much as an inch depth of wood, as if "rats had gnawed it." Of course, the "rasp" that cut away so much of Oswell's stock was in reality the wait-a-bit thorn bushes through which the hunter rode. Baker entrusted the Oswell rifle to a favorite tracker, who knew how to fire it—and did. He had to shoot the rifle, however, not at a charging beast, but at an "attacker." The ramrod was still in the bore of the rifle and, just like in the leatherstocking tales of the eastern pioneer, it sailed into the body of the assailant, according to Sir Samuel.

At any rate, the rifle was returned to Oswell minus its original ramrod. Baker found the rifle entirely satisfactory, and compared with his own firearms, quite mild-mannered. The recoil, said Baker, was "trifling." Baker found the rifle accurate for hunting to 50 yards. Oswell had pointed out that the taking of a large bull elephant with the 10-gauge longarm often required two hits, while the smaller female pachyderm was felled with only one ball. Incidentally, Oswell generally confined his shooting to male elephants only.

AFRICAN RIFLES, GAME AND PEOPLE

Oswell was not given much to writing, but fortunately was persuaded to pen a few of his stories of early hunting in Africa. One such reminiscence, "African Game and Rifles," was printed by Longmans Green & Company of London in 1902 in "The Badminton Library, Big Game Shooting" collection. All Oswell quotes here are

from that work. The book was accompanied by a set of action drawings by Joseph Wolf, noted wildlife artist of the day.

"I was never a crack shot," said Oswell. That personal sentiment predicated his hunting style. Oswell mentioned three of his rifles in the Longmans Green book, the 10-bore spoken of above, a 12-bore Westley-Richards light double gun, and a heavy single-barrel rifle firing a two-ounce belted ball. "This last was a beast of a tool," said Oswell. The rifle almost cost the hunter his life when it "stung" a bull elephant but did not drop the beast. The Purdey came through and saved the day.

In this tale, Oswell related the story of the ramrod. "Baker returned it [the 10-bore rifle] to me with a note apologising for the homeliness of the ramrod—a thornstick which still rests in its ferrules—adding that having to defend themselves against a sudden attack, his man Richard,

William Cotton Oswell, a white pioneer to Africa, roamed the Dark Continent when scenes such as this, taken from a 19th-century painting, were common.

The great Massai warriors as they looked when Oswell hunted in the mid-1800s. The natives of various regions were said to adulate Oswell, for they trusted him never to abandon a dangerous position for his own safety at the sake of his men's lives.

being hard pressed whilst loading, had fired the original ramrod into a chief's stomach, from which they had no opportunity of extracting it."

Oswell had many narrow escapes in his African hunting experiences. He relied on the lead ball to get him out of these jams. It seems odd to us that the large conical slug was not necessarily considered deadliest in the blackpowder muzzle-loading firearm of the era, but Oswell's incidental remarks echo those made later by Baker, Shakespear and Forsyth—that the spherical ball, which we know better as "round ball" as opposed to "conical ball," proved more effective than the elongated missile, even on dangerous game. While the laws of physics deny this position, the rules of experience seem to confirm it.

One of Oswell's narrow escapes had to do with a percussion cap failure, or misfire. Although Cotton revered the Joyce cap, one did fail him. It was "... *the only* miss-fire I ever had in thousands of shots," the old hunter explained. "... a fine bull elephant came close to the waggons. I rode to meet him, and fired, but failed to do any serious damage, though he pulled up. I reloaded and manoeuvred for his shoulder; but before I could get a shot he charged, and the cap of the right barrel snicked—fortunately the left stopped him with the first shot, and he fell dead."

The most dangerous animal in Africa? Some say it's the Cape buffalo, others believe it is the elephant. A ferocious creature, an elephant can attack swiftly and deliver almost instant death. Oswell hunted elephants on the Dark Continent during the blackpowder days and even pursued them on horseback.

Such was life in early Africa, not only for a hunter, but for anyone who happened to be there. Oswell's association with Livingstone is an important aspect of the man's importance, not only in shooting history, but in world history. For example, Cotton related the story of Livingstone's scrape with a lion in clear terms:

. . . the overlapping end of the broken humerus was visible enough when the body [Livingstone's] was brought home. The story of the accident was fresh with him and the Kafirs when we reached Mabotse. A lion had killed an ox near the village, and the Ba-Katla turned out, as they always did when the lion deserted his game, and attacked their herds. Each man, as is usual in a hunt of this kind, carried two or three assegais and a plume of ostrich feathers on a pointed six-foot stick. The lion was tracked. . . the dear old Doctor caught sight of its tail switching backwards and forwards. Up and off went a gun that would hardly have killed a strong tomtit. Livingstone was spun over eight or ten feet, and the lion was standing over him. The brute took his arm in its mouth and put a heavy paw on the nape of his neck, from which he pushed it off, for as he said, 'It was so heavy, man, and I don't like to be stamped on'. . . .

Cotton went on to observe that Livingstone might have made a fine hunter because of his courage, but "he could neither shoot nor ride (except on oxback)—this was not his business."

Oswell admired the fact that Livingstone could "talk to the Kafirs' ears and hearts, we only to their stomachs, and I would fain believe that his grand work was occasionally made a little smoother by the guns." Oswell was a good chronicler-hunter because he spoke of more than the game; he put down stories of the native peoples of Africa, their customs and character (such as the story of the woman who attacked a lion with a short-handled hoe in order to convince the animal to drop her husband, who was lodged in the lion's jaws at the time). "Would Mrs. Smith do as much for Mr. Smith?" asked Oswell. "Could she do more?"

He also gave tips on hunting, much as we find in modern writing on the subject. And he explained the nature of the animals he hunted along with his stories of how to best pursue these wild animals. He said the Cape buffalo was ". . . the bravest and most determined of all animals when wounded or at bay; courage is the instinct of the buffalo family." He related, along with his African tales, a few anecdotes about India. In telling of buffalo, he said, "In Collegal, an outlying talook of the district of Coimbattoor, in the Madras Presidency, I have seen the village buffaloes drive a full-grown tiger helter-skelter up the hills, pursuing him far beyond their feeding grounds." He also told of a tiger that sprang into the midst of a buffalo herd, only to be "stamped and gored to death."

Most interesting was Oswell's story of the man who was "licked to death" by a buffalo. When in Africa, I heard the story several times from different professional hunters in both South Africa and Zimbabwe, but no one remembered its source. This is Oswell's version:

The following short story illustrates the vengeful nature of the beast; it is told, I think, in Moffat's 'Missionary Travels,' but I have not the book by me, and cannot vouch for the exact words: A native, sitting by the water at night, wounded a buffalo, but not mortally. It made for the shooter, who ran and lay down under a projecting rock. Unable to get its horns to bear, but not to be baulked, with its long, rough tongue it licked off the flesh of the exposed part of the man's thigh down to the bone, and then left its victim, who died in the morning.

The version I heard was slightly different. The native made it to a thorn tree, which he climbed, but not high enough to escape the enraged buffalo entirely. The animal could reach the man's foot with its tongue. The buff then applied his rough tongue to that area, and the native hunter finally succumbed to loss of life-giving bodily fluids.

"The smell of blood seems to madden these beasts; they will turn on a wounded and bleeding companion and gore him most savagely," said Oswell, who had many hair-raising experiences with buffalo. On one occasion, he was literally trapped among a big herd of the animals. "They dashed about me like rooks after the wireworms in a newly ploughed field," wrote the hunter, "I had the sensation of drawing myself in very tightly about the waistband. . . then I knocked over six at exceedingly close quarters." The same happened with elephants. Oswell dismissed such adventure, saying "How they avoided or missed you—for they didn't seem to try to avoid—you can't tell. You come out of it without a scratch, and therefore, as a rule, think no more of it."

Oswell's position on the native peoples of Africa seems somewhat less narrow and demeaning than opinions stated by other English/European hunters of the era. Of course, he was a man of the times, and as such, elevated non-European persons only so high on the human scale. However, in telling of the courage of hunters facing dangerous animals, Oswell pointed out that "We all belong to the same family. . . Some men have more of their wits about them than others no doubt; but all pale faces must yield to the black skins in this particular." Oswell related a Livingstone story of a native chased by a buffalo. When literally pinned by the animal, and when it seemed that the native's fate was sealed, the man attacked the buff's nose, wrenching it so hard that the animal gave up the attack. Said Oswell, ". . . it is illustrative of such presence of mind as would hardly be found in a European—living amongst wild animals and inheriting from generation to generation the instinctive knowledge of their natures, it would be surprising if the blacks were not in such things our superiors."

William Cotton Oswell was noted by his peers as one of the finest of Africa's early "white hunters." But Cotton Oswell was much more than a hunter. He was associated with a famous man of history, and in more than a trifling way. He exhibited an understanding for, and an appreciation of, the native peoples who were his helpers and in many cases his friends. He passed on his feelings on firearms for our study, and he related hunting tales as well as anyone could. He respected his men and they respected him. He risked life and limb for their safety:

Jumping off my pony, I ran into the scrub, guided by the sound [of a man's shriek]. I had hardly got fifty yards when, bursting through a thicket in front of me, a man, covered with blood, fell at my feet, crying out that he was killed by the lion, and at the same instant I caught sight of the beast close up on three legs, his mane electrified into an Elizabethan collar, with the Kafir's dog in his mouth. As his head came clear of the bush, I put a ball through it, and he dropped dead by the native's foot.

Oswell cleaned the man's wounds, rearranged lacerated tissues, bound the stricken areas, and took the man to the village, where the native eventually made a full recovery.

Oswell's African adventures remained a part of the man for the rest of his life. He said, when asked if he would like to return to Africa to relive those experiences, ". . . were I not a married man with children and grandchildren, I believe I should head back into Africa again, and end my days in the open air." As Baker pointed out, Oswell gave honest testimony concerning a special time in the history of a country, as well as a special branch of hunting. His life spanned from 1818 to 1893. Baker called Cotton the "Nimrod of South Africa," saying that "all those who knew him, either by name or personal acquaintance, regarded him as without a rival; and certainly without an enemy; the greatest hunter ever known in modern times, the truest friend, and the most thorough example of an English gentleman. We sorrowfully exclaim, 'We shall never see his like again.' "

22

HARRY "H.M." POPE: PRECISION BARRELMAKER

We admire the professional hunters of Africa for their daring. We praise the riflemen who explored and tamed the West. We applaud the 19th-century marksmen who peppered their lives with adventure and shooting feats that delighted millions of onlookers. But Harry Pope fits none of these moulds. Why rank him among the shooting stars of history? Because of his quest for accuracy. For without accuracy, shooting is just making noise. Pope had a dream—to create the finest barrels in the world. His goal was perfection, and although that plateau was never quite reached, Pope carved out many steps leading to its realization. Barrelmaking obscured his life, but Pope does belong here among the great shooters because in his pursuit of the accurate barrel, he became a renown offhand shot as well as a gifted benchrest marksmen in his own right.

Pope studied barrelmaking and built barrels for the love of it. He was good at it and he knew it. Money was decidedly not the object. Ned Roberts stated in "The Match, Target or Free Rifle," an article that appeared in the July 1943 issue of *Hunting and Fishing Magazine*: "I know of Pope rifles that have been in use for more than forty years during which time they have been shot between 35,000 and 40,000 times and will now make perfect scores at 200 yards. . . ." Roberts applauded Pope and his work for years, as did so many of Harry's peers. Pope shared the same time frame with a number of the "big names" in

shooting, the experimenters and innovators of the era. He was contemporary with Dr. F.W. Mann, with whom he worked, Niedner, Donaldson, W.V. Lowe, Whelen, Roberts, C.W. Roland, and many others. Because he lived so long, his life both predated and postdated many whom we now admire as pioneers of accurate rifles and ammunition. He taught these men. He learned from them. He befriended them, and in his own Pope style, he also feuded with them.

The best. That term applied to Pope the man, his workmanship and his ideas. "Generally speaking, the Pope system has been found to be the best for lead alloy bullets," claimed Townsend Whelen in *Small Arms Design*. Phil Sharpe also ranked Pope as one of the best in the business. Then there was Pope on himself—he considered himself a mechanical engineer. He did have schooling. But was he a mechanical engineer? In a degreed manner, that seems doubtful. He also rated himself a highly skillful workman. That fact cannot be denied. Pope also said that "by preference" he was a "gun crank"—that was entirely true. He boasted that ". . . every man who shoots a Pope improves his scores." And "I do all nice work by hand . . . ," and ". . . quality considered, my price is very low." His letterhead reveals something of himself, too: "H.M. Pope—Small Arms Expert."

We know of the man from his work, from his reputation, and from a substantial collection of

Harry Pope as a young man was determined to make the ultimate, accurate barrel—one that would consistently fire one-hole groups. It has been said that Pope rifles used over forty years, and shot nearly 40,000 times, still made perfect scores at 200 yards.

personal correspondence compiled by Gerald O. Kelver in his book *Respectfully Yours, H.M. Pope*, a 1976 title. Letters reveal many aspects of a person's nature, while disguising other traits. Without feedback between two speakers, specific nuances of communication may be lost. Nonetheless, the Pope letters tell much of the man. His fellow arms experts told even more. Pope was well-known by anyone interested in the quest for the "one-hole" group. His work was coveted by target marksmen who wanted to replace old shooting records with new ones. Kelver said that Pope's one obsession in life was to make the best barrel in the world. From my research, Pope felt he *was* making the best barrel in the world. One Pope rifle was reported to have been fired 125,000 times with a total of 700 pounds of powder and 4,000 pounds of lead going through its bore. It was still accurate. Furthermore, its dimensional measurements showed a bore wear of only .001 inch.

The image John Scofield painted of Pope, "The Old Master," in his June 1941 *American Rifleman* article will forever remain on the canvas of my mind. Stooped over in his dimly lighted shop, except for the bright illumination of a bare bulb directly above his work area, in an environment so cluttered that only the man himself can lay his hand upon a given tool or piece of hardware, stands the grand master of barrelmaking. An ever-burning cigarette protrudes from a bearded chin—he "started smoking after the San Francisco fire, when grub was hard to get." He wears moccasins folded back under the heels of his feet, tattered work shirt and pants. A black hat with visor rests upon his head. "Don't Talk to me Now," reads one of his shop signs. It was a clue to the master's nature. Too much demand upon his limited time. Too many projects to accomplish, and with near perfection in rifling and metalwork.

**IF YOU WANT YOUR
HEALTH TO REMAIN
GOOD
LEAVE MY BENCH ALONE**

That was Pope. "Repairing is Not My Business." That was Pope, too. "No Delivery Promised, Take Your Work When Well Done or Take it Elsewhere." That was Pope. "I Did Not Ask for Your Work. I am Doing You Favors, not You Me." And that was Pope.

What moulded the man?

FROM BICYCLES TO BARRELS

Harry Melville Pope was a child of the Civil War era, born August 15, 1861, in Walpole, New Hampshire. As a baby of only one year old, he moved with his family to Worcester, Massachusetts. The year the war ended, Harry lost his mother, then his sister, to diphtheria. He was only four. His father, Charles M. Pope, died two years later. Notes pertaining to the passing of Harry's parents suggest that grandparents and an aunt raised the orphan as their own. But Pope said an aunt raised him. He also mentioned an uncle who taught him how to work with things mechanical. We know Harry worked in his uncle's bicycle shop as a mechanic, which supports the relationship of aunt/uncle guardians.

It was in the bicycle shop that young Pope rifled his first barrel. When he bought the shop, Albert Pope, Harry's uncle, acquired a supply of dart-shooting air pistols along with the bicycles. Young Harry reasoned that the darts would fly truer if they were rotated in flight. Scofield's pertaining quote goes, "Rifled my first barrel when I was 12 or 13 . . . when I worked for my uncle, Colonel Pope, in my spare time." This rifling was of a brass air pistol barrel. "One day when the shop was deserted I rigged up a foot lathe and ground a broach with a spiral twist and went to work . . . The grooves couldn't have been over a couple thousandths deep, but they served to straighten out those darts. My pistol did better than any of the others."

At age 20, Pope enrolled in the Massachusetts Institute of Technology. Herein lies Harry's claim to being an engineer. I found no other report of formal education beyond the primary grades. Six years later, Harry had a wife and a boy, and the usual expenses of a husband and father. He wanted to rebarrel a rifle. However, at a wage of two dollars and fifty cents a day, the cost of barrel work was out of the question. "I knew nothing of barrel-making," he reported to Scofield, "never been in a gunshop, but I had a foot-lathe and figured I might be able to make what I wanted."

He wanted a 25-caliber barrel. So he made

one. That in itself is significant. But the fact that Pope won a shooting contest with it is even more remarkable. "The record was 99, I forgot whose, shot at Walnut Hill. Anyway, I got a 99 with that rifle of mine, muzzle rest." That 25-caliber barrel was the first in a line of hundreds. Pope also handcrafted the cartridge cases to go with his rifle. He turned the brass cases from solid stock. Only 12 rounds of straight 25-caliber cases did he make, loaded with 100-grain bullets behind 25 grains of black powder.

Pope the inventor. Pope the innovator. Pope the barrelmaker. Yes. But Pope the marksman, too. It's easy to forget that Harry was a supremely good rifle-shot because his barrels and shooting ideas have loomed larger than his target work. He was hardly the first shooter to trod the path leading to that mythical "one-hole group" that today's benchresters continue to strive for. Nor was Pope a benchrest shooter as such, but he greatly furthered the sport through the precision of his barrels. It was he who invented a machine-rest in order to test the inherent accuracy of a rifle. He was not first to have such a gadget. But he was early in its use and in the attempt to remove as many human variables as possible from the testing of a rifle.

Pope considered the effect of "jump" in his machine-rest system. Whelen reported Pope's thoughts on barrel jump in Volume II of *Small Arms Design*, page 66. In his article in *Arms and the Man*, March 5, 1914, he says, "Next let us see what our old reliable H.M. Pope has to say on the matter:"

> The action of the recoil is straight back in line with the barrel, but the resistance is always below the line of the barrel; that is the center of gravity of the rifle, also the resistance of the shoulder. This low resistance causes the whole gun to try to revolve around the center of resistance, precisely as pressure on the crank of a bicycle wheel tends to revolve the wheel.
>
> This sudden pressure bends the gun in a curve, with the center below the barrel, and causes the muzzle to dip and the breech to rise out of line and shoot low.

Whelen included an illustration of the Pope Machine Rest in Volume II of *Small Arms Design and Ballistics* (page 162), a Samworth book first printed in 1946. Whelen suggested that the Pope rest was not adaptable to modern rifles of high recoil, but only to rifles of low recoil. He was not hard on Harry. Just honest. But Pope was sometimes hard on Whelen. In a letter to Riley Sanford written March 22, 1925, Pope criticized, "Don't pay any attention to Whelan [sic] or Winchester. Neither of them know a damn thing about a muzzle loading Schuetzen rifle. Whelan never did or will and the war work and efficiency experts at Winchester took all men out of the shop who really knew anything about rifles." Pope's acid tongue was tolerated because of the barrelmaker's success in creating super-accurate rifles. After a shooter produced groups bettering anything obtained earlier, he tended to forgive the crusty gunsmith. Whelen forgave Harry and continued to praise his work.

Pope barrels were *guaranteed* for accuracy. There were a few provisos, but on the whole, Harry guaranteed that with his barrel a group of 2.5 inches at 200 yards was attainable—except for the 25-caliber tube, which did not carry so bold an accuracy promise. Ned Roberts (in spite of Donaldson stating that Roberts was a lousy shot who could never produce an inch group at 100 yards with any rifle), C.W. Roland, and Donaldson himself, all registered 10-shot strings of one ragged hole at 200 yards with Pope rifles. Pope, ever the marksman, retained in his possession a target that sported a *center-to-center* group of five-eighths of one inch at 200 yards for a 10-shot string. There was too much proof to deny Pope either his ability as a rifleman or a barrelmaker. He was both.

Pope and his rifles won numerous shooting contests. Although he was an especially gifted offhand shot who was instilled with great target-shooting talent, it is his benchrest effort and search for the perfect group that earned Harry his place of honor in shooting history. But Pope would rather have been remembered for his offhand shooting ability. After the experimentation left off, Harry insisted on "shooting from the hind legs like a man!" In 1897 he set a record doing so at the Lake Lookout Range in Springfield, Massachusetts. The wind flags were frozen from flying snow, but Harry broke the range record—100 shots offhand at 200 yards. That particular record, a 917 score, remained intact when Scofield wrote his 1941 article.

POPE'S "PERFECT" BARREL

Pope's legacy of barrelmaking includes two important factors: his special style of rifling a bore, and his unique method of "muzzle-loading a breechloader." As for the rifling, some confusion exists. It has been said that Pope used the gain-twist method for all of his barrels. Not true. Gain twist was intended for muzzleloading Schuetzen rifles only. Gain twist was supposed to impart more energy to the bullet due to reduced bore friction. Whereas a standard constant rate of twist meant that the bullet was forced to engage immediately with the full effect of the rifling and with energy loss through friction, gain twist allowed easy starting in the leade of the bore, with a gradual increase in bore friction. A better gas seal was also propounded for gain twist, with improved obturation, or bullet upset, in the bore. Some of the attributes were exaggerated, in my opinion, as shown by the fact that the gain-twist style of rifling is seldom seen today. Furthermore, the results of a head-on-head test conducted by a modern armsmaker left me somewhat cool on the virtues of gain twist in a muzzleloader. Two gain-twist muzzleloader barrels of identical caliber and style were breeched, one regularly, the other *backwards*. Both shot equally well. No accuracy differences could be discerned, even though one barrel was reversed at the breech.

Pope used the 8/8 rifling system, eight wide grooves and eight narrow lands with corners "rounded off," left-hand twist, except for the 30-06, which was right-hand twist. He did not lap his barrels, and was supposed to have fumed

One manner of shooting the target rifle Pope was famous for barreling. Note that the barrel itself is rested at the bench, not recommended practice today. A stiff barrel helped to thwart bullet diversion.

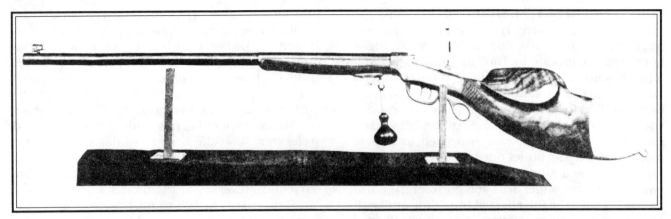

The Schoyen-Ballard was the kind of rifle Pope built barrels for. This one is a single-shot target piece in 32-40 caliber with double-set triggers, tang sight and palm ball for offhand shooting.

when asked if he did. He said a bore would never require lapping when made correctly in the first place! Groove depth was very shallow, about .004 inch. The narrow lands readily engraved the bullet, while aiding easy loading from the muzzle. They also marked the bullet sparingly, which was supposed to enhance accuracy through promoting bullet surface integrity. Choke bores were sometimes used. Bore diameter was gradually reduced toward the muzzle. In this manner, the shank of the bullet was ever kept in "perfect" relationship with the bore. Advantages of the Pope rifling system were enumerated as follows: better accuracy, less effort in muzzle-seating a projectile, central bullet seating, more precise obturation in the bore with the base of the projectile remaining perpendicular to the walls of the bore, and more efficient and effective burning of the powder charge. "Perfect workmanship" was Pope's byword. (Harry was not a humble man.)

Ability to load a Pope barrel either from muzzle or breech was also considered an attribute because the powder charge was not locked in to the capacity of the cartridge case. In fact, the powder charge could be widely varied. The wise shooter would experiment until he found the best charge, and that charge did not have to coincide with case capacity. More black powder than the case itself could hold was possible by seating an empty cartridge case in the chamber first, then dropping the powder charge downbore as with any muzzleloader. Therefore, the powder charge column could be taller than the cartridge case.

Shooters also learned to control ramrod

pressure for bullet seating uniformity. One simple method was to hold a finger over the top of the loading rod during the bullet-seating operation. The finger would be pinched between the end of the loading rod and the hand or finger doing the bullet seating. This way the shooter had a built-in gauge. He couldn't seat a bullet too firmly because his finger would be pinched hard. He could "get a feel" for seating the bullet with about the same pressure each time, which promoted uniformity and accuracy (a lower standard deviation from the mean velocity).

However, *safety measures were observed*. In relating the muzzleloading method of shooting the breechloading rifle, precautions may be left out today. Harvey Donaldson reminded shooters that Pope had a specific way of muzzleloading his breechloader. He wrote, "Pope taught me to place a dummy cartridge, with a plug in the mouth of the case (that stuck out a sixteenth of an inch) into the chamber of the rifle. Then the bullet was inserted into the false muzzle and pushed down *carefully*, until it touched the plug in the dummy case. If the starter rod is a little snug, one should withdraw the rod *slowly*, or it will suck the seated bullet part way up the barrel, and thus ruin that particular load. . . You then take out the dummy case and replace it with a loaded one with a greased wad on top. Also, to keep from shooting off the false muzzle, most shooters had it tied to the shooting bench with a short piece of heavy cord."

By using a false muzzle in loading the Schuetzen rifle, Pope promoted a nearly perfect alignment of the projectile in the bore. Harry credited Will Hays, whom he'd met at the Newark Schuetzenfest of 1888, with the idea of muzzle-loading a breechloader. The system of preparing a breechloading rifle as a muzzleloader had another advantage. No bullet crimp was necessary because the bullet was never seated in the cartridge case. It was introduced downbore via a loading rod. There was no problem with neck friction, because there was none. As we know, pressures can vary in accordance with the amount of force required to free the bullet from its place of rest in the neck of the cartridge case. No variation in neck friction existed with the muzzleloading method.

Incidentally, the case could be introduced to the chamber with or without its powder charge. One could install the powder charge in the case, slip the case into the chamber, and then close the action on it, or close the action on an empty case, with the powder charge dropped down the muzzle of the rifle.

BEYOND BARRELS AND BORES

Pope's impact did not stop with fine barrels or good loading methods, either. His universal mould was touted as excellent. There was also the Pope lead melting pot. Sharpe credits Pope with the design of a good front iron sight, too. "Did this author originate it? Positively no. The one and only Harry M. Pope, master rifle-barrel maker, was responsible. . . ." (*The Rifle In America*)

Pope also gained fame by working with ballistic student Dr. F.W. Mann. This was an interesting relationship, better understood by reading all of the Pope/Mann letters as presented in Kelver's book. There was respect. But discord was present. Disagreement between two experts on a given subject is as natural as spring water. Pope and Mann did not always see eye to eye. "You dulled in two places in your manuscript while criticizing my tests," said Mann in a November 1910 letter. "I have heard way down in Washington that you had the margins of my book all covered with criticism and that you were an authority." That was true. Scofield remarked that he saw the Mann book, and indeed it was riddled with Pope corrections. Pope was to say later that Mann was hard to work for, not because the good doctor was unfair—he paid promptly for the la-

bor—but because Mann did not always know what he wanted in the first place, and Pope had to tell him. There is cause to believe, after studying the particulars, that some of the Pope/Mann findings should be credited more to Pope than to Mann. An example is shooting close to planks in order to gauge bullet departure. While this plan is thought of as Mann-inspired, Pope may have originally devised it.

Pope was a writer, too. One article, "Offhand Rifle Shooting," appeared in the December 1941 issue of the *American Rifleman* magazine. It was instructional, bent on helping the shooter score better "off the hind legs." Although he was not prolific, he did pen a considerable amount in his time. Pope's image became well-known by readers of gun magazines, since oftentimes his photograph accompanied an article. But the barrelmaker was even better-known through the fiction of Lucian Cary, arms author and firearms editor of *True Magazine*. Cary used Harry as a model for the character, J.M. Pyne, and promoted shooting through his stories. The hero, Pyne (Pope), was a model of instruction, imparting shooting wisdom to the reader. Cary's fictional gunsmith was provided with a platform so he could talk about "old-time" marksmanship and winning shooting matches.

A typical Lucian Cary/J.M. Pyne article was run in the *Saturday Evening Post*, April 18, 1936. Called "Forty-Rod Gun," it began, "YOUNG BALLENTYNE didn't know, in the beginning, what J.M. Pyne meant by 'a forty-rod gun' or 'string measurement,' or 'the bud.' He had never heard of Enoch Worden or Adam Vondersmith. The plan he formed, as J.M. Pyne talked about the old days, was innocent. He did not mean to start a war." Vondersmith was the real-life George Schalk, another Schuetzen king, thinly clad in the veneer of Lucian Cary's fiction. While old rifles and methods of target shooting were not necessarily revived through the J.M. Pyne vehicle, precision shooting was sincerely promoted. Nobody interested in accuracy could walk away from the "old gunsmith" without a heightened desire to create smaller groups on the target.

Pope was recognized by the shooting industry as a revered authority and an important source of knowledge. He was so well thought of that J. Stevens Arms & Tool Company bought him out on April Fool's Day, 1901. Stevens retained Pope

The Harry Pope the shooting world knew was an uncompromising man of singular purpose. With but a single bulb acting as a beacon over his lathe, he devoted total concentration to every task. His workshop was cluttered beyond imagining and signs displaying such edicts as "No Delivery Promised, Take Your Work When Well Done or Take It Elsewhere" abounded.

to work on high-grade rifles only, continuing with what was to be called the "Stevens-Pope" rifling system. Phil Sharpe says in *The Rifle In America,* "The Stevens line of rifles has long included the services of that most famous barrel maker of all times, Harry M. Pope . . . Pope always made barrels right." If I am clear on the data, and that's always a question when dealing with no fewer than 30 resources on one subject, the guarantee continued with the Pope-Stevens barrel; however, not the same guarantee. The new promise was for 3.5 inches or better "across centers" at 200 yards for 10 shots with the 25-caliber barrel. The Stevens-Pope impact was real. Walker Greer, in a March 1930 *American Rifleman* said, "Some years ago Mr. Harry Pope was associated with the Stevens Arms Co. and while there made the gun which Mr. Sizer now has—a .32-40 of the de-luxe grade." The writer continued his praise, reporting that groups were made with the Pope rifle, at the bench, from 100 yards, and for 10 shots, not five, which could be covered with a dime . . . not center to center, but *covered* with a dime. Pope was noticed, too, by another faction of the industry when his name was attached to a particular Peters-22 rimfire load, the box marked: "50 .22 Stevens-Pope Armory Rim Fire Cartridges . . . Swaged Bullet."

Harry's eventful life wound down. The losses began to outweigh the gains. Pope had lost his parents as a child. He had lost his possessions in the San Francisco earthquake and fire of April 1906. He'd failed in his attempt to build a business in Los Angeles following the San Francisco debacle.

The 1920s were anything but roaring for Pope. Two years into Prohibition, he said he folded in a shooting match because he was too weak to hold the rifle steady—he'd had no lunch to eat that day because he could not afford to buy food. Harry wrote, ". . . I am dead broke, the price of two barrels would not help me at all. I owe almost everyone I have dealings with and my credit is exhausted. . . ." His clothing was so ragged he remained indoors much of the time, even forsaking the movies he loved so much. When a friend of Harry passed on, the widow gave her husband's clothes to Pope so he could go out again. A shotgun had blown up on him. His shop had been burglarized. And a fire, which did no appreciable mischief of itself, ended up costing 50 ruined barrels through water damage. Working alone was peaceful for Harry, but working solo had its trials as well, especially when old age befell him. In 1923, Pope cut a large muscle in his left wrist, after which he complained that he could no longer hold a rifle in the offhand shooting posture without pain. His Great Depression had begun early.

In 1927, an eye problem plagued him. He was way behind in his work. On March 5th of that year, he said, ". . . I do not fear death but only hope it won't be a lingering one. . . ." It appeared that Harry Pope, at age 66, believed the grains of sand in his life's hourglass were falling quickly to the lower bell. But he was wrong.

Pope lived another 23 years, and continued to build barrels and do custom work. In the 1940s he worked out of his own shop in Jersey City. An excerpt from a letter to Harvey Donaldson written November 27, 1971, by Pope's friend, Samuel

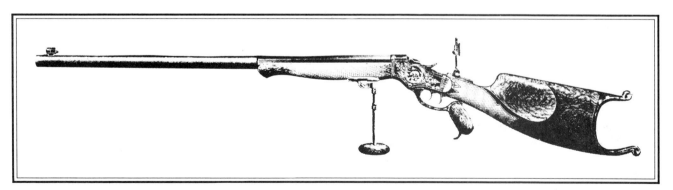

The Stevens "Ideal" Schuetzens were single-shot rifles of the Stevens-Pope era. In addition to extremely accurate barrels that served competitive shooters well, the arms have beautifully graceful lines. These higher grade models, discontinued about 1916, are today considered collector's items.

Clark, describes the barrelmaker's shop:

His location was at 18 Morris St. Jersey City and he was located on the third floor of a warehouse, down near the docks and looking right out at Staten Island and the Statue of Liberty, or possibly the Statue looked right in on Pope's shop, as Pope was the better example of Liberty, himself.

His shop measured about 50'×35'×15' and his bench ran along the south side where he had the best light all day from the windows which ran all the way across. The windows were never washed. There were only three hanging lights along that south side and they didn't give off much light. They were always on, but I don't think he depended on them much except when it was real dark and cloudy. I often heard him complain about how his work was slowed up by dull weather.

All the inside walls were of brick, painted a very dull brownish white. Maybe they were once white and the dust that coated everything had given them this color.

You got up to his place on the third floor by way of an outside stairway with galvanized outside walls painted red on the outside and unpainted on the inside. As you went up the stairs there were metal covered doors about 5'×7' that opened onto the third floor main warehouse. When you reached the third floor, up the stairway, you saw in black paint on the outside of his door, roughly displayed, "H.M. Pope."

If there was ever a speaking tube to the third floor, it was never in use while I was going there. I was informed by shooters at the Metropolitan R&R Club down near Mott St. in N.Y. where I was shooting that when I got over there, I should get in the street and yell "POPE" as loud as I could and he would stick his head out of the window and maybe tell me to come up. Later I learned from him that I could rap on his metal door as loud as I could with a silver dollar and he would come open up as he couldn't hear me if I yelled outside his door.

When you got in, walking was done in single file as all other space was occupied by boxes, crates, tools, machines, all belt driven with belts hanging from belt-ways above. There was an aisle from his entrance on the west wall straight across to the east wall and thence southerly for about 35' to his bench on the south wall and another aisle from the entrance door down the west wall. In the middle, between these aisles, were his drill presses, rifling tool and other belt-driven tools, but only one person at a time could get in there on account of boxes and whatnot piled all around. They were very effective in isolating Pope when he was using this machinery. No one was ever able to look over his shoulder.

His bench was really something with accumulation of years piled at least a foot deep, except for a small area in the middle of the bench which proclaimed that he worked there by reason of being free of dust. He said that it took too much time to arrange everything in an orderly manner, even if there was room for it. But he said that he well knew where everything was and I believe that he did after seeing him dig down through this accumulation and come up with some small tool.

Over on the east wall, back from the bench, was a pile of books on machine work and everything else that pertained to him, arranged in a sort of circle with an old torn leather chair in the middle. This was his office and letters were scattered around in piles on top of books. There was a box in there, too, which he used to write on, when he wrote, which was very seldom indeed. He brought his dinner with him and the "office" served also as an eating place.

He was never troubled to sweep out the place as there was no room to sweep. There were barrel blanks standing around here and there, but I never saw him rifling one but once. He said that he started by rifling on a foot lathe and I don't think that the rifling machine that he had there had advanced much except by the belt drive. As with everything else there were no frills to his machines, but I guess he made them work all right.

He was a lot of fun to talk with. He said his worst trouble came from people who came up there and asked a question and then

Harry Pope lived a long, interesting life during which he knew many of the shooting greats: Colonel Townsend Whelen, Adolph Niedner, Dr. F.W. Mann (with whom he worked), and Harvey Donaldson, to name a few. Here Pope is chatting with the granddaughter of George Schalk, another "artisan of accuracy."

asked him another before he had time to more than make a start at answering the first one.

There were mosquitos in his shop and so I had some fun with him. I knew that if one lit on your arm and stung you, if you would draw a deep breath, it would be impossible for the mosquito to withdraw his stinger. So when one of them lit on my arm as I stood beside Pope at his bench, I drew a deep breath and then began to stroke the mosquito with my finger lightly. Pope didn't turn his head, but he watched me closely out of the corner of his eye as I soothed the insect. When I held my breath as long as I could, I exhaled and let the mosquito go, remarking to Pope that his mosquitos were indeed a friendly lot. He was beside himself to know how this had been done and although he knew that there was a trick to it, I never let on, merely stating that I "had a way with mosquitos."

Those were great days and I wouldn't have missed them for anything in the world. . . .

Right before Pope's 80th birthday, the *American Rifleman* staff and the National Rifle Association praised Harry for his life's achievements. C.B. Lister, then Secretary-Treasurer of the NRA, wrote an open tribute to the great barrelmaker. In a letter dated July 15, 1941, Lister said, "Dear Harry, At the Meeting of the Executive Committee of the National Rifle Association, held on Monday, July 7th, here in Washington, a motion was passed directing me, as the Secretary of the Association, to extend our sincere personal and official congratulations to you on this, your eightieth birthday." On July 14th, the Metropolitan Rifle League membership drew a collection of $270.00, which was given to Pope as a birthday present.

Pope lived until October 11, 1950—almost nine decades. His days were harried, but long and interesting. He did what he wanted to do. He made barrels. He made the best barrels. And that's all he ever asked of life.

23

DR. LOU PALMISANO: CREATOR OF THE 22 PPC

Juliet Theodoro and John Joseph Palmisano were born in the United States of Italian immigrants, all of whom worked in the silk dye shops. This was in Paterson, New Jersey, known in those days as the ''Silk City of the World.'' Juliet's family in Italy was prominent in the literary arts. John's family members were mainly husbandmen. John was a mechanic by trade, employed by the Public Service Autobus Works in New Jersey, where he went from helper to mechanic to foreman. Following World War II, with the help of his son, Louis, who had been born on October 15, 1930, John built a repair and gas station, which he ran for the rest of his life. Mr. Palmisano's mechanical genius resulted in several automotive inventions. Lou's first jobs were associated with the service station, where his own inventive talents were nurtured.

The senior Palmisano noted with interest, but not pleasure, his son's gift for mechanics. When he discovered that Lou was working with fervor on automobiles, including the building of stock cars, he immediately confined the lad to the grease pit. He had other plans for his two sons, which did not include automotive mechanics as a trade for Lou. ''No mechanical work in this shop for you,'' John Palmisano told his boy, a rule he enforced. John's and Juliet's parents, being dye-shop workers, were unable to further their children's educations.

John Palmisano Sr. had made up his mind that his sons, Lou and younger brother John, would have educational opportunities. He greatly admired the Mayo brothers and Clarence Darrow. His dream was to have a doctor and a lawyer for sons, which is precisely what transpired. Meanwhile, both boys were obliged to learn to play musical instruments. Lou studied the accordion from a book written by the famous American accordionist, Charlie Magnanti. ''While the other boys were out playing ball, I had to practice the accordion for an hour and a half after school,'' said Lou. In the mid-1970s, Lou met Magnanti at a benchrest match. When he found out who the man was he approached him saying, ''I want you to know that you were the cause of much anguish in my youth.'' After explaining, both men had a good laugh.

Lou Palmisano's early education was in Paterson Public School No. 18, followed by Eastside High School, where he played football for four years. Then came Seton Hall University where Lou earned a B.S. degree. ''I met a Chinese boy at Seton,'' said Lou. ''He spoke little English. His father was a general in the Chinese Army; his brother an Admiral in the Chinese Navy.'' Lou helped the lad by placing carbon under his note-paper and explaining the notes. ''I later got an invitation to attend medical school at the University of Hong Kong,'' Lou said. ''Of course, I didn't, but my old classmate and I are still friends.''

Lou decided on medical school in Bologna,

Dr. Lou Palmisano, co-inventor of the 22 PPC USA and 6mm PPC USA cartridges. As a youngster, he learned shooting accuracy during woodchuck hunts with his father. Here, with 22 PPC Sako rifle, he pursues prairie dogs.

Italy (noted for producing fine surgeons), where he studied for five years. He returned to America, did a rotating internship at Barnert Memorial Hospital in Paterson, followed by further surgical training at East Orange Veterans Hospital. In his career as a vascular surgeon, he worked with many innovative practices and tools, including an instrument that sought and extracted clots from within the heart. Some of Lou's surgical instruments are still known by his name. Dr. Palmisano serves today as a surgical consultant. But he also devotes a significant portion of his life to the furtherance of precision shooting.

Lou harbored an early interest in shooting and hunting. His father had two firearms, a rifle and a shotgun, which stood in his parent's closet, with ammunition placed on a high shelf. Lou would dress in his father's traditional green hunting outfit with bandoleer of red shotgun shells, pretending that he was preparing for a hunt. His father encouraged Lou's early interest in firearms by teaching the youngster how to clean guns. "The fascination began right there," Lou reminisces, "in the cleaning of that shotgun and rifle." Lou hunted rabbits, pheasants and deer as

well as black bear in New Jersey—always with his father.

But it was woodchuck shooting that fascinated the young rifleman. Placing the bullet on target at long range demanded precision. And Lou was deeply interested in precision. Later, a back injury temporarily curtailed hunting, but promoted an interest in target shooting. Woodchucking also continued. In fact, Lou used a version of the PPC on woodchucks long before the cartridge entered the ranks of benchresting. Although he was a benchshooter early on, building his own 300-yard shooting range, it is interesting to note that with all he has accomplished in precision shooting, Lou did not compete with a rifle until 1974. He became involved in competitive benchrest shooting through Skip Gorden. Though Lou had already been working on several accuracy cartridges, he had no intention of competing with these rounds. He wanted to *study* accuracy.

Roy Vail of Warwick, New York, master engraver and gunsmith, had been building firearms of note, some of them for dignitaries, such as the Shah of Iran and President Eisenhower. Vail did most of Lou's early chambering of experimental

The 22 PPC USA (center), Palmisano's co-invention with Ferris Pindell. After testing the PPC Varminters made by Sako, the NRA staff said,"The 6mm and .22 PPC ammunition and rifles received for testing proved capable of accuracy levels not previously encountered in shooting tests of factory ammunition/rifle combinations."

wildcat cartridges. Among Lou's wildcat ideas were the now famous 22 PPC and 6mm PPC cartridges, first built on 220 Swift brass. Between a busy surgical career, Lou found time, or, more accurately stated, he *made* time for testing firearms. He transferred his medical skills to the world of shooting, ever looking for more precise machinery and methods. Lou aligned himself with many modern scientists of shooting, including the late Dan Pawlak of Pyrodex fame. Pawlak did considerable testing of the early PPC cartridges, as well as several earlier accuracy rounds that Lou designed. Phil Davis, ballistician and staff member of the NRA, also worked with Lou in testing concepts and cartridges.

Lou's association with Ferris Pindell in 1973, however, led to the finalization of the PPC cartridge and its name, Pindell Palmisano Cartridge, PPC. "Ferris Pindell is the Michelangelo of Steel," says Lou. "He is an honest man who believes in fully testing anything which bears his name and reputation." The two men got along well, and are still best friends because of a mutual interest in giving the shooting world the most precise *tested* instruments and cartridges possible.

Without a doubt, the PPC cartridges have brought the most fame to this inventive experimenter. The PPC round was born of a desire to gain ground on that elusive one-hole group. Having worked with Swift brass, Palmisano began taking a look at a cartridge case that would require less alteration to meet precision-shooting specifications. The ideal seemed to be embodied in a little foreigner, the 220 Russian. Lou dreamed of a cartridge that would surpass the 222 Remington, 222½ benchrest wildcat, 219 Donaldson Wasp, 6×47 and all others for accuracy.

He began working with the 220 Russian, an offshoot of the military 7.62×39mm cartridge. The new case would embody the tenets of accuracy: short, squat design, modest capacity, straight walls. The finished product has a case length of 1.50 inches, body slope of only .010-inches from base to shoulder, and a shoulder angle of 30 degrees (supposedly the ideal angle for proper interior chamber shape). Head size is, of course, .445-inches, and the flashhole, which Lou insisted be drilled, not punched, is .061–.062 inches diameter, as opposed to the more prevalent .081–.082 size.

"I'm not a famous shooter," Lou protested when elected to accompany the other greats in this book. I retorted that anyone instrumental in developing the most accurate cartridge in the world was indeed worthy of sharing company with the other noteworthy shooters honored between the covers of this text. Nobody has been able to compile an accurate figure on how many matches the PPCs have won. In the past decade, however, 179 IBS (International Benchrest Shooters) records have been broken. Of these, 149 fell to a PPC. The conservative NRA staff pronounced, after testing the PPC Sako Varminters, "The 6mm and .22 PPC ammunition and rifles received for testing proved capable of accuracy levels not previously encountered in shooting tests of factory ammunition/rifle combinations."

What the shooting world may not know is the fact that Palmisano has been working with other cartridges and bullet designs. I had the pleasure of shooting the tightest group of my life with a 300-meter rifle that belongs to Dr. Lou. The group was accomplished with the 6mm 105-grain VLD (Very Low Drag) bullet. Five bullet holes crowded into a shade over one-half inch center to center—at 300 yards. Bench-type rifle or not, that's exciting. Perhaps I could never repeat that group, not being a benchrest expert. But one thing is sure: without the precision elements built into the cartridge, the bullet, the load and the rifle, even good luck couldn't have produced that sort of bullet clustering at 300 yards.

Dr. Palmisano's wife and two daughters do not partake of the shooting world, but his son David, even as a boy, followed his father into the field, just as Lou had followed his father before him. Lou taught David the fine art of long-range precision shooting. David began shooting the PPC cartridge on woodchucks. Meanwhile, Lou made an initial impression on benchrest shooters by winning the 1975 Super Shoot (100 yard phase) with a PPC. But people were not altogether impressed. After all, Palmisano was a newcomer. His winning group could have been more luck than skill, or impetus of cartridge and rifle.

The next year something quite significant happened, though. David Palmisano, at age 14, won the 1976 200-yard IBS (International Benchrest Shooters) Championship in Johnstown, New York, shooting a PPC. David's shooting experience in the woodchuck fields paid off. He learned to dope wind and cope with mirage. Now the

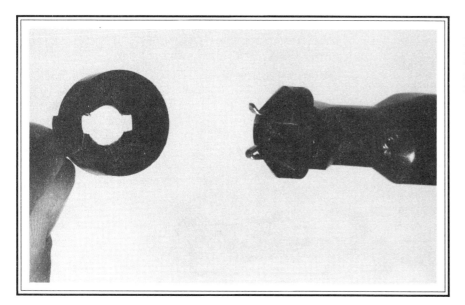

Dr. Palmisano was instrumental in introducing to the shooting public the PPC insert, which improves the internal relationship between bolt and receiver.

benchresters took notice. After all, the PPC had won again. It was to win again many times over, as all were soon to find out.

No matter how many titles fell, though, manufacturers did not take an interest in producing rifles or factory ammunition for the PPC. Lou calls it the NIH Syndrome, "Not Invented Here." He says, "I'm a little sad about that. The cartridges proved themselves over and over again, and yet I couldn't get an American company to produce either a rifle chambered for the PPC cartridge, or PPC ammunition." In 1988, a rifle and ammunition were factory-built—but not in America. It was Finland. The Sako company capitulated, making a Sako Varminter single-shot rifle in 22 PPC USA and 6mm PPC USA, as well as a repeater in the latter caliber. Sako also tooled up to make finished PPC ammunition and reloader's brass, which are now available in America. Consider the impact—the PPC rounds have been deemed the most accurate in the world. Lou's series of PPC cartridges include several designs that have not been seen by the public as yet, a couple which may prove to be good long-range hunting cartridges. The PPCs are an affirmation and furtherance of basic cartridge accuracy precepts, Lou feels.

There were other innovations. "I have always looked for a better way to do something," said Lou. "I start with existing ideas, of course. Only Leonardo da Vinci seemed to have gotten his ideas from out there somewhere." Years ago, Lou Palmisano taped mercury-filled tubes to a target bow to dampen its vibrations. He developed a long loading tube for blackpowder rifles to introduce all of the powder charge into the breech area. He found that certain burn ointments made good blackpowder patch lubes. He used soft clarinet brushes to clean rifle chambers. And he found that Flitz was a fine bore cleaner for removal of lead and copper fouling if followed by Shooter's Choice or similar agent to remove Flitz residue.

Dr. Palmisano was also awarded a couple of patents. With Orlin Gilkerson, Lou holds a patent on the PPC Locking Lug Insert, a device that ensures close chamber tolerances in a target rifle. With Charles Poff, Lou holds a patent on the 45-degree locking-lug bolt, which has undergone stringent tests. In one abusive trial, the entire barrel sheared away from the action proper, yet the bolt itself was not sprung. The locking lugs were intact. The 22-rimfire bolt with its 6 o'clock firing pin is a Poff-Palmisano patent. It has front locking lugs and a very fast lock time. A 22-rimfire target rifle made up on this action proved extremely accurate. Palmisano's "22 Rimfire Project" continues, the goal to produce the most accurate 22-rimfire ammunition in the world. As Lou says of this ammunition, "The 22-rimfire lead-bullet problem is a science unto itself, but I'm almost there. In another 20 years of study, I

One of the best benchrest shooters in the country, Dr. Palmisano won the 1975 Super Shoot (100-yard phase) with a PPC. He has also served as advisor to the Finnish Benchrest and Italian Benchrest clubs.

might understand the 22 Long Rifle cartridge.'' He laments the fact that the Soviet Union, not the United States, makes the most accurate 22-rimfire match ammunition in the world.

PROMOTER OF WORLD SHOOTING

Palmisano has worked with several others who are intent on improving shooting. One person is Bill Davis of Tioga Engineering. The Davis VLD (Very Low Drag) bullet is now a pet project of Lou's. VLD bullets (I have tested these in 6mm and 30 caliber) retain velocity remarkably. In one shooting demonstration, a 7mm Remington Magnum firing a 162-grain BT at about 3200 feet-per-second muzzle velocity was plied against a 240 Weatherby shooting a 105-grain VLD bullet at the same muzzle velocity. In a strong crosswind, the lighter bullet drifted significantly less than the heavier one starting at the same velocity. The bullet was used in one international match. "It's the first time I know of,'' Lou said, "where the Russians wanted to trade ammo, after our 300-

meter rifles beat their 300-meter rifles.'' Aligning himself with others interested in the furtherance of precision shooting, and supporting their studies, is typical of Lou Palmisano.

There is another side to this shooter that is perhaps as important as his inventive nature and that is his support of American shooting. "Now is the time,'' says Palmisano, "that the NRA must buy as many outdoor ranges as possible. You read every month of new places to shoot, but these are short-distance indoor ranges. When I was a boy I could bicycle to outdoor ranges near Paterson, New Jersey. Last week I drove for three hours to reach a good 300-yard range.'' If Lou has a crusade, it is to further shooting in America. "We have to show sport shooting on television. The only shooting young people see on television today is violence,'' Palmisano regrets. But to say that Lou is interested only in American shooting would be inaccurate. He contributed to a shooting range in Finland, and was in part responsible for a change in Italian law that forbade benchrest marksmanship. The law had been written in the days of Mussolini, and in effect stated that a rifle fired from a bench constituted a "fixed position," which was legal only for the military. Now Italian shooters are allowed to use a bench for sport-shooting, and an Italian Benchrest Club has been started.

Lou has been instrumental in offering many trophies and incentives to the shooting public, including the handsome Roy Vail Trophy, a 26-inch cup. Ten thousand dollars in trophies "to encourage women and men to continue the shooting game so that we shall remain a nation of riflemen (and women)" has been offered. The Juliet Palmisano Bronze Trophy—"Miss Liberty"—for shooting excellence (for women only) with prize money is a Lou Palmisano donation. A Bronze Palmisano Olympic Trophy is another. The Palmisano Trophy of Finland is one more. He is a sponsor of the Finnish Benchrest Club. A new range, the "John J. Palmisano Memorial Shooting Range" in Pennsylvania has already been enjoyed by many shooters. Not to embarrass the man, but his generosity in aiding shooters is becoming legendary.

Dr. Palmisano has been a member of the Executive Committee for the ISDS, a technical advisor for the United States Shooting Team, an ad-

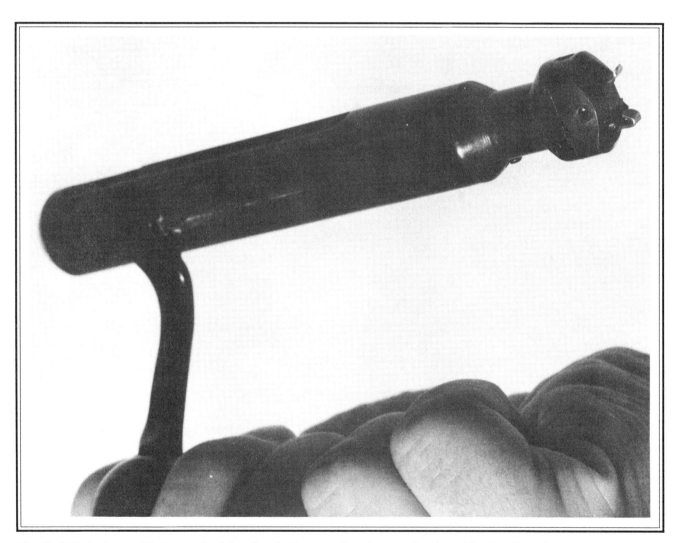

The Poff-Palmisano 45-degree locking-lug bolt is another innovation in which Dr. Palmisano participated. The resulting action is so strong that in one test the barrel blew away from the receiver, even though the bolt was not set back.

visor to the Finnish Benchrest Club and the Italian Benchrest Club, a member of the Board of Directors for the International Shooters Development Fund, a Lifetime Honorary Member of the Shooting Sports Research Council, and more. Gary L. Anderson, Executive Director of General Operations for the NRA, has said of Lou, "Dr. Louis Palmisano has been the leader in trying to apply America's unparalleled benchrest/accuracy technology to the challenge of producing the finest possible equipment for the U.S. Shooting Team."

Dr. Lou Palmisano's shooting interest has provided us with what has to be called the most accurate cartridge in the world. But his current crusade is for improved shooting conditions in America. "We need an educational program to teach the public the truth about shooting," he says. "I am especially worried about outdoor target shooting in America. Will there be ranges, especially in the East, where a shooter can try his skill at 200 or 300 yards?" He also hopes for "more shooters in the gun business," dedicated marksmen who wish to make shooting their "life's work." He says, "Our nation deserves the very best in firearms and ammunition."

Palmisano has been accused of being a flag-waver. His reply: "You are right. I am a flag waver. What better flag is there to wave than an American flag?"

24

GEORGE RUSHBY: AFRICAN ADVENTURER

A search for adventure was George Rushby's youthful fantasy, a dream born in his childhood and nurtured early into reality. Rushby was almost born too late to fulfill his destiny. Many modern American outdoorsmen wish for a plains filled with bison, mountains teeming with bighorn sheep, and unlimited opportunities to explore game lands untouched by civilization—but it is too late. Our land is in the grip of "progress." And progress calls for the raising of wheat—not bison, super highways—not game trails, and a place for people—not wild animals—to prosper.

Rushby almost missed his calling. His days in Africa were preceded by Oswell, Baker, Bell, Selous and many others. Africa was changing, but the huge continent resisted the hammer-blows of industry and the inroads of human population that demanded towns, shopping centers and indoor plumbing. That is why Rushby found adventure into the 1950s, including the hunting of what the *Guinness Book of Records* called the most devastating rein of marauding lions in the history of Africa. It was an episode that brought with it the strange and eerie practices of lycanthropy, animalism and cannabalism, as well as over a thousand human deaths by the man-eaters. While Rushby is remembered for hunting the deadly killer lions of the Njombe District, he is also called the last of the professional ivory hunters.

Rushby was born on February 28, 1900, in Nottingham, England, but his parents moved to Eastwood when George was a baby. The lad was one and one-half years old when his father died. His mother remarried a man who terrorized young Rushby. "I grew up with a stepfather, a drunken and bullying bastard," said George. His clouded youth had one sunny spot: Gypsies camped on his stepfather's land and took a liking to the boy. "The women used to carry me about slung in a cloth on their backs," said George. The men were "First class. They taught me to box." The youngster wanted to learn fighting so that "I could handle my stepfather when I grew up." But the abusive stepfather denied George that opportunity. The man sang in bars for drinks, and the alcohol caught up with him, killing him before Rushby could take his revenge.

The gypsies taught George how to hunt. He loved hunting from the first time he stepped into the field. The keen edge of his hunting desire was honed by "a few books my father left me. There was a three-volume work, *Worlds of Adventure*, with many stories about Africa, and there were Selous's great hunting books. I almost read the print off their pages. I never wanted to be an engine driver or anything like that. I just wanted to come to Africa to hunt."

Africa was in the grip of the post-war depression of 1921 when George immigrated from England "in search of adventure." Jobs were few. George possessed a basic education. He was familiar with electrical engineering from a job ex-

George Rushby—one of the greatest African lion hunters of all time. (from a line drawing in *The Hunter Is Death*, by T.V. Bulpin)

perience with Oakes & Co. after graduation from school. But there was no work for him in Durban, where he landed. He ate in a Salvation Army soup kitchen and slept on Hill 60 at the beach with other out-of-work men. ''Wanted, Electrical Mechanic.'' The man was nailing the sign up at Irvin, Maule & Mansergh garage as George walked by. He got the job. But there was no adventure in it. A notice for work in the Portuguese port of Lourenco Marques caught his eye. He moved on, landed that job, too, but no adventure there, either. In July of 1921, he moved on again and by August, Rushby was in Beira. Conditions there were squalid, but hunting opportunities close. George's eager hand reached out for the hunting life. Like Buffalo Bill, Rushby would begin his career as a meat-hunter for railway workers.

He had one problem, though: no rifle. An opportunity to work as a meat-hunter went begging for lack of a firearm. Finally, George located a fellow willing to make a trade—an old, battered 303 with ammo for some clothing and cash. George had his rifle. He worked the 303 over until it was fully serviceable, and thus began his adventure. After only 10 days, he found that working for his employer was impossible. The man was demanding, and cash had to be extricated from him like prying an oyster open for its pearl. He quit. He got his money, and something else—a few of his boss's trackers.

George decided to hunt on his own. He was keen for it, but he lacked experience. The largest game he had fired on prior to Africa was a rabbit. Rushby's first encounter was humorous. He tried a shot at an animal he thought was lying down. But the wart hog was standing up. The shot was a clean miss. The animal, not knowing where the shot came from, dashed toward George, who thought he was being charged. The wart hog swerved and disappeared in the bush. George's trackers burst into laughter. Rushby could only laugh with them.

His next hunt was more auspicious. Rushby got a redbuck, one of the finest-eating game animals of the Dark Continent. He was happy and so were his trackers. George hunted for the railway workers for several months. Next, he worked for the Senna Sugar Estate, again as a provider of meat for workers. He was now 22 years old. Satisfied with the Senna arrangement, he decided to stay for a long while, and he may have, except

for one thing—elephants. They fascinated George. They would, the young man announced, comprise his life interest. Rushby decided what many other professional hunters of Africa concluded, that the elephant is the most dangerous big game on that continent. He would be an ivory hunter. They were still in Africa at the time, although the life was waning. The elephant was too populous in many regions and black villagers as well as government officials and tribal leaders wanted them thinned out. Plus, the meat was of value and the ivory was precious.

George did well with the Senna Sugar Estate, but after four months the urge to hunt on his own overcame the desire to make steady money. He had become a good shot, sparing no ammunition in his practice. He was rugged, using only a canvas shelter as he traveled about the wilds. Then something happened. Rushby was asleep beneath his canvas lean-to. He heard a noise, woke up. By the light of the bright stars, he saw a man armed with a speer, a menacing figure. George's practice in fast rifle-handling was put to the test. He whirled the rifle barrel around, shot and killed the intruder.

Who was he? No one knew. Rushby's men decided that the spear-holder must have been a robber. But George would have to explain the killing to the Portuguese officials, a task he did not wish to do. The dead man was buried and George vacated the area on the good advice of older hunters who knew that ''there would be punishment enough for even a cold-blooded murderer,'' which is exactly what the spearman represented.

Far from his last hunting grounds, George secured a permit to shoot ''as many elephants as he liked,'' for the animals were running rampant through native villages, destroying crops and homes. ''They simply walked through villages, pulled the grain bins off their stilts, tore them to pieces to steal the contents, and did very much as they pleased in the fields and banana groves. The damage was very considerable.'' George wanted adventure. He would get it hunting elephants. The first charge came when a tuskless bull decided to thrash the two-legged intruder. George fired. But the shot did not drop the pachyderm. Rushby dashed for cover, kneeling in the bush. The elephant did not see him. He towered so close that his chest wound spilled crimson droplets over the man. George could not fire.

Although Rushby missed the heyday of African ivory hunting, he certainly crammed in enough elephant adventures in one lifetime for any two men.

Should the bullet drop the jumbo, the giant animal would collapse on top of him, crushing the life from his body. The elephant turned. George finished him.

So this was elephant hunting.

While the elephants in the district were many and dangerous, they did not carry good ivory. Next stop: Tanganyika. Here there would be profit. Ivory was selling at 20 shillings a pound on the world market. The next encounter brought tragedy, however. Rushby had a light rifle. The elephant came straight at George. He had to shoot. His bullet was well-aimed, but too small to drop the mammal on the spot. The bull caught one of the trackers. "The animal simply crushed the man into the ground and raced on for about forty yards before he fell dead with a tremendous crashing of grass." There was no way to stop him. "The tracker had been killed instantly." Rushby had learned a lesson at the expense of a human life; he grieved over it. He also vowed never again to use a light rifle for ivory hunting. Part of his profits were spent to secure a big-bore rifle. The next time he took to the field in pursuit of jumbo, he would be carrying a heavy double-barreled arm.

Although ivory hunting remained Rushby's life goal, the trade had its ups and downs. George tried gold mining for a while. Then he went back to hunting jumbos. However, when he could not secure the proper licenses, he joined the ranks of Pondoro Taylor in pursuit of ivory without proper governmental approval. In short, he became a poacher. There was a new element in the hunting now. Not only did Rushby have to find and dispatch his elephants while offering the best possible protection for his men; he also had to dodge the authorities. It was worth the bother, he felt, in adventure and in pounds sterling. George was socking away a tidy bit of cash for his efforts. But you pay when you hunt elephants. And the next confrontation would be of the bone-crushing kind.

Rushby had moved into a forested region for his ivory-gathering. Further permits had been issued, and he was once again hunting with the blessings of those in power. One day he brought himself carefully within range of a good bull carrying heavy teeth. George delivered a bullet to the heart. But you don't stop an elephant with one heart shot, even with a heavy bullet from a big-bore rifle. The bull quickly located the source of his problems and charged headlong after Rushby. Let no one tell you that a jumbo is slow on his feet. He's no cheetah, but he can *move*. Too quick for the hunter, the beast was on Rushby with its trunk wrapped around the man's thigh and a tusk pressed against his chest. Somehow, Rushby clung to his rifle. Good thing. The pressure of the tusk dented a groove into the wooden stock, a crushing force that would have otherwise split the man's chest open. It was time for George to die. However, the keeper of life's clock moved the second hand backward. An elephant could drop its victim to the earth, trampling the body lifeless. But this pachyderm flipped Rushby through the air like a spout of water over his hindmost parts—without further attack.

Rushby struck the animal's rump and bounced from it, rolling into the swamp. A desire to run was overcome by a silent pledge to finish the job. The hunter's ammunition had been flung from his jacket. Rushby searched for a cartridge in the muck of the swamp. He found three that had been caught in the thick foliage. George flipped his rifle open. The bores were clear of mud. He loaded the double gun and proceeded to run after the elephant. He didn't have to go far, for the elephant appeared to be standing 30 yards away. It was an illusion. The beast had dropped dead. The appearance of life came from the fact that the elephant had fallen on high ground and seemed to be standing up, its ears propped forward, suggesting a charge.

Rushby had three cracked ribs, bruises and scratches. He lay on the ground as his men removed the tusks of the bull. Word traveled through the "bush telegraph" that the hunter had been killed. Ivory hunting as a way of life was coming to a close. By 1927 the profession was breathing its last gasp. But adventure for George Rushby was not over. He would take a little time out to return to England, mainly for a nose job. George, who had worked for a time as a bouncer, had had his nose flattened. He wanted it repaired and now he could afford it. Off to England he went.

In London, he met a lady from Cape Town. Eileen Graham, who had been in England to study music, said she knew of a pretty young woman who might like George. And he would surely like her. Following the lead, George met Eleanor Dunbar Leslie. They hit it off. "She was twenty-four with auburn hair, a pretty face, and a neatly balanced figure." George was handsome again, with his new nose. Within fewer than 48 hours, George decided that Eleanor was for him. Eleanor agreed that George was for her. At the protest of the young lady's father, who wasn't sure that an ivory hunter was exactly the right mate for his school teacher daughter, the two were wed.

On January 1, 1931, the couple found themselves on a farm in Tanganyika. They felt that growing coffee made more sense than for Rushby to chase after what little ivory hunting remained. Eleanor loved the farm, but reluctantly returned home to Cape Town to have their first child, Ann. Little George followed on April 29, 1933. Coffee prices were down. George had to do something else. He became a professional hunter, a job he did not care for, especially in light of early experiences with rich and spoiled clients who came to Africa with a laundry list of species they wished to take, rather than a desire to experience the glory of the land. Besides, Rushby was not keen about having to concede to the wishes of clients, while at the same time staying in command of the safari.

At one point, a leopard was wounded. It vanished into thick foliage and had to be followed. The animal bolted from its lair like a clawed missile launched by a powerful spring. The object of its attack was one of the trackers. When a leopard leaps on you, it buries a forepaw behind each shoulder and with its powerful back legs rakes the life from your body. "The unfortunate tracker was completely disemboweled." That disaster was attributable to poor marksmanship. Lack of

shooting ability is always a negative factor in hunting. In Africa, poor shooting costs lives. The client's lack of talent with his rifle brought death to a man. Rushby had to go on with the safari as best he could. After two months, his contract was fulfilled. He wanted no more of the "white hunter" game. And so he returned to the plantation. But coffee prices did not escalate. George had to find other employment.

In 1936 following young Ann's birthday on February 8, Rushby moved on again. Ann was not doing well. The area did not agree with her health. The doctor said she would be better off in Cape Town. For a time, George worked the gold fields. Finally, the family had to separate. Ann and young George would be better off out of the wilderness for a while. The while turned out to be eight years. Rushby did not see his children

George Rushby experienced his share of close encounters with many big game animals, including man-eating lions and this fellow, the leopard.

once in that span of time, although Eleanor returned again and again to be with him. The family was temporarily fragmented. From mining gold to "mining" guano, Rushby moved again to secure a living. Eventually, there would be four children. And eventually, the family would reunite. This union was made possible by a new job. George took on a position as forester for the government.

Not surprisingly, Rushby took the first opportunity to leave off with the forester work. He became a game ranger at 360 pounds per annum. That was a fraction of his earnings as an ivory hunter, but it was steady money and he liked the work. He had no way of knowing that this job would lead to the greatest adventure of his life and the fulfillment of his youthful dreams.

SAVIOR OF THE NGOMBE DISTRICT

Rushby would go down in history as the savior of people besieged by man-eating lions of the Ngombe District. It was an odd affair. The maulings went on for some time without relief, while superstitions pervaded the issue. Rushby experienced little military duty in World War II because he was fighting a war against the man-eaters, and against the supernatural beliefs that prevented the lions from being dispatched.

There were men who indirectly made a profit from the killings. These witch doctors were given even more credence when the lions got away with their human predation, because they could be considered a form of lycanthropy. The werewolf story is an ancient one, as are other forms of the superstitious tale, in which humans take animal forms other than the wolf. The man-eaters were no doubt "werelions," just as there were "werehyenas." A hyena cult existed in the region of the Mbugwe people. A ranger reportedly killed a hyena, finding the dead animal to be wearing clothing. It must be a werehyena, the natives believed. Black magic was at work. Barbarous murders, not the work of lions, frequently occurred. These were associated with one or more of the cults functioning in the region. The "Watu-Simba," or lion men, were a strong force, with nefarious activities and barbaric cruelty continuing for years.

In 1920 an officer in the district was called in to investigate a staggering 200 killings, murders said to be the work of the lion men. Meanwhile, the witch doctors were having a field day.

They were not unlike certain modern religionists who take advantage of human frailty. The dirty work of the man-eating lions was camouflaged by the more evil deeds of humans, who were not killing for food, but for profit. Something had to be done about it. And a game ranger would have to do it.

The lions that would become known as the man-eaters of the Njombe District began their reign of terror around 1932. That year, solid reports of maulings formed a distinct geographical pattern. The officials involved surmised that the killings began with a lioness that had been injured in such a way that she could not hunt proper fare. She turned to eating humans, and trained her cubs to do the same. As she mated again and again, she trained new broods of young to become man-eaters. It was speculation, of course, but no better theory evolved. Furthermore, the police investigating these maulings agreed that they were the work of real lions, not werelions or lion men. The killer was genuine, with weapons of fang and claw. The corpses were typically devoid of flesh, the meat literally licked from the bone with rasplike tongues. In spite of armed men in the region, not one lion was killed. They seemed charmed. But the total area used by the marauding cats comprised 1500 square miles, a large realm difficult to survey.

From 1932 through 1940, the lions did their work with systematic zeal, although no specific records of victims was kept. People didn't want to talk about it. As Peter Hathaway Capstick pointed out in his book, *Man-eaters* (Petersen Publishing Co., 1981), people were so terrified "that should a parent lose a child during the night to one of the man-eaters, neither mother nor father would dream of mentioning the fact to even a close friend for fear that the simple invocation of the man-eaters by name would suffice to place the speaker next on the list." Capstick noted that George Rushby had a terrible problem on his hands, not only because of the man-eaters themselves, but also because of the witchcraft and lycanthrophy attending the killings. Gaining information was difficult, as was compiling leads, or tracing the deadly lions as they did their dirty work. People just didn't want to talk about it.

George did not even see a lion. The animals worked at night. They might jump upon the thatched roof of a native hut, their heavy weight bringing them down into the domicile. The occupants of the little dwelling were at their mercy. Then George was called away from lion hunting to the duty of locust control, not returning to Ngombe District until January of 1946. At that point, George put six trusted scouts on the job. Traps were set. Various baits were used, including goats. How many killer lions were there? Capstick says there may have been 22. Yet none was dispatched.

The lions attacked singly. They attacked in groups. When they did the latter, they might scatter afterwards so there was no chance of following a large number of tracks. There was no definite pattern. Tracking failed (and the black tracker of Africa is a master at his craft). Three weeks of hunting brought nil results. George's failure was regarded by some as proof that the beasts were supernatural.

Rusbhy instituted an information network. Using truck drivers and others, reports were ushered to the hunter in an attempt to discover the lions' whereabouts. They were strictly man-eaters. They did not bother the livestock; they went straight for the human target. The cattle became used to the man-eaters' habits, not stampeding or even stirring when the felines came to do their grim work. A cat might attack *through* a herd of

George Rushby (right) poses with his wife Eleanor and T.V. Bulpin who wrote *The Hunter Is Death*, a fine biography about Rushby and his adventures.

domestic animals in order to reach a herd boy, snatching the lad down from the back of his mount, while placing no claw in the cow that the boy rode. The cats killed wild pigs, which they seldom ate. Rushby worked his mind for the solution to this problem.

Then a truck driver brought word: in the night the village of Mambego had been devastated by man-eaters. Rushby moved immediately. Most of the villagers had fled the scene. A little girl answered the hunter's request to enter the village. Her mother and father were gone. The father fled; the mother had been eaten by the attacking lions, a group of four animals.

The hunter knew the killer cats would not return, but he had to watch the village that night anyway, just in case. In the morning, he began a tracking mission with one scout and a few village men who had returned in the morning. They cut fresh lion sign three hours later in thorn bush vegetation. It was terribly hot. George carried a comparatively lightweight double-barrel rifle chambered for the 9.3mm German Magnum cartridge. Suddenly, the party burst upon a scene of four lions standing in a clearing. Rushby placed his sights on one and fired. The animal was hit, but not fatally. He shot her again. Then twice more. He had to prove that this was an animal, not a devil. The tribesmen waited for the beast to transform into a human. It did not. George had the word spread far and wide that one of the man-eaters had been dropped—and it was no werelion. Almost immediately, word reached Rusbhy that the lions had attacked another village. He sped to the site.

Rushby had guessed their were nine killer cats. Now he knew there were more. But success continued, and the native people began to fight back. A young herdsman speared and killed a lion. Although it was not one of the man-eaters, the act raised the spirits of the tribesmen. Eventually, nine lions were down. George had a close call with a big male, but he froze as he came upon the animal at only five yards. Later, he would drop the same lion, one of the few trophies of his career. The stranglehold of the man-eaters was loosening.

But in March and April of 1947, 24 people were killed. Evidence pointed to "man"-lions in some instances. Two tribesmen who were reputed to be killers were found to be on drugs. They were in the employ of witch doctors. They dressed in lion skins and even ate of their human victims. Rushby and his scouts continued their efforts. Finally, 15 man-killers were accounted for. The people were now protecting themselves. Their confidence had returned. Continued vigilance paid off. Tribal leaders made an effort to curtail the "werelions," and there came a time when no more humans were killed by the lions of the Njobme District. In the course of the siege, however, over 2000 people had died by claw, fang or the knives of man-lions.

Rushby became a hero—one of the great shooters of Africa.

In June 1956, George Rushby retired as Deputy Game Warden of Tanganyika. After his retirement, he farmed for three years in Lupembe. Finally he set farming aside for good and moved with his wife to Cape Town, her original home. There the couple settled for their quiet years in a pretty naval port, Rushby content that his dream for adventure had come true.

25

TEDDY ROOSEVELT: 'ROUGH RIDING' PRESIDENT

Theodore Roosevelt's chariot of accomplishment was drawn by the steeds of ambition, energy and hyper-activity. His qualification as a great American shooter hinges more on hunting exploit than on pure shooting activity. However, T.R.'s story is too sweeping to be told from the hunting or shooting point of view alone. His role was broad. His life had impact—both immediate and long range. After all, Roosevelt was the 26th President of the United States. And although he did not look the part, he was an American hero.

Theodore Roosevelt—pronounced Roze-eh-velt, not Rooz-eh-velt—was born at 28 East 20th Street in New York City on October 27, 1858. The second of four children, he was named for his father, a successful businessman who died at the age of 46. "My father," extolled Theodore, ". . . was the best man I ever knew." (*Autobiography*) The Roosevelt offspring were true symbols of the American melting pot: Dutch on the father's side and an admixture of Irish, Scottish, Welsh, English, French and German on the mother's side. Despite being born into a well-to-do household—with tutors and whatever a child could wish for—Theodore was born frail and asthmatic. In his autobiography he said, "I was a sickly, delicate boy, suffered much from asthma, and frequently had to be taken away on trips to find a place where I could breathe." "Teedie," as he was called, remembered being carried in the arms of his father at night, and sitting upright in bed

struggling for air. He saw little of school in his early days. However, at age 10, he was off on his first tour of Europe, which he hated. At 14, he went abroad again, this time having sufficiently matured enough to enjoy travel. One gets the idea that Teddy was a serious youth. He always loved activity, when he was well enough to take part, but he also steeped himself in thought during quiet times.

Theodore was a reader. He read everything he could get his hands on, and later in life he would write the same way he did everything else, with an all-consuming drive. One biographer notes "2,000 works," which may be a modest count, if you include numerous magazine articles and thousands of letters. His list of books alone— over 30—is an author's dream. His first volume, *The Summer Birds of the Adirondacks*, was published in 1877 when he was only 18 years old. In some biographies, this title is omitted. *The Naval War of 1812*, a book he had begun while a student at Harvard, is reported as his first book publication. However, the latter was not published until 1882, two years after his graduation as a Phi Beta Kappa.

After he graduated from Harvard, on his 22nd birthday he married Alice Hathaway Lee, of a distinguished Boston family. She died four years later, after giving birth to their only child, also named Alice. That same day, February 14, 1884, Roosevelt lost his mother to typhoid fever. The

Teddy Roosevelt, the hunter—an image the famous statesman was proud to portray. It symbolized the "strenuous life" he lived and that he assured would "build character." After his first wife and his mother died on the same day in 1884, Roosevelt spent three years in the Bad Lands of the Dakotas "building character." This is a rare photo of him without his glasses.

double-shock was devastating to T.R. Friends said he never spoke of his beloved Alice again, and no mention of her is made in the man's autobiography. He fled by "taking to the hills" in the Bad Lands of the Dakotas. This experience showed the "stuff" out of which Roosevelt was created.

OVERCOMING THE ODDS

Sorting the wheat of truth from the chaff of fiction is never simple in tracing a life history; however, it is clear that T.R. was not a coward. At some point in his youth, he had determined to overcome his smallish size through physical development prompted by hard work. He couldn't change his size, but he could cultivate whatever strength he did possess. At age 25, for example, he was only about 5 feet 7 inches tall and weighed 135 pounds. As I stated earlier, Roosevelt was hyper-active, a term others do not apply to him. I think it fits. He played 91 games of tennis in one day in 1882. He ran four miles through "muck" that sucked his shoes off. And he boxed, although he admitted that the rumor of his being light-weight boxing champion of Harvard was false. He loved boxing, but hated "prize-fighting," believing it was wrong for two men to pound on one another for showmanship or money.

But picture him in the Wild West—Dakota country—where he'd bought a couple of ranches along the Little Missouri River. He was a spectacle. In fact, he wore them—spectacles, that is—and in those days, being a "Four Eyes" was a sign of weakness. Better to put salt in your coffee than run around with eyeglasses stuck to your face. Teddy had begun wearing glasses when, at 13 after he'd received his first gun, he could not hit the bull's-eye. He was nearsighted. The cowboys on T.R.'s ranches snickered when they saw the little dude. At this time Roosevelt was still in the lightweight class, a fellow roughly five and a half feet tall weighing about 150 pounds—now add eyeglasses. Furthermore, Teddy did not swear. He did not drink liquor. He did not smoke. He did speak with a New York accent laced with Harvardese. He had a lot to overcome.

A grizzly bear helped Teddy conquer the "Eastern Dude Syndrome." The fierce bear charged. Cowboys were scattering like dynamited logs in the river. Meanwhile, Four Eyes stood his ground slinging lead from a lever-action Winchester rifle. A cattle stampede also helped T.R. crush his EDS. When the animals went crazy, thundering over the range, Four Eyes rode farther and faster after them than anybody else. When his horse rolled with him, T.R. gathered himself off the ground to continue the chase. According to witnesses, Teddy also overcame any stigma of dudishness in a saloon when a bully—just a bar-room bully T.R. noted in his autobiography—insisted that the little chap from the East pay the bar bill. Here is how Roosevelt told it: "As soon as he saw me he hailed me as 'Four Eyes,' in reference to my spectacles, and said, 'Four Eyes is going to treat.' I joined in the laugh and got behind the stove and sat down, thinking to escape notice." The fellow then stood over T.R. brandishing two guns. "He was foolish to stand so near," said Teddy. "As I rose, I struck quick and hard with my right just to one side of the point of his jaw, hitting with my left as I straightened out, and then again with my right. He fired the guns, but I do not know whether. . . he was trying to shoot at me. When he went down he struck the corner of the bar with his head."

Research convinces me that Roosevelt was an honest-to-goodness cowboy, a "working hand," not a stay-at-the-ranch house boss. He rode the range with the rest of the hands until the work was done. He also took the opportunity to provide most of the ranch meat. This task gave him a great deal of hunting experience in a hurry. His autobiography notes, "Getting meat for the ranch usually devolved upon me. I almost always carried a rifle when I rode, either in a scabbard under my thigh, or across the pommel." However, T.R. says, "I never became more than a fair hunter," proclaiming that whatever success he did have in the field came with perseverance more

Roosevelt became so widely known as a hunter that caricatures such as this, with him in his "hunting costume," were common.

than hunting skill. That is a manly pronouncement. Not all guided hunters realize, or admit, that they are not real outdoorsmen, that they tag along until the guide locates the game. They do the shooting, but the hunt ends for them right there. The guide dresses the animal and sees that the hindquarters get back to headquarters. Teddy recognized that although he did hunt on his own, he was not a great outdoorsman of the Nessmuk class. He appreciated the animals for themselves, individually, and he was one of the founding fathers of the Boone & Crockett Club in 1887, an organization geared to "promote manly sport with the rifle."

But hunt he did, and he loved it. He went after any and all game available to him in the Dakota area immediate to his ranches. He hunted elk. And he hunted mule deer, "black tails," as he called them in keeping with their common name in the area, an appellation that stuck into the 1950s. He shot white-tailed deer, too. And wolves. Grizzlies. Bison. Sheep. Mountain goats. He also ranged beyond the Dakotas into the

> "There were all kinds of things of which I was afraid at first, ranging from grizzly bears to 'mean' horses and gunfighters; but by acting as if I was not afraid I gradually ceased to be afraid." —Theodore Roosevelt

northlands for caribou and moose. He wrote of his adventures in several books: *Ranch Life and the Hunting Trail* (1888), *The Wilderness Hunter* (1893), and later after the "big" hunts, *African Game Trails* (1910). *Ranch Life and the Hunting Trail* (published by The Century Company, New York) deals with ranch life, cattle country, the range, round-up, and winter-time in these vast reaches. "When the days have dwindled to their shortest, and the nights seem never ending, then all the great northern plains are changed into an abode of iron desolations." He wrote of the "Frontier Types" and the "old-style" hunters, ". . . their battered pack-saddles carried bales of valuable furs—fisher, sable, otter, mink, beaver."

He spoke of the Indians of the region, "Red and White on the Border," and of his tour of duty as sheriff. "In our own immediate locality we have had more difficulty with white desperadoes than

with redskins," observed T.R. "At times there has been a good deal of cattle-killing and horse-stealing, and occasionally a murder or two." Teddy handled some of the badmen himself, rounding them up on his own.

Interwoven with his love of action was his passion for politics and power. While he dabbled at ranching in the West, Roosevelt could not divorce himself from the workings of government. As early as 1882, he had been elected to the state legislature in Albany. In 1886 he ran for mayor of the City of New York, losing to Tammany Hall-backed Abram Hewitt. The December following his defeat, Roosevelt married his childhood friend, Edith Kermit Carow, with whom he later had five children. Edith was strong-willed but cool-headed. Some historians credit her with a steadying effect on T.R., the President. She may have been a greater force in decision-making than history records. After a ceremony in London, the couple wintered in Europe. That spring, after learning that most of his cattle had succumbed to blizzards, he finally abandoned his Dakota "retreat."

ROOSEVELT'S INFLUENCE ON THE SHOOTING WORLD

Throughout his life, Roosevelt nurtured his zeal for hunting, shooting and firearms. Although the rifleman in Roosevelt does not show in all of his outdoor writings (late 19th and early 20th-century quill-pushers like Selous, White, and Bell usually wrote more of hunting exploits than armament, too), Teddy's penchant for fine rifles surfaces from time to time. In his book on ranch life and hunting, he talks shooting in the chapter "The Ranchman's Rifle on Crag and Prairie." He said, "Personally, I prefer the Winchester, using the new model, with a 45-caliber bullet of 300 grains, backed by 90 grains of powder, or else falling back on my faithful old stand-by, the 45-75. But the truth is that all good modern rifles are efficient weapons; it is the man behind the gun that makes the difference." That summed up the big game rifle for T.R., although we know of his influence on the Springfield rifle, and that he owned a custom Springfield early on.

He used and wrote about the Model 1894 Winchester soon after the rifle was introduced in 30-30 caliber, and he liked its flat-shooting nature and smokeless powder manners. In *Outdoor Pastimes of an American Hunter*, Scribner's 1923

Roosevelt loved Africa with its brimming vitality and wildlife. He also felt that the Winchester 1895 lever-action was *the* rifle to carry, especially in caliber 405 Winchester. No doubt, it is Teddy's Winchester that the professional hunter on the left is holding.

text, T.R. said of the "little 30:"

In the fall of 1896 I spent a fortnight on the range with the ranch wagon. I was using for the first time one of the new small-calibre, smokeless-powder rifles, with the usual soft-nosed bullet. . . .

The last shot I got was when I was out with Joe Ferris, in whose company I had killed my first buffalo, just thirteen years before, and not very far from this same spot. We had seen two bands [of antelope] that

morning, and in each case, after a couple of hours useless effort, I failed to get near enough. At last, toward midday. . . we got within range of a small band. . . I did not have a close shot, for they were running about 180 yards off. The buck was rear-most, and at him I aimed; the bullet struck him in the flank, coming out of the opposite shoulder, and he fell in the next bound. As we stood over him, Joe shook his head, and said 'I guess that little rifle is the ace'; and I told him I guessed so too.

Roosevelt was well-known for his love of the Model 1895 Winchester lever-action rifle. He had the Winchester company custom-build several '95s for him, with many variations, often in sights. Perhaps T.R. was trying to devise a way to see his sights better, for his vision was never perfect. George Madis, in *The Winchester Book*, shows a special Roosevelt Model 95 (page 426) with 24-inch round matted barrel, Lyman sights, checkered stock of figured walnut, cheekpiece, sling swivels, and "soft rubber shotgun butt-plate." Madis also quotes Roosevelt, showing his faith in the rifle: " 'Tarlton took his big double-barrel and advised me to take mine, as the sun had just set and it was likely to be close work; but I shook my head, for *the Winchester .405* is, at least for me personally, THE 'MEDICINE GUN' FOR LIONS.' "—a rifle that really got the job done.

Roosevelt had an impact on shooting. He was a rifleman, of course, and a hunter. He was also a collector of firearms, the collection of which embodied a history of arms evolution. Furthermore, he was indirectly helpful in furthering the development of the Springfield rifle.

When Congress declared war against Spain in April 1898, Teddy was ready for action again. He resigned his post as Assistant Secretary of the Navy under President McKinley and became a lieutenant colonel in the Volunteer 1st Cavalry. Cowboys from the West and polo players from the East joined Roosevelt in the outfit that became known as the "Rough Riders." Their success in the Battle of San Juan Hill, Cuba, had Roosevelt's name all over the papers, and helped clinch his political career. When Teddy returned home from the Spanish-American War, he pursued the adoption of the Mauser rifle chambered for the 7×57mm Mauser cartridge. While not successful in that, his insistence escalated the development and acceptance of a bolt-action military rifle. This turned out to be the Springfield Model of 1903, chambered for what we now call the 30-06 Springfield cartridge. Furthermore, T.R. directly influenced the eventual configuration of the Springfield, for he insisted upon its redesign to accept a knife bayonet rather than an internal rod bayonet. This alteration forced a change in the rifle's appearance. Finally, Teddy had the first Springfield sporter that we know of. He was so early with his sporter that the custom rifle was not chambered for the 30-06 cartridge, but for the 30-03 Springfield cartridge that preceded it. (For more about Roosevelt's influence on the Springfield, see *The Springfield 1903 Rifles* by Lt. Colonel William S. Brophy.)

By 1900, Theodore Roosevelt had been Police Commissioner of New York City, where he was noted for enforcing the Sunday closed-saloon ruling; he had been easily elected Republican Governor of New York State; and now he found himself Vice President of the United States. Campaigning in his Rough Rider hat, he had toured the nation, making energetic speeches while McKinley tended to business at the White House. Roosevelt's book, *The Strenuous Life* that appeared in 1900, describes the man's philosophy: "Go for the gold." Give your all. Never quit. He lived this way. And his attitude rubbed off on many others of his time, including Stewart Edward White, the novelist/hunter who has his own place in our book.

Fate sped Theodore's rise. When President McKinley died on September 14, 1901, from an assassin's bullet, Roosevelt became the youngest man, at age 42, to hold the highest office in the country.

He was a popular president and won by a wide margin in the following election of 1904. In keeping with his ambitious nature, he accomplished much: success in making the Sherman Anti-trust Act stick, negotiating for the building of the Panama Canal, mediating in the Russo-Japanese War, which made him the first American recipient of the Nobel Peace Prize, establishing the Food and Drug Administration—and much more that history books recount.

Roosevelt is also known as the natural resources president because he, along with Gifford Pinchot and F.H. Newell, shaped many plans for conservation. Yellowstone National Park and other reserves of this type exist today because of Roosevelt and men like him. T.R. saw first-hand the many changes that took place in the West. He wanted to avert "landgrabbing," as he called it, and the wasting of natural resources that included needless wildlife loss through uncontrolled development of natural habitat. Roosevelt was directly responsible for the Forest Service firefighting code. His hunting, of course, brought political pressure. And Roosevelt did what a trained politician would do; he made statements to appease

T.R.—the politician, the statesman, the President. The youngest man to hold the highest office, Roosevelt operated from a platform of strength. "Walk softly but carry a big stick" was his motto.

the detractors: "I don't approve of too much slaughter," or "I like to do a certain amount of hunting, but my real and main interest is the interest of a faunal naturalist." His *real* interest was in picking up a sharp-shootin' rifle and "making meat" with it, and he proved it over and over again. He was, however, a dedicated sportsman. "To make a very large bag, whether of deer, or prairie chicken, or ducks, or woodcock, or trout is something of which to be ashamed and not to boast of." Harvest, but don't waste.

Biographers have always treated Teddy's hunting as a mystery. Remember that T.R. was the first dedicated hunter since George Washington to live in the White House. How could a man who loved animals shoot them? That was the paradox. In a recent movie on T.R.'s life, the question arose again as the narrator lamented the ex-President's "blood lust." But Roosevelt understood population dynamics and wildlife carrying capacity quite well. He knew that species left to multiply would "crash," as they always have, Dame Nature taking a toll through disease and starvation, as well as winter hardships. Theodore Roosevelt was no hypocrite, eating domestic meat, or fruits and vegetables raised on ground that had once been habitat for wild animals, while at the same time promoting a sentimental but senseless stand. As other hunters of yesteryear and today, T.R. was interested in setting aside areas that were to remain pristine. He used his political clout, his stature as a public figure and his popularity to encourage conservation.

T.R. did not consider himself a great shot. He thought of himself as part of a vast middle ground of riflemen, those with average ability who had honed their meager skills with dedicated practice. He also felt that being a fine target marksmen did not necessarily make a man a good game shot. In keeping with his love for adventure, his greatest thrill was possibly the grizzly bear charge, saying "the only narrow escape I met with was not from one of these dangerous African animals, but from a grizzly bear." Teddy wounded the beast, following it into a stand of lodgepole pines. The bear attacked. The President shot again. The bear kept coming. Through the black-powder smoke came a paw, but the bear was about finished. The grizzly expired before it could grab the hunter. Unfortunately, Roosevelt's chance to be with and learn from the greatest bear

hunter of the era was never realized. B.V. "Ben" Lilly (*see* separate chapter) was commissioned the Chief Huntsman for a Roosevelt hunt in 1907, but conditions were such that Ben never had a chance to prove his merit. The President went away considering Ben a religious fanatic, and perhaps a lunatic as well.

Roosevelt did have a chance to enjoy the company of a special partner—his son, Kermit. After deciding not to run for high office again, Teddy and Kermit enjoyed a great African safari, as related in the 1910 book *African Game Trails*. On this trek, Roosevelt hunted under the guidance of R.J. Cunninghame. In stalking Cape buffalo, T.R. said of the man: "Cunninghame, a veteran hunter and first-class shot. . . [is] no better man to have with one when after dangerous game. . . ." After almost a year, they bagged nearly 300 animals and collected what was at the time the most complete array of fauna to have been gathered.

Roosevelt was a product of his time, but he was also well ahead of it in many ways. On the one hand, he harbored many of the same attitudes held by the vast majority of men of the period. Few Westerners of his time considered the jackrabbit edible fare. Ranchers relegated the animal to varmint, eight of them eating what a domestic sheep could survive on. Today, biographers note with horror that Roosevelt considered the jackrabbit good for little else than "target practice." As these people speak, rabbits in Australia occupy the same station in the hierarchy of wildlife that jacks have held in the American West for a couple hundred years. Biographers and critics marvel that Roosevelt was both naturalist *and* hunter. However, when a modern hunter looks at T.R. he sees himself: concerned with the continuance of wildlife and habitat, interested in animals for their own sake, gaining as much from being in the outback as from collecting a proud trophy, honoring the game more than the taking of it, using game meat as food, working hard to be a proficient outdoorsman, loving the camp life, enjoying quality firearms and crackshot marksmanship, and being realistic enough to know how nature really works.

Because he was President of the United States and so widely known, Roosevelt was able to influence views on shooting and hunting. He made a terrific impact on shooters and hunters, as well as conservationists, ranchers, farmers

President Roosevelt poses with hunting companion Captain Slater, after T. R. dropped the rhino at Kilimakiu during his almost year-long African safari in 1909.

and all persons interested in the outdoors. His personality, drive and unique character made him the great hunter-rifleman that he was. He was no Ben Lilly, tracking game all by himself in a vast wilderness for weeks. Yet he was as devoted to hunting. He was no Ad Topperwein, able to shoot little wooden blocks out of the sky with a 22 rifle. But Teddy led the strenuous life, worked hard with the natural ability he was granted and shaped the raw material until T.R., the man, was the best he could be.

By 1912, Roosevelt again decided to heed the call of the Presidency. He declared himself a candidate and ran on the independent Progressive ticket. Right before a campaign speech, he was shot in the chest by a political zealot who did not agree with his philosophy. Roosevelt delivered the speech anyway. He recovered rapidly and within weeks was up grandstanding for votes. Although he came in second, he was pleased that outgoing President Taft, who had not upheld Roosevelt's firm hand against big business, trailed in third against Woodrow Wilson.

In the winter of 1913–1914, Theodore Roosevelt, true to the wanderlust and adventure in his soul, explored the River of Doubt territory in central Brazil. He fell ill from a tropical fever and never fully recovered. When the U.S. entered World War I, all four of his sons signed up. He wanted to lead a division to France himself, but Wilson rejected the offer. In 1918, near the end of the conflict, Quentin, Teddy's youngest son, was shot down behind German lines. Roosevelt planned a comeback for the 1920 presidency, but the illness contracted in South America, plus the loss of Quentin, made serious inroads on his health. Roosevelt was in and out of the hospital during 1918. On January 6, 1919, at his home in Oyster Bay, Long Island, T.R. died in his sleep.

26

BILL RUGER: CLASSIC DESIGNER

Bill Ruger was born to design two things: guns and cars. Those of us who shoot are fortunate that this self-educated engineer chose firearms as his life's major interest. At only 32 years of age, he co-founded the Sturm, Ruger Company, which has been successful in producing firearms of uncommon quality at uncustomary prices. Ruger, the man, has been involved with designing, promoting and shooting firearms throughout his entire life. As a result, Ruger, the company, has been able to give to the shooting public high-grade arms that pushed the industry into the 20th century long before its due.

William Batterman "Bill" Ruger's birthplace was Brooklyn, New York. He arrived on the summer day of June 21, 1916—two years into the Great War. It is perhaps not surprising that he loved machine guns. His mother was the former May Batterman. His father, Adolph, was a lawyer who enjoyed shooting and hunting in his leisure time. He owned a duck-hunting lodge on eastern Long Island in the prestigious Shinnecock area. At age six, Bill was accompanying his father on forays through the woods. He felt comfortable and happy there. He loved the outdoors, and even more he yearned to be around firearms of any sort. Guns held great fascination for Bill.

The family rifle, a Stevens 22 rimfire, was in Ruger's hands at a tender age. When Bill was about 12, he was laid up with scarlet fever. His papa told him that for his upcoming birthday he'd

get him a Remington. The boy couldn't allow himself to believe that it might be a Remington rifle, for at the time Remington knives were popular as well. "It must be a knife," mused the sick boy. But the Remington turned out to be none other than a Model 12 pump gun. As soon as Bill could get around again, the sleek little shell shucker was crooked in his arm as he traced over the wooded trails of Long Island.

Adolph Ruger died shortly thereafter. Bill went on with his schooling, attending Alexander Hamilton High in Brooklyn. He did all right, but when presented with a choice of school assignments or studying firearms, the latter got the nod. In high school, Bill experimented with as many firearms as he could get his hands on. The *American Rifleman* magazine was his bible and General Julian Hatcher, his mentor. Every gun book in the school and local library was assaulted for knowledge. The tall blue-eyed researcher poured over all he could find on firearms design, fingers running through his sandy hair as he studied.

Bill was a member of the high school rifle team, and enjoyed shooting indoors. But finding a place to shoot outdoors was tough, even in the Brooklyn of the 1920s. Bill and his shooting compadre, Bill Lett, fixed up a basement range for their 22s so they could get in some extra practice without leaving home. They also tramped the countryside whenever they could get away. On one outing the boys encountered a fellow shooting

Bill Ruger, the man behind the guns of the famous company that bears his name. He was once likened to a ''Renaissance merchant prince.''

a 30-06 rifle. That was a revelation. Here was a "real" rifle, with considerable boom and snort to signify its potential.

It wasn't long before Ruger and Lett put their hands on their own "real" rifle. As soon as Lett's parents said OK, a war surplus 30-40 Krag was ordered at $9.75. Lett figured it would be a good idea to test-fire the new rifle in the basement, but young Ruger vetoed that idea. The lads wound up shooting their new prize in a vacant field at the end of the subway line.

Bill collected guns, too. Colts, Sharps and Springfields comprised his high school holdings. He also owned a Luger pistol he considered a favorite. Keep that in mind, because Bill Ruger's first step to the peak of the gunmaking pyramid was taken with a Luger-like pistol he designed. That gun made his fortune. While still a student, Bill, at 17, sketched a firearm design on paper for a light machine gun. He wanted a prototype built, but had no cash to pay for the work. At Bill's insistence, sufficient trust monies left by an Aunt were freed by the courts of New York, and a rough model of his machine gun was made. Ruger was already a man of action. Ideas were only as good as their realization.

Although blessed with high intelligence, Ruger applied his mental abilities where his interests lay—firearms. He wasn't a crack student; he didn't have time for that kind of study. He did scan the books at a Salisbury, Connecticut, prep school, however. No guns were allowed there, so Bill kept a firearm off campus. He wasn't going to be without a shooting machine of some sort. When home in Brooklyn on holiday, Bill could be found in one machine shop or another. He was totally captivated by the concept of taking raw metal and turning it into something functional. Ruger went on to college, for two years, and while at the University of North Carolina, he converted a Model 99 Savage lever-action rifle into a semiauto. He did it right. The story of his conversion appeared in a 1942 *American Rifleman* magazine.

Bill married in 1939. After an extended European honeymoon bankrolled with $10,000 inheritance money, Bill and bride returned to America a lot lighter financially. Ruger decided to walk away from college and get to work. He sought employment as a designer with one of the large gun companies. Even though they showed little interest in the young man, he kept dogging after

a job anyway. He showed his machine gun design to members of Army Ordnance. Several officers were impressed. Although the design was not accepted, Ruger's talents could not be denied.

Finally, a job came through. A telegram from the Springfield Armory called him to work. He remained there from 1939 through 1940. But the pay, 65 dollars every two weeks, was hardly enough to support a wife, a new son, and himself. Besides, there was little room for advancement at Springfield. Bill was somewhat bored. He had to move on. He returned to North Carolina, where he worked on a new light machine-gun design for the Army. The prototype of the gun was demonstrated here and there, but interest was mild. Remington didn't want a machine gun. Neither did Winchester. Nor Smith & Wesson. But the last two offered the young designer jobs. He went to work for neither. Rather, he hired on at Auto Ordnance Corporation, the company responsible for building the Thompson submachine gun. There, he labored over his own machine-gun design for three years, beginning in late 1940. The company liked Ruger's gun and contracted with the young inventor for patent rights. But by 1944 nearing the end of World War II, the government was no longer interested in his updated battle gun. Bill was putting in 80 hours a week, though, making about a hundred dollars—terrific pay for the times—and loving it.

Auto Ordnance was good for Bill Ruger. His mind was free to explore avenues of intense interest. He learned metallurgy. He also got a look at a Douglas Hammond design that intrigued him. Hammond had a first-rate idea for building a firearm from joined sheet metal, a method that would save costly machining. And the end product worked fine. Two halves of a receiver, for example, could be built economically and then put together as a single unit.

Bill did well at Auto Ordnance, but he was forever urged on by a desire to break out on his own. He was compelled to open a manufacturing shop, even if the enterprise did not build guns. In 1946 the Ruger Corporation of Southport, Connecticut, was born. The fledgling company produced a line of carpenter's tools—screwdrivers, hand drills and the like. It wasn't guns. But it was manufacturing. It was a beginning. It was a dry run. In a way, Bill's tools were too good. They had to cost a little more than others because they cost more to make. A demand for the tools never materialized and the flame of the little company flickered out in 1948. Besides, Bill was still pondering guns—not just building them, but doing so in a way never accomplished before.

STURM AND RUGER BOLDLY LAUNCH A CAREER

Enter Alexander M. Sturm—graduate of Yale Art School, painter, writer, gun collector, and husband to Paulina Longworth, Theodore Roosevelt's granddaughter. Sturm and Ruger got along famously. Sturm had faith in a special idea of Ruger's—a 22-rimfire semiauto pistol that could be sold for less than the competition's, but that still offered reliability and accuracy. The heart of the concept was joining two simple pieces of metal to form a more complicated unit. The frame of the pistol could be built sturdily and accurately without expensive machining. Ruger had the idea. Sturm had the 50,000 dollars to invest in it. A company was formed.

Consider for a moment that even in 1948, when Sturm, Ruger & Company, Inc. got underway, $50,000 was minuscule capital with which to launch a gun manufacturing enterprise. Had the men ruminated over this fact long enough, the Ruger semiauto pistol may have remained on the drawing board. Instead of allowing obstacles

The Ruger Standard Model, a classic 22 Luger-like Automatic, was the first sidearm Sturm, Ruger & Company manufactured, beginning in 1949. After Sturm died in 1951, the red eagle medallion was changed to black as a memorial. Today the gun in its original version is a collector's item.

to interfere, however, the men dove in. Sturm was in charge of advertising and marketing; Ruger, of design and production. And the shooters of America were responsible for the success that followed.

Sturm, Ruger & Company has never had to borrow one cent to promote the company because the operations have always been carried on by the dollars of profit. In 1949 a little advertisement appeared in the *American Rifleman* magazine. Essentially, it said you could own a totally reliable semiauto 22-rimfire pistol for $37.50. $37.50? Yup. And that price stayed in effect for a long time. No wonder orders poured in. Word soon spread that the little pistol was worth every penny it cost. No, *more* than you paid for it. Before the enterprising men could say, "We've made it," a thousand units were shipped off. A strong review by Major Hatcher, whom Ruger called "my great sponsor and mentor—almost like a father" promoted sales even further. Bill Ruger never looked back. The future lay before him.

For Alexander Sturm, however, the story ends differently. In 1951, at the age of 29 and only three years after he and Ruger set up partnership, Alex died. Bill's studied opinion was that he had succumbed from "hard living." Ruger's sorrow at the loss of a true friend would forever show in a change of color for the Ruger logo. Sturm had designed the trademark himself, a round medallion featuring a hawk with outspread wings, although it is popularly known as the Ruger Red Eagle. Sturm had admired the past—he'd decided that the human condition reached its peak somewhere in the twelfth century, Bill said. The color of the falcon image was red. After Sturm's passing the bird was changed to black as a memorial on all 22 semiautomatic pistols, and so it remains today.

Bill Ruger went forward with design after design. The 1949 Luger-like Standard Auto was followed in 1951 by the Mark I Auto. The second 22 semiautomatic pistol had target sights instead of fixed sights. Also, whereas the Standard wore a barrel of either 4⅔ inches or 6 inches in length, the Mark I was furnished with barrel choices of 5¼ or 6⅞ regular, or 5½-inch bull barrel.

In 1952, Ruger considered a 22 tip-up pistol. His appreciation for the best designs of the past promoted the idea. But even before the plan could materialize, he upgraded it. A single-action re-

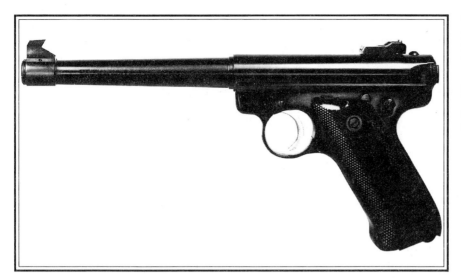

The Mark Series, I and II, that followed the Standard Model has met with extraordinary success. The Mark II Target Pistol (left), introduced in 1982, features a tapered 6⅞-inch barrel with undercut target front sight, in blued or stainless steel finish.

volver would be better than a single-shot. In 1953 the Ruger Single Six, a Colt-like sixgun, was on the market. By investment casting (lost wax process) the frame, costly milling once again was omitted without sacrificing quality. The company couldn't make enough of the new revolver to meet the demand. Ruger had another winner. The Single Six was accurate. It wore adjustable sights. And in the future it would be offered with an alternate cylinder for 22 WRM (Winchester Rimfire Magnum), giving the shooter, essentially, two handguns on one frame. The semiauto pistol was a whale of an idea. But the Single Six was a whole ocean.

A Single Six Light Weight came along in 1956—successful to the tune of 200,000 pieces. A year earlier Ruger had been studying a big-caliber sixgun alteration. A number of shooters, including gunwriter Elmer Keith, were beefing up the old-timers to handle modern loads. The old guns were also fitted with good sights. In 1955 Ruger had a solution for all of those who wanted a powerful and reliable sidearm. It came in the form of the Blackhawk. Here was a single-action sidearm that came muscled up from the factory, with fine target-type sights so the shooter could hit something. Bill Ruger had another hit on his hands. Chambered initially for the 357 Magnum, the modern Blackhawk sixgun was soon offered for many powerful rounds, including the 44 Magnum. Furthermore, various Blackhawk styles were brought out, every one of them a winner.

Other Blackhawks included the 44 Magnum of 1956, the Super Blackhawk 44 Magnum (with unfluted cylinder) in 1959, the Blackhawk 41 Magnum of 1965 and a Blackhawk 30 Carbine in 1967.

The word "cute" does not often pertain to sidearms, but the term fits Ruger's Bearcat, a tiny non-fluted revolver with 4-inch barrel brought out in 1959. Fixed sights may have helped to scuttle this 17-ounce beauty with its engraved cylinder. Buntlines were also a part of the Ruger handgun lineup.

The Ruger Hawkeye, a 1963 innovation, may have been too far-reaching. It looked like a sixgun, but it was instead a single-shot chambered for the zippy 256 Winchester cartridge. It never achieved record sales. The cylinder of the Hawkeye was replaced by a rotating breechblock, which gave this pistol, for that's what the Hawkeye is, a truly powerful lockup. It could have been chambered for many interesting and worthwhile cartridges, and it is my humble opinion that the Hawkeye would have blown the roof off of sales if offered in a variety of hot handgun rounds, such as the 221 Remington Jet, which appeared in 1963, or the 22 BR Remington, or 6mm BR Remington, or perhaps a 7mm BR Remington, as well as other hotshot rounds. In fact, a Hawkeye chambering for the 221 was announced, but never realized.

Along with the many variations of Ruger sidearms came a bevy of the most popular long

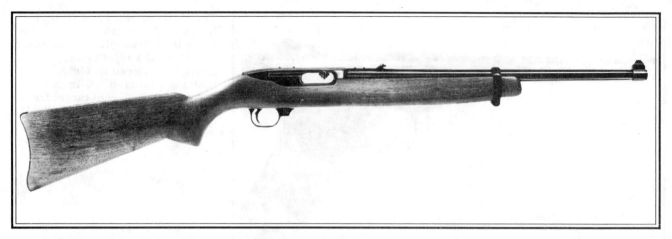

One of Ruger's many innovative firearms designs is the Model 44 Carbine, a semi-automatic chambered for the 44 Magnum cartridge. At a shade under six pounds, this fast-action arm is a winner in the brush, and is still being produced—almost 30 years now.

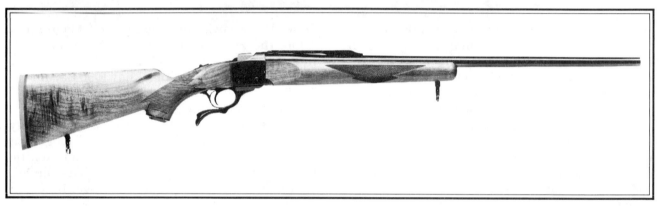

On the hunch that American shooters were not finished with the single-shot, big game rifle, Bill Ruger introduced the No. 1 in 1966. He was right. It's still popular today and is chambered for many different rounds, including the 458 Winchester.

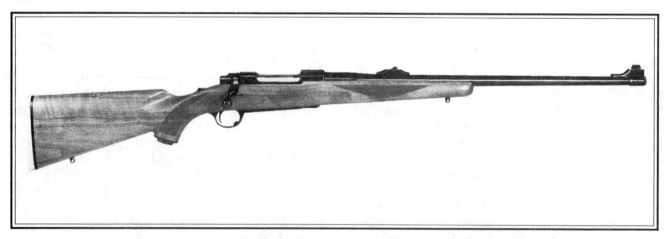

Ruger combined many features from different bolt-action rifles before deciding on the design of his own Model 77, above. Offered in numerous variations, this Mauser-like big-game baby has plenty of extraction power and has pleased many a hunter over the years.

arms produced in modern times. In 1961, Ruger's gas-operated 44 Magnum semiautomatic carbine hit the bricks with a ton of force. With a handy cross-bolt safety, the 44 Magnum Carbine was a winner in the brush. It weighed under six pounds and was just a shade over three feet in length. The 18.5-inch barrel boosted 44 Magnum ballistics significantly. Here was a fast-action autoloader that was perfectly at home in close cover. Today, with so many different 44 Magnum loads, including Garrett Cartridge Company's Super-heavyweight with 280-grain Truncated Cone bullet, the Carbine becomes a close-range, one-punch artist on deer-sized game. A blowback 22 rimfire called the 10/22 because of its 10-shot detachable box rotary magazine showed up in 1964, soon to follow with variations on the theme. Bull's-eye again.

Then Bill Ruger introduced a product that even he had to wonder about. Who would buy a single-shot, big game rifle in the 20th century?

Answer? Thousands of satisfied shooters. The Ruger Number One was introduced in 1967. It represented one of the biggest chances Bill ever took. Single-shot big-game rifles were for all practical purposes defunct in 1967. The Number One branched out into many variations also, every one of them excellent. Different barrel lengths and chamberings for just about any high-intensity cartridge a big game hunter could want lured many buyers. The Number One could wear a 26-inch barrel without looking like a vaulting pole, too, because the single-shot action was a bit shorter than the standard-length bolt-action. Right up to 375 H&H Magnum and 458 Winchester, the Number One was ready to serve its waiting audience of shooters.

The very next year following the Number One's debut came what we all knew would have to follow—Bill Ruger's idea of what a bolt-action big game rifle should be, a Mauser-like model with plenty of extraction power, and ample strength to contain any high-power cartridge. It was the Model 77. Again, numerous variations emerged, including a nifty full-stock International model and a handsome lightweight. Calibers? Many, from the lightning little ones to the big boys.

A GUN FOR ALL SEASONS

Ruger continues to surprise us with his innovations. The goal of the Ruger company is ob-

vious: to produce a model in each of the different action designs. Should you think not, look at the Ruger Red Label over/under shotgun. The crystal ball reveals a classic side-by-side double-barreled shotgun that might one day bear the Ruger name. Meanwhile, there is the Ruger P-85, a semiautomatic 9mm pistol carrying 15 shots. Ruger has already come out with a blackpowder firearm, in case you're wondering. It's the Ruger Old Army in 44 caliber, blued or stainless steel. It's won many shooting contests at modern-day rendezvous. The six-shot cap 'n' ball revolver sports target sights and it has cylinder safety notches similar to those found on the Model 1858 Remington Civil War revolver (not all 1858s had safety notches, but most did). The GP-100 is Ruger's answer to a handy, strongly built double-action revolver, while Ruger's Redhawk and Super Redhawk in 41 Magnum and 44 Magnum give the shooter a powerhouse double-action revolver in standard or stainless steel. Then there is the Mini-14 semiauto 223 and a Mini-Thirty semiauto chambered for the 7.62mm Russian cartridge. About the only models not forthcoming from Ruger are a lever-action, big game rifle (Bill has always looked upon the lever gun as being outclassed by other action styles) and a double-barreled rifle. And I'd wonder about the latter.

As noted, the Ruger company operates debt-free with a solid profit margin. Investment casting and computer-controlled milling promote the company's success. Over the years the company has branched out. There is the Pine Tree Casting Division of Newport, New Hampshire, a Ruger plant that takes up over 135,000 square feet of operation space. This ''secondary operation'' is in fact larger than the home office in Southport, Connecticut. A plant in Prescott, Arizona, produces the P-85 pistol. Assets for the Ruger operation total around a hundred million dollars now.

But all of this has not changed the character of Bill Ruger. Sure, he's a rich man. His home reflects that wealth, with fine taste that includes priceless paintings and other collectibles. Bill's love for cars manifests itself in a collection of fine vintage automobiles. He even manufactured a Ruger Car embodying the eye-catching lines of the past, but with a hot 427 Ford 425 horsepower engine. Ruger's Sports Tourer was one of the few ''replicars'' that earned high praise from experts. Ralph Stein said, after lambasting most replica

Cars are Bill Ruger's second love and he manufactured them with as much care as the firearms. The Sports Tourer, above, with double-walled fiberglass body and Ford 427 V-8 engine, won high praise for durability, performance and beautiful engineering. Besides, say auto buffs, it is fun to drive.

cars, "There is, however, one replicar, the Ruger Sports Tourer, over which purists can enthuse. Although this sporting four-seater looks like a 1929 4½ liter Vanden Plas-bodied Bentley, its builder, William Ruger of Sturm-Ruger, Inc. (the gunmaking firm), says that he has no intention of making a Chinese copy of a Bentley."

Bill Ruger kept up the hunting interests he shared as a boy with his father. In almost three-quarters of a century, he has hunted far and wide—in the Lower 48 States, in Alaska, Canada, Scotland, Iran and Africa—and his fine collection of mounted trophies proves it. Today, the unfortunate ravages of rheumatoid arthritis make it dif-ficult for the designer/entrepreneur/shooter to get around as he once did, but he still remains active. Living a full life was one of the marks of the man. Along with the myriad successes in gun design and business, Ruger is a family man. He and his spouse, the former Mary Thompson, have two sons, William B. Ruger Jr. and James Thompson Ruger, both high up in the Ruger company. There is also a daughter, Carolyn Amalie, now the wife of Stephen K. Vogel.

It is safe to say that no modern marksman will spend a career in shooting without owning, or at the very least, shooting a Ruger firearm. That is impact. That is Ruger.

27

F.C. SELOUS: FRONTIERSMAN OF AFRICA

Imagine being transported by night to a distant planet—alone, left with meager supplies among a people who do not speak your language, whose culture is not yours, amidst a flora and fauna unlike any you have known, a place where death can flame from the bush like a grassfire fanned by a hundred mile-an-hour wind. This scene greeted the young F.C. Selous on his first trip to Africa.

Born in Regents Park, London, in 1851, Frederick Courteney Selous (*Sell-oo*) was afforded a good education, primarily as a naturalist. After Rugby, Frederick completed his formal learning in Switzerland and Germany. He was being polished into a pearl of wisdom, a diamond of knowledge, a ruby of manners. Had he never read of Africa, Selous might have taken his place among the anonymous, living the life of a gentleman, rewarded with cool drink in summer and warm quarters in winter. Joining the ranks of high society, his greatest hardship would have been choosing which tie to wear to tea. But it was not to be. Adventure and curiosity were more magnetic than propriety.

His fellow students agreed that Selous was a good runner, a fine football player and an accomplished swimmer. They believed, too, that he enjoyed a refined degree of hearing and sight. These traits, coupled with innate intelligence and tenacity, would blend to create one of the greatest hunter-riflemen of his or any other era.

On September 4, 1871, Selous's boots trod upon African soil for the first time. He was only 19 years old. His net worth was 400 English pounds. With this coin he was to pay for an undetermined stay on the Dark Continent. He would become a professional elephant hunter, a quest for ivory leading him into some regions previously unseen by the eyes of white men. His few wagons containing provender were often left for months at a time as the hunter wandered in search of pachyderms. Selous was overcome by the freedom of Africa. He dressed, or undressed, appropriately for the part. He must have been a sight, this white man clad only in hat, shirt and shoes, nothing else, a big-bore blackpowder rifle in hand in preparation for whatever might have come his way.

The hunting method was simple and grueling. Shoot—run—load—shoot again if you have to—all of this with a muzzleloader. On his first adventure, his small double-barrel Reilly rifle was stolen from a wagon, leaving only a Vaugham double-barrel 10-bore, which "threw its bullets across one another," and a "little double gun that shot well with both shot and bullet." Selous often hunted during the day as his ox team took shelter out of the sun. The game he got he carried back to camp on his own shoulders—duiker, springbuck, bushbuck, kipspringer and rheebok. He learned many things, as we all must at times— the hard way—and through an accident. On his first hunt, Selous was working with loose gun-

Frederick Selous, the great 19th-century hunter of Africa. He hunted many varieties of game in Africa and other continents. Using his skills as a naturalist, he studied animal behavior and also contributed valuable specimens to museums.

powder. A companion, Dorehill, walked over to the wagon. A spark from Dorehill's pipe fell into the powder, causing the propellant to flash. It burned both men "all over our necks and faces." The flame also burned Frederick's eye. He was a long time recovering fully, but he did regain full sight.

Selous fell in with a good man, his earlier mentor and comrade, Cigar, a Hottentot native. Cigar was not a servant, but rather a partner. He would hunt alongside Selous for ivory, often working into an elephant herd with the goal of placing a ball into one or two pachyderms, aiming for the heart. The big-bore muzzleloader was not sufficient to drop the elephant on the spot with such bullet placement. As the tuskers raced away, Selous and Cigar followed on the dead run, reloading as they went. One mile. Two miles. Whatever it took, they followed. Often, they caught up with the herd and dispatched one or two additional animals. Four jumbos in a day was not unheard of. Cigar, Selous and their men lived on elephant meat as well as any other game that came their way. The rest of their diet consisted of corn in the form of a meal, sometimes called sudsa or mealy meal.

Although he delighted in the fauna for, after all, he was a trained naturalist, the young English hunter was to learn much more about Africa than its game. Selous discovered Africa—the land. Early in his career, he became lost. "I began to think that I was in stern reality lost in the veldt, without even a bullet to obtain food for myself, and no water within heaven knew what distance away. . . And where was that road—was it behind me or in front?" The young hunter stayed lost. Soon he was without horse. He woke stiffly from a night of fitful sleep to find the animal gone. "All that day I walked as I have seldom walked since. . . devoured by a burning thirst." He finally found his way to a village. He asked a man for water. The man said, "Buy the water," which Selous would have done had he had any money. But he saw a boy coming in from milking goats, so he traded the lad a large clasp knife for a calabash full of milk and a gourd of water.

He was also to learn the ways of his adopted country, sometimes lenient, sometimes harsh and abrupt. An attempt to gain permission to hunt a given territory ended with kind permission. Matabele Chief Lobengula teased at first, asking if the lad in front of him were not in fact chasing Stembok (very small antelope) and not elephants. "Why, you're only a boy." Selous admitted, yes, he was only a boy, but he was also an elephant hunter. He was allowed. On the dark side, the young hunter was one time near witness to an execution. A Hottentot native had murdered a camp helper "in cold blood," because the young man had not responded swiftly enough to a demand for water. The murderer was caught and turned over to the camp. The men demanded his life in expiation of their comrade, and the Hottentot was bludgeoned to death, his body left for the hyenas. Selous remarked, "I was glad I did not see him killed."

Of course, there was always the constant danger imposed by the large animals of the Dark

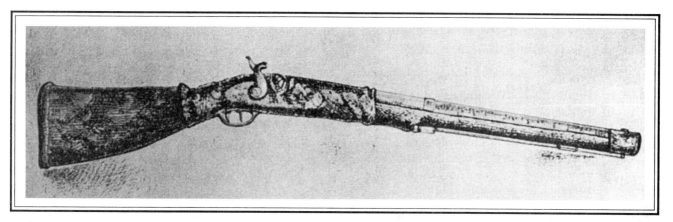

Before breechloaders came into use, Selous hunted with blackpowder rifles. Here is the huge 4-bore he used in his early years of African hunting.

Continent. African big game "shoots back." While on horseback, Frederick was charged by a Cape buffalo. He could not get a shot off. Man and horse were pitched through the air. Selous fired in the process of being thrown. The heavy recoil of the rifle sent it sailing in one direction, the man in another. The horse galloped away, but the buffalo's horn had disemboweled the steed. Selous ended up on the ground in a sitting posture. Facing him was the bull. The animal charged. Dodging aside, only the hunter's shoulder was contacted by horn. The buffalo, satisfied that Selous was smashed, moved on. Then the hunter had to dispatch his hopelessly wounded horse.

Later Selous was treed by another buffalo. The animal had been wounded by a lion and was in a foul mood. Although Selous did not fire on him, the bull charged anyway. Frederick had no rifle. His gunbearers had sought safety off the ground. The hunter climbed a tree and was spared. There were other attacks, one by an elephant that came close to ending the Englishman's career. He was on horseback. Seeing the charge coming, Selous urged the animal forward, but it struck out at a walk instead of a gallop and would not respond to the rider's urgent command to get out of harm's way. The jumbo caught horse and rider, dashing them to the ground. Then it sank its tusks into the earth trying to pin Selous. "She was on her knees, with her head and tusks in the ground, and I had been pressed down under her chest, but luckily behind her fore-legs." His rifle broken, Selous secured another from a gunbearer and dispatched the angry pachyderm. He had a bruised eye and "all the skin was rubbed off my right breast." A lucky escape he called it.

The hunter graduated to horseback riding rather than walking all the time. Although he switched from muzzleloader to breechloader, he was often compelled to use the old-time firearm on many of his hunts. His four-bore muzzleloader was a single-shot. Cigar, hunting alongside Selous, carried a six-bore muzzleloader. Often, Frederick would leave the wagons and most of his men behind, traveling with only one young tracker, who would carry a blanket and spare ammunition makings. Selous "shouldered" his four-bore and a leather bag filled with black powder. He also toted 20 four-ounce "round bullets" (While we tend to use the term "round ball," round bullet is equally correct—a bullet is any missile fired from a gun.) In the heat of the chase, the powder charge might not be measured at all. Selous just grabbed "a handful" and poured it downbore. As noted, in spite of the huge bullet, over an inch across, pachyderms did not always fall to one shot. Selous often used his 10-bore rifle on Cape buffalo. This was a single-shot rifle firing the round ball. A charge of "6 drachms" of powder was the normal hunting load. The term "drachm" was used for dram at this time and equaled 27.34 grains weight. Therefore, the powder charge for the 10-bore was 164 grains weight.

Selous was in it for the hunt more than the coinage. While his tally seems great by our standards—about 175 Cape buffalo and 106 elephants, others of the era scored far more heavily. Frederick became a lion hunter, too, with about 31 to his credit, as well as being in on 11 other lion kills. He became, in fact, an expert on lions.

Selous was in love with Africa, with the adventure, and with his work. He had learned to speak various dialects and could converse with the native peoples. He was no longer an alien on a foreign planet. He was at home. Paint this scene on the canvas of your mind: An elephant charge ". . . suddenly the trunk of another elephant was whirled round, almost literally above my head, and a short, sharp scream of rage thrilled through me, making the blood tingle down to the very tips of my fingers." Selous had emptied his rifle already. He was without defense. He could do only one thing: run. He dashed into the heart of the thorn bushes. The elephant followed, screaming as she charged. Suddenly, the trumpeting ceased. Selous was barelegged "as I always am when hunting on foot." He was wearing only a flannel shirt, a belt and a hat at the charge. These were ripped away by the thorn bushes. He stood after the charge with only part of the ragged shirt clinging to his torso and not "a square inch of skin left uninjured anywhere on the front of my body!"

His natural history background was called into use on a daily basis, and he kept notes on animal behavior. He discussed the lives of African animals with accuracy and clarity and did not ascribe human traits to them. His book, *A Hunter's Wanderings in Africa*, reprinted by Wolfe Publishing Company of Prescott, Arizona, reflects the hunter's interest in wildlife for its own sake. He also did some museum hunting to gain specimens

Patient death—a large male lion waits in the long grass. Although the male is known for his lazy nature, allowing the females to do most of the hunting, a lion this size is very dangerous. He can cover a hundred yards in a few heartbeats of time. Selous became an expert at hunting these creatures.

for display. His vast experience in both hunting and natural history ranked him high as a 19th-century authority on wildlife. He went on to visit many countries—Asia Minor, Transylvania, Canada, Newfoundland, Norway, as well as many parts of America. A 1918 book about Selous, entitled *The Life of Frederick Courtenay Selous, D.S.O.*, by J.G. Millais, also supports the contention that Selous's interest was not nearly as mercenary as it was adventuresome. (The spelling of the middle name, incidentally, is usually Courteney rather than Courtenay.)

THE CHALLENGE OF AMERICAN HUNTING

Selous visited America—to hunt, of course. He also wrote of his North American adventure, which transpired in the Rocky Mountains of 1897. He no longer carried blackpowder guns, rather, a 256-caliber English-made boltgun. The little 6.5mm rifle fired a 160-grain projectile at 2300 feet per second muzzle velocity from a 26-inch barrel, muzzle energy rated at 1880 foot-pounds. It was like our own 30-30 in terms of "power." Selous also carried a 303 British, firing the 215-grain bullet at about 2000 feet per second

Selous used ox wagons to carry supplies into the backcountry of Africa in pursuit of ivory.

for a muzzle energy of 1910 foot-pounds. The great ivory hunter of Africa enjoyed his American safari, for he returned only one year later, still using the 303 British cartridge, but this time chambered in a single-shot falling block rifle. He must have decided upon slightly greater ballistic authority between trips, because included in the battery for his second American hunt was a 375-caliber rifle using Cordite powder and firing a 275 grain jacketed missile at 2000 feet per second for a muzzle energy of 2,443 foot-pounds. Incidentally, Selous's American rifles were iron-sighted, with folding leaves zeroed for 100, 200, 300 and 400 yards.

On his second American hunt, Selous arrived in Sheridan, Wyoming, on August 29, 1897. He traveled by wagon across the Big Horn Mountains to the eastern boundary of Yellowstone National Park. Selous found the hunting more demanding than it had been in Africa, in terms of game wariness and seclusion, although here there were no elephant or Cape buffalo charges to worry about. He enjoyed the hunt very much and even claimed that being alone in the Rocky Mountains

was a special thrill.

He loved his Wyoming hunt and greedily bit into the hardship of it, once wading a stream barefooted in a snowfilled area, his footgear draped over a shoulder as he splashed through the icy water. He was on the trail of game. When that game again crossed the stream, Selous repeated his ice water wading in order to follow.

Selous fared well in the cold country, remaining in camp in spite of snow half covering the tent, and cold that froze the game carcasses so solid that steaks had to be sawed off. He called the weather and circumstance a "charmingly novel experience for my wife and myself, who had never before travelled in a cold country."

Selous was a trophy hunter. His biographers concluded that he tried to hunt as many species as possible. This attitude prevailed in American hunting as well. When he dropped a bull elk on a steep ridge, the animal rolled into a deep canyon. "Standing at the top of this and looking downwards, my heart died (as the Kafirs say) for I did not think it possible that a dead animal could fall down such a place without smashing his horns all to pieces." Selous was delighted to learn that only a few inches of tine had been broken from the antlers of the bull in its fall. And the naturalist in him prevailed in America as it had in Africa. He weighed his game and found, for example, that one big mule deer buck weighed 17 stone and four pounds—242 pounds to us.

But for all its indigenous excitement, Selous mildly complained about the lack of game in comparison with Africa. He said in *Sport and Travel*, a 1900 book, "I can imagine no more perfect country in which to hunt than the Rocky Mountains must once have been, when game was still plentiful. A few fair heads can still be got by hard work and perseverance, but for every head obtained, a good deal of hunting must now be done. . . ."

Selous feared that the game of Wyoming was doomed, except for the animals residing within the borders of Yellowstone Park. He suggested enlarging the park to include more winter range for wildlife. He felt that although game laws existed, they were not being observed at the time, and that many of the residents believed game laws in the United States were unconstitutional, because the game belonged to all of the people. Fortunately, Selous's fears never materialized. Today, Wyoming is one of the best big game hunting states. The Big Horn Mountains teem with deer and hold good populations of elk and moose. However, Selous's remarks were well-founded for 1897.

Selous was a student of riflery and ballistics. He never admired his muzzleloaders. They were of the time and he put up with them. But once the frontloader "died," Selous never looked back. He preferred the modern firearm. He once said he was "heartily sorry" for ever having touched the huge-bore blackpowder rifle. It recoiled severely, and was not that reliable on lung shots, for the lower velocity missile did not deliver the "shock" associated with a modern high-speed bullets. Today's blackpowder hunter often discovers that a shot *in* the shoulder proves deadlier than a shot *behind* the shoulder, verifying Selous's position. On the other hand, Selous found the 6.5mm inadequate for elk. He describes the loss of a bull elk struck with the 6.5mm rifle, blaming his own "bad shooting," as well as the bullet. "I have made many bad shots in my time," he said, "but never, I think, quite so bad a one as this." He

continued, "A Mannlicher bullet sometimes goes wrong, I am told, owing to the nickel coating parting from the lead core as it leaves the muzzle of the rifle."

At age 64, Selous went to war—World War I in East Africa. He attained the rank of captain in the Royal Fusiliers and was awarded the D.S.O. for his service. In January 1917 as he led his men

This very old picture portrays the great Selous in his later years on a safari. At age 64, he joined the British forces fighting in World War I; in 1917 he was killed in battle in East Africa.

against forces four times their strength, he was shot to death.

Selous spanned the bridge between the blackpowder era and the smokeless powder age. He went from the muzzleloader to the breech-loader. He passed from single-shot to repeater. He saw the transition from big bore blackpowder power to the force of smaller projectiles at high velocity. He used them all. Fortunately, many of his experiences were recorded by his pen so that his memory survives to this day as one of the great hunters of all time.

28

AD TOPPERWEIN: GREATEST TRICK SHOOTER

The greatest trick shooter in the world. If you want to be known as that, you have to *earn* it. Many marksmen of note developed through the years, including the marvelous Annie Oakley. But those qualified to judge such things lift Ad Topperwein to the pinnacle as the world's best exhibition shooter—the best aerial marksmen of them all.

Adolph Toepperwein, sometimes called "Top" or "Ad," was born in Bejar County, later known as Leon Springs, Texas, about 25 miles north of San Antonio. His father Fred had settled near New Braunfels, Texas, in 1869 with plans of farming. Mr. Toepperwein was also a shooter, a gunsmith and a firearms designer. He even obtained a rifle patent, which he sold to Winchester. Although the pilot model never enjoyed manufacture, Ad was very proud of his father's accomplishment and recognition.

Herr Toepperwein had a strong influence on his son. He had been a Schuetzenfest marksman in the Old Country. Since there were a number of Bavarian settlers in Bejar County, Toepperwein organized them into a shooting club. He was among the best riflemen of the group. He harbored a great respect for marksmanship, a sentiment he passed on to his son. Young Ad Topperwein— who later dropped the "e" in his last name—loved to hunt. His early interest in hunting led to his later aerial target shooting. However, Ad's first adventure with a firearm was associated with the procurement of game meat, just as Annie Oakley was introduced to shooting through hunting.

Food for the table was Ad's goal. He first hunted with a 40-caliber muzzleloader, which he replaced with a Winchester Model 73 lever-action rifle chambered for the 44 WCF (Winchester Center Fire) cartridge. The rifle had a 24-inch octagonal barrel. While he sustained an interest in hunting, he became devoted to target shooting. The young marksman acquired a Winchester Model 1890 slide-action 22-rimfire rifle. With this he accomplished feats of marksmanship unseen by his friends and unknown to the great majority of shooters. His ability was uncanny. The tall, slim, blue-eyed Topperwein would someday entertain multitudes with his gifted ability.

In the meantime, he shot for enjoyment, while his friend Louis Heurmann tossed pebbles, blocks of wood and other targets into the air for the rifleman to shoot at. Ad, as far as his biographers know, was not interested in putting holes in a paper bull's-eye. All of his rifle targets were of an aerial nature. He leaned heavily toward the 22-rimfire rifle and standard bullets, not shot cartridges, although he did use shot cartridges in the early part of his career.

A Winchester Model 1903 autoloader, firing the 22 Auto cartridge, eventually replaced the pump-action 22 Model 1890 rifle. Then a Winchester Model 63 semi-auto 22 rifle came along, firing 22 Long Rifle ammunition. This rifle over-

Ad Topperwein—greatest trick shooter of them all. Blessed with supreme coordination, he could "shoot the pips out of an orange" and the orange didn't have to be stationary at the time.

took the Model 1903. The latter required special ammo. With this Ad fired the 22 Winchester Auto round only. The Model 63 digested all 22 Long Rifle ammunition. Ad shot as often as he could. But before trick-shooting fame would rest upon his shoulders, he would pursue another line of work.

Ad Topperwein was gifted with artistic talent as well as shooting talent. He could draw. In 1887 at age 18, he left Leon Springs for San Antonio, at that time a thriving town of 10,000 souls. There, after a short stint as a sales clerk in a clothing store, according to Colonel Charles Askins who knew and wrote about Top, he became a cartoonist for the San Antonio *Express* newspaper. (Another source says Top drew cartoons for the *San Antonio Light*.) The cartoons can still be seen in archival materials and in the original chalk plates, which were part of the printing process. Ad's cartoons were well-received by the public.

But a great romance was blossoming. On just about any afternoon, the cartoonist could be found plinking, for that's what Top preferred to do, standing along the river, zipping holes into tin cans with 22 rifle bullets. He wanted to shoot more than he wanted to draw. Now enter the Sells-Floto Circus. Touring San Antonio, the circus owners were not looking for a new act. They already had a trick shooter who fired in the Buffalo Bill style, from horseback, at balloons with shot cartridges. Word reached the circus owners that San Antonio was home to a man whose ability surpassed their trick shooter's talent. Ad would have a chance to prove that ability.

Ad could do with a 22 rifle what his predecessor managed with shot cartridges. Details of Top's demonstration for the circus people were not available from the resources I investigated. We do know that the young good-looking man got the job, and that he moved on with the circus to its next engagement: Mexico.

Top was well-loved by the Mexican audiences. His 12-minute performance included pistol and rifle shooting. His act was soon considered the best in the show. However, Topperwein had to switch from 22 bullets to shot cartridges. Twenty-two missiles supposedly undermined the efficacy of the circus tent a little at a time until the Big Top collapsed. The circus manager was not happy.

Top's shooting fame spread. One of his feats, demonstrated previous to 1894, included the breaking of 955 out of a thousand 2¼-inch clay discs tossed into the air—not with shot cartridges, but with lead 22-rimfire rifle bullets. Topperwein did not rest on his laurels. His shooting steadily improved. Reshooting the same trick, he broke 987 and 989 of 1,000 aerial targets. He took on the standard "clay pigeon," firing at 1,500 of them and breaking 1,500 without a miss, the first 1,000 from a distance of 30 feet, the final 500

LINCOLN WAS RIGHT

By Ad. Toepperwein

§

You may hit some of your targets most of the time.

And most of your targets some of the time

But you can't hit all your targets every time all the time.

No matter how great your skill and how hard you try, sooner or later you'll let one go by.

But no matter whether you hit'em or miss' em you are always having a lot of fun.

Keep up your shooting. You will never regret it, and you may make a better score tomorrow.

from a distance of 40 feet. Ad Topperwein was now in his late 20s. He would soon build a long list of shooting tricks with many different firearms.

Topperwein was a great showman. He purposely invited criticism of a given trick, so that the audience would doubt its veracity. Then Top would prove his ability. For example, Top shot at a metal washer, claiming that the bullet was passing through the hole in the washer. When someone challenged the trick, the aerial marksman covered the hole, as with a postage stamp.

Three weeks after their marriage, "Plinky" Topperwein, who had never fired a shot, was hitting bits of chalk Ad held between his fingers. She once hit 1,460 square 2¼-inch wooden blocks out of the air with a 22 rifle—without a miss.

Then he would fire again. When the washer touched the ground after its short flight, there would be a hole in the center of the postage stamp. A 32-20 cartridge was tossed into the air. Using a 22-rimfire rifle, Ad shot the bullet out of the cartridge case without hitting the case itself.

In the early 1900s, Winchester Repeating Arms Company hired Ad Topperwein as its new exhibition shooter. By my calculations, Ad must have been around 27 years old at the time. He liked his employer. And his employer apparently appreciated him, for Topperwein was Winchester's exhibition shooter for 55 years.

Edwin Pugsley, well-known Winchester Company figure and executive with the firm, often related the story of how Ad met his wife. It seems that the trick shooter had never questioned the quality of his ammunition, until suddenly he acquired a concern for every round that he took on tour, insisting upon personal inspection of each batch of ammo before using it in demonstration. Pugsley pondered the situation, but he let the sharpshooter go on testing ammo at the plant. Winchester's executive became quite suspicious when Top wanted to return all the way from Oregon to ensure that his exhibition ammo was of the best order. Puglsey said OK, but he kept an eye on the sharpshooter. It seems that Topperwein was much more interested in a lovely young lady working in the ballistics lab than he was the ammo itself. That lady, Elizabeth Servaty, was to share Top's life. The couple was married in 1903. Everyone who knew Ad and Elizabeth said it was a happy union.

Top nicknamed the pretty lady "Plinky." She became a renowned aerial shooter in her own right. Her accomplishments with a shotgun were remarkable. Firing a Winchester Model 97, then a Winchester Model 12 when that shotgun surfaced, Plinky set records. In 1916, she broke 1,952 of 2,000 regulation clays in three hours and 15 minutes (another source says five hours and 20 minutes) at the Montgomery (Alabama) Country Club. Runs of 280 straight, 139 straight, 111 running and 109 in a row were established by Mrs. Topperwein.

Mr. Topperwein was a pre-television walking/talking/living advertisement for Winchester. He train-traveled from one town to another, covering vast stretches of America and Canada. Part of Top's job was to visit local gunshops that sold Winchester rifles and ammunition, there to chat with local shooters whose feats of marksmanship often topped Top's—at least in the telling.

After meeting and speaking with his admirers, Top would repair to the edge of a city—cities had edges in the early 1900s. There he plied his trade, mainly the shattering of frangible aerial targets with a 22-rimfire rifle. Top tossed in a little handgun and shotgun aerial trickshooting to balance the riflery. Ad handled a shotgun as well as he fired a rifle. He exhibited equal grace and the same unerring results with the scattergun, hitting five clay targets out of the air, tossed simultaneously. The targets were flipped while Top's back was turned. At the command, Ad would do a backflip and nab his shotgun, regaining his composure in time to shuck five rounds from his Model 12 Winchester 12-gauge pumpgun, smoking each clay target before it could reach the earth. Apparently, there were variations on this theme. One was a fast run with a forward flip following the tossing of the clay targets. After the flip, top regained his feet, grabbing his shotgun from a table and powdering the clay targets. But even that level of shooting was not sufficiently lofty to satisfy Ad Topperwein.

Picture this. Top holds a Model 63 Winchester so that its ejection port faces skyward. He fires the rifle. A spent cartridge case leaps out of the port and upward, at which Top swings into action, pinging the empty case out of the air with one 22 Long Rifle bullet. The hand-eye coordination required for this feat defies measurement. A 22-rimfire cartridge case is less than two-thirds of an inch long. Hitting one stationary on the ground requires good shooting.

Another of Top's tricks included the shooting of two sixshooters simultaneously. The marksman aimed one revolver in the standard fashion, but to give the feat a higher level of difficulty and interest, he held the other pointed rearward. The second 22-rimfire revolver was aimed over the shoulder by aid of a mirror. A tin can in front of the shooter and a tin can in back of the shooter shuddered and flipped at the unified crack of the two revolvers.

Meanwhile, wife Plinky would shoot the ash from a cigarette as it rested in Top's lips. As Colonel Askins pointed out, Ad did not smoke, but the cigarette made a good prop when fired at with Plinky's 38-caliber revolver. Top took aim on a progression of aerial tin cans—first two, then three, four and eventually five, all in the air at once. Not one can reached the ground before it was punctured by a 22 bullet.

Although I never saw Topperwein shoot, his Uncle Sam and Indian chief outlines were repeated by many other shooters, if not with quite the definition of Ad's "drawing with bullet hole" technique. A local shooter in the Yuma, Arizona, area drew figures on tin with bullet holes, and remarked to the gun club group looking on that it was Ad Topperwein's shooting that prompted his own marksmanship efforts. Sadly, our local sharpshooter did not have the cartoonist training

The great Topperwein shot a Winchester Model 1903 Autoloader firing the 22 Auto cartridge at aerial targets.

that Top possessed, and some of his drawings were a tad lopsided. While our local marksman accomplished his artwork with between 300 and 400 bullets, he observed no time limit. Top made his bullet hole outlines with 350 to 450 bullets, firing about a bullet a second. Not one puncture was out of line. These bullet hole outlines sometimes ended up as souvenirs. Colonel Askins has a Topperwein Indian chief in his collection. The great exhibition shooter was known not only in his era, but well after it.

Topperwein lived when trick shooting was world-popular. He was hardly alone as an expert showman with a firearm. While Ad was not laying claim to being the best aerial rifleman in the world, others were, especially one Doctor Carver, who never worked as a hospital orderly, let alone a physician. But Doc was good. And he had tenacity aplenty. He shot for records, proclaiming himself world champion trick shooter after breaking a multitude of 2½-inch glass balls. These glass spheres were very popular aerial targets during the era. They could be considered a standard target of the trick shooter. Doc went on a shooting spree that included over 60,000 glass balls. He kept several Model 1890 Winchester trombone-action rifles steadily spewing bullets, while helpers removed the fouling produced by semi-smokeless powder. By using 11 rifles and staying with the program for 12 shooting hours each day for 10 days running, Carver disintegrated over 55,000 glass spheres. Later, Doc repeated the feat, missing only 650 targets out of 60,000.

It should be noted that the target-tossers were practiced in their art, too. They learned to flip the target into the air with about the same speed and direction each time, providing a uniform arc. The consistent style of tossing targets helped the aerial shooter hit them. Top's upcoming shoot on wooden blocks would include six boys as target-tossers, not trained aids.

Records are made to be broken. Practically before the smoke cleared the bores of Dr. Carver's Winchesters, one B.A. Bartlett was hard at it. Bartlett warmed his Winchesters up and fired for 144 hours, shooting at the same regulation-size glass balls. After 60,000 were tossed in the air, Bartlett quit shooting. He had missed only 280. He was king of the broken glass ball hill, for a very long time. In deference to Bartlett's shooting

Tom Frye, the Remington shooter, broke Topperwein's record by shooting 100,010 wooden blocks in the air, while missing only six. Frye died in 1978.

spree, when Ad Topperwein decided to produce a shooting record of his own, it was not with glass balls. Top never explained his switch from the "standard" glass ball target. We wish today he had stayed with it, because we could have compared apples with apples instead of apples with oranges. Nonetheless, Top did not fire on the glass ball.

Top shot wooden blocks instead. These blocks were square—2¼ by 2¼ inches—each one precisely cut. In 1907, Top entered the San Antonio Fair Grounds with 10 Winchester 1903 autoloaders and 50,000 rounds of ammo, along with seven wagonloads of the little wooden blocks. Another mystery—since the normal number of aerial targets fired on "for the record" was 60,000, why did Topperwein elect to supply himself with "only" 50,000 wooden blocks? We don't know, and never will. However, we do know that 22,500 of the blocks were shot at twice. "Get him more ammo!" was the cry. When the 50,000 rounds, plus additional ammo were exhausted, Top had hit all but nine of 72,500 tossed blocks in a shooting time of 120 hours. Obviously, he had B.A. Bartlett whipped. Since he did not use the little glass balls, however, the Bartlett record was in a way unchallenged.

In the 120-hour shoot, Top had a run of 14,500 straight. But he wouldn't quit. Most of the blocks were splintered, so Ad shot at the pieces. When these were broken, he continued to shoot at pieces of the pieces. It was a record, glass balls or not, and the record was to stand for about a half century before it would be broken.

The shooter who broke Ad's record was a great marksman in his own right, although not employed as an aerial shooter. Tom Frye was a salesman for Remington. He grabbed a Remington Model 66 nylon autoloader and commenced firing upon 100,000 square 2¼-inch wooden blocks. By the time Tom had popped 43,725 blocks, his misses tallied only two. At the end of his shooting marathon, Frye had fired on 100,010 blocks with only six misses. Who congratulated Tom Frye on his remarkable accomplishment? Adolph Topperwein, of course, who wrote him a letter of acknowledgment.

EXPERT WITH RIFLE, SHOTGUN OR SIDEARM

Research shows somewhat different sets of figures for the various feats of marksmanship; however, the discrepancies do not detract from the accomplishments. Give or take a hit or miss, the trick shooters of the day were terrific. Top fired many different guns over the years. He is noted as a 22 rifle expert, but he was an expert with a 401 Winchester self-loading rifle, a 30-30 Model 94, many handguns, even an 18-pound BAR.

The story goes that Winchester was putting on a demonstration of the BAR for the Secretary of War. John Browning himself fired the BAR without a hitch. But Winchester had a clincher at the end of the test. Out came Ad Topperwein, who hit aerial targets with full-throttle 30-06 ammo. But he made an embarrassing mistake. One of his sky-borne targets was a tomato can, with the tomatoes still in it. The wind was not favorable. Ad fired. The tomato can erupted like a volcano, splattering its juicy contents into the air--and back to earth guided by that unfortunate wind. The Secretary of War was decorated with tomato "puree." Topperwein changed his act from trick shooter to magician, disappearing from the scene.

A reader reported in a July 1942 issue of *American Rifleman* magazine that he saw Top-

perwein perform a shooting stunt with a 44 handgun. The feat transpired at the N.C.R. Gun Club at Dayton, Ohio, in 1905 or 1906—the reader was not certain. Top used a single-action revolver chambered for the 44 S&W Russian cartridge, which he held cocked in his right hand. Using his left hand, Ad tossed a two-inch square block of wood into the air 20 or 30 feet high. Then Top hit the block of wood—not once, but twice. Remember that the single-action revolver had to be cocked again after the first shot. Consider, too, that after the block of wood was struck by the first bullet, it would fly crazily in the air, propelled farther away from the shooter. Mr. Earl E. Hole of Dearborn, Michigan, the author of the *American Rifleman*-published letter, stated that he saw this trick only once, although he attended many other Topperwein exhibitions. The great marksman obviously possessed uncanny hand-eye coordination in order to perform his rifle and shotgun aerial tricks. But to do with a sixgun what Top could accomplish demands a sense of space and bullet flight that would exist only in fiction if the world had not seen the man perform.

Another good Topperwein tale concerns an archaeology professor at the University of Texas and an Indian pictograph. Top and the professor apparently frequented the same area of rimrock country, although not in each other's company. On a short vacation, Ad was shooting in the location. He saw an interesting granite ledge and decided to draw with bullets his famous Indian caricature upon the face of that ledge, which he did. Later, the professor approached Top with exciting news—a heretofore undiscovered pictograph had been found. It was a wonderful likeness of an Indian chief in full headdress tattooed right into the side of a granite ledge. There was nothing else like it anywhere. It was quite a discovery. Ad agreed.

Ad Topperwein lost his beloved Plinky unexpectedly in 1945. Top left off with trick shooting about that time, but he did maintain a shooting camp and range 20 miles from San Antonio. The place was enjoyed more by his friends than by him, for failing eyesight finally wrote "the end" to his famous shooting career.

Ad Topperwein made a great impact on the world of shooting. While the era of the trick shooter slipped away, Top continued to attract many disciples. He inspired L.L. "Tex" Cline, for

Ad was a wonder with the handgun as well as the rifle and shotgun—and a great showman, too. He purposely invited criticism of a given trick, so that the audience would doubt its veracity. Then he'd show them what he could do.

example, who followed the tradition of trick shooting because he admired the great marksman so much. Topperwein lived into 1962, dying at age 93. With him went a slice of history. Professional exhibition shooting may be gone, but the memory of the greatest trick shooter of them all lives on.

29

STEWART WHITE: AMERICAN EXPLORER

"For some occult reason people never seem to expect me to own evening clothes, or to know how to dance, or to be able to talk about anything civilized; in fact, most of them appear disappointed that I do not pull off a war-jig in the middle of the drawing-room," said Stewart Edward White in his book *The Mountains* (1904). No wonder. If you read the first-hand accounts of his African safaris, the dangers he defied, the primitive tricks he used to survive, you might share the same reaction.

Stewart Edward White was a noted American rifleman, an explorer, an adventure-seeker. To say that he was an outdoorsman is total understatement. To him the outdoors—the more remote the better—was life-giving. It sustained him, nurtured him and provided his "raison d'etre." Of Africa he said, "It is the only country I know where a man is thoroughly and continuously alive." He enjoyed firearms and he learned of them and their loads from field experience. He often hunted alone, or with one other partner, being a "disbeliever in the common habit of trailing along a small army." He sucked up hard life on the hunting trail as medicine for the easy life back in the city, thinking that real hunting would ". . . require altogether too much work and skill for those 'softlings,' " as he called hunters who traveled to the outback with every creature comfort.

The year 1873 was not particularly momentous for those who lived in Grand Rapids, Michigan, except for Thomas Stewart White and his wife, Mary. In that year, their son, Stewart Edward, was born. Mr. White was a millionaire lumberman and an enthusiastic outdoorsman. It is from his father that little Stewart learned of firearms and hunting, interests that eventually took him to exotic reaches in search of excitement. As a boy, Stewart never studied in public schools; he was educated at home by tutors. And although he later attended law school, he did not receive a degree. He was good with words, however, and the law studies may have helped polish his writing skills.

Thomas Stewart bought a ranch in California, to which the family moved in 1884 (they lived there for four years before returning to Michigan). There White acquired the mortar that cemented the bricks of his writing career and bonded his love for hunting and shooting. From age 11, he kept a daily journal and faithfully entered notes in it up to July of 1946, two months before his death.

Stewart was not afraid of hard labor and in 1901, at age 28, he lumberjacked in the north woods of Michigan. The following year, he wrote his most successful novel, *The Blazed Trail*, based upon his lumbering experiences. By then he knew that he wanted to be a writer and a hunter. Writing would be Stewart White's vocation; hunting, his avocation. On many occasions, the two blended as the author's work, both fiction and non-fiction, arose from hunting experiences.

White married Elizabeth Grant, a rich girl who had no outdoor expertise, but who, after a camping-trip honeymoon, became a willing partner of the wilds. She shared many trips, including the 22-month African safari White later wrote about. Meeting Teddy Roosevelt when White was a tour guide in Santa Barbara, California, made a large impact on the author's attitudes. A long friendship with Roosevelt ensued, and Stewart adopted the "rough-and-ready attitude" of the great statesman, admiring hard work and the rugged life, which would, according to both men, build character. Even after being attacked by a leopard, White's disposition was upbeat. It was worth taking the risk, for the adventure of it he said. ". . . that is why, at the age of fifty- three, I am sitting here in a clay and thatched hut, in the wildest part of untouched Africa, joint king of the city of Nyumbo, somewhat chewed by a recent leopard, but still going strong." (from *Lions in the Path*)

An active lifestyle was extremely important to White. Sportsmanship and taking chances were an integral part of his personality: "If you do not like that sort of game, stay out of it entirely." (from *The Land of Footprints*) "The man too old or fat or soft to stand walking under a tropical sun should stay away, for, owing to prevalence of tsetse, riding animals are impossible." (*The Rediscovered Country*) And from the same, "The hard work will discourage the fellow who likes his shooting brought to his bedside." White's attitude of getting the most from life, of keeping in decent physical condition, of remaining active well into one's later years, seems more modern than the man. Many of his constituents, however, believed that growing out of shape was a right of passage with age. Not Stewart. He worked hard. He played hard.

TO WRITE WHAT YOU BREATHE

White's prolific writing career spanned about 64 years—with almost a book a year to his credit. In his captivating style, he created 24 non-fiction and 34 fiction titles, some with autobiographical overtones. Because of his fame and financial backing, White was able to hunt in many different locales, but he was best known for his exploits in Africa. His three safaris—in 1910, 1913 and 1925—gave him a large reservoir of hunting knowledge from which to draw. *The Land of Footprints*, first printed in 1912, is more than armchair adventure and travel guide. White's novelist background allowed the writer to lure the reader into the written page, where the latter dangled breathlessly 'midst the charge of leopard and lion. During the 1913 safari, which lasted almost two years, he was confronted by Germans who suspected that he was mapping the area for possible future military exploit. (Remember that World War I would begin in 1914). Although the Germans were suspicious of the American hunter, they did not detain him.

'*Footprints* in 1912, *African Camp Fires* in 1913, *The Rediscovered Country* in 1915 and *Lions in the Path* in 1925 were four of White's travel-oriented titles. But he also wrote books such as *Arizona Nights*, *The Claim Jumpers* and *Wild Geese Calling*. It is not true that good writers pen only from experience. Stephen Crane wrote one of the best Civil War stories of all time, yet he was never a soldier during the war between the states. However, White did launch his ship of fiction upon the ocean of reality. He craved adventure. And the adventure created a platform for his work. From *Lions in the Path*: "I have been, many times, at the receiving end of lion charges. There is a great thrill in it. The instant the beast starts, you realize two things: One is that he has made up his mind to get you . . . the other thing is that it is now up to you and to you alone."

Although he fit the 19th and early 20th-century posture of the sportsman hunter in Africa, his writing shows a special reverence concerning the natives of the foreign lands he visited. Of the gunbearer he said, "In close quarters the gunbearer has the hardest job in the world. I have the most profound respect for his absolute courage." ('*Footsprints)* He applauded these men who stood the charge, often without a tool of defense, or the thorough familiarity of its use. Sometimes these faithful trackers took the brunt of a charge. White tells the story in his own words:

All I knew at that moment was that the leopard had uttered a roar, and as I levelled the rifle toward the only spot from which harm could come to us, there was a flash of yellow as the beast leaped, bearing Suleimani down. He let off the Springfield, but of

Michigan-born hunter and writer, Stewart Edward White, is best known for his adventures in Africa. He authored three books based on his dramatic safari experiences, plus additional works on firearms and other outdoor experiences. His refined features belie his rugged nature and his belief that hard work and risk-taking "build character."

White frequently pursued lions during the hunt, as depicted in this 19th-century painting by Philip R. Goodwin. White was one of the first well-known hunters of his day to have the Springfield 30-06 sporterized and believed that the 30-06 was an all-around "meatmaker."

course missed. There was no chance for me to shoot, although they were by now fairly at my feet. Rolling over and over as they were, I should almost certainly have killed the man with my heavy bullet. It was a horrible sight. Never had I imagined such fierce, quick ferocity.

At this point, another man, Kisumu, opened fire on the leopard with a 22 rimfire rifle. This brought the leopard at him. White fired as the animal charged Kisumu. The bullet passed through the leopard just over the heart. The cat leapt instantly on White. Both went down together. White fought the leopard, but it was, of course, the effect of the bullet that saved the hunter's life. "To my great relief," said Stewart, "I felt him weaken,

then relax to limpness. He was dead." White looked around him. "We were scattered, as the cowboys have it, from hell to breakfast—guns, hats, knives, cartridges. Suleimani half sat up, covered with blood, his scalp half off, apparently one eye gone."

White looked for his hat first. Then he rounded up his Springfield 30-06 rifle—not for the weapon itself, but because under the buttplate Stewart carried permanganate crystals in a vial, which in fact was a 405 Winchester cartridge case. The crystals were an aid for septic poisoning. White treated Suleimani first. "His scalp was torn and furrowed by a dozen long gashes down to the bone, and was in one place ripped loose. A fang had gone through an eye socket. A flap of flesh hung down his cheek below the eye. His arm was torn and mangled. I did the best I could. . . ." Next he doctored Kisumu. And lastly, himself. There were no more permanganate crystals for White's wounds, but he managed to ". . . collect enough that had stuck to my bloody fingers to get some into each cut of my own."

That was the life for Stewart Edward White—rugged, unpredictable. You have to like White, to admire the way he treated people who were working for him. When Suleimani called to him, Stewart went over and held his hand. "This seemed to give him great comfort, for he perceptibly relaxed. After a few moments, his poor mangled face contorted into a grin and he chuckled.

"Ah, he was a very bad leopard," said Suleimani.

As for permanganate crystals in an open wound, White explained the burning pain this way: "Don't attempt to get the idea by applying a red-hot iron to yourself, or some other feeble subterfuge. The Spanish Inquisition certainly missed a trick there."

White also authored "how-to" articles on the topics of hunting and firearms. He wrote as widely as the "outdoor writer" of today, on personal experiences and studies in both shooting and hunting. Although able to afford the guided hunt, he was more than a tag-a-long, waiting to be led to game by a local "professional." In 'Footprints, White discussed stalking, "sinking down slowly out of sight" when game was spotted, and he talked of glassing for game and stillhunting. Mostly, he attempted to impart the *feeling* of the hunt. He promoted a strong sentiment for the land itself, and for the native people he hunted with. The instructional nature of today's outdoor writing sometimes denies that approach—of telling the story side of a hunt. In White's time, that style of writing was welcomed.

BALLISTICS DISCOVERIES

White was interested in and concerned with terminal ballistics. In many ways he was far ahead of his time in reporting on the effects of various cartridges and firearms. Many of the sportsmen of the era made mention of their rifles and rounds, but gave no great detail of the results. Others rarely spoke of the firearms used. White was interested in field autopsy, studying wound channels for clues of bullet effectiveness or failure. He preferred, for example, a "light repeater"

for lions, and he killed 73 of the big cats in his time. But he found that with his favorite 30-06, the 180-grain open-point bullet, though good on side hits, broke up on frontal shots. "The 220-grain delayed-action bullet for the same weapon is much better," he said. (*Lions*)

He felt as many of us do now that "A bullet that penetrates well and mushrooms is what is wanted." One of his favorite bullets for lion hunting with the 30-06 was the Improved Short Exposed Point in 220-grain weight. "It penetrates first and mushrooms later," he said. That is a profound statement, for as the initial bullet upset goes, so goes the wound channel due to the shock wave. White seemed to have an intuition, if not a factual grasp, of this condition. He wanted more than two shots for lion hunting, preferring a repeating magazine rifle, especially after an episode in which four lions charged simultaneously.

White used a Holland and Holland double rifle for rhino and Cape buffalo, as well as other dangerous game. He found the 465 Cordite round quite effective. According to John Taylor in *African Rifles and Cartridges*, (offered in reprint through Wolfe Publishing Company), the 465 H&H Cordite drove a 480-grain full-patch bullet at 2125 fps. That would give close to modern 458 Winchester ballistics. Taylor thought well of the round. White was not a double-gun fan, however, and his penchant for the lever-action Model 95 Winchester in 405 Winchester caliber was well established. The custom Springfield 30-06, stocked by Ludwig Wundhammer, wore a Lyman aperture sight. White range-tested this rifle thoroughly, finding it would produce 3.5-inch groups at 100 yards, with groups slightly over seven inches at 300 yards. His record of hits/misses with the custom '06 were 395 cartridges fired and 307 hits while in Africa. Many animals, most of which were needed for camp food, required a second strike, because the 307 hits brought a tally of 185 carcasses.

White carried the 405 Winchester extensively in Africa, as did Roosevelt. Taylor did not think much of the 405 as a lion-stopper and he noted that when Roosevelt used his, he was probably backed up by the professional hunter's big-bore double-barreled rifle. Nonetheless, the 405 was a White favorite, though he did not always rave of its authority on all large game. The 405 was much preferred for lion over the 30-06, but

White admitted that its looping trajectory made long-range shooting questionable. He stated that beyond 125 to 150 yards, he preferred the '06.

Even though he admired the rifle and round very much, White found himself in a see-saw situation with the 405. "I had now the 405 Winchester," he said in 'Footprints, "a light and handy weapon delivering a tremendous blow." When referring to Cape buffalo hunting, however, White later stated, ". . . he opened fire with his 405 Winchester, a weapon altogether too light for this sort of work." But another experience enhanced his opinion of the 405 on buffalo. He observed that "The shock of the bullet actually knocked that great beast off his feet! My respect for the hitting power of the 405 went up several inches." Ordinary bullets do not shove game over, of course, but White was speaking from his visual experience. It appeared to him that the buff was knocked off its feet by the thrust of the 405. White's assessment of what he saw is non-scientific, as the bullet most certainly did not push the buffalo over.

That last buff, by the way, got up and had to be struck by a second 405. That didn't do the job, either. A third strike in the ribs from an "elephant rifle" was administered. The buff still did not take the ten count. Five more shots from the 405 followed, creating, it was noted, a pattern that could be covered with the hand.

The 405 Winchester was another White favorite, but he see-sawed in its ability to handle big game. On one hunt, though, he was able to kill 14 animals with 14 shots.

A versatile and resourceful hunter, Stewart White even tried the longbow on lions during one safari in Africa.

The lever-action, with its fast-shooting nature, appealed to White, even after hitting a zebra five times with it at long range with less than telling effect. "The fifth shot emptied the rifle. As I had no more cartridges with me, I approached to within sixty yards, and stopped to wait for him to fall, or for a very distant Memba Sasa to come up with more cartridges. Then the zebra waked up. He put his ears back and came straight in my direction. This rush I took for a blind death flurry, and so dodged off to one side, thinking that he would of course go by me. Not at all! . . . It was a malicious charge. . . To be killed by a lion is at least a dignified death; but to be mauled by a zebra!" ('*Footprints*)

Although good bullets were available quite early from several companies, many failures observed for various cartridges in the late 1800s and early 1900s were really bullet shortcomings, not cartridge inefficiency. Overall, the 405 Winchester performed well for White. He noted that on one trip he fired at 14 animals with the 405, killing all 14. He also shot 33 times for 29 hits. But the 30-06 was Stewart's workhorse. He immediately contracted for two customized '06s as soon as he gained familiarity with the cartridge. On the same safari noted above, the 30-06 enjoyed far more use than the 405, with 135 animals dropped, 98 of them one-shot kills. White fired 260 rounds at 161 animals, missing 26 times. He further notes the longest shot as 421 paces. In 'Footprints, White pronounced, ''Evidently the very high velocity of this bullet from its shock to the nervous system had delivered a paralyzing blow sufficient to knock out the lioness for the time being.'' White was early to recognize a high-velocity advantage. He noted that the 30-06 dispatched game more quickly than cartridges shooting similar bullets at slower velocities.

In his own 30-06s, he used the 165-grain Winchester spitzer bullet, a 172-grain spitzer bullet from U.M.C., and the 150-grain service bullet. The last one he did not like. The ammo he carried on one safari lends credence to his faith in the 30-06 as an all-around meatmaker. For two men, the ammo supply was 100 each of ''heavy rifle'' and 405 Winchesters plus 400 ''New Springfield.'' He felt the 280 Ross with its ''grooveless oval bore'' rifling was not accurate beyond 100 yards, but he had faith in his 30-06 at 300 yards and beyond, noting that ''Three hundred and fifty yards is a very long shot. It is over four city blocks—New York size.'' So he was well aware of the requirements of long-range shooting.

In his writing, White made every attempt to relate his shots factually, especially in terms of distance and effect. He condemned one writer of the period for claiming to have dropped an African antelope at 800 yards. White took the trouble, when in the district, to check with the marksman's professional hunter. The latter confirmed that his client had made a fine long shot, but not at 800 yards. It might have been 350 yards, he admitted. White would often pace a shot to get a good idea of the actual distance. He knew that some long shots were best made with pencil and notebook back in the camp lounging tent.

Stewart Edward White was a successful writer and a noted American rifleman of his time. But he was more than rifleman, more than hunter. He assessed the environment around him. He froze blocks of time with words, verbally illustrating historical notes for readers of a future time. Of cowboys, he commented freely. He preserved many colorful quotes from these princes of the range: ''I wouldn't speak to him if I met him in hell carrying a lump of ice in his hand.'' And ''If you're brains were all made of dynamite, you couldn't blow the top of your head off.'' (The Mountains) Reasonably good gun savvy pervaded much of his writing. In The Long Rifle, White said,''In our country 200 years ago shooting was the national pastime and people shot guns as today they shoot golf.'' His book of the long rifle was actually a historical dedication to the leather-stocking trailblazers of the West, with firearm information pertaining to the various Early American shooting periods.

The modern shooter is fortunate to have White's clear stream of written experiences to take long drafts from. White was an interesting man, a product of his time, as we are products of ours. But he was also abreast of his era, and perhaps even ahead of it in his empirical study of firearms and cartridge behavior. White looked forward to the future, while at the same time preserving the treasured values of the past in both marksmanship and hunting. He tried everything from bow and arrow (on lions) to elephant rifles, making mental and written notes of the results. White was a novelist, a travel writer, and although he may not have known it, an arms author as well. How does history view him? A writer first, perhaps, but definitely based on a career as a great shooter.

30

COL. TOWNSEND WHELEN: DEAN of the GUNWRITERS

Colonel Whelen had a way of convincing us to make up our minds in his direction on matters of shooting. He was an expert—for years and years. The dean of all firearms authors, his impact on the world of shooting is undeniable. "Only accurate rifles are interesting," he said. Those words linger today, repeated over and over. He left a legacy of handloading. And a love for wilderness hunting. "No man is competent unless he is able to *stalk alone and armed through the wilderness,*" said Whelen. Overstated? Perhaps. But modern courses in wilderness living are credited with building confidence as well as the human spirit.

Ink flowed from Whelen's prolific pen starting at the turn of this century. Born in Pennsylvania on March 6, 1877, in blackpowder days, Townsend lived to see the space age, dying in 1961. But his beginning was not so auspicious. He was a frail boy, a failure in sports. A physical fitness expert declared young Townsend the poorest physical specimen in the school. "I could not compete well with other boys either mentally or physically," Whelen later admitted. "I always stood at the tail of my class at school." He had a poor memory to match is equally poor stature. That changed. The frail boy would become a powerful backwoods hunter. The last in the class would be the first in gun writing.

The outdoors put Whelen on his trail of life. "There in a thicket I built a little wickiup," he

recalled. He wandered the woods alone for hours. And later for days. His father was a doctor who often worked away from the city. Young Townsend took advantage of the Pennsylvania geography by hiking and hunting, and by shooting whenever he could.

Tall and thin, Whelen decided at age 19 to exercise himself into shape. He needed a more rugged routine to build himself up, so he joined the Pennsylvania National Guard. His daily regimen gave him confidence in his body and in his intellect. He took command of the National Guard shooting range at Essington, Penn. After two years of this, he made the U.S. Army his career, which lasted about 40 years. Teddy Roosevelt commissioned him a 2nd Lieutenant of Infantry in 1902. During his career he was ordnance officer in charge of Frankford Arsenal, and also responsible for research and development at the Springfield Arsenal.

Although Townsend eventually became a family man with grandchildren, it was shooting that enveloped his thoughts, actions and writing. Whelen's story is, therefore, one of shooting, hunting and the great outdoors. He was particularly good with the Springfield Model 1873, shooting the 45-70 Government blackpowder cartridge. He used mainly the standard load: 405-grain bullet, 70 grains of Fg or FFg powder. He later turned to a Winchester Model 1985, caliber 40-70, for which he cast his own 330-grain bullets. He also

Townsend Whelen was a great wilderness hunter and a powerful man who could go it alone in the outback. Here he packs a moose head and cape back to camp.

liked the 30-30. Even at the end of his career, he supported the little cartridge when most gunwriters did not.

Colonel Whelen was a student of Dr. Mann. He knew Pope and Niedner. And he earned the respect of all the impactful shooters of the era—with only a few harsh words heaped on him from one or two of these gurus of guns. He was an experimenter. Whelen's testing was empirical—he was not a wizard of physics and did not spout scientific jargon like a Roman fountain. But did he shoot! When the 243 Winchester and 6mm Remington hit the gunstore shelves, the Colonel decided to learn something of these cartridges.

Most gunwriters were content to shoot a couple boxes of factory ammo and the same for handloads, after which a verdict was rendered. Not Townsend Whelen. His bench-testing sessions included firing 600 rounds of ammo. He thrived on testing. He loved burning powder. Patiently, the Colonel shot a rifle and load until he knew the idiosyncrasies of both. He studied trajectories, powders, bullets, and cartridge-case designs. If he didn't own a particular rifle he wanted to test, he borrowed it.

Because of his dedication, his patience and his thorough approach to shooting, he captured the admiration of men such as Jack O'Connor, who said:

The late Colonel Townsend Whelen was a good friend of mine. I believe I have read almost everything of his that has been published, as I started reading his stuff back before World War I when I was a gunstruck adolescent and he was still only a lieutenant. I consider him one of the most sensible, honest and reliable gun writers ever to practice the rather doubtful trade in this country. He started hunting big game in the blackpowder days.

O'Connor summed it all up in three words—sensible, honest and reliable. That was Whelen.

The hunting field was Whelen's classroom. In 1901 he and partner Bill Andrews took a little hunting trip to British Columbia that lasted nine months. They carried flour, sugar, beans, rice, dried fruit, cereal and a few incidentals. They had a tent or two and some Army blankets. Whelen described the experience in a December 1906 *Outdoor Life* article: "For cooking utensils we had 2 fry pans, 3 kettles to nest, 2 tin cups, 3 tin plates and a gold pan [for stream panning for gold]. We took 300 cartridges for each of our rifles. Bill carried a .38-55 Winchester, Model 94, and I had my old .40-72 Winchester Model '95, which had proved too reliable to relinquish for a high-power small bore." The Colonel would later change his mind on that score, voicing great admiration for the high-speed 22-caliber varmint cartridge, the 270 Winchester and many other "high-power small bores." Whelen was a true wilderness hunter, a breed as scarce as dinosaur eggs. He might strike out with: rifle, mess kit, oatmeal, matches, tea, salt, tarp, knife and hand axe—no sleeping bag—(he dozed by a fire with his clothes on)—making it on his own in the backwoods. He remained a wilderness hunter all his life. At age 80 he planned a backcountry trip. Only a broken hip prevented his going. Otherwise, he would have been on the trail.

Whelen was influenced by the great outdoorsman, George W. Sears, better known as Nessmuk to his readers. Nessmuk could have made a real-life model for James Fenimore Cooper's leather-stocking tales. Nessmuk out-wildernessed Natty Bumpo. When Townsend was a boy, he met the great trailmaster. He recalled lifting Nessmuk's special canoe and marveling at its lack of weight and strength of construction. Whelen may or may not have used Nessmuk as a role model, but he certainly followed in the woodsman's footsteps. His method of staying warm without a sleeping bag, by starting a fire and rekindling its flames from time to time throughout the night, was of the Nessmuk style—go light. Carry only what you need and nothing more. Colonel Whelen had two rifle-testing grounds. One was the range with its benchrest. The other was the field. His firearms writing was supported on the broad shoulders of solid experience.

Whelen's book, *Wilderness Hunting and Wildcraft*, published by the Small Arms Technical Publishing Company in 1927, saw a second life in a 1987 reprint by Wolfe Publishing Company. A hunting text through and through, Whelen filled it with chapters on the habits of big game—deer, elk, moose, caribou, sheep and many other wild animals. He talked about finding your way in the outback, clothing, wilderness marksmanship, even photography. "Good shots are made, not born," he believed, and said a good target shooter could be a good game shot, a good game shot a good target shooter. He advocated learning to shoot from all field positions. He discussed proper sight-in.

Whelen practiced what he preached. One time he led a deer with his old 40-72 Winchester rifle, firing three shots. The buck fell with "three bullet holes in his hide just back of the foreshoulder." Whelen's advice on hunting apparel parallels the man's rugged nature. "In choosing clothing for a hunting trip," he said, "particularly in the northern part of the United States or in Canada in the fall of the year, many sportsmen make the mistake of selecting garments that are entirely too heavy. The temperature, even pretty far north into Canada, is delightful right up to the middle of November. . . ." Yes, Colonel. Just like Florida. You have to love his spirit. Generally, winter hasn't spread its icy cloak over the northern landscape by mid-November. But leave your safari shorts at home.

If he wasn't writing a book on his favorite topics, rifles and hunting, he was teaching through his articles. A typical Whelen topic for

the big game hunter, "Some Real Dope on Packing Equipment," appeared in the March 1930 issue of *American Rifleman* magazine. "Scopes for Hunting Rifles," written much later for a December 1950 *American Rifleman* reveals the Colonel's feelings about the glass sight. His statement concerning target magnification and consequent improvement in bullet placement should be heeded today, especially among hunter-riflemen who buy a variable scope, and then leave it on 4X instead of boosting the magnification when appropriate. Whether writing on backpack hunting or scopes, the Colonel was ever an expert through

As a young shooter, Whelen was quite a lever-action fan, and in fact did not change his stance even after he switched to the bolt-action rifle, a firearm he did much to promote.

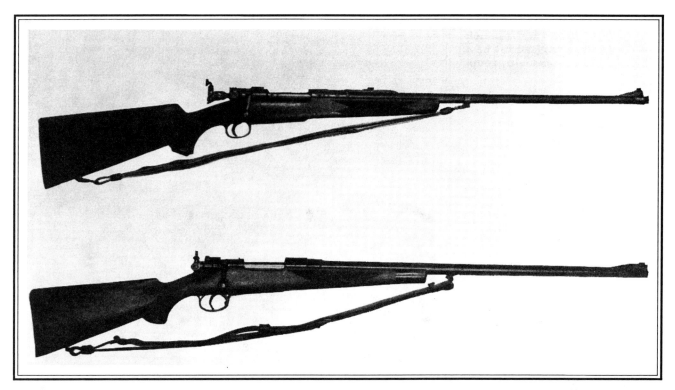

In promoting bolt-action rifles in his book, *Wilderness Hunting and Wildcraft,* Whelen particularly liked the Springfield (top) and the Mauser sporters.

doing what he wrote about. He was no paper hunter. He was a big, strong man, six feet, two inches tall with good health and a rugged constitution. He always looked a decade behind his years. Many of us picked up on Whelen's backcountry hunting tactics in emulation of the man who knew how to make it on the trail without the kitchen sink.

The Colonel's code of ethics was worth following. For example, he used what he harvested and bade others to do the same. On one trip, he was more interested in filling a grizzly bear tag for the meat than the trophy. He insisted that grizzly meat, from a relatively young specimen, was tasty. It was the old monarch that made stringy eating, said the Colonel. Many good hunters of yesteryear scarcely mentioned their firearm, much to the sadness of today's enthusiasts. Whelen was different. His fervor for firearms and loads cemented his hunting adventures with veracity and information. Whelen was concerned not only in the high-performance load for big game hunting, but also with squib loads for big game rifles. He assumed, with entire correctness, that small

game and mountain grouse should be used for food on the backtrail. In wilderness areas, both varieties of wildlife are seldom hunted. Therefore, Whelen built and tested dozens of underpowered loads for big game cartridges intended as meat-savers for on-the-trail edibles. A number of us have followed the Colonel's tracks, using mild loads in big game rounds for harvesting trailfood.

When he spoke of cartridge performance, his words flowed from a deep well of documentation. As an adult, he had a good memory. But he also had notes to back his ballistic claims. A Whelen article, such as "Guns and Gear on the Trail," which appeared in the 1957 *Gun Digest,* was predicated on solid data. In that article, the Colonel discussed knives and walking shoes as well as cleaning kits and gun cases. Whelen loved optics and strongly advised the serious hunter to carry and *use* binoculars. This notion is given lip service today, but few hunters employ the binocular as a game-finding tool. They use it to look at what they have already discovered with the naked eye. Whelen praised hunters who used binoculars as instruments for finding big game.

Whelen was willing to change his mind in print, though. As any expert grows in knowledge, ideas change. The Colonel originally believed that the older blackpowder cartridge, firing heavy bullets of large caliber, was better than the high-speed round that followed it. Remember, of course, that the so-called high-velocity number that came tripping down the cartridge trail after the big-bore blackpowder cartridge was the 30-30 Winchester. Whelen liked the 30-30. However, he did not see the smaller cartridge stomping all over his 40-72 and similar blackpowder cartridges in harvesting power. Then like the mighty oak

tree, our man began to bend. He started to look upon the 30-30, for example, as a fairly decent cartridge after all. And he said so. He even said in a 1930 *American Rifleman* article that the 30-30 was better for the average sportsman than the 30-06: "Nine out of ten of our sportsmen would be very much better fitted, I think, with the Winchester Model 94 in .30-30 caliber than they would with the same rifle in .30-'06 caliber." Whelen meant, presumably, that the 30-30, in both cartridge and rifle, was easier to manage than the '06 and therefore more effective for the hunter who hit the field a few times a year in pursuit of a deer and maybe a black bear.

By 1947 Townsend had much good to say about the 30-06 Springfield cartridge. "The .30-'06 is Never a Mistake" was the title of the December *American Rifleman* article in which Whelen was just a little smoky under the collar. "With writers it has been customary of late to malign the .30-'06," Whelen wrote. "Some have declared that it is not powerful enough for game larger than deer. It has few defenders, perhaps because the large body of sportsmen who have been using it with perfect success for forty years consider that its efficiency may be taken for granted, and it needs no defense." Whelen went on to explain, "I shot most of my game with the .30-'06 before the days of motor cars and planes, and before I had the money to hire guides." He concluded that "I got to love it as I have loved no other rifle since."

In a little while, however, Townsend was courting a new romance—she was called the 270 Winchester. He decided that if he were obliged to carry but one rifle into the wilderness for all big game hunting, it would be chambered for not the 30-'06, but the 270. Whelen was honest. He altered his views when he felt he should, rather than cling to them to avoid controversy.

Whelen did well with a variety of cartridges because he was a good hunter. Due to his proficiency in the field, his deer hunting experiences with the 30-30 were happy ones. When it became fashionable for many gunwriters to degrade the 30-30 (one said the cartridge was useless on deer past 50 yards), the Colonel defended the little cartridge as fine for harvesting deer-sized game.

PROMOTED ACCURACY IN BIG GAME HUNTING, AND MORE

Whelen's real impact, however, was in the arena of big game hunting rifle accuracy. The Colonel's criterion for big game rifle accuracy would be considered a little soft by today's standards. He considered a 100-yard, five-shot, one-inch group extraordinary, with two-inch and even larger patterns quite satisfactory. While it's true that a factory bolt-action big game rifle, out of the box shooting most factory ammo, is well above average if it meets the minute-of-angle goal, numerous rifles today better that level considerably. In Finland, I fired an out-of-the-box Sako rifle in an underground 100-yard range. Using 30-06

Sako factory ammo, several five-shot half-inch groups were produced, all witnessed. Accuracy, thanks to men such as Whelen, has improved. Another example: five-shot one-inch 200-yard groups have been the rule from my Storey 7mm Remington Magnum rifle with heavy Douglas air-gauged premium barrel.

While Colonel Whelen was conservative, he was not afraid of progress. His love for accuracy led him to reloading. Long before handloading was an American pastime, as it is now, Whelen was making thousands of handrolled rounds annually, and promoting the activity. Handloading has been around since the advent of the cartridge case. But Whelen helped to promote the process in modern times. Furthermore, cartridges were handloaded strictly for economy and out of necessity. When the smokeless powder cartridge took over, home-rolling ammo went into a lull. Whelen, among others, helped to revive this sport within the sport—and this time, economy and necessity were secondary considerations.

Handloading was practiced in the name of better accuracy, ballistic authority and cartridge versatility. Through the latter part of 1935 and into the early part of 1936, Townsend Whelen wrote a fine five-part series on handloading for *American Rifleman* magazine. The Colonel explained in his own careful and complete manner how to select components and how to create the best possible loads, all in perfect safety. In Part I (November 1935), "An Introduction to Reloading," Whelen asked and answered several vital questions for would-be handloaders: Is reloading practical? Does reloading pay? Is reloading economical? And so forth.

Whelen was one of the principals associated with the commercializing of the 22 Hornet cartridge. He handloaded for the round and disseminated the results. While Whelen did not develop the Hornet, he helped to promote it through reader/shooter interest. Without him, the Hornet may have remained behind the stage curtains a long time. This and other cartridge work brought the Colonel to more experimentation through handloading, which led to further books. His popular *Why Not Load Your Own?* title is still checked out of libraries across the land.

The Colonel also edited *The Ultimate in Rifle Precision*, a text that provided a wealth of valuable information for benchrest shooters. Townsend Whelen was not in the forefront of the benchrest shooting movement. Other names pre-date his in the promotion of benchshooting. But it was Colonel Whelen who provided an example for benchresting, not in terms of winning contests, but as a platform for the betterment of rifles and ammunition. The photograph of Colonel Whelen most often printed shows the man at his bench, intent behind a high-power target scope.

Whelen's pragmatic books continued to support shooting, helping readers all over the country. Fortunately, enough were printed so that there are still copies available today, quite often through used book dealers. Some of Townsend's titles have been reprinted. Wolfe Publishing Company offers several, including *The Hunting Rifle*, a 1940 work. This was a nuts-and-bolts work, enjoyable and instructive. Many gunwriters often quote Whelen's remark on killing power in his chapter of the same title. Colonel Whelen's summation of harvesting force makes sense. It stands as a foundation for understanding, and acts as a launching pad for further discussions on the topic:

> The killing power of a bullet in flight depends entirely upon the average size of the wound channel it makes in an animal, and upon nothing else. The size of the wound channel in turn depends upon the size, weight, construction, and shape of the bullet, and the velocity with which it strikes, and upon no other details.

Colonel Whelen was highly responsible for the widespread use of the rifle sling. His theories were sound, well-founded and provable. Millions of shooters today use a sling to promote rifle stability. Shooters who do not understand the function and employment of the sling should take heed of Whelen's advice and learn to use the device. A short time ago I had an opportunity to present the use of the sling in its least desirable mode, the "hasty" method, in which the left arm, for a right-handed shooter, is merely entwined in the strap. I demonstrated shooting beverage cans at 100 yards offhand with and without the use of the sling. My scores with the sling were much better than my scores without it, and I was trying equally hard with and without the strap. Whelen proved the efficacy of the sling by winning several target

matches with its use. His modified Whelen sling style is perhaps the best for the dual purpose of promoting rifle stability and carrying efficiency.

Colonel Whelen also advocated the peep or aperture sight before scopes were widely used in America. He proved that this excellent aiming device offered a more precise aimpoint over the open iron sight. He attached an aperture sight to several of his hunting rifles. However, when the telescopic riflesight gained prominence, the Colonel was right there pushing all the way. His regard for the scope, plus his many positive words on the subject, no doubt swayed many shooters to the use of the instrument.

In his quest for accuracy, this famous rifleman/hunter fell in with the bolt-action style rifle. He was without doubt one of the foremost proponents of the bolt-action rifle in the hunting field as well as the military arena. He helped promote the use of bolt-action rifles for hunting big game.

Townsend Whelen did grow adamant on some points. However, the majority of his beliefs hold up, even under the light of modern scrutiny. The colonel absolutely hated the super lightweight hunting rifle. He found featherweights unstable. In his usual manner of two-sided commentary, he admitted that super light rifles could be accurate when "pinned down" at the bench. However, he found flyweights too light in the hand, therefore unsatisfactory in the field. The argument that you carry a rifle a lot more than you shoot it on a hunt did not convince the Colonel. The moment of truth comes when the bullet leaves the muzzle and speeds to the target. You can carry an empty water bucket uphill to the cabin. It's going to be a much lighter than a full one. But you won't have anything to drink when you get there. You can merrily dance over the mountains with a super light rifle, but if you can't make that shot because the rifle won't settle down for you, your easy carrying was for nothing.

I suggested earlier that the Colonel was conservative, perhaps a bit too much so, concerning accuracy and other shooting tenets. Whelen loved "averages." He did not discount any information. He never dismissed the individual off-shot. In my own testing, I occasionally use the "weighted average" approach. Statistically sound, it removes a single wild figure from consideration. If I have a rifle that fires three five-shot groups with 14 bullets going into one inch and one expanding the

Whelen wrote prolifically because he had experienced much as a hunter, benchtester and all-around shooter. Here he enjoys a cool drink at a shooting match.

group to two inches, I will toss out the one wild shot, blaming it on the shooter rather than the rifle or load. Naturally, if the trend persists, it will be investigated to see if indeed the rifle does throw one bullet askew out of fifteen. Townsend preferred to include the flyers, even if they ruined an otherwise fine group. Some of his averages were compiled from groups totaling 100 shots. Remember that as you read the results of his testing. Townsend was adamant on another point—hunting rifles must have free-floated barrels. He would not back off on this one, believing that the free-floated barrel would hold its zero better than a barrel that made considerable contact in the stock channel.

Whelen was not a slide rule man, not in the sense that Admiral R.J. Schneider, Navy ballistics expert with a background in physics, was. However, he did write a two-volume set of books well worth reading, *Small Arms Design and Ballistics*. Whelen fans should look for these book. Volume I, published by Samworth in 1945, deals with the basics of small arms in general, the rifled bore, barrels, stocks, and sights, with a great deal on ammunition, from primers and powders to cases and bullets. Volume II, Samworth, 1946, covers interior ballistics, pressures, velocities, recoil, exterior ballistics, trajectory, killing power, handloading and more.

Whelen was involved in many shooting developments, including the 35 Whelen cartridge. James V. Howe of the famous Griffin & Howe firm is usually credited with the invention of a 35-caliber cartridge based on a neck-expanded 30-'06 Springfield case. The wildcat appeared in 1922 and named the 35 Whelen. History suggested that Howe named it in honor of the Colonel. But further documents researched by Ken Waters of *Rifle Magazine* revealed that Townsend built it. The cartridge was recently given factory status. Remington did not change the name of the round because the company reasoned there were few serious shooters who weren't familiar with Whelen's name.

"Only accurate rifles are interesting," said the Colonel. He was right. But after all, Colonel Townsend Whelen was right about a lot of things. His legacy to shooters will not soon fade.

31

ROY WEATHERBY: INNOVATOR PLUS

"Tomorrow's Firearms Today." That was Roy Weatherby's creed for a very long time, and it is still the platform supporting Weatherby, Inc. today. Everyone has a right to vote for the single individual who has had the greatest impact upon the modern firearms industry. John Browning? Charles Newton? Perhaps. But Roy Weatherby's name often heads the list. As arms author Jim Carmichel said, "The most influential personality in sporting arms ammunition design during this half of the 20th century is Roy Weatherby. It's as simple as that. There really isn't a second place. . . ."

Roy Weatherby made a lasting imprint on sporting arms because his thinking was special. Even the lover of the American classic design, which is the antithesis of the Weatherby configuration, has to admit—"Those Weatherby rifles do shoot, and they fit right, too." That's what one modern American classic stockmaker said to me. Weatherby's philosophy of armsmaking has always been progressive. But progressiveness was never allowed to overshadow function. Many shooters believe that the major reason you own a Weatherby rifle is prestige. Even Roy admitted that his rifles were just about as much for ownership as shootership. But never mistake the fact that a Weatherby is made to get the job done in the hunting field.

Charles Newton was called the "Father of High Velocity." His cartridge designs match, and

in some instances surpass, ammunition we shoot today. But it was Roy Weatherby who carried the practice of "fast bullets" to the highest plateau of success. Where Newton failed as a businessman and purveyor of his products, Roy succeeded. While Newton's rifles were diverted by a world war, only a few reaching the hands of American shooters, a Weatherby rifle is as close as your local gunshop. Newton's fine cartridges went out of manufacture years ago. Roy's line of ammunition not only thrives, but has spurred the development of similar cartridges offered by other manufacturers.

Mr. Weatherby was an inventor, too, as we shall see, although he did not claim to have sired the first high-velocity hunting cartridge. He worked with existing cartridge designs, but when he was finished he had a complete line of rounds unlike any the world had seen before. Roy remained true to his first love—speed. And something else—the Weatherby rifle would be among the most recognizable styles ever produced. No shooter can mistake a Weatherby for anything else. Roy's rifles remain as streamlined as firearms come.

Roy believed early on that velocity was the key to success in a modern hunting cartridge. He shaped the idea, polished it, and presented the finished product to the world of shooters. He was known as the velocity king, and he never apologized for the title. My phone rang one afternoon and, as was typical of Roy, his voice came on the line with words of encouragement first, "Nice job on that article, Sam." From there we talked about—what else?—shooting. "Get the bullet going fast enough and it'll kill anything," Weatherby told me many times. He never backed away from that concept. But he was a down-to-earth person. He did not support the use of a peashooter for Cape buffalo, for example, even though he was accused of it. He knew the importance of *what* projectile you propelled at high velocity.

Roy did not advocate varmint rifles or varmint bullets for big game hunting. "People who heard that I shot a Cape buffalo with a 257 Weatherby Magnum think that's a recommendation," Roy related. "I never said that. I was coming in from the field and there was a buffalo standing in front of me. I shot it with what I was carrying, a 257 Weatherby." The beast dropped dead. Get the right bullet going fast enough. That was Roy's byword. Shooters asked if Weatherby meant that his 300 with a 180-grain bullet at 3200 fps mv was on par with an English double rifle. He said, "Sure it is, if you have the right bullet." But for those who mistook the gleam in Roy's eye as that of a dreamer, just remember that

Roy Weatherby shooting—what else—a Weatherby rifle in Africa. Roy believed that if the bullet could be driven fast enough, it would cleanly harvest game. He succeeded in persuading many hunters that his theory was right.

when Weatherby decided to build a cartridge that would put any game animal on earth to its knees with one blow, he designed the 460 Weatherby Magnum to do the job, with a 500-grain bullet, soft point or solid, at 2700 fps mv for a muzzle energy of over 8,000 foot-pounds.

Roy took his share of criticism. Magnum. The very term makes some shooters bristle. "Magnumitis," they call it. "Who needs a magnum?" But Roy's magnums were aptly named, except for the 224, which carries the magnum title because it is in the Weatherby lineup, not because it is the fastest 22-centerfire cartridge. Critics forgot why Weatherby favored the magnum. High speed for a quick big game harvest? Sure, that was the main reason.

But trajectory was also a consideration. Roy wanted a rifle that would be flat-shooting. He often said that high velocity was a boon to the modern hunter whose opportunities were limited by seasons and bag limits. Give this man a fast bullet, and he would not have to guess about holdover until very long range. For example, Roy's 257 Weatherby Magnum with the 100-grain bullet could be sighted dead on at 300 yards, with the bullet rising less than 3.5 inches at 200 yards, which won't cause a miss on any big game animal. The hunter can place his crosswires right on a deer-sized target at long range without guesswork.

"If a fellow got out all year the way the pioneers could, he could learn the trajectory of just about any rifle and do well with it, even at the longer ranges," Weatherby said. But the modern hunter doesn't enjoy the field all year long. When he sights in a Weatherby correctly—even the big 300 Weatherby Magnum can be sighted in for 300 yards without undue bullet rise at 100 yards or 200 yards—you don't have to worry about Arkansas elevation from muzzle to any reasonable shot in the field. Bullet drop is just a term until you're past 350 yards with such a firearm. Roy's early experimentation proved that high velocity was not only superior for killing power, but that it meant the "average shooter" could be more successful in the big game field, especially in the West where opportunities might come from afar. It was this aspect of the Weatherby rifle as much as its lightning punch that sold the rifles.

Born on the flat plains of Kansas in 1910, Roy Weatherby spent his early life doing mostly manual labor at farm chores. His father was a tenant farmer and money was far from overabundant. The Weatherby story runs like a silent film, with a toiling lad so poor that he had to stuff cardboard in his shoes to keep the snow out. But Roy did put cardboard in his shoes to gap the holes. And when he went hunting and fishing, it wasn't for the sheer sport of it, but rather to see what he could bring home for the table. The Abe Lincoln log cabin story of American success fits Mr. Weatherby quite well. If Roy wanted something, he had to earn it. He wanted a Daisy BB rifle and he earned it by selling garden seed. "I sold every seed package by walking from neighbor to neighbor," Roy recalls, "with none living closer than a mile from one another." That sort of tenacity carried Roy far in life.

Perhaps it was an aid later on that Roy had trouble making ends meet as a young man. His early years in the firearms business were not blessed with monetary reward. After all, it took Roy 37 years before he owned all of his own company. He bought out his last partner in 1983. He had a great deal of proving to do before he captured success. Roy always had great respect for education and his early vision included a college education he never attained. He attended the University of Wichita for a couple of years, but could afford to go only at night. Working for Southwestern Bell at the time, it was slow progress toward a degree. This was 1937, when America was still in an economic straitjacket. Roy decided to move on, but he did not quit his job. He judiciously got a leave of absence in case he failed in his venture. But Roy never had to turn back.

With his wife, Camilla, who supported him all the way, Roy headed west. He ended up in southern California and landed a good job as an insurance agent with the Southern California Automobile Club. Weatherby did splendidly. Consider a 600 dollar-a-month salary in the late 1930s/early 1940s. That was "good money," and Roy was bringing it home regularly—until he quit.

A magnetic force known as ballistics pulled him away from the job. Not only did Roy love ballistics; he lived ballistics. He wanted to be close to firearms, to work with guns on a daily basis. He bought a lathe from Sears—$189—and an $89 drill press, and took his first step on the path of making a living with firearms. He had "his own company," a little sporting goods store, with firearms the foundation of the enterprise.

What he did not have was money. Capital was more scarce than a Model T in a road race. Roy had a small payroll to meet, too. When he could not, he borrowed money from his friends. In 1946, he sold half of his enterprise for the sake of capital, gaining $10,000 in the transaction from an attorney who had faith in the Weatherby firearms concept and who liked Roy's work.

The money bought some new equipment, but the dollars soon evaporated in paying old loans.

Cash flow was not torrential. Mrs. Weatherby, at this time, inherited $21,000 from the sale of the family farm in Kansas. Weatherby used some of it to buy back his share of the store from his attorney friend; the rest he spent on a new supply of rifle parts. But even this infusion of dollars was insufficient. Roy offered stock in the company, even though his attorney said the company was in the red, and eventually, stockholders invested about $75,000 in the Weatherby company. Roy knew from the start that his particular brand of

Welcome to Weatherby's. Started as a little sporting goods outlet, with firearms the foundation of the enterprise, the South Gate, California, store draws customers and onlookers from all over the globe. Roy Weatherby built an international reputation for himself and his firearms.

firearm was not going to catch on overnight. It was no surprise, then, that Weatherby was still buying out his own company until 1983. Every businessman is in it for a profit, but as with other dedicated men, Weatherby's love of firearms went far beyond his love of cash. He stuck it out because he wanted to pursue his life's interest, and because he had faith in his idea—the Weatherby rifle and cartridge.

The history of the Weatherby company, the sacrifices of its president, and the roaring success that the company would enjoy are perhaps diminished by the inroads Roy Weatherby made himself. Roy was often asked if he would do it all over again. He admitted that working 12 to 15 hours a day, seven days a week, forced him to lose time with his wife and three children. Would he do it over again? He didn't know. But there was no question about his belief in the Weatherby rifle and cartridge. Those ends he would have pursued, regardless of the financial ups and downs. For our purposes, the best way to understand the Weath-

Roy Weatherby in his office, surrounded by the mementos of his life and his adventures. He holds, of course, the Weatherby rifle in 300 Weatherby Magnum, the most famous round in the lineup.

erby impact on modern shooting is to look at the Weatherby rifle and cartridge.

FUTURISTIC ONE-UPMANSHIP

Weatherby's first firearms were built by re-chambering Winchester Model 70 rifles, or by making customs on Mauser actions. In the mid-1950s, however, a Weatherby wish came true—a "real" Weatherby rifle, from scratch. The Mark V action was born at the hand of Weatherby's inventiveness. Roy was quick to give credit where due, and he readily conferred part of the new action's design excellence on company engineer Fred Jennie, a fine mind in the gun business. Innovation was Roy's middle name, however, and whether in combination with others or not, good ideas blossomed into *workable* ones when Weatherby was at the helm.

The Mark V action was strong. Early detractors said that its nine locking-lug design was more for show than strength; it was unlikely at best for nine lugs to recess perfectly into the receiver. Whether or not the lugs recessed perfectly, the bottom line was strength proved by tests. When a 180-grain bullet was fired out of the barrel by another 180-grain bullet from a 300 Weatherby Magnum cartridge, the action took it. Guesstimations of pressure were in the 90,000 psi range. The bolt lift was only 54 degrees, not the usual 90 degrees, on the Mark V action. That made the action slick—fast—smooth. The encompassed cartridge casehead with shrouded bolt precluded the claw-type Mauser extractor, but the Mark V extractor proved to grip enough of the fired case to withdraw it without a hitch. In short, the action was in perfect tune with the Weatherby concept of a rifle—call it "futuristic one-upmanship." Roy was never interested in duplicating the designs of the past, even when he liked them. His new action would fit perfectly in the overall artistic line of the Weatherby stock—the "California" style, with Monte Carlo cheekpiece, diamond-shaped grip cap inlays, charging lions, and many other embellishments.

"I'm just an idea man." That was one of Roy's favorite quotes. Just an idea man, indeed. When the great stockmaker Leonard Mews was commissioned by Weatherby to design a truly different, even racy, stock to adorn the Weatherby rifle, he came up with a number of radical ideas. Roy's input helped to tone and blend these ideas into the now famous Weatherby stock design. I call it "fit with flair." You never want to forget that Roy's stocks work. They do fit. They do seem to help control the effects of felt recoil. I've never been "kicked around" by a Weatherby rifle, including the 416 and the 460. I have benchtested the 378 and lived to tell about it—bruiseless.

The Weatherby style caught on. It interested "the right people." Posing with a Weatherby rifle were many notables, including John Wayne, the Prince of Iran, Governor Joe Foss, the King of Nepal, Robert Stack, and a host of others. When I was a kid I knew I'd never own a Weatherby, because I had no plans or hopes of becoming a movie star, nor was ascension to any throne in my horoscope. When I got my first Weatherby, the most interesting single aspect of the rifle was how well it worked, not its lineage. It was trim, neat, small for its caliber, and yet it shot with fine accuracy (half-inch 100-yard groups with my handloads) and without undue shoulder punishment. There was the true Weatherby legacy. . . not the racy lines of the rifle or futuristic style of the round, but the fact that both rifle and cartridge functioned as promised.

The famous rifle was enhanced by the just-as-famous Weatherby cartridge. Roy was working with, or at least thinking about, wildcat cartridges barely beyond his BB gun stage. The first wildcat to bear a Weatherby birthmark may have been the 22 Weatherby Rocket, also known as the 220 Rocket. This was a blown-out 220 Swift. Although the wildcat cartridge looked advanced over its parent round, it was not. (There was another 22 Rocket built from the 303 British case, incidentally.) Weatherby's goal was quite clear—to lift the "ordinary" velocity of a given bullet. We look at the wildcat design engineered to do this with an eye to advancement, and yet we can also look at the original cartridge in light of its lackluster. Sloping shoulders were supposedly useful in guaranteeing cartridge case extraction, yet no wildcat or straight-shouldered design has given the least problem in case extraction—then why the slope-shoulders, as with the 300 H&H Magnum? Roy and others asked the same question, then eliminated the slope.

Weatherby's original notion was to gain all that could be gained from a given caliber through a case design built to maximize powder capacity while efficiently burning the charge. That the

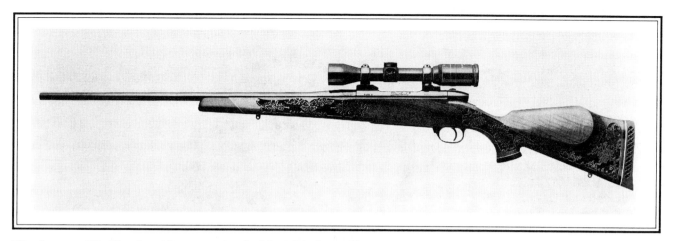

The famous Weatherby rifle—unmistakable. This beautifully carved bolt-action Mark V Lazermark is equipped with Monte Carlo stock and a Weatherby 3X-9X variable scope sight on Buehler mounts.

Weatherby design is altogether unique has never been claimed. In the late 1930s and early '40s Roy was working with many different wildcats—including a 270 PMVF and 300 PMVF—wildcats of the "Miller K-cartridge" series. The 30 Newton was certainly an obvious Big 30, too. Freeboring was well-known at the time. The Venturi shoulder was also extant. But Roy put these and other ballistic enhancements to work. (The Venturi design can't be called an enhancement, but it's interesting.) Then he presented the finished products to the public. We still tend to think of the Weatherby cartridge as a sort of wildcat. It isn't. And that's the whole point. Roy's line of interesting and powerful rounds are factory fodder. You buy them over the counter and have been able to for many years. With Roy Weatherby—experimentation and imagination blended into reality.

By 1944 Roy had tested many wildcats, including the blownout 27s and 30s. He was involved with penetration demonstrations on metal plates and with discovering potential accuracy levels of big-cased rounds. Today, we look askance at some of the findings of the '40s, not only because of claims that seem outlandish, but face it—the Oehler and other good chronographs were not generally in the hands of the shooting fraternity. Some guesswork was going on. My initial doubt has been replaced with wonderment at the ferocious pressures the wildcatters were playing with. The wildcat-loving lads of the forties did achieve those outrageous velocities, but only with very high pressures. And for a price. Roy

had a 257-30-06 Magnum wildcat of his design in those days. He was driving an 87-grain bullet at 4000 fps mv and a 100-grain bullet at 3700. My best 257 Weatherby Magnum loads from a 26-inch barrel gain about 3900 fps with the 87-grain bullet and 3600 fps for the 100-grain projectile, *but with safe pressures.*

Weatherby wisely abandoned the 30-06 case. His dreams for super velocity would have to be realized with a bigger cartridge case. In 1943 he developed his 270 Weatherby Magnum sans 30-06 brass. He had found his case, a belted one. While the belt itself was of minor significance, improved case capacity was. Roy had selected the 300 H&H Magnum case, which he shortened and fireformed to make his 270. The 270 Weatherby Magnum was a ballistic improvement over its standard cousin, but not enough to deserve a ticker tape parade. However, Weatherby had improved the performance of a famous cartridge.

The cartridge that was really something to write home about surfaced in 1944. The 7mm Weatherby Magnum was born 18 years before the 7mm Remington Magnum, which is now third in popularity west of the Mississippi River where hunters pronounce it a superior performer for Rocky Mountain big game hunting. It is my favorite of the "all-around" cartridges. Weatherby had the same round, ballistically speaking, in 1944, but the 7mm Weatherby Magnum never gained the following it deserved. Another cartridge did, however, the most famous Weatherby, the 300. Americans love 30-caliber rounds.

Weatherby did a lot of hunting with his own rifles. Here he poses with one of the world's great prizes, a mature polar bear.

bearing his name. The first presentation was made in 1956 to Herb Klein. Many notables received the award; some also presented them. Even arms writers won them, including Warren Page and Jack O'Connor. Among those who presented the award were General Doolittle, Robert Taylor, Lorne Greene and Dr. Wernher von Braun.

Roy Weatherby's impact on the world of shooting is self-evident. Weatherby was an innovator. He had drive. When an idea struck, he kept at it until he made it "real." He said, more than once, that the sacrifice, the long hours, the concern, even the worry, were perhaps more than he would have endured had he a chance to do it all over. However, even though many rifle and cartridge designers were at work as his contemporaries, it is Roy Weatherby's name that has come to symbolize a specific style of firearm, and a high-performance cartridge to match it.

On April 5, 1988, Roy E. Weatherby passed away following heart surgery. The Weatherby imprint, however, remains emblazoned on firearms and cartridges today as it will for the shooters of tomorrow.

It took only one look to see what this Big 30 could do. It was a long-range powerhouse. Roy had his 300 off the drawing board by 1945, and in the field by about 1948, maybe earlier. This round became the favorite of the "world beaters." You could hunt mule deer in Montana or Wildebeest in Zimbabwe with the 300 Weatherby. Sheep hunters working on the Grand Slam often chose the 300 Weatherby Magnum as insurance against the long shot. The round suffered for a while from soft bullets meant for 300 Savage velocities, and even today true 300 Weatherby performance occurs only when the round is fed bullets designed for high velocity. But with correct projectiles, it's hard to whip a 300 Weatherby for long-range big game hunting.

Weatherby's genius filtered into many areas. He knew what he wanted. When he wanted fine optical sights for his rifles, he investigated the matter until he was satisfied. In recent tests, a Weatherby Imperial scope performed much to my satisfaction. Weatherby did something else, too, which would increase his fame. He initiated the annually conferred Big Game Trophy Award